Time and the Word

Time and the Word

Figural Reading
of the Christian Scriptures

Ephraim Radner

WILLIAM B. EERDMANS PUBLISHING COMPANY
GRAND RAPIDS, MICHIGAN

Wm. B. Eerdmans Publishing Co.
4035 Park East Court SE, Grand Rapids, MI 49546
www.eerdmans.com

Hardcover edition 2016
Paperback edition 2021

ISBN 978-0-8028-7997-4

Library of Congress Cataloging-in-Publication Data

Names: Radner, Ephraim, 1956- author.
Title: Time and the word: figural reading of the Christian scriptures / Ephraim Radner.
Description: Grand Rapids, Michigan: Eerdmans Publishing Company, 2016. |
    Includes bibliographical references and index.
Identifiers: LCCN 2016002489 | ISBN 9780802879974 (pbk.: alk. paper)
Subjects: LCSH: Bible—Criticism, interpretation, etc. | Bible—Hermeneutics.
Classification: LCC BS511.3 .R335 2016 | DDC 220.6/8—dc23
LC record available at http://lccn.loc.gov/2016002489

Chapter 1, "Figural History as a Question," is taken from the forthcoming book to be published
by InterVarsity Press, tentatively titled *Exile and Biblical Theology,* edited by James M. Scott.
Copyright © 2017 by James M. Scott. Used by permission of InterVarsity Press, P.O. Box 1400,
Downers Grove, IL 60515, USA. www.ivpress.com

To my students at Wycliffe College, from whom I have learned much,
and whose love for the Scriptures of Christ is a
deep encouragement and inspiration.

Verbum Domini manet.

Contents

A Brief, Personal, and Figural Apology

In 1991, I was among several doctoral students at Yale Divinity School who gathered for lunch with Old Testament scholar Brevard Childs. We came together to discuss a small book by Andrew Louth entitled *Discerning the Mystery*.[1] Louth is a writer of some note on Patristic theology, and in this book he had made a vigorous and unabashed call for a return to the kind of allegorical reading of Scripture that, he claimed, was both practiced by the early Church Fathers, and continued well into the Middle Ages.

The topic of our luncheon meeting was the degree to which this call of Louth was or ought to be compelling. I think all of us at the time shared with Louth his sense that the reign of historical criticism, along with the presuppositions undergirding its intractable and domineering use in reading the Bible, had proven perverse. They had, in fact, hogtied our ability as churches to be led by Scripture into the knowledge and life of God. We were agreed on this. But this was becoming a common enough sentiment then, and had been for some time, just as today it is now an unexceptional truism (if rarely acted upon). But none of us really thought that specifically *allegorical* reading of Scripture, understood in its broad sense as figurative reading in the mode of the pre-modern church, was the solution. Among Protestants certainly, and Catholics today as well, it is still rarely seen as the avenue by which to retrieve the creative authority of God's Word, and this despite an explosion of interest in just these pre-modern interpretive traditions.

Louth, in his book, made his own case for such a hermeneutic retrieval.

---

1. Andrew Louth, *Discerning the Mystery: An Essay on the Nature of Theology* (Oxford: Clarendon Press, 1989).

1

But although it intrigued and even attracted us, we were all left somewhat unsettled as to its actual force. What Louth seemed to leave unaddressed was the degree to which the figurative reading of Scripture could have any real conceptual purchase on our modern intellects. As practiced by the Church Fathers and Doctors, the "spiritual" reading of Scripture was sustained by metaphysical outlooks or broad philosophical (mostly neo-Platonic) conceptions of the relation between the text and the natural world that are no longer tenable, certainly not widely shared. And without such sustenance, *can* the case for figurative reading of Scripture be coherent any longer, except as a postmodern Scaramouche? What other recourse does one have, then, for escaping the draining imperatives of materialist historicism?

Childs was beginning to wrestle with this question himself. He would later surprise many by engaging Origen positively in a way that would have been unthinkable for him thirty years earlier. But by 1991 the topic was already in the air, even if not quite in the explicit terms it quickly came to take. The theological faculty at Yale, mostly at the Divinity School, had been engaging in an array of approaches of theological *ressourcement*, mostly from a Protestant perspective. Research, courses, and discussions abounded with reference to the early Church Fathers, the Reformers, and, through George Lindbeck, Aquinas. And in almost all this work the Scriptures assumed the central role — theologically, via Barth, but also through Childs's own commanding presence, along with a large and creative Scripture department grabbing our attention. Hans Frei's *The Eclipse of Biblical Narrative* was already over fifteen years old,[2] and had shaped discussions in my seminary years during the late 1970s by attuning us to the way that Bible reading had radically contracted its vision in the 18th century, in comparison with the 16th. But digging into the past and questioning the present was not, in itself, a way forward.

For despite speaking of figure and typology in a central way, Frei had never really engaged the practice and shape of figural reading concretely, and his early death closed the door on that possibility. It probably would not have ever come anyway. Frei's Barthian sympathies seemed to mute for him the lure of Patristic practice, with all its seemingly extravagant and arbitrary Catholicism. (Not that Barth was not himself a practicing figural reader; but he was explicitly opposed to Origenist proclivities, and so both gave the appearance of being anti-figuralist as well as blocked off easy passage into the Fathers' exegetical practice.) Yale professors of the late 1970s had pressed the Christological centrality of Scripture, as well as, implicitly anyway, its corresponding

2. Hans Frei, *The Eclipse of Biblical Narrative: A Study in Eighteenth and Nineteenth Century Hermeneutics* (New Haven: Yale University Press, 1974).

self-authenticating divine character. But the appropriation of figure into the category of "narrative" had, in any case, quickly turned the entire enterprise over to the literary critics and the pneumatic core of scriptural speech that Frei himself wondered over was quickly smothered in the discussion. Even so, in a liberal Protestant context like Yale's, the turn back to Scripture and its "magisterial" interpreters was nonetheless revolutionary. It was a revolution, however, that was never really assimilated into the churches for which the school was training pastors. In fact, many of those most shaped by this renewal of focus went on either to be marginalized pastors and teachers, or to leave their denominations altogether, such was the inhospitable environment in most modern churches to this renewed vision. And in this respect, they never quite got off the mark on publicly pursuing the consequences of these commitments. The Scripture was asserted; but it was never quite "unleashed," as Stanley Hauerwas would say.[3]

In 1991, Childs's long sense of unease with the commitments of his own biblical guild had reached a point where he could see that his carefully calibrated methodological arguments, themselves founded in part on historical-critical presuppositions, had not been able to budge the ecclesial impasse in which Scripture had become stuck within the mainline churches. Even Catholicism and Evangelicalism were now mired in it. He was beginning to reassess "allegory" as a potentially positive interpretive approach to the text, and now began to read extensively (as he always had up to a point) in earlier Christian interpretation.[4] His late volume on the history of Isaiah's Christian exegesis was a testimony to what had become for him a new stage in his search for a renewed exegetical path.[5] But even here, he seemed to leave Isaiah, in the eyes of many of his readers, more as a question mark in the tradition — a struggle — than as a working book whose continuity of power and purpose in the tradition was still being deployed today. (In fact, Childs's view of "struggle" was, I believe, marvellously in line with the ascetic character of figural exegesis I speak to later in this volume.)

Meanwhile, younger Christians and scholars were being faced with similar obstacles of conception and trust, but perhaps fewer debts owed to our historical-critical forebears. After all, we could simply watch as John Spong and Marcus Borg became adult education standard fare, showing up at clergy

---

3. Stanley Hauerwas, *Unleashing the Scripture: Freeing the Bible from Captivity to America* (Nashville: Abingdon, 1993).

4. Some of this is traced in Daniel Driver's superb work, *Brevard Childs, Biblical Theologian: For the Church's One Bible* (Grand Rapids: Baker Academic, 2012).

5. Brevard Childs, *The Struggle to Understand Isaiah as Christian Scripture* (Grand Rapids: Eerdmans, 2004).

conferences to "open us up"; or while various versions of the "documentary hypothesis" of J, E, D, P continued to rattle down the pike of "serious Bible study" and denomination-oriented adult teaching, only to surround our attempts at preaching, teaching, witnessing, and praying among the living Body of Christ with hedges, ditches, nets, and stones. Our people seemed increasingly skeptical and political, driven by more and more blatant late-20th-century consumer cultural bias, unexamined and uncriticized. The inevitable battle with Evangelical tradition that arose on the political front quickly turned into a stale confrontation of "critical intellect" vs. biblical truth-assertions whose opposition missed much engagement with the cultural problem: how to engage, not defend, the Bible's truth-telling power in a context of deliberate impermeability to the divine life shaping our world. Rarely, in our churches, did we hear the question raised, let alone faced: shall God, through his Word, change me and what we call the history of our race?

In my own case, I came to a positive answer to that question as a young priest in the 1980s, among African Christians in Burundi, where I had gone to work within the Anglican Church. It was an ambivalent discovery, but just because of that, all the more powerful. The Anglican Church in Burundi lived within an evangelical revival setting, in which the Scripture was turned to, read, and shared from and among the least to the greatest.[6] The Bible was the one bridge between cultures, roles, social strata, and political distance or even hostility. It framed our gatherings, prayers, meetings, decisions, and struggles. All this was part of the Christian culture of the church there, no more, no less. It was not a virtue held by individuals. Indeed, just the opposite! It was only because I quickly came to see the huge holes and disparate ingredients of character and integrity, or moral courage and even divine love in the midst of a deeply torn society and church itself, that the Scripture's strange role among us came into relief: the Bible was actually *moving* in its work, stirring up, overturning stones and exhibiting unpleasant growths, judging even as it led and encouraged. I began to see people more clearly — the depths of their hearts, for good and ill. And, to be sure, I began to see myself as such. The political and moral complexities, corruptions, and agonies of Burundi at that time were easy enough to grasp with the wounds of the 1972 civil war and genocide still fresh. Most visitors could articulate them. But exposed to the Word, I saw a reflection of a much deeper set of needs and hopes in the face of human loss that we shared, whose truth my own naiveties and self-righteousness could

---

6. For a historical discussion of the East African Revival, and its impact on Burundi, see Kevin Ward and Emma Wild-Wood, *The East African Revival: History and Legacies* (Farnham, UK: Ashgate, 2012).

not obscure and whose demand they could not escape. I committed a host of personal and ecclesial sins, even as I was built up in a greater host of ways. The Word, I found, was truly more than a "two-edged sword," "dividing asunder" "soul and spirit," "joints and marrow," and discerning "thoughts and intents of the heart" (Heb. 4:12). But it proved also a wind-blown fire, sweeping away the green and leaving stubble (Isa. 5:24; Jer. 23:29). Trying to navigate the dark complexities of national dissolution and church-building at the same time, under the shadow of a pressing divine Word, I found that the Scripture had begun to frighten me, even as it also drew me in and wrapped me up.

Some of what I had learned in seminary not long before came back to me then — Barth, the urgent engagement of Childs, open-ended yet textually focused, Leander Keck's insistent questioning of our assumptions before Paul's unrelenting gospel, even Abraham Malherbe's patient teasing out of the text that, I realized, was also a means of staying present before it to the point of finally having one's intellect cracked open by its acute meaning. But even more than these somewhat intellectual provocations, I was overcome by the pressing sense that I was the product of a culture, including an ecclesial culture, that had more generally and long sought to domesticate the Bible than, as they ought, to be undone by it. This message, in the end, was what Frei's historical work seemed to come down to, and its truth became more and more evident to me. My own time in Burundi, which involved knotted human failures in both the church and civil culture, left me emotionally torn. I came back to America hardly certain of my own ability to stand before God's articulate speech. But what this journey did assure me of was the call to go with the movement that the Word's own life had set in motion; this, at least, was the only path worth following, precisely because the alternatives could not survive.

On this basis, carrying on with ministry in parishes, in prisons, and elsewhere, I did so convinced that the Scriptures were a word that was actually doing something, shaping the lives of those with whom I worked and lived, along with me. By and large, I was never sure of what exactly this might mean. To read a text from Isaiah together with a group of prison inmates was immediately to enter into a world where God spoke directly in the Scriptures to those of us gathered. It was clear that Jerusalem stood among us, or perhaps over and against us; and that Tyre or Edom took up their stations alongside. And to read the Gospels thus was not to move to a new place and new time, but rather to have Jesus and the Samaritan woman, or Martha and Levi, or the two thieves on the cross, step into the same location inhabited by Jerusalem and Tyre, which was here, in a windowless room watched over by grim corrections officers.

Certainly, I came to see that none of these biblical figures were really "dead"; and that their relationship one to another was given in a strange kind of time that did not quite parse itself along the lines of a three-year chaplaincy or a twenty-year sentence; or even an ongoing marriage and fatherhood, of births and aging, such as I was beginning to experience. "'I am the God of Abraham, and the God of Isaac and the God of Jacob.' . . . He is not the God of the dead, but the God of the living" (Mark 12:26-27). If nothing else, reading the Scriptures in such places and with such growing sentiments — no different, really, if less pervasive, than in Burundi — kept pressing the point of the mystery of God and the life he has given us, into which the Scriptures speak. Within a Sunday service and among the fragmentary lives that constitute any "normal" congregation, I slowly, and unconsciously almost, began to preach as if this mystery and its Word were really the case. But at the same time, I also sensed that this matter of fact was a quantity none of us knew quite how to handle.

It was only in the early 1990s that I returned to graduate studies, and found myself having conversations about the "return of allegory." And only then did I deliberately re-engage a world of Christian reading — the Fathers, medieval monks and commentators, and indeed, as I began to learn, Catholics and Protestants well into the modern era. It was a world that had in fact long shared this sense of the Word's work of, as it were, configuring our realities, including those of time and space, life and death. I rediscovered Augustine, for instance, not as the stranger he had seemed in my seminary days, but as someone with whose wilderness world I too was now somewhat familiar. And the excitement of this rediscovery pressed me to dig more deeply among the church's Scripture readers of the past. Here was a world where, as it were, Burundi Christians shared the table of the Word with European scholastics and antique monks and Catholic and Protestant missionaries of the 18th century — not to mention men in jail in the late 20th century and even a few Christians in the pews of embattled suburban American congregations, along with scholars like Childs and Christopher Seitz. I had in fact discovered a densely populated land, flourishing with riches of Christian understanding and imagination, watered by the flowing currents of a living scriptural word. By the time I was having lunch with Childs and discussing Andrew Louth, I had been reading Jansenists and Puritans in some depth, as well as living seriously with charismatics and Haitian Pentecostals; and I knew that the "mystery" had been well discerned by many over the centuries — Platonists, Aristotelians, nominalists, capitalists, natural scientists, missionaries, mothers, children, peasants, sailors, and soldiers — and that Louth was only speaking, as it were, to the weaknesses of a few, at least historically speaking.

I have taken up the phrase "the figural reading of Scripture" to indicate this populated world of Christian hearers of the Word over the centuries. It stands for the general approach of reading the Bible's referents as a host of living beings — and not only human ones — who draw us, as readers, from one set of referents or beings to another, across times and spaces, whatever these may constitute. The phrase "figural reading" derives from the broad literary trope of having one name (or referent) represent another — "figure" it — and to that degree, is much like the term "figurative."[7] By the 18th century, especially, the "figural" sense had taken on the comprehensive meaning that the "spiritual" sense held among the Fathers, a sense that could be contrasted with or at least distinguished from something called "historical." This figural sense includes what later came to be explained, in the Middle Ages, in terms of the three non-literal levels of meaning: allegory (pointing to matters of faith), tropology (matters of morals), and anagogy (matters of our final end). It also embraces the later Protestant dyad of typology and allegory. But the term "figural" extends even farther than this, and also includes what we would indeed describe as "figurative" rhetorical tropes: metaphor, metonymy, etc. Part of the problem in any of these categorizations is that the contrasts are, as it turns out, all equally vague: "literal" and "historical" are themselves of uncertain reference, with the former including "figurative" readings often (as narratively embedded tropes) and the latter depending on various construals of temporality that have shifted within different cultural settings. "Figural," as I will try to explain in this volume, finally refers to the "everything" of God's act in creation, as it is "all" given in the Scriptures. And "figural reading" of the Bible is that reading that receives this divinely-given "allness" — who is the Christ "through whom are all things and through whom we exist" (1 Cor. 8:6), who "is before all things, and in [whom] all things hold together" (Col. 1:17) — from within the breadth of the Word written.

But if this is so, figural reading is not really a "method," and I hope to make clear why not. Instead, it is about the nature of a world that God has made in

7. The term "figural" is already in use in English by the 15th century and seems to stand as a general synonym for "allegorical," or more general non-literal readings of Scripture especially. It was also a synonym for "figurative," which proved the more common term in this context. Understandable attempts have been made to distinguish "figurative" from "figural" on the basis of the former's purely semantic focus — a trope that carries a detachable "meaning" — from the latter's form historical and "performative" character. J. David Dawson has made this argument, and while I think he is absolutely right in his theological claims on this score, especially as they relate to Origen's own usage, the history of the term "figural" is simply too varied to rule out its blurred reference. See John David Dawson, *Christian Figural Reading and the Fashioning of Identity* (Berkeley: University of California Press, 2002). Dawson's argument about the divinely performative nature of scriptural figure, although couched in more literary terms, is coherent with my own argument in this volume, especially as I lay it out in terms of the relationship between Scripture and temporality in Chapter 3.

relation to which a certain divine text rises up, hovers over, and orders. Certainly such reading involves doing some very particular things when it comes to engaging the Bible. But these things are really the natural outflow — the "common sense," I will argue — that emerges from the character of Scripture as the living, breathing, acting Word of God that it is. Figural reading, that is, is a natural response to the character of the world as God's creation, which God relates to in a certain way. And discussing this involves central *theological* affirmations and is a centrally *theological* task. That is why the question of figural reading cannot simply be left in the realm of optional literary postures, one of many techniques, in this case rather antiquated, in the toolbox of the textual investigator. Some practitioners of historical criticism have been quite willing to hold on to claims about God as Creator in Christ but, at the same time, to let go of the fundamental figural character of Scripture. That has proven to be a religious (and moral) failure. Despite being the preferred mode of much modern Christianity, such a decoupling of fundamental dogma from figural reading has had the effect of slowly eviscerating God's creative being from our consciousness and apprehension, leaving in its place the traces that we have filled out with our dim memories, mostly of ourselves and of our fading loves.

But perhaps the loss of figural reading within the church is itself the result of something much larger than genealogies of pastoral and theological practice. While tracing the development of ideas and the shape of Christian formation is important in retrospectively indicating the path of experience, it cannot, in itself, disclose the meaning of such trajectories. If, that is, the Word is indeed the living hand that shapes events, then we should rightly seek the meaning of such events in their figural identity. And that would, ironically, include the fate of figural reading itself. This, at any rate, is the conclusion to which my own thinking has pressed: to speak of the "history of the figural reading of the Bible" in a consistent fashion is to see it as itself the shape of God's creative act in bodily process. In giving an account of figural reading, then, I must indicate this final set of steps that move, in my case, from discussions around tables, whether in seminar rooms or dining halls, or even around circles of prayer, to grappling with the actual form of the church's destiny within the currents of time.

As I have mentioned, the context of my own discovery of the Bible (or it of me) was one of enormous human struggle — politically, relationally, morally. Inevitably, one tries to make sense not only of such experiences, but of their location within the gifts of divine grace, in this case, of the Scriptures themselves. How is it possible to be taken up by the living Word, and yet find all around oneself only the rubble of human hopes, among them those commended by the Word itself — loyalty, forgiveness, gentleness, family ties and trusts? How, finally, integrate the grace of God's Word with the church's own spurning of its divine gifts?

Many Christians have, of course, struggled with this discontinuity. It forms, from one perspective, one of the major intellectual and experiential contexts in which the theological discipline we call "ecclesiology" has emerged, first within the internal struggles of the early church, more concretely in the quest for renewed integrity in medieval Europe, and finally and formally, in the ecclesial fragmentation, with its many perplexing wounds, of the 16th century and beyond. Responses to the seeming contradiction between scriptural commendation and ecclesial witness have been various. But they have often, in my mind, ended simply by embracing the discontinuity rather than by integrating it within God's own gracious work (which, for me and for many, remains considerable in the midst of whatever challenges). One response has been to eschatologize Christ's fullness of Lordship, by putting off to some future, transcendent or not, the visible confirmation of scriptural claims. Another response has been to demean the church altogether, limiting it to an entity exhaustively explained in sociological terms. Again, and more recently, some have sought to relativize the gospel itself within the forum of human religions, thus embedding the discontinuity within some more general human and cultural incapacity vis-à-vis God's truth. And so on. These kinds of responses manage, in a way, to cordon off the unseemly elements of the world from God's purity. But they also seem, finally, to deny the very Scriptures that purportedly generate Christian hope in the first place.

All of us have tried to navigate these possibilities, and in doing so, throw this and that store of freight from the vessel. I have been no different. So, for example, in the late 1980s, trying to understand the character of Christian mission within difficult inner-city contexts, I revisited the "exodus" imagery that was so prevalent in discussions of economic justice at the time, and that shaped ecclesial discussion relentlessly. The liberationist embrace of this image, as rationale and basis for a certain activism, was not without power. But it also obscured many of the already-embedded gifts of Christian life within poor communities, ones often nurtured in small apolitical conservative tabernacles that were, at the time, often dismissed as "quietist" by church leaders who funded ministry in these areas. Likewise, the focus on "exodus" masked many of the moral challenges needing to be addressed, involving eroded communal and behavioral virtues whose personal aspects did not fit well with the larger interest in systemic change. As an exclusive vehicle for change, the "exodus" image was not only limited, I felt, but often acted as an albatross to serious Christian reflection and patient ministry. I began to wonder whether Scripture's full range of illuminating metaphors was being properly deployed

9

in social self-understanding: might not, for instance, "exile," with all *its* social and political implications, be just as truthful to the facts?[8] There was, of course, nothing novel in such a question (as the first chapter in this volume emphasizes rather bluntly). But in the context of the emancipatory assumptions of the times and my own ecclesial home, it seemed to many counter-intuitive.

But simply raising up vying images or "models" cannot finally resolve missionary arguments. It was not until I began, in my doctoral studies, a careful investigation of the 18th-century Jansenist movement's ecclesial pneumatology, however, that I was forced to consider how limited were these illuminating, or strategically practical, scriptural "images" we were fond of raising up as rationales for our organized ecclesial work. I had been drawn to the Jansenists initially as a way to study the intersection of miracle and theologies of grace, both of which were central to their movement. But what I discovered was a doorway into a different way of reading the Bible that finally, in its self-explication, began to make sense of things I had until that time only inchoately intuited. Jansenists insisted that the "figures" of Scripture actually shape the world; they have historical substance, from a divine perspective, and thus describe what human history is all about, from the inside out as well as the outside in. There is no point in my muting the crystallizing role the Jansenists have played in my thinking, though it is obvious that they were hardly unique or novel in their understanding of Scripture, as I point out in Chapter 2 below. Still, Jansenist theology was provocatively clear in how it managed to integrate robust doctrines of creative grace, incarnational Christocentrism, and scriptural literalism in a way that was able to face squarely the demands of an increasingly sceptical culture to qualify all these elements. Their approach was tied to a discipline of Patristic reading and ascetic discipline. And together, these aspects provided the ill-fated reform movement which Jansenists constituted with the lenses to apprehend how both that fate, in its ecclesial disappointments, and the world in which it is suffered reveal the very God in Christ whom we worship and thankfully adore. That was, for me, the key theological resolution we were after.

What was the church and where was she going? The Jansenists read the Old Testament, and discovered an answer in the forms of Israel; they read the New, and discovered yet more in the figures of Jesus' own existence. They insisted that the two Testaments be read together in just this way. While the Jansenists were hardly personages to emulate on a host of levels — in many cases argumentative, rigid, without humor or joyful gentleness — I remain

---

8. For my rather jejune reflection of the time, see Ephraim Radner, "From 'Liberation' to 'Exile': A New Image for Church Mission," *Christian Century* 106:30 (Oct. 18, 1989): 931-34.

fascinated and astonished at the clarity of their vision and, in certain respects, witness, especially on the level of Bible reading. Following through on Jacques-Joseph Duguet's simple, but still revolutionary, proposal for "figural" reading, despite its ultimately pinched and unhelpful regulative mode, spurred my thinking, as it did for many in his own day.[9] I cannot help but think, if only unconsciously, that it managed to inform a more general Catholic attitude towards history that permitted many French Christians to survive as they did the convulsions of the Revolution. And these are convulsions that bear some analogy to the contextual life of many Christians today.

My own interest, in any case, lay in ecclesiology, informed, not by the French Revolution, but by its many social epigones and contrary rejoinders, which continue to vibrate through the past two centuries. These were ones that I experienced in the immoral complicities, impotence, and division of Christians in Africa, America, and, more broadly now, in the Anglican Communion. How is "the church" that we see around us and live within — from African and American, European and Asian centers of expansion and decline, moral failure and sometimes courageous resistance and mission — how is this church that is given in many struggling churches the place wherein God's grace in Christ is offered and lived for the sake of the whole world? The Scriptures tell us this, I have come to believe, even as the churches are engaged within these divine contexts that the Scriptures themselves are constituting. This church-in-the-churches-in-the-world is precisely the shape and history of what Scripture presents and creates through its "figures" — its stories, images, strictures and exhortations, established primordially in the forms of Israel and then of Christ Jesus. Everything we live is given first there and in the shapes so articulated. The figures of Scripture are not "themes" or reminders or attitudes or spurs to reflection: they actually *are* what we are created as both being and becoming in time.

This is, I realize, as much a philosophical question as it is simply religious. The religious problem was one we were living (and live still!) within the Anglican Communion's struggles, and colleagues like Christopher Seitz and Philip Turner provided the encouragement of personal witness. But they also urged all of us on to greater theological clarity — Turner through his incisive analysis of ecclesial life and Seitz through his fertile and intensive pursuit of the "two-testament" character of the Scriptures.[10] Among other places, I tried to

9. Jacques-Joseph Duguet, *Règles pour l'intelligence des Stes Ecritures* (Paris: Jacques Estienne, 1716). Duguet was among the foremost scriptural commentators of his era, and was a leader in the popular renewal of scriptural exposition within Jansenist circles.

10. It is worth noting Seitz's recent *The Character of Christian Scripture: The Significance of a Two-Testament Bible* (Grand Rapids: Baker Academic, 2011) and Turner's forthcoming

explore the issue of a figural ecclesiology historically in *The End of the Church* and more recently in *Brutal Unity*.[11] In both books, I examined how the Christian church can be said to be both that church referred to and promised in the New Testament, and that church that has in fact blasphemed its God and contradicted its faith through violence perpetrated against non-Christians, Jews, and other Christians over the centuries. The coincidence of this one church in these references, promises, and acts is a theological problem, as well as — and this was my larger argument — a divine revelation in time, given in the Scriptures: we know who we actually *are* today as Christians and as the Christian church by seeing ourselves in-the-making within Scripture. In *Brutal Unity*, I even attached figural readings of Scripture that dealt with the church to each of the chapters engaging intellectual and ecclesial history, and so attempted to clarify the theological issues through just such a figural biblical discussion.

But these attempts were admittedly somewhat allusive. They provided examples of figural theology in practice, but only up to a point. And their combination with standard historical theology has proven confusing to some. Promises of good "post-liberal" thinking, or hard-hitting "conservative" apologetics, or critically sophisticated politics have not been forthcoming from this approach, and this has disappointed some readers. While I think that the combination itself is, at least in theory, practicable, none of us are probably yet adept enough at figural reading to do it well, least of all myself. And my attempt at an actual figural "commentary," on the book of Leviticus, seemed to frustrate others who sought more applicable messages (not to mention those who were looking for more meaty philological and historical scrutiny of the Hebrew text).[12]

Certainly, my own limited job as a theologian is not done. The reality and character of Scripture is one of the central aspects of the Christian gospel, and thus is always calling for our unrelieved and joyful engagement. But Scripture itself tells us of the insistence of special times and places, unveiling itself even as it illumines the condition of the world and of the church. Such a special time is ours. And thus, in the present volume I seek to focus more narrowly and explicitly on the topic of scriptural figuralism itself: what is it? Where does it come from? What theological presuppositions undergird it? What are its theological implications? And finally, how do we approach it in our read-

---

Christian Ethics and the Church: Ecclesial Foundations for Moral Thought and Practice (Grand Rapids: Baker Academic, 2015).

11. Ephraim Radner, *The End of the Church: A Pneumatology of Christian Division in the West* (Grand Rapids: Eerdmans, 1998); *A Brutal Unity: The Spiritual Politics of the Christian Church* (Waco, TX: Baylor University Press, 2012).

12. Ephraim Radner, *Leviticus* (Grand Rapids: Brazos Press/Baker, 2008).

ing and preaching of the Scriptures? As figural readers from the early church through the monastic and parish precincts of the 14th century through the American wilderness of the 17th century all knew, the Bible impinged upon their existences from the ground up, and to hear it and receive it gladly is to be and become a certain kind of person. Conversely, to turn away from the Scriptures or receive them with resistance is to be and become another sort of person. The same is true, surely, *mutatis mutandis* for the church and her churches — each becomes who they are according to their posture before and with the Word. Perhaps both sorts will meet each other coming around — the welcoming and the spurning. In an embrace?

Certainly, both will find their place in the one world that God creates according to the Scriptures. This fact has its range of doctrinal, moral, and political consequences, which I hope others will pursue. But the greatest of consequences, I believe, is simply reading the Bible in such a way that its power to form becomes a matter for constant thanksgiving. All of us will do something. Josiah rent his garments when he heard the Word read (2 Kings 22:11); Job clapped his hand upon his mouth when he saw it spoken (Job 40:4); Mary wondered at its feet (Luke 10:39). I would climb a little higher (Luke 19:4) — and others with me? — to see its passage into my midst.

PART ONE

THE HISTORY AND THEOLOGY OF FIGURAL READING

CHAPTER 1

Figural History as a Question

In this first chapter, I want to provide a kind of case study: what does it mean when we say that the Bible talks about history and historical events? We may think that this is an easily grasped common-sense notion that requires little examination. In fact, however, Christians (and Jews, as we will see later) have, until only recently, understood "common sense" on this matter in a very different way than we do today. Much theological debate in our day is founded on the question of "did it happen?" From this question, many other questions can be answered. But this basic issue of "happening" has become the entry way into almost all other interpretive discussions. In this first chapter, then, I want to engage the issue of figural reading by complicating the modern question of "did it happen?" without yet drawing any clear conclusions. Taking a well-known topic, "exile," I will simply provide a straightforward summary exposition of its figural explication within the Christian tradition. But I present it within the context of a discussion of N. T. Wright's historical-critical argument regarding the idea of "ongoing exile" as informing the expectations of 1st-century Judaism, and hence of Jesus, and of Paul's own attitudes regarding the divine promise for Israel's restoration.[1] My point in doing this is twofold. First, I want to show how it is quite natural to expand the reach of the historical-critical argument itself: the notion of ongoing exile has a paradox-

---

1. See, in general, his *Jesus and the Victory of God* (Christian Origins and the Question of God, Volume 2) (Minneapolis: Fortress Press, 2010), pp. xvii-xviii, 126-29, 428-30; *What Saint Paul Really Said: Was Paul of Tarsus the Real Founder of Christianity?* (Grand Rapids: Eerdmans, 1997), pp. 29-35; "Continuing Exile: Paul and the Deuteronomy/Daniel Tradition," lecture given at Trinity Western University, November 17, 2010.

ical signification even at the time of Jesus. Second, I want to suggest that the figural interpretation of exile not only rightly engages this paradox, but also (and therefore) relativizes the historical-critical temporal framework itself. If in fact ongoing exile, as understood or grasped after in 1st-century Judaism, transcends unitary temporal limits, what are we talking about exactly when we speak about "history"? My hope in making this two-fold point is to narrow somewhat the gap in mutual understanding that has, alas, arisen between historical critics and figural exegetes. It is a gap that has unhelpfully made antagonistic two necessary aspects of scriptural reading.

In what follows, I want first to present the figural approach to scriptural exile, and then reflect more broadly on some traditional significations of this referent. One of the key issues is to gauge their historical meaning, that is, the way they conceptualize history itself as a scripturally-informed reality. Next, I will briefly try to locate these traditional significations within the scriptural text itself, addressing the basic question of whether they have any *prima facie* plausibility as valid readings of the Bible on its own terms. Since my conclusion is that they *do* have such plausibility, I will then want to assess more broadly what a Christian "theology of exile" might constitute, and how it in fact might relate to historical experience. Only from this perspective, finally, will I seek to evaluate the *historical* meaning of concepts like "continuing exile" and "restoration" as exegetically useful tools. My conclusion is that, while they are indeed useful, they are so only on a limited basis, and only insofar as they find their place in a more supple understanding of the Bible's historical referentiality itself. It is this suppleness, demanded by the shape of historical experience and its articulation itself, that opens the window onto the compelling character of figural reading.

I. The Figural Challenge

Let me begin with a classic example of simple figural explication as a way of setting out what has been called the "pre-critical" challenge. What does the word "exile" refer to scripturally? In Calvin's view it was a textual term with a multiple range of simultaneous referents. So, in a famous letter written from Geneva to Jacques de Bourgogne, Monsieur de Falais, whose Reformed convictions had set him at odds with the French authorities, Calvin takes the contemporary political referent as a tool to leverage out several scriptural meanings.[2] First, he calls de Falais to accept *being exiled* from France for the

---

2. Yan Brailowsky, « Mis au ban de la terre promise? La mythographie des exilés religieux

sake of his faith. But this exile, similar to the one that Calvin accepted for himself, refers to Christ's own banishment, something implicit in his passion and death. Here is a case where one must follow the Master. But one does so, according to Calvin, in line with Abraham's earlier exile, one in which he "hastened forth without hesitation."

> We have no express revelation commanding us to leave the country; but seeing that we have the commandment to honour God, both in body and soul, wherever we are, what more would we have? It is to us, then, equally that these words are addressed, *Get thee out of thy country and from thy kindred.*[3]

Calvin's appeal to Abraham, on the basis that "we are his children," proved a frequent move in seeking a referent for the experience of contemporary exile.[4] But he also made use of other referents, slightly less exemplarist, and more situational: the Roman Church was the Babylon of old, into which one might in fact be carried away in captivity — so be careful! But as a place of idolatry, the Roman Church was also to be fled in bodily suffering, much as the early Christians had demanded flight from the Babylonian Rome of the book of Revelation. In such a Rome as this, after all, Anti-Christ had set himself up, in the form of the papacy.[5]

Yet more broadly and perhaps deeply, Calvin could view the scriptural — and hence contemporary — referent of exile as the "world" itself, a place of material limitations and suffering, a place of perverting fleshly satisfactions and unfulfilled spiritual desires, a landscape of passage in contrast to one's true heavenly "home." Here, the "banishment" of Christ takes form in the body of his incarnation itself, something to be suffered for the sake of a final exaltation and reign. "In Christ," the true Christian also lives through such an existential exile, now synonymous (as already in Abraham's case) with the act of "pilgrimage" and wayfaring.[6]

---

sous le règne de Mary Tudor », in *Le bannissement et l'exil en europe aux XVIe et XVIIe siècles,* Pascal Drouet and Yan Brailowsky (Rennes : Presses Universitaires de Rennes, 2010), pp. 15-30, which offers an overview of 16th-century Protestant, especially English, understandings of scriptural exile.

3. John Calvin, *Letters of John Calvin,* ed. Jules Bonnet, trans. David Constable (Edinburgh: Thomas Constable and Co., 1855), vol. 1, p. 374. The letter is dated October 14, 1543.

4. Calvin, *Letters,* vol. 1, p. 401; John Calvin, *Letters of John Calvin,* ed. Jules Bonnet (Philadelphia: Presbyterian Board of Education, 1858), vol. 2, p. 121.

5. *Institutes of the Christian Religion,* IV.2.4 and 12; IV.2.10, 23.

6. Calvin, *Letters,* vol. 2, pp. 208-9; "Even if no necessity compelled you to quit the nest, yet you were no daughter of God, if this earthly life did not seem to you a pilgrimage. But now when the sacrilegious tyranny of Antichrist expels you from it, and God calls

Of course, this is all a familiar application of spiritual — multivalent — signification, much as the Christian tradition had been engaging for centuries. And with respect to the referent of "exile," Calvin draws on an established and rich legacy of exegesis, beginning at least in the early church, as well as in Rabbinic Judaism. (To what degree it is embedded, as it were, in the scriptural text itself is a question we will raise later.) In what follows, I want to explore this interpretive phenomenon, less as a matter of historical description than as a matter of engaging the historical effect given by the meaning of the scriptural text itself. When Scripture speaks of "exile," what are we "meant" to understand by the verbal referent? What do our times, which are given by God, press us into apprehending?

The theological stakes are obviously high in answering this kind of question. N. T. Wright's own influential reading of the meaning of the Christian gospel, founded on Jesus' recorded preaching and Paul's central proclamation, derives from a particular claim regarding the meaning of exile "for" Jesus and Paul, and therefore the meaning of exile's resolution or healing.[7] The claim itself is based on a self-consciously "critical" examination of the Scripture. On a straightforward level, we might wonder if Jesus' understanding of exile and its overcoming, in scriptural terms, was simply different than Calvin's, and therefore if Calvin's understanding of the gospel was somehow off-base. This might seem a (methodologically) simple historical problem to address. But what if the traditional and "pre-critical" reading of exile as holding multiple referents is evangelically valid, that is, what if it properly — in the sense of deriving from the message of Jesus Christ — founds the gospel? How might this inform our *historical* thinking about the meaning of "exile" in its scriptural enunciation, even in the context of Jesus' own specific teaching, and hence "self-understanding"?

II. The Christian Figural Tradition of Exile

We have already seen some of Calvin's understandings of the scriptural referent for "exile": there is such a thing as a politico-religious exile, in which individuals (like himself) leave their country and go to live in another. Gen-

---

you with a loud voice to go forth; let not the condition of your peregrination seem painful to you, till the time when at last he shall bring us all together into his eternal inheritance (pp. 452-53).

7. "Theology, History and Jesus: A Response to Maurice Casey and Clive Marsh," *Journal for the Study of the New Testament* 69 (1998): 105-12. This offers a succinct view as to how he views this topic within the context of a critical historian's task.

erally Calvin sees this as a necessity to be borne for the sake of fidelity to the gospel. (As some commentators have pointed out, he was here following an "Athanasian" tradition of defending the Christian acceptance of exile, over and against the tradition of Tertullian that argued for the Christian acceptance of martyrdom *in situ*.)[8] "Conscience" and the freedom to worship God faithfully might well demand that one leave one's home. But Calvin places this concrete experience of politico-religious exile within the "reality" of Jesus' own experience of exile, now viewed in various ways: his "exile" from heaven to earth in his incarnation; deriving from this, his passion and death; but upholding this, his own politico-religious exile given in the form of his persecution and arrest, and thereby his being "driven" from the nation of Israel. It is out of this fundamental Christic character and experience of exile that Calvin identifies a number of other specific scriptural exiles: Abraham's, the Jews' exile from Jerusalem, and so on. Likewise, he frames the Christian life as a whole in terms of Christ's exilic-incarnational form: the world in "this life" is a place of exile, cast in terms of a difficult journey or pilgrimage leading back to one's heavenly "home" or "inheritance," and defined in terms of temptations and the assaults of Satan, the latter of which is given historical force especially through the form and action of the Roman Church and her pontiff.

The context of his usage was firmly grounded, from one perspective, in lived experience, that is, in his own exile from France and in that of countless others whom he either knew personally or about whom he had heard. This fact is important to bear in mind, for the same can be said for other scriptural interpreters of the era, especially among Reformed readers of the Bible: to speak of "exile" as a "scriptural" referent was to speak of something whose lived contours were familiar. So, for instance, William Tyndale's interest in exile as a theological category was clearly informed by a life whose very shape was bound to his own exilic existence. Yet it was also one that he had to reflect upon theologically in terms of Scripture's own referents. Tyndale's usage is, in his case, more continuous with early church understandings in the tradition of Tertullian, where persecution and martyrdom were seen as specific demands

---

8. Tertullian's *De fuga in persecutione* is the classic text for the argument that persecution is to be accepted, since (according to Tertullian) its ultimate author is God, who uses it for the good of the suffering Christian and for the unveiling of a clear witness to the gospel. Flight — or, as it were, the acceptance of exile for the sake of one's faith — is by contrast a form simply of cowardice and disobedience. Tertullian deals with scriptural examples of flight by consigning them to a now-overcome dispensation. Athanasius, on the other hand, in his *Apologia de fuga sua*, offers the contrasting position of one who views persecution as inherently satanic, and thus properly resistable, until the point that death is simply unavoidable. His own use of scriptural figures is less dispensationalist than is Tertullian's.

of faithfulness and also finally prizes for it as well. In general, he does not speak explicitly of "exile," but rather of "captivity," in the terms of Egypt or Babylon. And in this regard, the pope embodies, for example, Pharaoh, aiming his evil wiles against an Israel that embraces "all" of God's people, including, of course, the true church. In this, however, the dynamic of oppression is historically extensive, moving throughout the entire scriptural history, where "prophet" and king stand in a kind of primordial struggle, with the pope standing for all the enemies of the truly faithful, subjecting them to "bondage" and "captivity," and finally personifying "the world" itself, who "hateth them [Israel] for their faith and trust which they have in God." It is precisely because the nature of this struggle is thus intrinsic to the world's history as a whole that Tyndale will take the route of Tertullian (despite his own personal flight to the Continent) and urge patience in one's place of witness. Hence, scriptural "exile" as "captivity" is in fact the experience of persecution itself, in all its forms, and such persecution becomes the identifying mark of the true church. Yet even here, one can go further: the church is true insofar as she rightly and honestly lives out the true historical condition of humankind: "captivity" is, at its most fundamental, the condition of the sinner bound by Satan; and the scriptural events that recount forms of bondage are but instances that figure sin's domain. Salvation, then, derives from this recognition and the turn to God's grace in Christ for forgiveness and empowered love.[9]

Calvin's "calling out" of his French friends *into* an experienced exile was, in its most pragmatic orientation, a contrasting "Athanasian" response, and made use of its own set of scriptural figures. But whether Tyndalian or Calvinistic, what shaped the Christian tradition that each shared in common was a sense that "exile" was something that was intransigently a part of the Christian existence, something to be grappled with and navigated, including and most especially in its scriptural demarcation. We tend to forget this in our own day, as we imagine exile in terms of an almost ideal form or experience, requiring somehow existential translation for the modern mind. But from the ancient world to the 16th century (and obviously beyond) the actual experience of exile was a central part of social life. It is only recently that historians and cultural critics have begun to pay attention to this fact.[10] Banishment and exile,

9. For the various references to Tyndale above, see respectively his *Obedience of a Christian Man, Prologue to Exodus, Prologue to Jonas*, and *Parable of the Wicked Mammon*, all found in *The Works of the English Reformers William Tyndale and John Frith*, ed. Thomas Russell (London: Ebenezer Palmer, 1831), vol. 1, pp. 17, 58, 343. The quotation itself is from the *Prologue to Exodus*, p. 17. While this edition is critically outdated, it is easily accessible, and accurately provides the major texts.

10. In addition to the volume of Drouet and Brailowsky above, see Jan Felix Gaertner ed.,

of individuals or of whole groups and peoples, were a regular practice over the centuries, used generally for purposes of political and sometimes simply personal control, display, and vindictiveness. These repeated, remembered, experienced, and often expected elements of "displacement" were memorialized by great writers (e.g. Ovid, whose attitudes joined with Scripture in informing exilic experience in the Middle Ages), as well as by the folk wisdom of widespread adepts. Popular traditions of the fugitive (e.g. Robin Hood) bumped up with sophisticated literary articulation (e.g. Dante and Cino da Pistoia, or François de Villon), but in both cases these publicized attitudes were bound to actual lives whose pointed details were broadly familiar. Furthermore, exile continued to be something aimed at the center of Christian existence quite specifically in various ways, including within a context of legal expectation and even sanctioned authority.[11] Hence, "excommunication" becomes a form of "exile," or simply the life of disciplined subjection within the Christian church's authoritative structures, sometimes under bishops, sometimes as bishops (e.g. Beckett and Anselm) under the secular arm. The so-called "Babylonian Captivity" of the papacy in Avignon is a formidable example of how "exile" becomes a specifically *Christian* ecclesial condition that gathers within its concrete forms, often quite painful, not only the full scriptural weight of meaning but the expectations of the early Fathers and saints who had already borne these figures.[12]

The fact that the experience of exile not only failed to diminish in the early modern and modern periods, but actually expanded its reach, and at least initially did so on the basis of religious realities, is again something we tend to forget. Calvin's own discussion is a specifically religious discussion, but one whose demands are existentially ineluctable, as they continue to be through-

---

Writing Exile: The Discourse of Displacement in Greco-Roman Antiquity and Beyond (Leiden: Brill, 2007); and Laura Napran and Elisabeth Van Houts, eds., *Exile in the Middle Ages* (Turnhout, Belgium: Brepols, 2004). The introductory chapters by Gaertner and Napran respectively provide overviews of the burgeoning literature for these periods. See also the two volumes edited by James M. Scott, *Exile: Old Testament, Jewish, Christian Conceptions* (Leiden: Brill, 1997); and *Restoration: Old Testament, Jewish & Christian Perspectives* (Leiden: Brill, 2001).

11. The development of ecclesial laws and canons governing "exclusion" on various grounds follows the ramification of the actual practice of exile. Elizabeth Vodola, *Excommunication in the Middle Ages* (Berkeley: University of California Press, 1986).

12. Cf. Brian Briggs's discussion of the 12th-century Osbert of Clare, "*Expulsio, Proscriptio, Exilium*: Exile and Friendship in the Writings of Osbert of Clare," in Napran and Van Houts, *Exile*, pp. 131-44. Osbert's exiles seem to have been due to ecclesiastical conflicts. But Briggs shows how, in his letters, Osbert made use of an astoundingly broad rhetorical repertoire of exilic figures, whose imaginary purchase was due less to the monk's learning than to their insistent pertinence.

out the 17th and 18th centuries, and for many beyond. Catholics, Protestants, Dissenters, Sectarian trouble-makers, Anabaptists, and so on were driven out of their homes, fled, or were imprisoned and banished by the thousands (and in the case of the French Huguenots, by the hundreds of thousands).[13] The "modern" and contemporary experience of exile, as it has tended to attract commentary, has been more political in its ramifications.[14] One speaks today of a "political refugee" rather than an "exile," although the causal base of each is usually similar, and the contemporary nomenclature tends to stress provisionality over permanence (something with its own existential implications, especially if unreflected by actual outcomes).[15] But one can properly project backwards the considerations of contemporary "exilic" writers in their response to experiential constraints, reading the tropes of their self-understanding within the traditional stream of religious figuralism, and discover how the meaning of their philosophies and political science in particular have taken on peculiar nuances in ways inexplicable except from within this tradition.[16]

These concrete experiences, furthermore, were only fragmentary — if often overwhelming — elements of a larger picture of human existence, where

13. Christopher D'Addario, *Exile and Journey in Seventeenth-Century Literature* (Cambridge: Cambridge University Press, 1999); Philip Major, ed., *Literatures of Exile in the English Revolution and Its Aftermath, 1640-1690* (Farnham, Surrey: Ashgate, 2010); Bertrand Van Ruymbeke and Randy J. Sparks, eds., *The Huguenots in France and the Atlantic Diaspora* (Columbia, SC: University of South Carolina Press, 2003). For a rather sobering account of the confusing fruit of the exilic experience, religiously and politically, see Abraham Friesen, *In Defense of Privilege: Russian Mennonites and the State Before and During World War I* (Winnipeg, Canada: Historical Commission of the US and Canadian Mennonite Brethren Churches, 2006).

14. Terry Eagleton, *Exiles and Émigrés: Studies in Modern Literature* (London: Chatto & Windus, 1970); this was an early examination of modern English writing in this vein. Many other studies have followed, concentrating on different political locales and geographical origins: e.g. David Bevan, *Literature and Exile* (Amsterdam: Rodopi, 1990); Sophia A. McClennan, *The Dialectics of Exile: Nation, Time, Language, and Space in Hispanic Literatures* (West Lafayette, IN: Purdue University Press, 2004); John Neubauer and Borbála Zsuzsanna Török, eds., *The Exile and Return of Writers from East-Central Europe: A Compendium* (Berlin: Walter de Gruyter, 2009); etc.

15. According to Refugees International (basing their numbers on UN statistics), there were in 2011 over 15 million cross-border political refugees, and over 24 million "internally displaced" refugees. See http://www.refugeesinternational.org/get-involved/helpful-facts-%2526-figures#top.

16. The more nihilistic strand of thinking, e.g. by Emil Cioran, can only be grasped from within this specifically European and Christian stream of exilic perspective. See also Leszek Kolakowski, "In Praise of Exile," in *Modernity on Endless Trial* (Chicago: University of Chicago Press, 1997), pp. 55-59. Kolakowski is explicit in trying to relocate contemporary exilic consciousness within a more traditional scriptural context.

material, social, and geographical instability were constant features of most people's lives. Again, modern Westerners tend to forget this perennial element of our race's heritage. Philosophical judgments about this fact were in any case long in play, from a range of antique visions regarding the fleeting character of human life to developed metaphysics of material alienation. Plotinus' famous framework of *exitus-reditus* (the increasingly burdensome departure of being from its source of oneness, and its eventual return into unity) was given a common conceptual stamp at the celebrated end of his *Enneads*: "This is the life of gods and of the godlike and blessed among men, liberation from the alien that besets us here, a life taking no pleasure in the things of earth, the passing of solitary to solitary."[17] The standard MacKenna translation just quoted colors the Greek perhaps too strikingly, but Plotinus's vision is clear enough: the things of this earth are "other" ("alien") to the truly "godlike" human being, and divinity consists of "liberation" from their grip and literally "fleeing" to the One.[18] It was this framework that simply fit into the widespread categories already in use, politically, economically, and religiously for some time: "flight" or "exile" from the world of useless passions and besetting suffering, and searching instead for some kind of union with that which lasts. Even in the late 20th century, Kolakowski can affirm that "exile is the permanent human condition."[19] But as permanent, its alternative — redemption or release — is obviously located elsewhere than in the "world" itself. This is, in fact, Tyndale's claim about "the world" (in a certain Johannine and perhaps Pauline reading of the matter) and Calvin's too.

But they were well established long before. Origen had his own Christian version of the Plotinian paradigm of exile, driven by a sophisticated scriptural ascetic. Figurally, it was given in the sin of Adam and Eve and their expulsion from Paradise, into a world of mortality, suffering, and sinful debasement. But it was this reality that the historical narratives of the Bible, and indeed therefore their historical weight as temporal experiences, signified.[20]

Therefore, when you hear of the captivity of the people, believe that it did indeed happen according to the historical narrative, but then go on to un-

17. Plotinus, *Enneads*, trans. Stephen MacKenna, 2nd edition by B. S. Page (London: Faber and Faber, 1956), p. 625.

18. Cf. the Greek text in Plotinus, *Ennead VI:6-9*, trans. A. H. Armstrong (Cambridge, MA: Harvard University Press, 1988), p. 344.

19. Kolakowski, "In Praise of Exile," p. 59.

20. See Joseph Trigg, "Origen, *Homily I on Ezekiel*," in *Ascetic Behavior in Greco-Roman Antiquity: A Sourcebook*, ed. Vincent L. Wimbush (Minneapolis: Fortress Press, 1990), pp. 45-67.

derstand that story as a sign of something else. Following that sign you will discover the mystery. You, if you call yourself a believer, when you experience peace — Christ indeed is our peace — inhabit Jerusalem. If you then sin, God's visitation leaves you, and you are handed over captive to Nebuchadnezzar, and so led captive into Babylon. When then your soul is troubled by vices and disturbances, you are taken into Babylon [. . .] Adam was indeed in Paradise, but the serpent caused his captivity, and brought it about that he was expelled from Jerusalem or Paradise, and entered into this place of tears.[21]

Jesus, then, the Son from heaven, "descends into corruption," into the place of "captivity" that is Ezekiel's, the other human prophets', and ours. But because we are made one with him, Jesus can say to us "Come out!" — out of Babylon, out of captivity, out of the "storms of life," out of the fallen world, out of sin — and rise into forgiveness, sinlessness, immortality, glory. The world is a place of purgation's "hot wind"; Jesus, the means by which we reach the pacific cool of heaven.

The purgative character of the world, at least for the believer, was taken up robustly by the ascetic vocation of the monastic movement. Hence, "exile" is increasingly filled by Christian writers with a paradoxical value, and just as "discipline comes from the Lord" (Heb. 12:3-11), suffering is granted a divine purpose whose end lies beyond this life. Jerome, for instance, can call exile a "crown" for the Christian, turning political oppression on its head as a prize. But he goes on to point out that the life of the monk more particularly is itself a kind of positive "exile": "is not every monk an exile from his country? Is he not an exile from the whole world?" The public authorities have no power over one whose retreat into the ever-present Christ releases him from the landscape of physical arrest and banishment.[22] And this is only because there is no difference between such political exile and daily existence itself. Human life, in its bare form, is intrinsically captive. So Chrysostom expresses himself on the Christian life, whose sojourn in this world is one of the "foreigner" (*xenos* — as used in Hebrews 11:13, and then joined conceptually to 13:13-14) from heaven.[23] As the Latin, and finally Vulgate, translation of Hebrews 11:13 made use of the term *peregrinus*, the "pilgrim" figure took wing,

---

21. Trigg, "Origen," p. 52.

22. Jerome, Letter 82.10, to Theophilus of Alexandria, in *Nicene and Post-Nicene Fathers, Second Series*, vol. 6, p. 172.

23. John Chrysostom, Homilies on Matthew, in *Patrologia latina*, 58:548. Chrysostom's own embodied fate in an exiled death was more than fitting to his exegesis.

classicized in the West by Augustine and Gregory.[24] We are all sojourners on earth within this mortal life, and the Christian "alien" is particular in that his or her eyes are rightly cast upon the true *patria* in heaven. By the Middle Ages, devotionally upheld by a complicated network of geographical pilgrimage routes, this consciousness moved far beyond monastic vocation and became a standard lens for popular self-understanding.[25] Books treating human life as a pilgrimage proliferated, often in multiple translations, and in fact successfully migrated into the epoch of printing, as well as crossing the Catholic-Protestant frontier into the 17th century. From Guillaume de Digulleville to John Bunyan, mutations of the Augustinian outlook shaped a comprehensive cultural interpretation of human life.[26] And it did so, in large part, because it "fit" the felt ordering of human existence.

We can take Bede's summary of the threefold meaning of Psalm 136 (137) — "By the waters of Babylon . . ." — as a crystallization of this entire outlook in

24. Irenaeus was in fact one of the first to stress this theme. See Emmanuel Lanne, "La 'xeniteia' d'Abraham dans l'oeuvre d'Iréné. Aux origines monastiques de la thème de la '*peregrinatio*,'" *Irenikon* 47:2 (1974): 163-87. Augustine uses the *peregrinus* image frequently. In the *Confessions*, for instance, in 3.6; 9.13 (the pilgrimage of earth away from the eternal Jerusalem); 10.5. The *City of God*, of course, is replete with examples, especially where the "City of God" is itself described as an "earthly pilgrim": 1.35; 15.1; 18.54; etc. See M. A. Claussen, "'Peregrinatio' and 'Peregrini' in Augustine's 'City of God,'" *Traditio* 46 (1991): 33-75. Further, see Augustine's commentaries on the Psalms, 38.21; 49.22; 64.2; 119.6-9 etc. On Augustine and his role in the Western tradition here, see Manuela Brito-Martins, "The Concept of *peregrinatio* in Saint Augustine and Its Influences," in Napran and Van Houts, *Exile*, pp. 83-94. For other patristic discussion, see Wendy Pullan, "Ambiguity as a Central Condition of Early Christian Pilgrimage," in Jaś Elsner and Ian Rutherford, eds., *Pilgrimage in Graeco-Roman and Early Christian Antiquity: Seeing the Gods* (Oxford: Oxford University Press, 2006), pp. 387-410. Gregory provided the foundation for the medieval tradition of "spiritual pilgrimage," often spoken of in terms of early "exile," yet specifically colored by a range of affective elements, such as "desire" and "yearning" for heaven. See his *Moralia*, 18, in *Patrologia latina*, 76:63. For an extensive treatment of the tradition here, see F. C. Gardiner, *The Pilgrimage of Desire: A Study of Theme and Genre in Medieval Literature* (Leiden: Brill, 1971).

25. Cf. the standard analysis by Jean Leclercq, "Monachisme et pérégrination du IXe au XIIe siècle," *Studia Monastica*, III (1969): 33-52.

26. For references to studies of Digulleville's three popular "pilgrimage" poems (translated a century later into English by John Lydgate, and then one of the earliest books printed in England), see Maureen Boulton, "Digulleville's *Pèlerinage de Jésus Christ*: A Poem of Courtly Devotion," in *The Vernacular Spirit: Essays on Medieval Religious Literature*, ed. Renate Blumenfeld-Kosinski, Duncan Robertson, and Nancy Warren (New York: Palgrave Macmillan, 2002), pp. 125-44. More broadly, see Dee Dyas, *Pilgrimage in English Literature, 700-1500* (Cambridge: Boydell and Brewer Ltd., 2001). For an overview that covers material from the early church to the 17th century, see Juergen Hahn, *The Origins of the Baroque Concept of Peregrinatio* (Chapel Hill, NC: University of North Carolina Press, 1973).

terms of its explicit scriptural referents. There are three "captivities" to which Babylon refers, he writes: there is first, of course, the captivity of the Jews at the hands of the Babylonians themselves; there is, second, the captivity of the human race in sin, brought by Adam's fall and expulsion from Paradise; and there is, third, the captivity into which the Devil would ensnare the church's members during their earthly pilgrimage.[27] "Captivity," more generally, can be rendered as "the world," just as "Jerusalem" can be rendered as Christ's salvation and as heaven.[28] The *Glossa* takes this further, and, as with the tradition as a whole, ramifies captivity's reach in terms of a range of assaults — "carnality," "cupidity" and so on.[29] But the range of referents is clear and relatively stable. As the tradition reads "captivity" or "exile," Christian writers also reference various scriptural figures.[30] Besides Babylon, we have Abraham and his own exile from Ur; the Egypt of Pharaoh; there is also David, especially in the Psalmic location of his laments — flight from Saul and exile in Philistia, flight from Jerusalem, and so on; the prophets as a group become figures of exile, whether before or after the key moment of Babylonian captivity, for they struggle with Israel's sinful leadership and are always, as it were, standing "outside the camp" in their truthful witness. Moving to the New Testament, figures like John exiled at Patmos and his own visions in the Apocalypse are commonly taken up; as is Paul in his final journey, and so on.[31] Overarching all of these is the dual figure of Adam and Christ, each exiled in their own way, yet with the latter carrying through the former's restoration precisely through his own subjection to captivity's fundamental grasp in sin and death. It is in this movement that the Christian is caught within the world, neither wholly free, nor yet wholly imprisoned. Hence the notion of progression, the journey and pilgrimage *towards* freedom, the "Jerusalem above," somehow already spiritually touched.

27. Certain ecclesiological elements conformed to as well as made possible some of these distinctions, for instance, the common view that there were different levels or even referents for "the Church's members" in this regard, e.g. the perfect, the imperfect, and the evil, to which aspects of "captivity" might apply differently. See Marcia L. Colish's discussion of medieval psalm exegesis in her *Peter Lombard* (Leiden: Brill, 1994), vol. 1, pp. 162-88, esp. p. 172.

28. The discussion by Bede (or probably a much later follower) on Psalm 136/7 is found in *Patrologia latina* 93:1093-94.

29. For the *Glossa*, see *Patrologia latina*, 113:344 and 1056-58 on Psalm 136/37 in particular.

30. In fact, the Vulgate rarely uses the word *exilium*, and hence *captivitas* came to be seen as equivalent (though sometimes the distinction was played upon). See C. P. Lewis, "Gruffudd ap Cynan and the Reality and Representation of Exile," in Napran and Van Houts, *Exile*, pp. 45-46.

31. These common figures can be gleaned from the various discussions in Napran and Van Houts, whose wide scope of focus, from Viking to Italian culture, nonetheless maintains a consistent set of exilic scriptural texts as they are applied to contemporary experience.

III. A Scriptural Figural Tradition?

Where do these referents for captivity and exile stand in terms of a scriptural textual tradition in itself? Part of Wright's own project, along with others, has been to found the notion of a "continuing exile," even after the nominal "return" from Babylon, within biblical texts themselves, like Daniel and Ezra, and he has done that well.[32] Likewise, he has insisted, again rightly, that inter-testamental texts raise the exilic demand into an eschatological pitch (something I will return to shortly). He also notes that Israel-as-expelled-Adam was already rooted in Jewish tradition in the inter-testamental period.[33] If nothing else, this leads one to assume at least the potential resonance of such thinking regarding the figural reach of the exilic condition within the intentionality of New Testament writers, including Jesus himself. But even without such specific exegetical (and to some extent difficult-to-date) resolutions on hand, one cannot escape the fundamental exilic projection into the full range of scriptural figure by the canonical Psalms themselves, whose superscriptions alone demand a multi-referential application: chronological exclusivity is rejected in favor of a historical simultaneity that must include, by definition, the "now." This, after all, lies at the base of Jesus' own usage of the Psalms to indicate his place within them.[34]

It is, of course, this drawing together of Jesus and David, and through this, David and a host of other realities, from Adam through the exodus and beyond, that makes of exile, as in Psalm 136/7, a referentially multivalent reality. When Jesus speaks of a future destruction for Jerusalem, he does so in terms of this psalm (Luke 19:43-44). But he also places his own disciples (along with himself) within this turmoil. Many of the discipleship sayings are in fact cast in exilic terms, as are the end-time sayings: Chapter 9 of Luke, for instance, is filled with references to the impoverishment of wandering and homelessness, while the final age is to be one of flight from home and land (Luke 21:21), just as the disciple must not be like "Lot's wife" (Luke 17:32). The Johannine translation of some of these elements into the language of the "world" and its sufferings (John 16:33) does not, for all that, eliminate the specific chronological aspects of divine demand and historical crisis (John 15:19; Rev. 7:14). Existence and crisis are conflated, and take the form of the persecuted Christ (Acts 14:22; 1 Thess. 3:4; 2 Tim. 3:12). Specific notations of exile (e.g. Matt. 10:23;

32. Wright, "Continuing Exile."

33. Wright, *The Climax of the Covenant: Christ and the Law in Pauline Theology* (London: T&T Clark, 1991), 18-40.

34. Most famously in his cry of dereliction from the Cross (Ps. 22:1) and self-commendation (Ps. 35:5).

Ps. 105:12-13) are located within the general vocation of a discipleship whose normalcy is defined in the terms of the Last Days (Matt. 10:5-42), and these in the specific form of Jesus himself (John 15:20). Paul's and the other letter writers' diasporal (Gal. 6:16; James 1:1; 1 Pet. 1:1; Heb. 13:14) and two-age discussions (e.g. 2 Cor. 4:18-5:2; Phil. 3:2-21) are inseparable from this framework, and they are founded on elements of spiritual expectation already embedded in the Psalms especially (Ps. 73:25).

These texts and their scripturally-networked meanings provide a fairly straightforward basis for the Christian tradition's appropriation of their intersecting referents. The movement from historical *exilium* (or *captivitas*) to existential *peregrinatio* becomes not only a fluid possibility but a permanent connection: "this world" is a world of "exile" in which we "make our way" — both in terms of endurance but also perhaps progress — to something "better," to "Jerusalem, our home," the divine *patria* or *civitas vera* who is God's own self. And the way to this goal is the way of Jesus himself, in him and after him, as patient disciple. The stable meaning of this vision is given in its multi-traditional and cross-denominational popularity, from monastic outlooks to 19th-century (and beyond) American Protestant spirituality. "Jesus, my all, to heav'n is gone . . . I'm on my journey home";[35] "I feel like, I feel like I'm on my journey home";[36] "I'm a pilgrim and a stranger, rough and thorny is the road";[37] "O who will come and go with me?";[38]

> O who will come and go with me,
> I am on my journey home;
> I'm bound fair Canaan's land to see,
> I am on my journey home.

35. Text by John Cennick (a young acquaintance of Wesley), originally in *Sacred Hymns for the Use of Religious Societies*, 1743; frequently reprinted, with the chorus, in America, e.g. *Southern Harmony* no. 11; *Baptist Harmony* no. 70.

36. The verses, beginning "When I Can Read My Title Clear," are by Isaac Watts (included in Richard Allen's 1801 hymnal for the African Methodist church), but the famous chorus and tune derives from 19th-century America. See Howard W. Odum, "Religious Folk-Songs of the Southern Negroes," *American Journal of Religious Psychology and Education*, vol. 3 (July, 1909): 265-365 (originally published as Odum's doctoral dissertation at Clark University), where Odum provides a range of examples from African-American hymnody that fall squarely into the *exilium-peregrinatio* scheme, and that drifted between Black and White spiritual in their adaptations.

37. Text by Mary Hamlin Maxwell. This hymn became popular within the Salvation Army at the turn of the 20th century.

38. Stith Mead, ed., *General Selection of the Newest and Most Admired Hymns and Spiritual Songs Now in Use* (Richmond, VA: Seaton Grantland, 1807), no. 89.

O come and go with me,
O come and go with me,
O come and go with me,
For I'm on my journey home.
Farewell vain world, I'm going home,
I am on my journey home;
My Savior smiles and bids me come,
I am on my journey home.
Sweet angels beckon me away,
I am on my journey home;
To sing God's praise in endless day,
I am on my journey home.

What is crucial to grasp is the way this stable tradition finds its vital tap root, not simply in a congenial and long-lived devotional style, but in the very referential exactitude of the Scripture's description of exilic existence as it is in fact historically located in the ongoing lives of Christians.[39] That is part of the insistence of African-American theologians, whose rejection of the compensatory theory of "slave religion" in favor of its scriptural fidelity has done so much to revitalize the proper recognition of each reality's nature — the Scripture's inherent meaning and power, and its just appropriation by African-American Christians.[40]

All this is not just an interesting piece of intellectual or devotional history. It must, if only as a matter of usage, raise the question, "to what does the scriptural referent of 'exile' 'actually' refer?" If "actually" is taken in a strict historical sense, it is nonetheless just this historically inescapable experience of "ongoing exile" in the lives of those reading the Bible that cannot be avoided in a first-order way. It is an experience whose formal similarities with the shape

39. Kiri Miller, *Traveling Home: Sacred Harp Singing and American Pluralism* (Univ. of Illinois Press, 2008) pp. 201-7, with its attempt to restate the central Christian tradition of exile and pilgrimage in a modern psycho-cultural dress, something whose post-modern self-referentiality must still bow to the assertive and explicit practice of this spirituality.

40. The theological seriousness of the "Spiritual," in its lived context, was emphasized in the early 20th century by critics like James Weldon Johnson. More recently, see James Cone, *The Spiritual and the Blues: An Interpretation* (Maryknoll, NY: Orbis, 1991). For a discussion that touches more acutely on the topic of this essay, see Cheryl Sanders, *Saints in Exile: The Holiness-Pentecostal Experience in African American Religion and Culture* (New York: Oxford University Press, 1999). Michael Stone-Richards, in *Logics of Separation: Exile and Transcendence in Aesthetic Modernity* (New York: Peter Lang, 2011), draws together African-American and African, as well as modern European authors like Paul Celan, in a contemporary revision of exilic consciousness (see above).

of 1st-century exile provides a consistent standard for judging referentiality as a scriptural category. One can note simply the perspective of Jewish readers of the text, for whom "exile" can only refer to a *sequence* of realities, and does so in fact: not only to the tense prolongation of Babylon's captivity through Roman hands — the purported "intended" meaning of the term at the time of Jesus; but also the already recognized expectation, only budding or fully formed, of a captivity whose breadth stretched backwards and forwards more mysteriously. It was, and remains, a reach that would include the Temple's destruction, further dispersion, Christian and Muslim oppression and persecution, and most recently a conflagration of unimagined magnitude in the Holocaust.

Indeed, that there *is* a historical question of the moral relationship between the Jews and the Christian church — a question whose answer has been ominously given in terms of a profound Christian culpability that cannot help but resonate with the words of Romans 11:21 — must touch upon *any* interpretive claim regarding this or that "historical" meaning attached to "ongoing exile" and "return from exile." The classic observances of the fast day of Tisha B'av (the "Ninth day of the month of Av"), lamenting the destruction of the two Temples, and later the mourning of other Jewish calamities, has, for all its debated significance as a holiday, long pointed to a chronological notion of "expectation" that obviously has extended far beyond the 1st century, *and, historically speaking, well ought to*. And if this is so, for the reader of the Scripture seeking the proper referent of "exile," there remains a real question: to which Jews are we asked to listen in order to ascertain correct scriptural "intentionality"? If the referent of "Israel" is already scripturally extended beyond the spatio-temporal location we identify as Babylon in the 6th century B.C., how far shall this go?

There is also the issue of the church's experiential outcome when taken as the fruit of a corporate entity: how does the church relate to "exile," not only under Rome — the book of Revelation's initial historical locale — nor under a range of experiences in the East and Near East, but under diverse *Christian* governing groups, and then within non-Western political and cultural alienations after especially the 16th century? In all this, individual Christian lives, in their many particulars, have moved to recast the character of exile in a temporally extended or at least multi-layered simultaneity with respect to scriptural descriptions, so that formal frameworks of referential interpretation like Bede's made common sense.

Part of both Jewish and Christian extensions of reference is bound up with the simple but inescapable theological and moral demands of theodicy: if the Scripture is somehow true in its reference, then its referents cannot be limited to chronologies of signification that exclude a clear relationship to the present. If "exile" is truly dealt with in the Scriptures — "restoration" — then that truth, whether it be "restoration" or not, must somehow include the historical exiles of the present. These demands have been properly tethered to renewed and repeated scriptural discernment, with the result that scriptural reality resolves exile in different ways: exile, for instance, may refer to a discipled participation in the Cross; or to an ascetic denial and yearning; or to some transtemporal pneumatic embrace; or an agonistic resistance to evil; to penitence; to the long practice of prayer. Paradoxically, from a Christian perspective, such referents *also* signify some true aspect of a *restoration from* exile, insofar as they are bound, in their enactment, to Christ Jesus.[41]

For on a scriptural level all of these resolutions of signification have been given through their enfigured realization: here is where we return to the specific question of scriptural reference. If the resolution is given "in Christ" somehow, then the character of "exile" itself encloses the standard referents of exile as "now," as "still true" in the same way as "Jesus is raised" or "Jesus is Lord" demands a rethinking of the "life" and "nature" of Jesus of Nazareth. Adam, Abraham, David and Saul, Jewish Babylon, Psalm 137, and so on, must now be determined by a character that is chronologically complex, for "He is the God of the living" (Mark 12:27). Their resolution as referents is given in their "ongoing" "life." Jerusalem as true "home" is expected because inhabited by various kings in David's line, to be sure; but this is so because it is, in a first-order way, lived as Jesus, Jerusalem's Lord, whose own exile "outside the camp" becomes, however oddly, the fullest expression of her restoration. Since all find their "home" in him, exile and return are coincident in Christ.

---

41. N. T. Wright, in his more popularly-oriented *Evil and the Justice of God* (Downers Grove, IL: InterVarsity Press, 2009), properly links the scriptural thematic of exile to theodicy (pp. 46-63), but is less clear about the properly figural reach of such a thematic into the character of "restoration" itself. He prefers, instead, to lay these links out on a still fairly strict serial chronological basis, as if what can prove to be the case in Old Testament terms — a figural exile that is broached for theodicy reasons by Israel — must no longer apply when it comes to Jesus himself (pp. 95-96). He goes further in engaging the Cross's "extended" temporal role in Paul's ministry in "Redemption from the New Perspective? Towards a Multi-Layered Pauline Theology of the Cross," in *Redemption*, ed. S. T. Davis, D. Kendall, and G. O'Collins (Oxford: Oxford University Press, 2006), pp. 69-100, especially pp. 94-98. But even here, there is a commitment to maintaining a commonsense past-present-future schema in a rather rigid, if not always illuminating way, where "anticipation" (i.e. of restoration's "full" accomplishment) as a temporal category bears more weight than it can with clarity. I am not here arguing that "figural time" provides a *better* theodicy, in the sense of being more morally realistic, than serial chronology, but such an argument could probably be made. More to the present point, I am arguing that theodicy probably requires both.

The coincidence here is important. For the temporal framework presupposed by these resolutions does not correspond neatly, let alone exhaustively, to the serial chronological scheme that expectation and fulfillment — along with its assumed phenomenologically identified experienced referents — might indicate. From a temporal standpoint, these resolutions point rather to a certain kind of simultaneity and historical extension (or distention), such that, at least in this kind of case, sequential and mutually discrete (and exclusive) events cannot properly identify a given scriptural referent at all. They can only provide an often limited perspective upon it. From a scriptural perspective, that is, what we learn from the text — its referents — are not fundamentally single narratives, but rather, in Jacob Neusner's phrase, narratives that act as "paradigms," whose forms actually found temporality's very nature in a primary fashion, and provide coherence to what could otherwise appear as only random experiential surd.[42] In a specifically Christian sense, it is the formative emergence of these paradigms — let us say, for instance, Adam and Abraham and Paul and John — within the experience of this or that individual and the church especially, that discloses the single temporal character that is Christ Jesus' own life. History consistently looks like Jesus, even as that one narrative is ordered by its appropriated narrative figures.

This is, in fact, a standard way of understanding "figural time," as it upholds a certain way of reading the Bible. It does not contradict the kind of claims N.T. Wright might make about a "single narrative drama" that informs the whole of the world's time, nor of the accumulating expectations that inform the religious orientations of 1st-century Jews like Paul. It can affirm that he was indeed, in his own view, living in the "middle stage" of a single overarching Deuteronomistic narrative of which we are a part, encompassing Sin, Exile, and Restoration.[43] That middle term is simply temporally extended. But how far? And in what directions? Within figural time, "extension" itself becomes part of the practice of phenomenal referentiality. Furthermore, Jesus as the Restorer does not somehow undercut or bring to an "end" such temporal extensions, but rather simply complicates them in upon himself yet more fully. "We thought he was the one to restore Israel" (Luke 24:21). The Restorer reengages the middle stage in one sense, his resurrection underlining its experiential form. But more importantly, the Restorer is, as Wright has argued, granted his prophetic leverage within the coming of the *eschaton*, and thus,

---

42. For an accessible entrée into Neusner's notion of temporal "paradigm," see his *The Theology of the Oral Torah: Revealing the Justice of God* (Montreal and Kingston, Canada: McGill-Queen's University Press, 1999), I.6, pp. 241-79.

43. Wright, "Continuing Exile," p. 8.

"eschatological time" takes over the dynamics of the grand narrative itself. And this is precisely where chronological sequence as an arbiter of referentiality breaks down, and where the historian's task trembles before the facts of God.

IV. Critical Realism and Its Probative Limits

Wright's own approach to the historian's task, which would uncover to some fair extent the meaning of a historical text like the Bible's, is governed by what he calls a "critical realism."[44] A critical realist will interpret a text according to the ongoing testing and adjustment of perspectives brought by reader, author(s), and cultural context, but also with the assumption of a stable and objective meaning to the text whose critical engagement must properly constrain interpretive directions and conclusions. These, finally, properly find their expression in the narrative forms by which textual meaning is always articulated in human terms.

> [Critical realism] is a way of describing the process of 'knowing' that acknowledges the *reality of the thing known, as something other than the knower* (hence 'realism'), while also fully acknowledging that the only access we have to this reality lies along the spiralling path of *appropriate dialogue or conversation between the knower and the thing known* (hence 'critical'). This path leads to critical reflection on the products of our enquiry into 'reality', so that our assertions about 'reality' acknowledge their own provisionality.[45]

> A critical-realist reading of a text will recognize, and take fully into account, the perspective and context of the reader. But such a reading will still insist that, within the story or stories that seem to make sense of the whole of reality, there exists, as essentially other than and different from the reader, texts that can be read, that have a life and a set of appropriate meanings not only potentially independent of their author but also potentially independent of their reader; and that the deepest level of meaning consists in the stories, and ultimately the worldviews, which the texts thus articulate.[46]

44. See N. T. Wright, *The New Testament and the People of God* (Christian Origins and the Question of God, Volume 1) (Minneapolis: Fortress Press, 1992), pp. 32-46. A lucid presentation of this topic is given by Robert Stewart, "NT Wright's Hermeneutic: Part 1. Critical Realism," in *The Churchman* 117:2 (2003): 153-76. References to some of the informing and parallel philosophical categories at work in critical realism are usefully provided.

45. Wright, *New Testament and the People of God*, p. 35.

46. Wright, *New Testament and the People of God*, p. 66.

Wright's version of critical realism is in fact an approach that is widely pursued, in a practical way. Biblical commentators share varying degrees of worry over whether the approach implies a "purely" perspectival view of knowledge or some even more fundamental skepticism. But most practitioners of the critical study of the past, in whatever field, employ some form of the "method," if that is what it is, if only because it is obvious that the past needs to be "studied" in part precisely because its form is somehow "missing" elements that must be hypothesized in order to be apprehended; and these hypotheses are ordered by a range of assumptions that are to be tested in concert with the evidence as one attempts to engage it.[47] At one clear end of the spectrum, one can observe how archaeologists, given a very limited collection of artifacts, must create contexts for them ("stories" or "narratives") whose shape can only be "critically" — that is, arguably on the basis of persuasive but rarely definitive evidence — theorized in order to elucidate the meaning of their contents.[48] But even here, precisely because the critical concerns are brought to bear on found objects and actual locations, there are parameters to skepticism, as well as immovable prods to potential truthful explanation. And as the evidence becomes more extensive, as artifacts proliferate, the critical edge becomes finer as do the promises (and pitfalls) of understanding.

Most practicing historians do in fact subscribe to such a general method. Even a delicately attuned phenomenologist like Paul Ricoeur, whose concern with historical understanding proved a lifelong intellectual project, affirmed its fundamental and unavoidable soundness.[49] Indeed, as a phenomenologist, Ricoeur sought to describe what is taking place when we perceive the world and encounter it. To that extent, Wright's critical realism is common sense, almost by definition: this *is* what is going on when, not just a person of higher

47. Cf. Wright, *New Testament and the People of God*, p. 42, which presents just such a standard critical process in terms of "question, hypothesis, testing of hypothesis."

48. The self-understanding of "interpretive" or "post-processual" archeology has been consciously driven by this critical edge. For a well-ordered example of this, see Julian Thomas, *Understanding the Neolithic*, rev. ed. (New York: Routledge, 2002); more relevant perhaps to biblical parallels, see Susan Alcock's *Archaeologies of the Greek Past: Landscape, Monuments, and Memories* (Cambridge: Cambridge University Press, 2002). The slide off the realist spectrum, however, can perhaps be seen in something like Barbara Bender, Sue Hamilton, and Christopher Tilley, *Stone Worlds: Narrative and Reflexivity in Landscape Archaeology* (Walnut Creek, CA: Left Coast Press, 2005), where the constraints of artifact and its ambiguously defined location dissolve into almost complete interpretive *jouissance*.

49. See Paul Ricoeur, "Philosophies critiques de l'histoire: Recherche, explication, écriture," in *Philosophical Problems Today*, vol. 1, ed. G. Fløistad (Dordrecht: Kluwer, 1994), pp. 139-201; also, Ricoeur's *The Reality of the Historical Past* (Milwaukee: Marquette University Press, 1984).

consciousness, but any normal person — the "we" of the common reader — perceives and comes to knowledge. And with this articulation of common sensing comes, as with Wright, an assertion that what is common sense is embedded in what is in fact the case, what is "true." Not in a way that is exact in its expression; our common sense is always "more or less" true, and thus must be critically examined to gauge its place within this continuum of probabilities. But this ongoing critical practice is good enough.

But is this *actually* enough? It is precisely the "more or less" of reality that opens up what metaphysically — the truly true — remains a chasm of ignorance within our daily and pragmatically compelling common actions. There is always something "missing" in our accounts of the past, let alone our simple apprehension or knowledge of it, even as we move in the direction of filling out our accounts. Indeed, "accounting" itself can never represent the past except analogically, that is, as some kind of human narrative, cognitively incommensurable with the *bruta facta* whatever they may be. This is not to say that such narratives are untethered to reality. One need not embrace the skepticism of Oakeshott on this matter.[50] Narratives themselves can be readjusted in order to take account of facts that arise anew. But Ricoeur and Oakeshott both demonstrate how, at best, this readjustment is not something straightforward or commonsense in the least: it involves a morally complex engagement with the reality of death and of "dead things," of disappearance, ignorance, fear, hope, and so on. Historians engage this challenge less as pure historians than as those who simply must live as human beings, before the demands of a present whose connection to something we call "the past" is mysterious yet inescapable. Ricoeur, in my mind, rightly acknowledges this ongoing stage of historical inquiry as primarily moral. Just so, theodicy as a historiographical discipline drives theological renewal.[51]

The point is, even a commonsense "critical realism" must *open up* a realm of mystery about the past and its actual status as "real" in relation to the present; and it cannot narrow that gap except to the degree that it seeks to ignore "history" altogether.[52] When Scripture refers to something in "the past," this is

50. Among his several essays on the topic, see Michael Oakeshott, "The Activity of Being an Historian," in *Rationalism in Politics* (London: Methuen, 1962), pp. 137-67.

51. Paul Ricoeur, *Memory, History, Forgetting* (Chicago: University of Chicago Press, 2004), pp. 350-70, on history and disappearance, and the way that remembering and forgetting, as a historical practice, is driven by the facing or avoiding of death. The book gathers together many of Ricoeur's themes around the moral demand of a certain kind of remembering and historical practice.

52. One of the great defenders of this view, from what is in fact a working "critical realist" perspective, was the social theorist, famous for his work on film, Siegfried Kracauer. See his

itself to raise a question about the nature of our relationship with God, in any and every aspect: how are we made by God and towards God that we can be ordered towards a "knowledge" of something that lies outside the immediacy of our experience? Indeed, is this even possible? Is this not, in fact, something analogous to our relationship with our creation and our death, boundary realities that defy clear reference? From a theological point of view, just as it intersects with common sense, we must wonder if "the past" to which Scripture refers is not simply a divine mode of the present, whose nature exceeds comprehension even as its moral demands can never be evaded. And this question, raised and answered if only cautiously and uncertainly, is precisely what lies behind the straightforward figural reading of something like "exile" that we have been examining.

If, for instance, we look at how Wright himself deals with a traditionally understood "figural" discussion within Scripture, we see some of this "opening up" language being used. In a case like that of 1 Corinthians 10:1-14, where Paul's use of the exodus-church figure is presented in the language of historical event rooted in the actuality of Christ's trans-historical existence, Wright chooses to use an array of historically allusive but also historically specific terms at once: the exodus is "like" the Christian church's experience in Paul's day; there is an "analogy" at work; Paul's usage of the figure aims at making a certain "point"; aspects of the comparison are "unnatural"; but the Corinthians are actually located (historically?) in the "same drama"; the literal idea of the Rock following the Israelites is nonetheless "fanciful." Some of these terms indicate an ill-defined area of reality that can somehow encompass diverse historical moments and understandings (e.g. the same drama, or an analogy), but others seem to resist such an embrace (likeness, the real point, fancifulness).[53]

The seeming inexactitude of these terms taken together, however, is surely inevitable in this case. For the question of "what happened" or "what does this (present event/experience) mean" as it is related to the past has always been seen, in certain respects, to be non-straightforward. Consider, for instance, the category of "the forgiveness of sins," especially in the scriptural language of "wiping away" or "being no more": largely because the character of these disappearing actions of the past are given in relation to God, their status as actions and now as past actions is governed by a divine reality that in itself surpasses humanly temporal definitions. One may wish to speak in terms of

---

final, unfinished work, *History: The Last Things before the Last.* Completed by Paul Oskar Kristeller with a new preface (Princeton: Markus Wiener, 1995). Coincidentally, the historian as temporal "exile" is an underlying theme.

53. N. T. Wright, *Paul for Everyone: 1 Corinthians* (London: SPCK, 2004), pp. 121-25.

"analogical" description here, but even so, this only underscores the historical mystery involved in "forgiving sins" from the side of God. Likewise, the existence of the dead, in terms of their relationship to temporal sequence and its unidirectional "flow," must raise, but without ever being able to resolve in commonsense historical terms, a profound question regarding the nature of past and present. If God is the "God of the living" (Mark 12:27), precisely in his relationship with those who seem to be "dead" in historical terms, then the "past" cannot be accessible to the present *only* as the past. When dealing with these kinds of examples, we are thrust into an area of exegesis that must make use of more commonly accepted figural categories (if rarely applied as contemporary currency), such as that between the "earthly" and "heavenly" Temples (e.g. Exod. 25:40; Ezek. 40; Heb. 8:5; 9:23; Rev. 4; etc.), where some kind of articulated historical form is proposed whose actual temporal, though not necessarily spatial, character is displaced. To speak of "simultaneity" in this case is itself only an analogical term, and certainly a misleading one if taken in terms of historical sequence. The kinds of claims made about temporal chronology in a book like *Jubilees,* for instance — which provides a Jewish framework for figural referentiality culturally close to Jesus' period — are too uncertain to sustain clear historical categories of any kind.[54] But "simultaneity" as a divine "mode" of creative referentiality is one that, I think, appropriately indicates the direction historical thinking must take if it is to make sense of scriptural signification.

Broadly speaking, a careful critical realism will allow these elements to pry apart the exhaustive character of serial chronology, in this case, in its application to scriptural referents; that is, it will encourage a critique of such chronology on the basis of data that do not fit its contours.

That critique has been explored most self-consciously (and, perhaps, still most fully) by Augustine and some of the tradition he inaugurated (e.g. Wycliffe). What does it mean for God to "create" something in which time itself is invented out of a divine will that is both logically and ontologically prior to it? Although he never systematized his thoughts on this, Augustine at various points indicated that the very reality of a divine Word who creates must somehow include within his (i.e. Christ's) own self the referents of all

---

54. James M. Scott's treatment of the Book of Jubilees in this regard, in his *On Earth as in Heaven: The Restoration of Sacred Time and Sacred Space in the Book of Jubilees* (Leiden: Brill, 2005), is more interested in the chronological framework of the book's vision; but his detailed discussion of the heaven-earth mirroring axis of this vision offers a solid approach to the figural exegetical claim. This kind of axis goes beyond an explanation of extended exile in terms of "extended metaphor" (e.g. as argued in Martien A. Halvorson-Taylor, *Enduring Exile: The Metaphorization of Exile in the Hebrew Bible* [Leiden: Brill, 2011]).

historical particulars, something that founds the figural exegetical enterprise as central to scriptural historical understanding.[55] These kinds of reflections, for Augustine and others, have rightly made exegetical notions of "ongoing exile," for instance, temporally dense, but also chronologically mysterious and opaque. They have reshuffled temporal identities, with respect to referents like "exile" and "restoration," making such reshuffling a constant of their referencing altogether. Exile and restoration, from a temporal perspective, are indeed elements that not only can but must coexist in a fundamental existential and moral simultaneity, whose precise explication remains a challenge.[56]

Theologically, a number of elements come to bear in such conclusions, as their conditions: obviously aspects of divine transcendence and creation are primary. But so too is the priority of the scriptural text as a divinely creative agent in the articulation of temporality itself (this, at least, touches on the ideas of a "heavenly Torah" in Judaism, and of Wycliffe's scriptural ideas): the Word and its "words" are logically prior to historicality as it is experienced in any commonsense way.[57] (Here, obviously, the Christian theologian — and historian! — must go further than the atheistic phenomenologist.) It is not so much that exile and restoration are temporally simultaneous realities as that they are comprehended together in the metaphysically prior reality of the Word, of the living Christ. Therefore, Christ's reality founds the history of exile and restoration both, and their relation to him "in time" is secondary to his originating and exhaustive comprehension of their very being at any

55. Augustine's concerns with time have been treated extensively, and continue to engage interest. For the current general argument, see his *De Genesi ad litteram* (*Literal Meaning of Genesis*), Bk V (e.g. cc. 30-45 especially), and the *Confessions*, Bk. XIII, 34-38. More broadly on the philosophical aspects of this, see Richard Sorabji, *Time, Creation, and the Continuum: Theories in Antiquity and the Early Middle Ages* (Ithaca, NY: Cornell University Press, 1983), which remains the most thorough and serious synoptic treatment of Augustine's (among others) inherited arguments and concerns in this regard.

56. I have used the term "existential" loosely thus far, standing in for historical, personal, and social experiences whose actual significance could well overlap with the kind of sociological-political concerns we find in a treatment of exile such as Daniel L. Smith-Christopher's *A Biblical Theology of Exile* (Minneapolis: Fortress Press, 2002); "experience," on Smith-Christopher's model, instigates social "responses" (e.g. by Israel or Judaism) that may turn to biblical tropes in order to form adjustive meanings for otherwise cognitively difficult situations. At issue in the present essay, however, is the character of these tropes as "divinely given," and if so, as given by the divine agent of final restoration. What is "existential," then, must also refer to the way that human experience is scripturally founded in a prior way, which necessarily raises the question of temporal sequence.

57. On Wycliffe, a good place to start is Ian Christopher Levy, "John Wyclif's Neoplatonic View of Scripture in Its Christological Context", *Medieval Philosophy and Theology* 11 (2003): 227-40. I discuss Wycliffe further in Chapter 2.

temporal moment. We do not look to history to find Christ; but at Christ to find history, in its divinely constructed form.

But this also means that in the history we have, we *do* find Christ. Here, the theodicy character of much Christian exile literature gathers an inevitable theological demand: whatever "restoration from exile" might mean — what *Jesus* means when he speaks in these scriptural terms — must cohere with the divine justice that orders the events of human suffering *in* exile, even within the church's redeemed life. If the words of Christ are divine words, then their meaning must explicate the fact that the freedom brought by Christ is one that takes place within the existential experience of *continued* exile itself. This is where the question of scriptural reference becomes so specific. In this case, the *peregrinatio* theme (or better, the various historical instantiations of *peregrinatio*) — Abraham perhaps, or John the Baptist, or Paul's journeys, or Hebrews 11, or simply Adam and Eve's expulsion — provides the primary figural limits to the words of Jesus. In the same way his own divine life of incarnate pilgrimage and expulsion (John 1 and Heb. 13) must tether the semantics of his restorationist discourse and its resurrection focus. And it is just this semantic constraint that will therefore provide a new energy to the historical challenges of Jewish Israel's "ongoing exile" as well, in particular as it has been shaped by the reality of vicitimization at specifically Christian hands. If the witnesses of Christ, who themselves recorded the words of Jesus in their integrity and order, are yet to be "true" witnesses of the promises Jesus offered, then their own ethical denial of this or that implied referent must be taken into account in evaluating the "intent" of the words themselves. To say, that is, that "this is what Jesus meant when he spoke of exile and restoration," is useful and true only to the extent that it coheres with the historical outcome of the words themselves. Scripture and the Christian tradition (the latter often despite itself) in fact offer lines of interpretation that permit the articulation of such coherence. But these lines do not necessarily follow the clear path of the semantic contextual reconstructions of the historical critic, nor should they.

V. Figural History

Wright has long insisted that the Christian gospel — and the Scriptures that articulate it — is concerned with "flesh and blood" referentiality, as opposed to abstracted religious categories: Jesus, his death on a cross and resurrection are "real" in the sense of having existentially temporal foundations.[58] It is this

58. Cf. Wright, *Evil and the Justice of God*, p. 94, 116, etc. The fact that one prominent

reality that grants their power for temporal beings like ourselves. Hence the historical critic's role is, for the church's practical witness as much as for the truth's sake, essential in uncovering and buttressing this kind of reference. Surely Wright is correct in this insistence. And his defense of the centrality of the historian's contribution to evangelical witness is thus also well-founded. But such concerns become evangelically limiting if they are satisfied by the identification only of punctiliar temporal reference within the scriptural text. For one thing, the "flesh and blood" target of historical criticism must itself uncover the moral ambiguities of such reference. Naming "exile" and "restoration" as "just this" or "just that" in historical terms, from a scriptural (that is, in Christian terms, theologically substantive) perspective, is to invite the objections of historical contradiction: "ongoing exile" is seemingly never overcome in a historically precise way. That is Calvin's tacit assumption because it is his explicit experience. And if this contradiction is ignored in favor of such limited temporal reference, "exile" itself therefore threatens to become a theologically irrelevant category in scriptural terms.

In this case, I have suggested that theodicy represents, in part, a wedge in historical criticism's scriptural application, but also perhaps a continuing prod: the ramification of historical reference that figuration assumes is itself the product of historical criticism's inherent moral force. Secondly, however, the historical-critical enterprise must always face into its own incapacities in the face of a reality — of "history" understood simply as a temporal set — that is resistant to definition and comprehension. Here, Wright's treatment of the resurrection offers a kind of parable: one can walk to the edge of the tomb and confront its empty confines, but at this point a threshold of understanding is encountered that defies the categories of temporally referential precision.[59] It is not so much that the figural exegetical approach "takes over" at this point — faith picking up where science leaves off — as that this approach orders scriptural referentiality *in congruence* with this reality of such a threshold existing at all, given the truth of God's creative being. The referents of temporal experience themselves emerge across this threshold as co-extensive gifts of God's own self, "in Christ." That is a discovery that, once made, historical ex-

---

secular investigator of the theoretical physical basis for what might be viewed as a figurally-ordered history, the physicist Julian Barbour, calls the actual universe of time's experience "Platonia," may well confirm Wright's worries. See Julian Barbour, *The End of Time: The Next Revolution in Physics* (Oxford: Oxford University Press, 2001). Yet such a worry, nonetheless, emerges from a confusion of "flesh and blood" with a particular definition of temporality, and so begs the question in a way.

59. Cf. N. T. Wright, "Christian Origins and the Resurrection of Jesus: The Resurrection of Jesus as a Historical Problem," *Sewanee Theological Review* 41:2 (1998): 1-13.

perience itself confirms, over and over. And once made, as Calvin, or Origen, or Augustine and so many others did, it reasserts itself within the continual and repeated reading of the Scriptures, again and again. Exile and restoration are both aspects of the form of the one Lord, Jesus Christ, Son of David, of Abraham, of Adam, and "Son of God" (Matt. 1:1 and Luke 3:38). But if this is so, historical reality, "happenings," cannot be so discretely managed by the apprehending human subject as modern historians suppose. We turn now to the earlier Christian tradition on this matter.

CHAPTER 2

The Fate of Figural Reading

The last chapter broached the question of the historical references of the text and their relationship to God the "Almighty, creator of Heaven and Earth." Facticity as a concept or category is certainly a part of this question, and it has captured almost the entire attention of biblical historians. What Hans Frei called the text's "ostensive reference" has defined this interest in facticity, at least since the 18th century, in almost purely chronological terms.[1] Although Frei himself, as is well known, saw this voracious interest as ultimately deformative of scriptural understanding, we all know that it is a concern that cannot be thrust aside easily, if only because it defines the vehicle by which the Bible is delivered to many readers in our contemporary world. But facticity is in itself a subset of the larger relationship of time to God — what is given to us as real, but "to us" in the sense of our necessarily temporal apprehensions. What do we find "in time," what is "the temporal," and how does it inform the scriptural text and its meaning?

The figural use of exile is challenging here. Simple moral, or tropological, parallels and functions break down, precisely because the figure itself seems to permeate historical realities that, in a sense, it shouldn't logically. So, for instance, one might argue that the relationship between exile and return is one that "teaches" us something about the proper posture we ought to bear in the face of sin and redemption in Christ. That would be the "moral" purpose of considering this past event of exile, and its anticipated resolution. One might,

---

1. Hans Frei, *The Eclipse of Biblical Narrative: A Study in Eighteenth and Nineteenth Century Hermeneutics* (New Haven, CT: Yale University Press, 1974), pp. 76-78, where he develops the concept in reference to the 18th-century English thinker Anthony Collins.

furthermore, claim as a result that this posture stands, temporally, in a way that is simply independent of the actual historical status of exile and return, independent, that is, of something that is, in theory, "datable" in chronological terms. The scriptural problem, however, is that this presents two possible bases for the tropological meaning of a text, both of which are challenging. First, it might be that, from a tropological point of view, the datable character of the metaphoric images is simply irrelevant. In this case, the figures from "the past" function rather as moral images whose "facticity" becomes secondary and arguably irrelevant to the force of the image itself. In this case, these past figures are scriptural loose change at best or ultimately dispensable. This has been the option generally chosen by developing liberal historicism since the 18th century. A second possibility is that their historical facticity is insisted upon. In this case, as we have seen, the datable reality of one seems to inject itself into multiple temporal realms, so that "exile and return" in the 6th century BC seems to refer as well to "slavery and exodus" in the 14th century BC and "sin and redemption" in the 1st century AD, and evil and release in the 16th century AD. The tropological point's consistency depends on there being some kind of referent that is stable within multiple temporal frameworks, and indeed, which somehow can merge these frameworks.

In general, and until quite recently, the Christian tradition has committed itself to the latter, logically problematic option — one in which temporal disjunction is dissolved in the figure somehow. Furthermore, even as contemporary historicism has opted for the former option — dehistoricizing the tropological referent for the sake of maintaining a historicist consistency — just the kinds of theodical concerns we noted in the last chapter have made this move highly problematic from a moral perspective; indeed, it could be argued that, in this case anyway, the reduction of figure to "mere tropology" is logically correlated to the thinning out of theistic scriptural commitments in general: after all, of what value is a book whose tropological status has no tools for connecting singular historical claims — e.g. the cross and resurrection — to the historical experience of subsequent generations? The standards for instruction, in this case, would be utterly untethered to any final reality, and would thus be without compelling stability of application.

Hence, the challenge of reengaging the traditional figural notion of history is a moral one. But it is also a logical one. That is, only by attending to the logical status of the figural history — that is, by reassessing the claim that option one above is *in fact* "illogical" — can one at least provide some grounding for a robust scriptural history.

This brings us back to the issue of the historical "threshold" alluded to in the last chapter and above: what constitutes the character of what we call "history" or "the historical," or perhaps even, broadly, "the temporal" in the face of its created dependence upon God? That this is in fact a deep conundrum with Christian significance is indicated by its central place in simple exegetical reflection. In the remaining part of this chapter, I will indicate some of the central ways the Christian tradition, in both East and West, engaged this conundrum in a manner that provided a basis for scriptural figuralism as an expression of the world's order which is in fact God's creation, rather than simply as a rhetorical strategy. And on this basis, the Scriptures themselves were read as divine words received, rather than as human words applied. In the next chapter, I shall propose some fundamental theses about the nature of Scripture, time, and the world that attempt to capture some of the implications of this wider tradition in all of its radical confrontation with the pinched sensibilities of much contemporary experience. Philosophers have been puzzling over these matters with renewed energy over the past few decades, and it is worth bearing in mind some of their questions and general answers, even if one might not wish (as I do not wish) to roundly assert the structures of their thinking. We shall see, after all, that early Christians, and Augustine in particular, were sensitive to the possibilities at stake, but also to their more thoroughly theological foundations than purely metaphysical projections. If, then, in the next chapter, I suggest something akin to aspects of medieval philosophical views of time, with their mix of eternalist and presentist notions, it is only because this way of approaching matters provides a useful analogy to the theological claims about reality and Scripture's central ordering of that reality that other unconsciously assumed and habitual modes of construing reality do not provide.[2]

So first: what modern historicists unthinkingly assume, early Christians understood from the start as inherently problematical; that is, the "time" that we experience as human beings and the "time" the Bible presents in story and exhortation are mysterious categories. It is simply wrong to assert that early Christian exegetes approached the Bible naively, and hence drew out their "fanciful" figural readings from a kind of primitive ignorance about how the world functioned. (This was the widely experienced cultural myopia of 19th-century critics like Frederick Farrar, and is still commonly suffered.[3]) Not that early

2. See the article by Taneli Kukkonen, "Eternity," in *The Oxford Handbook of Medieval Philosophy*, ed. John Marenbon (Oxford: Oxford University Press, 2012), p. 529. The possibility of combining eternalism and presentism is demonstrated in several essays in Gregory E. Ganssle and David M. Woodruff, *God and Time: Essays on the Divine Nature* (New York: Oxford University Press, 2002), especially the opening chapter by Brian Leftow, "The Eternal Present," pp. 21-48.

3. Frederic Farrar's *History of Interpretation* (1885 Bampton Lectures) (London: Macmillan, 1886) was the standard history for over 50 years in the English-speaking world. For

Christians framed their exegesis on the basis of carefully construed metaphysical theories. Most reading of the Bible proceeded from habits of understanding rather than from conscious methodologies. But they were well aware that
exegesis was inevitably shaped by the nature of the reader's perceived reality
and thus that it was morally incumbent upon the reader of Scripture to think
through these assumptions at some point and to test them repeatedly. One
place we see this happen regularly is with the interpretation of the opening
verses of Genesis — not surprisingly, since this was a key place where the very
categories of human thought would be supplied to the scriptural interpreter,
even as that interpreter was in the process of gleaning them from a text yet at
issue. While Augustine is the most famous and extensive in his multiple approaches to Genesis on this basis, other readers were equally captured by this
text. What we find in all of them, in the early church, is a clear sense of both the
mystery of the topic broached here, but also the undergirding implications for
the Christian exegetical project itself that were enclosed in this text.[4]

I. Basil and His Era

We might begin, for example, with Basil.[5] Basil is well aware of the paradox
of a text that would speak of creation's "beginning," of "beginnings" at all, in
a world that is fundamentally God-construed. If, as Genesis 1 affirms, there
is a beginning to the world, how is this associated with God? The notion of
"beginning" cannot obviously apply to God, Basil argues; and perhaps not
even to spiritual creatures. A "beginning" refers to temporality, and hence can
only be referred to temporal creatures. There is a tropological value to talking
about beginnings in Genesis, since it can metaphorically indicate the way that
all things are given by God and depend upon God. But just here, the metaphor,
if it is to be taken seriously, gives way to a metaphysical challenge: can we say

a far better modern discussion, general but properly framed, I recommend Gerald L. Bruns,
Hermeneutics Ancient and Modern (New Haven and London: Yale University Press, 1992),
which, although not devoted solely to Christian interpretation, provides a good overview of
early, medieval, and Reformation exegetical approaches, along with a fine discussion of Jewish
midrashic reading.

4. A very good overview of some of the issues discussed below and more broadly is Paul
M. Blowers, *The Drama of the Divine Economy: Creator and Creation in Early Christian Theology and Piety* (Oxford: Oxford University Press, 2012), especially Chapters 5-8. Blowers's focus
in his larger argument, on a divine "economy" as "drama," "performed" within Christian life
and liturgy, however, is less germane to my own interests here. See my next chapter.

5. Basil, *Hexameron*, Homilies 1-2, trans. Sister Agnes Clare Way (Washington, DC: Catholic University Press, 1963), pp. 3-36.

even that time "begins," since time itself is the standard of any beginning? For God, as the true standard, is beyond beginnings. Thus, however much we might wish to read Genesis as metaphor, such a reading still forces us into the mystery of God, and the perplexing miracle of creation, whose "instantaneous" appearance — there are no beginnings to the beginning — defies comprehension. Intriguingly (see my 5th chapter), Basil admits that, in this kind of discussion, metaphor must be reconstrued more specifically as synecdoche (a part for the whole), in the sense that anything Genesis says about "things" must inevitably thrust us directly upon the reality of God, in however a limited form of reference. If, that is, Genesis speaks of light and dark, it is not so much that these referents are constructed metaphors for something else, but that their very substantive factual reality marks a mysterious passage into the much more enveloping being of God.

For Basil, it is the divine priority that sets in place the parameters for engaging reality as proposed in Genesis. The proper way, for instance, to construe temporality is as the creaturely form of asserting this priority. Hence, Basil approaches the Genesis narrative within a clear ascetic/transformational framework, not because such a framework governs the tropological character of the text, but because tropology itself is an aspect of the fact that human beings can only speak of God in terms of their own transformed relationship of subordination and service *to* God. Only the holy person can understand God: this is a typical Patristic (and scriptural) claim. But it is rooted in the reality of God as creator, the nature of which is graspable only from the posture of the creature *being* fully creaturely. If, as Basil insists, time is given for the *change* of human beings, for their "pedagogy" — if time is a "school" for holiness, as he says — it is simply because creatures are infinitely other than God, and temporality-for-transformation is how this difference is expressed. And not only that, it is expressed this way insofar as God is such a creator as to create for the sake of the creation's ultimate life, or salvation. "Becoming" is a human/salvific reality.

Time's nature is thus, for Basil, defined in a specific way: change or flow. There is no stable point within it; the past is vanished, the future ungraspable, and the present gone before it is known. It is important to dwell on this claim for a moment, for it surfaces just some of the perplexities regarding history that we have been noting above. Time, understood this way, stands as the unveiling of the ultimate and utter priority of God; time as becoming, but just because of this, as itself a kind of empty referent, is a way of speaking about God's creative mastery of all things, especially of human life for the sake of divine and purposeful love. While it is appropriate to speak of human creatures as "changing," the temporality of that change, in its metaphysical evanescence, is the expression of its divine ulteriority and ultimacy. What Robert Pendleton calls "change without time," drawing on the work of A. N. Prior, is a non-theistic way of putting this: things, such as they are, simply change; but their temporal quality is a perceptual human construct (a "supervenience") upon these basic changes.[6] Theistically, "things change" not because they are temporal, but because this is the grace of God by which God is God and the creatures God makes are drawn to him. That this happens to us, we call "time."

From Basil's perspective, what is most important here is to see how God's creative character determines the discussion of time in Genesis in a figural manner. God creates as an "artist," according to harmony and form. Obviously, God is different or separate from all "matter." But because of this, the form that matter is given — and indeed, the shape of all created reality, such that we can name it — is God-derived. This constitutes the synecdochic character of figuration, rather than the purely metaphorical. Day and Night — prior to the actual creation of sun and moon — thus represent the "measure" of time by which God forms all things. They "stand for," in their humanly experienced 24 "hours," an *a priori* divine "measure" that logically precedes, although it does not obliterate, their created expression. Similarly, Basil takes up the issue of the "light": it pre-exists temporal creation (that is, it comes with the spiritual world of angels etc.), and is then applied, somehow, to the temporal creation. It is not that light is a metaphor; rather, the very thing that touches us, and that we experience as light, in fact derives from a more fundamental ordering act of the Creator — it is the echo or whisper of this act. When we see light, we are in fact seeing the gleams of this deeper act of God.

Hence, Scripture articulates the way that the world is related to God as creation, such that each part of its reality, however temporally conceived, be-speaks the fundamental reality of God's creative being and act. More than temporal beginnings, Genesis speaks of "substantive" beginnings, in the distinction made by R. R. Reno.[7] What we experience as "history" or "historical" exists *as* a referral to this fundamental reality. So, when Basil says that light and dark express the character of good vs. evil, the transition into the tropological is not arbitrarily imposed by his exegetical preference: the struggle against evil marks temporal existence and purpose precisely because such existence is ordered

---

6. Robert L. Pendleton, "Change Without Time," 2007 webpaper, at http://pendletonscholar .net/.

7. Reno, *Genesis* (Brazos Theological Commentary on the Bible) (Grand Rapids: Brazos/ Baker, 2010), pp. 30-38. Reno makes the distinction on the basis of a wider Patristic exegesis, and it is one in which Basil finds a comfortable place. I do not think, however, that we should press the distinction so far as to contract the "temporal" character of the biblical text's refer-ence altogether; its synecdochic figuralism precludes such a contradiction, and finds a place of temporality within it, however radically reconstrued.

as one with the shape of the world, the whole of which *is* the purpose of God in creating and in being Creator. Everything is this one complex reality, and the articulations of Scripture must necessarily speak of them in just this way. Basil's approach to the classic question of the nature of "one day" spoken of in Genesis 1 reflects this complex unity of reality. Each "day" of creation is a measure (synecdochically enacting the ordering work of God), but its expression in Scripture is also a tropological aid leading us, who reflect upon the text, to eternity. Genesis 1:5's "first day" is "dayness" itself in its eternal form, "circling back on itself," to "lead our thoughts" to God. And just because of this, each of Scripture's "days," wherever they appear, even within the days of Jesus' death and resurrection, must do the same, and can and should be read as such. Since all of history speaks of one thing in its temporally articulated fashion, each part of history can rightly speak of another, albeit only insofar as its divine origins and meanings are kept as the signifying purpose of their speech.

Many aspects of Basil's discussion find parallels in other writers of his time. John Chrysostom focuses more deliberately on the temporal aspects, and puzzles, of the Genesis account. In particular, he picks up, as others do, the strange fact that the "measure" of time seems to be created *before* there are planets that actually physically impose such measures, i.e. before sun and moon determine our experience of day and night, light and darkness even. John sees this more fundamental divinely created measure as ordering the very character of created existence: our lives are all about limits, he says, and this reality informs his paranetic approach to the Genesis narrative more broadly. Once made physically clear in the ordering of day and night, human beings can see that the world's order itself proclaims our need not to overstep boundaries of all kinds and, more profoundly thus, to follow the *ordo salutis* of the divine economy, both in time and personally. This order, however, is completely God's; and what we experience therefore as "time" is the sole province of God's will. John even admits that God could have done otherwise with respect to time's shape, raising the question of whether this temporal shape even really exists independently of God's own direction.

Ephrem, likewise, also faces the challenge of time somehow being given prior to the creation of the planets and of light and dark. He opts, as does John, for a kind of divinely created "measure" independent of the rest of creation. In his case, though, something new is asserted that will be important in later discussion: that is, the actual shape of creation in its multiplicity — its "substances" — so utterly depends upon God that we must derive the form of its substances from the very center of God's existence as Trinity. Inasmuch as Scripture attributes the creative action of God to the Son, Ephrem insists that the substances of creation are thus "inscribed" within the "mysteries" of the

Son's being. This will become a key area of reflection among later theologians, and its implications for understanding history and temporality are significant: does the world, as it were, which is given to us in temporal terms, somehow "already" exist in God's own mind or will or being?

Part of the spur to this kind of question comes from the assertion of divine priority in every aspect of creation. All commentators underline the *ex nihilo* aspect of God's creation, a common thread that goes against modern suggestions that Genesis assumes God taking some kind of pre-existing matter.[8] Not only does the *ex nihilo* assertion provide a good logical weapon against idolatry — for there could then be no alternatives to God, at least of an equal unoriginateness — but the very order of human attention is ordered inevitably God-ward by God's sole and exhaustive creative power. Thus, Basil, John, and Ephrem, among others, all stress the *ex nihilo* aspects of Genesis' account, despite the fact that its truth is at best implied rather than stated explicitly in the text. It is, of course, a deeply important issue with respect to time and history, and thus to the meaning we apply to what we call events and actions, whether scripturally described or otherwise: if everything comes from God's creative will and act, then the very shape of our temporal experience has as its "measure" only God, ultimately. As Chrysostom noted, God might have done otherwise. Which means, of course, that the interpretation of temporal events or factuality is granted its fundamental criterion by, with, and through God alone. The consequences of this simple, if radical, claim for the character and understanding of Scripture are enormous, especially if one assumes that the Bible represents the direct expression of just this criterion. The movement from fact to synecdochal figure to temporally networked referent is granted essential plausibility and perhaps necessity.

II. Augustine

It is Augustine who most fully explores this common framework.[9] It is remarkable how extensively, for instance, he raises very modern questions regarding time, and this in the context of his discussions of Genesis in his *Confessions* (e.g. Book XI). There is the issue of the meaning (and confusions) of common

8. On this topic, see again Reno, *Genesis*, pp. 39-44.

9. Jean Guitton's was for long the standard work, *Le temps et l'éternité chez Plotin et Saint Augustin* [1933], 4th ed. (Paris: Vrin, 1971). But there has been wide study on the topic since. See also Jaroslav Pelikan, *The Mystery of Continuity: Time, History, Memory and Eternity in the Thought of St. Augustine* (Charlottesville, VA: University of Virginia, 1986); and Roland J. Teske, *Paradoxes of Time in St. Augustine* (Milwaukee: Marquette University, 1996).

temporal language, e.g. the problem with the existential "copula" of the verb "to be" — to say "*x* is *y*" need not imply *x*'s existence, although our speech about the past and the future often sets us up to assume that it does. Augustine struggles, then, with the non-existence of the future and its problems for the notion of "prophecy": "is" there a set of realities we call "future" that are somehow real? What would this mean? We will commonly say that tomorrow is such and such; or that yesterday was so and so. But does that mean that there *is* something that exists metaphysically as future or past? And if future and past things are not real, how can one "see" them?

With respect to the past, Augustine famously locates its existential character within the memory. But if this is so, can one properly speak of a "real" past? In addressing these kinds of questions, Augustine seems to adopt a kind of impressionistic understanding of knowledge, and in particular of knowledge of past and future. That is, we know things via the apprehension of present impressions that are then rationalized into past or future. (I will make use of one construal of this theory in the next chapter.) This in turn raises the paradox of temporal "measurement" in the face of instantaneous experience of the present: what exactly *is* one "measuring"? Is a "long" or "short" "time" some kind of objective container, or is it a subjective construction? Finally, Augustine proposes that we might think of God as having an atemporal knowledge, one that grasps all things and all reality in a way that does not partake of our own human past/present/future parsing. And if this is so, the implications this might have for what we regard as reality within our temporal experience become mind-boggling, as even he admits.

> In the sublimity of an eternity which is always in the present, you are before all things past and transcend all things future. . . . Your "years" neither go nor come. Ours come and go so that all may come in succession. All your "years" subsist in simultaneity, because they do not change. . . . Your Today is eternity. . . . There was therefore no time when you had not made something, because you made time itself. No times are coeternal with you since you are permanent. (11.13.16-11.14.17)

> You are my eternal Father, but I am scattered in times whose order I do not understand. The storms of incoherent events tear to pieces my thoughts, . . . until that day when, purified and molten by the fire of your love, I flow together to merge into you. (11.29.39)

The juxtaposition of human temporal existence with divine, yet in a way far more fundamental, with divine eternity, is impossible to comprehend. Yet it is also something that properly impinges on our understanding. For Augustine also sees this very challenge in comprehension as uncovering a tropological demand. There is, after all, a religious claim and value regarding temporality vs. eternity in terms of the human need to rely on God alone. This will necessarily involve apprehending eternity in a spiritual/moral sense itself, one of cleaving to God's reality above all. One logical consequence of this is that the reading of Scripture itself, as Origen and the Patristic tradition more broadly asserted, is an instrumental means of such cleaving, of entering into an apprehension of eternity.

Without this backdrop, it is easy to misread Augustine's more didactic pieces on Scripture-reading as thin bits of rhetorical regulation, and then to judge his turn, in the midst of these, towards theological speculation, as lapses in critical rigor. His great *Literal Commentary on Genesis* has in fact caused interpretive problems on just this level: how could an effort that is so explicitly geared towards avoiding allegory end up mired in so much metaphysical brush? A key point is simply that the divine-human and eternal-temporal divide is so drastic that inevitably any discussion of, in this case, "creation" or "the world" must engage the foundational mysteries of this chasm as to impinge on any "literal" reading. What, after all, is the "literal meaning" of the creation of "time"?

In any case, Augustine's notion of *ad litteram* is less constraining than some suppose.[10] It seems to indicate a broad presupposition that Scripture, taken in the specificity and order of its distinct words, *means something* concrete (cf. IV. 25).[11] "How" it means something is another matter, and although Augustine, in e.g. *De Doctrina Christiana*, will provide regulative outlines, his own practice is much closer to his broadly expansive and wondering approach in the *Confessions*. "Ad litteram" requires a certain kind of attention, rather than a defined method.

---

10. See, among many: Kathryn Greene-McCreight, *Ad Litteram: How Augustine, Calvin, and Barth Read the "Plain Sense" of Genesis 1-3* (New York: Peter Lang, 1999). Frederick Van Fleteren offers a straightforward discussion of the relation of literal to figurative exegesis in Augustine, with a useful chronological overview, in "Augustine's Principles of Biblical Exegesis, *De doctrina christiana* Aside: Miscellaneous Observations," *Augustinian Studies* 27:2 (1996): 109-30. R. N. Hebb, in "Augustine's Exegesis *ad litteram*," *Augustinian Studies* 38:2 (2007): 365-79, wants to ground Augustine's notion of "literal" in the *res* of the Word who becomes incarnate, according to the "rule of faith"; this then provides the contours for all "things" of the world, including the creation narrative of Genesis, and, as it were, metaphysically orders the figurative sense. Hebb's overall argument makes sense, except that Augustine himself is less than consistent in the way he speaks about this.

11. Augustine, *The Literal Commentary on Genesis*, IV.25. I have consulted the translation of Edmund Hill, entitled "The Literal Meaning of Genesis," in Augustine, *On Genesis: A Refutation of the Manichees; Unfinished Literal Commentary on Genesis; The Literal Meaning of Genesis* (Hyde Park, NY: New City Press, 2002), whose enumeration I follow.

This becomes clear when he approaches, in Genesis, the question of creation, time, and history, especially in his *Literal Commentary on Genesis*.[12] With far more speculative detail than Basil, for instance, Augustine will draw out the possibility (and it is only that for him — a theory that allows him to dwell upon the words and their implications) of God's atemporal ordering of a temporal world. Here Augustine proposes his famous claim that everything "pre-exists" in God, timelessly, as the "causes" or *rationes seminales* of all things. Time is the unfolding of these causal connections already given in their divine determination. Nothing is "added" later/in time.

All things are "in God" primordially before creation.[13] This includes even a pre-existing church and angels.[14] Thus, time is an "unrolling" of a kind of singular reality "already" ordered in concentrated form. This unrolling of time is God's "still working" aspect.[15] It also explains what we mean by Providence, not to mention predestination, which itself is "prior" to creation's simultaneous givenness and its unfolding in time.[16] Thus, to think "literally" about Genesis 1 is to be thrust squarely into some of the most knotted and distinct doctrinal questions of Christian reflection.

With respect to the issue of Scripture's temporal referentiality, there are several key inferences to be drawn from Augustine's reflections here. For instance, when it comes to historical "facts," we must imagine them as "taking place" according to a set of atemporal referents/references that somehow give rise to their experience within our apprehension. Providence — the divine order of the given unfolding of temporality — is geared to the Word's primordial significatory purposes, whose truth involves a kind of comprehensive form, or *gestalt*. Hence, there is *always*, at root, a conjunction of meaning between two or more things and events. This is an aspect of the divine "presentism" of creative action that, as we saw with Basil, is implied in Genesis. For Augustine, the historical "causes" that we discern among things are given simply to disclose this conjunction of meaning within the temporal framework of created apprehension and experience.

Thus, the exodus as resurrection is a central Christian figural claim: "Christ our Passover is sacrificed for us!" (1 Cor. 5:7). God's mind, as it were, conjoins these two, even as Scripture indicates, but also as we can be assured simply by the nature of things. Time is the outworking historically of this conjunction, with respect to our own created apprehension of this eternal

12. Especially in Books V and VI of the *Literal Meaning*.
13. V. 30-39.
14. V. 38.
15. V. 40-42; see 41 esp., drawing on John 5:17.
16. VI.17-19.

form, through the history of Israel, whose life contains a network or language of conjunctions within the reality of the one Word who *is* this conjunction in divine givenness. Why, or to what end, might this arrangement obtain for human creatures? So that Scripture can itself be of use to us . . . in the present, as Paul himself indicates in 1 Corinthians 10:11: these things are "written down" "for us." Scripture is our access to the mind of God (the Word) and hence to our "rest," in Augustine's terms, that is our life *with* God.

And so the literal gives rise to, even demands logically, figural investigation of the Scripture. In this light, Augustine on Genesis in the *Confessions* is not in tension with the *Literal Commentary*. If Scripture is God's eternal word, "spoken" timelessly by God, it is also perceived *in time*, via the Holy Spirit (XIII.29). The predestined truth of the eternal Word — infinitely fertile — is put into the world through time; and this gives rise to "spiritual" readings (XIII.34). These readings are bound to a *multiplicity* of meanings for any given text, that is, if only because the conjunctive aspect of God's timeless speech must take the whole of reality in its reach "at once." From a pneumatological perspective, by which we describe the ordering of our understanding, we can speak of these multiple meanings as "intended" by God, whose human discernment is an ascetic practice of growth in love (XII.18, 23, 24, 25, XIII.24). As the reader is able to grasp ever more widely the potentially infinite reach of a text's meaning, he or she is moving more deeply into the fertility of creative purpose that *is* the Holy Spirit's own generosity of being (cf. XIII.14).

Spiritual readings of, in this case, Genesis 1 and 2, are necessary for Augustine, simply by the nature of things — things of this temporal world, in which we are embedded and which define us. While he will, as in *De Doctrina*, offer guides for when and how to engage such reading, I am not convinced that these are meant as anything more than occasional orderings of approach. Even there, Augustine's constant fallback upon the "rule of charity" bespeaks his sense that the multiplicity of meaning that must emerge from the character of Scripture as God's creative Word in time, apprehended pneumatically, is ultimately enveloping rather than systematically controlled. His reading, in the *Confessions*, of God's command that Adam and Eve "multiply" relies on this default presupposition: note that the command's linkage to the sea beasts seems arbitrary. Should we not see it, then, as peculiar in its signification when applied to human beings? Eventually, he decides that, beyond procreative fertility, the command to multiply must refer to just this aspect of Scripture reading: rational thought in its profuse engagement with God's truth, as tied to the Holy Spirit and the Word.

On this basis, we can see how Augustine's figural use of exile, to which we referred in the last chapter, is a natural reading, in the sense that it derives from the nature of both text and time. His paradigmatic reading of exile is given in terms of the Two Cities, with the Christian's life away from the true Jerusalem counting as the ultimate embodiment of what the Old Testament refers to when it speaks of Israel's captivity. This, for instance, is how he explicitly reads Jeremiah 29:7, where the prophet writes his letter to the exiles of Babylon.[17] Applications of this figure of Augustine have been prolific in their own right.[18] But he also will derive a similar meaning, with a host of nuance, from other exilic figures, ones that engage the moral life of the church and the heart of the Christian, but also link up with a range of contrastive dualities found elsewhere in the Bible, such as the two covenants, Paul's allegory of Sarah and Hagar, and so on.[19] The ecclesio-historical and anthropological referents of exile here emerge out of a more fundamental chasm of created limitation, such that "distance" becomes a defining parameter of all experience. All temporal form exists along the axis of this divide in some way, and if the Scriptures in any fashion represent the Word of God they will also express this divide within the referents of their speech. The "figural" import of the text is simply built into the structure of reality as created. The redemptive aspect of the scriptural "revelation" is tied, conversely, to the fact that this creation and its articulation is given in the Word who is Christ Jesus.

III. Summary of Early Christian Figuralism

Rather than going through more individual cases, let me simply summarize what I take to be some key elements in Patristic spiritual exegesis that derive from, or are at least fundamentally joined to, elements of temporality reframed

17. In *De Civitate* 19.26: "for as long as the two cities are commingled, we also enjoy the peace of Babylon. For from Babylon the people of God is so freed that it meanwhile sojourns in its company. And therefore the apostle also admonished the church to pray for kings and those in authority, assigning as the reason, 'that we may live a quiet and tranquil life in all godliness and love.' And the prophet Jeremiah, when predicting the captivity that was to befall the ancient people of God, and giving them the divine command to go obediently to Babylonia, and thus serve their God, counselled them also to pray for Babylonia, saying, 'In the peace thereof shall ye have peace,' — the temporal peace which the good and the wicked together enjoy" (NPNF1-02, p. 419).

18. See, for instance, Luke Bretherton, *Christianity and Contemporary Politics: The Conditions and Possibilities of Faithful Witness* (Chichester, UK: Wiley-Blackwell, 2011), which organizes a complex and historically concrete discussion of Christian politics on the basis of just this figural move by Augustine. See the "Introduction," esp. pp. 4-6.

19. Homily on Psalm 119 (120), in Mary T. Clark, ed., *Augustine of Hippo: Selected Writings* (Mahwah, NJ: Paulist Press, 1984), pp. 206-12.

by a reflective encounter with the reality of divine creation. I have not offered a historical overview, and have indeed left out all of the ante-Nicene development which, it could be argued, was distinct (although we shall return to Origen and Athanasius later).[20] But I believe certain generalities can apply more broadly.

- First, and to repeat: the God/creation distinction is fundamentally given in both ontological and cognitive terms: the over-riding perspective given by an *ex nihilo* reality of creation renders temporality/materiality and conceptual definition an impossible referent when applied to God.
- Second, the incarnational reality that is the Son's historical life in and as Jesus of Nazareth provides the basis for defining both fundamental distinctions. But it also allows for the distinction to inform the meanings of time and Scripture both. What will become the Chalcedonian definition later often acts as a key template for discussing this.
- Third, the vocation of the human creature within this framework is given in the movement, via Christ somehow, from temporality to, in, and into relationship with the non-temporal reality of God. While the terms of the movement constitute a much vexed debate, not only among theologians of the time but among their interpreters, one central element stands out in common and informs the ascetic outlook of both East and West: that is, history, as a collection of experienced events, is thereby granted a form or schema that is rightly read off of the incarnational elements of human life as described in Scripture.
- Fourth, the "at-onceness" of God's creative will stands as a background reality to our traversing this divine purpose temporally, creating all kinds of oddities of referential relationship both in life and in Scripture.
- Finally, the forms of exegesis that will eventually be articulated as regulative modes of Scripture reading — typology, allegory, tropology, and

20. On the development of Patristic exegesis as a cultural process more widely, see Frances M. Young, *Biblical Exegesis and the Formation of Christian Culture* (Cambridge: Cambridge University Press, 1997). Lewis Ayres has deployed the notion of early Christian exegesis developing within the context of specific doctrinal disputes, and making use of classical pagan interpretive techniques, in "'There's Fire in That Rain': On Reading the Letter and Reading Allegorically," *Modern Theology* 28:4 (October, 2012): 617-34. Ayres adopts an ecclesiocentric approach to explain the rise of allegory, in a way that is theologically defensible, but also somewhat to the side of my concerns regarding more fundamental aspects of history. Certainly Irenaeus's notion of reading the Scriptures literally according to a synthetic *hypothesis*, which Ayres makes much of, goes to the issue of divinely creative temporal comprehension; but that strikes me as more important in ordering figural reading than the ecclesiological demands he highlights.

anagogy — are less technical tools, at least among most readers in the early church, as they are attitudes of perception and reading that assume the ontological/historical relationships noted above and engage them practically. These attitudes and practices reflect the movement of the individual towards God — what is properly termed an *ascesis* — and hence reading Scripture in a certain way is itself a *Christian* practice, with all of its attendant virtues, rather than only a rhetorical technique.

Note how *ascesis* — the area of life that today is often talked about in terms of virtue — is simply an expression of the character of temporality, and that it is *this* that binds it to Scripture reading as a constitutive element of God's creative purpose. It is not so much the ethical aspect of Scripture reading that is primary (as it is often described today[21]), as it is the fact that ethics is a consequence of created subordination to God which Scripture itself embodies. Scripture, as God's Word in time, is the locus of human "becoming" within the scope of God's creative purpose. The challenge to this view is arguably its potential collapsing of human transformation with subjective knowledge, as a kind of *gnosis*. This has often proved the critique aimed at Origen, and through him, at all figural readers of Scripture from the early Christian tradition on. So it is worth pausing on this issue.

IV. The Origenist Standard

Although unconstrained by the explicit categories that became traditional in the wake of Chalcedon, Origen makes use of a contrastive dynamic of spirit and matter that parallels in some way the divine/human duality of later Christological definition. The key to both history and reading the Scriptures for Origen, then, is bound to the movement from the "seen" to the "unseen," from "flesh" to "Spirit." This, in turn, is founded on the reality of the Word — the Son of God — as goal, form, and means. The Word is what we seek; the Word's (scripturally described) life is the way we seek it (in humility, etc.); and the Word provides the Spirit that is constantly unveiling (and being apprehended) in the process or history of our movement towards our assimilation in spirit. Since, for Origen, scriptural history is a kind of image of this process — given in the contrasts, for instance, of Old Testament/New Testament, Law/Gospel; Letter/Spirit — there is in his view a certain eternal emblematicism that in-

21. For an example, as well as references to recent literature, see Richard Briggs, *The Virtuous Reader: Old Testament Narrative and Interpretive Virtue* (Grand Rapids: Baker, 2010).

forms the thematics of "change." The movement from one side of the contrast to the other, as well as the movement in *apprehension* from one to the other, ends up describing the temporal flow of reality. But that flow is also equivalent to the way that the one Word is refracted in its — his — relationship to creatures.

One can indeed engage all this in a dynamic fashion, experientially. And surely this is evident in, for instance, Origen's comments on scriptural exile, to which we have alluded in the last chapter. But in ontological terms, there is not so much a "movement" within, as a layered character to reality: the Spirit is always present under the flesh/time veil; the Word is always "coming" or "incarnating" itself in time so that the Spirit can be grasped by those who can penetrate more deeply. Again, this was evident in his discussion of personal "captivity," in which the literal sense of the text in Ezekiel was a kind of embodied veil to be constantly rustled and pulled off. Hence, the reading of Scriptures — and of time — can be seen as involving the uncovering of the *unchanging* ontological order of things at any given instant: Spirit perceived through the Word. This is true in the Old Testament and in the present.[22] Here is where the charge of gnostic stasis — an argument, as we shall see, made against rabbinic exegesis — tends to be lodged. Where is the dynamism of history in this scheme, since *any* point in time offers the same strata of obscuring flesh and disclosed spirit? Is redemption another word for apprehension?

The charge is plausible. But given the Creator-creature divide, into which temporality's character irretrievably hurtles, it is not clear that the concept of "historical dynamism" can escape reformation any more than can temporality itself. What we call "dynamism" — a sense of undetermined movement and change — is, as with all temporal qualities, simply the way that human beings appropriate, live out, the character of God's transcendent creative reality. It is a reality that is certainly inclusive of humanly-grasped dynamic elements.

22. See, for example, Origen's Homily 9 on Jeremiah 11:1-10: "According to the appearance of our Lord Jesus Christ as historically told, his dwelling was in a body and a kind of universal event which illuminated the whole world. . . . However, it is necessary to know that he was also dwelling prior to this, yet not in a body, in each of the holy ones. And after this visible dwelling, he dwells again in us. And if one wishes to have proof of this, take note of the passage, The word which came to Jeremiah from the Lord saying: Hear . . . , and so on. For who is the word which came from the Lord to Jeremiah or to Isaiah or to Ezekiel or anyone except the one in the beginning with God? I do not know any word of the Lord other than the one concerning whom the Evangelist said, The Word was in the beginning, and the Word was with God and the Word was God. But we need also to see that the dwelling of the Word is with each of those who can especially benefit. For what profit is it for me if the Word has dwelt in the world and I do not have him?" In Origen, *Homilies on Jeremiah and Homily on 1 Kings 28*, trans. John Clark Smith (Washington, DC: Catholic University Press, 2010), p. 85.

This is the syndechodic character of the creative figure that Basil insisted upon — the "literal" basis of the spiritual, in the sense that the gift of our lives is synonymous with materiality and temporality. But as a *gift* rather than as a self-generated reality, materiality and temporality are always implicated within a prior divine life that surpasses them. Their dynamic quality is the least we can say about them; but, as the "least," it is a quality to be subordinated to a whole that is much greater than this particular aspect.

For the contrast of Spirit/flesh — eternity/time — means that the latter must always be somehow inadequate and disproportionately limited with respect to the former. The reading of Scripture involves necessarily the encounter with realities that outstrip our limitations, in meaning, number, form, and so on. The spiritual meaning of Scripture is infinite in comparison with our understanding now; and this determines the multiple and unconstrained forms of our interpretations, whose touchstone is only transformation and participation in the Spirit[23] (cf. Origen 192-206). The *real* dynamism of life is given in this transformation-according-to-Scripture, which is inexhaustible in its forms, although exclusively tied to the reality of the Word made flesh in Jesus.

It is arguable, then, that the specifically *metaphysical* system of Origen, Augustine, or later, say, of Maximus — a certain kind of Platonism, one might say — is an essential cause of, and therefore support to, the figural elaboration of Scripture that becomes standard in East and West. It is true that the language of "prototype" and "micro-" and "macro-cosm," with their Platonic and Neoplatonic cast, becomes ensconced in figural discussions that proceed through the Renaissance and beyond.[24] But the movement of ascetic transformation (or its frustration) that *is* the dynamic of human history is put into play by creation's own deployment by an uncreated and creator God, a logical antinomy whose assertion — by Scripture itself — leaves open a variety of ways of expressing this metaphysically, none of which can, by definition, become exhaustible in the terms set by temporal speech, even as they are ineluctably

23. See the various selections in Hans Urs von Balthasar, ed., *Origen: Spirit and Fire. A Thematic Anthology of His Writings* (Washington, DC: Catholic University Press, 2001), pp. 96-102.

24. On Maximus, see especially his *Mystagogy*, which is organized around micro/macrocosmic reflection (*eikon*); translated by Dom Julian Stead, O.S.B., as *The Church, the Liturgy, and the Soul of Man: The Mystagogia of St. Maximus the Confessor* (Still River, MA: St. Bede's Publications, 1982). For a contextual analysis, see Pascal Mueller-Jourdan, *Typologie spatio-temporelle de l'Ecclesia byzantine: la Mystagogie de Maxime le Confessuer dans la culture philosophique de l'antiquité tardive* (Leiden: Brill, 2005). One of the most well-known discussions of the Renaissance context of this, with background, can be found among the essays in Ernst Cassirer, *The Individual and the Cosmos in Renaissance Philosophy*, trans. Mario Domandi (Oxford: Oxford University Press, 1963).

articulated somehow.[25] The question, as cultural changes take place within Western understandings of the Bible, is whether the Scriptures can hold a unique place in positing and instancing this antinomy, so as somehow to define it. I shall take up the question of metaphysical systems and figural exegesis in the chapter after the next. But for now I can simply suggest that contemporary attempts to "systematize" the antinomy of Creator-creature in a Christian fashion, like Robert Jenson's comprehension of temporality within God's own self, are perfectly legitimate approaches, insofar as they themselves represent "figural" construals of the infinitely fertile, if otherwise opaque, articulations of Scripture itself, the Word spoken in time by the Word.[26] To the degree, however, that they represent ontological systems — Hegelian or otherwise — whose claims would subordinate the scriptural articulations themselves to their framework, they have moved from Christian theology into another and non-Christian realm. It is Origen who should offer a decisive assertion in this regard: "You are, therefore, to understand the scriptures in this way: as the one, perfect body of the Word."[27] It is the connection of Scripture to Christ, in analogy with his incarnation, that defines the relation of Creator to creature; any metaphysical system that goes beyond this fundamental definition risks deforming its truth.

V. Medieval Developments

Such ontological systematizing, which drives the Scriptures in their self-explication into a subordinated position within a previously established metaphysical framework, has always been a temptation to articulate advocates of the Bible's figural meaning. If nothing else, the Protestant reformers' limitation of such meaning is often seen as a reaction to such systematizing as it was pursued in the centuries immediately before them. But while it is true that the Western medieval church took figural readings of the Scriptures in some

---

25. On the question of antinomy, see Chapter 6 below. I will pursue the metaphysical question more particularly in Chapter 4.

26. Robert Jenson, *Systematic Theology* (New York: Oxford University Press, 1997-99), vol. 1, pp. 221-23; vol. 2, pp. 29-49. As will be seen in Chapter 4, I can go a certain ways with Jenson on his understanding of the "event" character of God — God's prior being as person even in temporal terms — but not all the way, since I would want to accept the ultimately unassimilable difference that is God's, despite his utter self-giving in the Son.

27. This is from a fragment of a homily on Jeremiah; see von Balthasar, *Origen: Spirit and Fire*, p. 88. Some of the scriptural metaphysics involved in this can be seen in Origen's *De Principiis*, 1.2.2-4.

new directions — how could they not, simply by living through diverse and developed contexts in comparison with their forebears? — it is arguable that they did so primarily within novel philosophical bearings. Even Wycliffe, as I will note in a moment, who was among the most elaborate in his metaphysical explication of Scripture's authority, deployed his theories for purposes relatively at one with Patristic predecessors. In many ways, the Middle Ages seem simply to have carried on the interpretive practices of the Fathers. And, in the West, this meant especially the general ordering of an Origenistic dynamic of Old and New, Flesh and Spirit.

One major development in medieval figuralism lay simply in its historical and material extension, as compared with earlier practice. This seems to be linked to perhaps a different experience of time, subjectively speaking. Friedrich Ohly, the great cultural philologist of the Middle Ages, locates this experience primarily in the development of typological thinking.[28] In the first place, Ohly argues that the "typological" view of history actually stands as a conceptual frame *over and against* other historical outlooks, including a more modern historicist one. The latter, he suggestively argues, does not really push the typological view out until into the 18th century — a fact that should alert readers to the relative novelty of the historicist perspective. In this sense, medieval typology was part of a long-standing outlook that remained in place, *mutatis mutandis*, well into the early modern period, something worth pondering as we consider the supposed anti-modern character of figural reading. More specifically, typology is bound to a certain conception of time, one presented in terms of *historical unity*. It is a unity, as the typologist sees it, given by God in time that is articulated through revelation, but just because of this, it is more than a humanly subjective perception. It is a "real" unity that draws all periods into relation one with another. Indeed, the human interpretive act of periodizing history is important, for it provides a means of sorting what will otherwise be simple divine juxtapositions. Finally, the logic of this sorting is through "factual" (vs. "verbal") fulfillments of events/persons in Christ (type/anti-type).

All this is familiar, and perhaps overly so given the systematizing of Protestant typology within especially Reformed circles.[29] What is peculiar to the developing medieval outlook is the deliberate *extension* of this framework

---

28. Friedrich Ohly, "Typology as a Form of Historical Thought," in *Sensus Spiritualis: Studies in Medieval Significs and the Philology of Culture* (Chicago: University of Chicago Press, 2005), pp. 31-67. Recent assessments of Ohly's influential work, from within an art-historical context, can be found in the issue of *Gesta* devoted to him, 50:1 (2012). The opening essay, by Aden Kumler and Christopher R. Lakey, "*Res et significatio*: The Material Sense of Things in the Middle Ages" (1-17), offers an overview of some of Ohly's main ideas.

29. See notes on Allison Coudert (notes 58 and 59 below).

to wider and wider realms of existence, including natural objects and fabricated artifacts. Thus, the typological synthesis of the Middle Ages becomes ever more exhaustive in its reach in comparison with the practical typological schemes of earlier Christian interpreters. This makes the "present" a kind of intensification of "all that is" already given by God. Hence, we live "in the New," the period of the covenant given in Christ, and that newness stands perpetually as the given order of time, and in a given relationship to "the Old." So far, this assertion simply draws out Origen's outlook. But medieval philosophers and theologians attempted to explore this temporal dynamic more persistently than their predecessors, including its implications for concepts of grace and free will. Applying the fundamental principle of divine creative priority, which proponents of an extreme theo-etiology like Bradwardine made exhaustive, even something as vexing as human contingency was deemed to be utterly God-derived.[30] Each instant of human decision, that is, finds its existential location within the specific act of God's creative grace. The occasionalist aspects of such claims are clear, and even if they were generally rejected explicitly, they tended to lurk behind the logic of many medieval reflections about temporality. It is not surprising that Berkeley is today seen by some as a kind of philosophical flowering of this kind of medieval vision.[31]

More practically, this kind of "intensified newness" of God's acts also extends the typological revelation of reality to the full breadth of the present as well, including the natural world. This renders the world as an ordered whole, if grasped from a spiritual perspective, where everything must (and does) in fact refer to everything else. The universe exists as a "language" in and of itself, given that reality is a kind of divine speech before all else. While the first articulation of the notion of the "two books" of God — Scripture and created Nature — can be traced at least to Augustine, it is only in the Middle Ages that this framework becomes vital for understanding reality.[32] The demand

30. Bradwardine's *De Causa Dei* exercised a certain amount of influence, e.g. on Wycliffe. Regarding his views of time, see Edith Wilks Dolnikowski, *Thomas Bradwardine: A View of Time and a Vision of Eternity in Fourteenth-century Thought* (Leiden/New York: Brill, 1995).

31. While drawing some different conclusions, see the material laid out by Costica Bradatan, *The Other Bishop Berkeley: An Exercise in Reenchantment* (New York: Fordham University Press, 2006). Also Michael M. Isermann, "George Berkeley's language of vision and the occult tradition of linguistic Platonism. Part II," *Language and Communication* 28 (2008): 57-92.

32. Cf. Augustine, *De Civitate Dei* 16. The general trope is found in other Fathers. On some general discussion, including the developments of the Middle Ages, see Olaf Pedersen, *The Book of Nature* (Vatican City/Notre Dame, IN: Vatican Observatory Publications and University of Notre Dame Press, 1992). More specialized studies can be found in Jitse M. van der Meer and Scott Mandelbrote, eds., *Nature and Scripture in the Abrahamic Religions: Up to 1700*, 2 vols (Leiden: Brill, 2008); especially in Vol. 1.

and complexity of seeing the world this way is described by Eco as almost "neurotic" in its profusion.[33] But its overwhelming potential is held in check by the fact that such a vision is finally limited by the single reality of Scripture itself: the "one speech of God" is given in such a way that the world's linguistic meaning is always congruent with and explicated according to the singular voice of the Bible. While that voice, heard with Augustinian ears, might itself be of infinite depth and meaning, it is nonetheless the constraining feature that grants reality its fundamental coherence.[34]

Someone like Wycliffe takes up earlier Patristic/Platonist categories within this context. But his interest is to reapply this symbolic profusion — a kind of divine power in itself — to the scriptural text more immediately.[35] Wycliffe takes something like Basil's basic insight regarding creation's forms as lodged in the mystery of the Son, and establishes it on the basis of a sophisticated Neoplatonic metaphysic.[36] But the philosophical argument seems clearly aimed at a more subsuming point regarding Scripture's nature as creative authority.[37]

33. Umberto Eco, *Art and Beauty in the Middle Ages* (1959) (New Haven, CT: Yale University Press, 1986), pp. 52-64.

34. The level of generality at which I am speaking in this context masks enormous differences and even disagreements. The differences between Bede and Hugh of St. Victor, for instance, and the distinction of each from an Augustine they studied closely, is great, especially on issues of the nature of history in its relationship to scriptural figure. On Bede, who seems to have resisted the latter extension, see this question explicitly engaged in Timothy J. Furry, *Allegorizing History: The Venerable Bede, Figural Exegesis, and Historical Theory* (Eugene, OR: Pickwick/Wipf & Stock, 2013).

35. Why he does this is debated: A sense that new modes of philosophizing were breaking down this symbolic universe? As part of a moral battle against church corruption and corrupt authority? The issue of theodicy, alluded to in our earlier chapter, raises itself with respect to the context of demographic and economic dislocation in the wake of the Plague: the sense of just *this* world must be found in the Scriptures, and this presses for a readjusted sense of history.

36. This, at least, is Ian Levy's argument, and it is convincing. See Ian Christopher Levy, "John Wyclife's Neoplatonic View of the Scripture in Its Christological Context," in *Medieval Philosophy and Theology*, II (2003): 227-40, which draws on a range of Wycliffe's philosophical writings.

37. The pungent — and some would find also somewhat tediously expanded — outline of this deeper purpose is given in his *De Veritate Sacrae Scripturae*, ed. Rudolf Buddensieg, in 3 volumes (London: Trübner & Co., for the Wyclif Society, 1905-07). It has been translated (in an abbreviated edition) by Ian Christopher Levy as *John Wyclif: On the Truth of Holy Scripture* (Kalamazoo, MI: Medieval Institute Publications, Western Michigan University, 2001). See especially ch. 5, on the relation of literal to figurative or mystical meanings of Scripture. Earlier scholars, like Buddensieg, highlighted Wycliffe's press for the "literal sense," in a way that deliberately painted him as a precursor of Protestant arguments. But in fact, Wycliffe's approach to the "literal" is similar to Augustine's, as I understand him: the emphasis is on every word, "iota," as being "true" in its divine origin and purpose. Figurative readings that

With respect to primary definition, Wycliffe locates Scripture's truth in the "Book of Life," that is, in the "mind" of God himself as the Son. Thus, there is an actual metaphysical connection of created entities with God, through the natures that derive from God's simple intentions, which constitute the Word: God wills creation, and the particulars of that creation are given in God's "ideas." The material signs of Scripture, which derive directly from these ideas in a way that the creatures that are their material consequence do not, are thereby ontologically linked to eternal divine verities: they *are* Christ in a way analogous to, indeed actually connected to, the union of his two natures, as defined by Chalcedon, such that temporal history's synecdochic meaning has an ontological basis. The defined ontology, however — and here the notorious meandering of Wycliffe's arguments is disclosive — is of secondary importance: it is his ready-at-hand tool for pressing the creatively vital and logically prior reality of Scripture in relation to all creatures; and on this basis, the authority of Scripture in shaping and governing the life of church and society is established.

For our discussion, what is at issue then are the time-related implications for the way that Wycliffe construes scriptural authority in terms of its "literal" divinity: the words of Scripture are "certain," because their temporal limitations are in fact bound to their "tenseless" truth in God. The past and future are "necessary" with respect to their divine ordering, and because of this are

---

he rejects are those that are humanly constructed so as to bypass the signifying or referring claims of individual words and phrases. In this way, the "literal" may in fact be "figural," if the latter serves to maintain the revelatory character of the scriptural words. Certainly, the literal cannot be pitted against the mystical or spiritual reading of a text. Wycliffe will, after all, uphold the classic medieval distich, *litera gesta docet, qui credas allegoria/oralis quid agas, quo tendas anagogia* (Buddensieg, p. 119), but explains it, classically, in terms of each meaning's coherence, in a kind of ascent of manifestation that unveils itself to the faithful reader who takes hold of the text's fundamental "literal" truth. The spiritual reading — which makes use of the humility livened by the Holy Spirit in the reader — is a tool by which the letter is upheld, that is, is capable of being taken in its discrete truth. In Chapter 5 (Buddensieg, p. 92) Wycliffe first notes the reality that governs figural reading: all things find their origins in Christ, so that the specificity of creatures themselves find their common source in him, and can thus be mutually referencing through him. The intertextuality of the Bible's signification is but the expression of all of created reality's common presence, as it were, "in Christ." See also pp. 94-96, on the human being as a *minor mundus* or microcosm, in whom is contained all the natural world, via transferral from Christ's human nature. Chapter 6 (pp. 107-38) provides Wycliffe's non-metaphysical version of his view of the Bible, well-known in his five levels of meaning for the word "Scripture," beginning with the highest truth who is Christ as the Book of Life, and ending with the material marks on the parchment. These correspond to his ontological distinctions, which Levy draws from his other writings. See also Beryl Smalley, "The Bible and Eternity: John Wyclif's Dilemma," *Journal of the Warburg and Courtauld Institutes* 27 (1964): 73-89.

somehow "at one" with the present. Our temporal task as rational and moral creatures is to figure this out in scriptural terms. The world, that is, is a place where the Christian is called to know God; and this involves getting "behind," cognitively as well as in terms of our hearts, temporal or tensed realities. Scripture — for Wycliffe, but also it seems, in a more general way for most medieval thinkers and readers — is a special way of accessing this atemporal reality that is God's, via "concordance" (as Eco says): the particular aesthetic vision of nature is given through the exercise of a scriptural imagination figurally oriented and deployed upon the things of this world.[38]

But for Wycliffe, even more, it is the scriptural imagination — literally, God's mind as the Word — that is prior to all things and that draws their created being into the dynamic of concordance. This states, as forthrightly as possible in Christian terms, the way that the world's existence is both dependent upon Scripture and teleologically ordered towards it.[39] There is an Origenist color to Wycliffe's vision here, but it is now stated with such intense and concentrated assertion as to engender puzzlement almost at the radical assault it constitutes upon otherwise common sense. A critic of Wycliffe like Smalley assumes that his approach amounts to a "murder" of Time, but because of its dependence still on the Bible's narrative, it is forced to let Time's "corpse" sit around and rot.[40] What she cannot fathom, however, is that in Wycliffe's view the tenselessness involved in construing Scripture as embody-

38. Eco, *Art and Beauty*, pp. 55, 62.

39. Wycliffe's understanding of Scripture as a cosmic reality, so to speak, goes to the heart of what we mean by "Scripture" itself; and his own struggle with delineating the proper place of the "written" word in this is an indicator of this more cosmological vision. That it was not so odd to view things in these terms — at least until really the later modern era — is argued, more generally in religious terms, by Barbara A. Holdrege, *Veda and Torah: Transcending the Textuality of Scripture* (Albany: State University of New York Press, 1996), which aims at a certain typology of "Scripture" that is probably too constricting, but that nonetheless stimulates a rethinking of the basis of the Word's ordering character from a Judeo-Christian perspective at any rate.

40. Smalley's reaction voices openly what many perhaps suspect with reticence: "We have enough evidence now to compare him with Plotinus and Augustine respectively. The comparison suggests a metaphor. Plotinus murdered Father Time and dissolved the body in acid, so that no trace remained. Augustine subdued Time and fettered him, while still keeping him alive. Wyclif, a murderer like Plotinus, but less expert, killed Time, but did not get rid of the corpse. Wyclif's Time is dead time, dead but unburied. He therefore resembled Plotinus more than he did Augustine, just as his type of conversion was more Plotinian than Augustinian. To make the comparison at all is to risk an estimate of Wyclif as a thinker. It exposes him as too rigid and backward-looking to rank very highly. On the other hand it brings out the fact that he had the power and courage of his metaphysical convictions" (Smalley, "The Bible and Eternity," p. 193).

ing the "ideas" of God is intrinsically *creative*. Because it is thus creatively divine, it lies beyond the qualities of stasis or movement as we experience them. As I noted above, it is a peculiarly modern sensibility whose imagination cannot posit a dynamism thrilling enough to surpass human constraints. And in any case, Wycliffe's asceticism is not oriented towards the acquisition of *apatheia*. From his perspective, our own experienced temporality is wrapped up in the engagement of this intrinsically and infinitely creative Word, whose forms gather us up into God's life. The human, and humanly Christian, life is bound up with struggle and change. Indeed, the direct connection Wycliffe draws between the forms of Scripture — what we can now call "figures" in a wholly non-rhetorical way — and the immediate shape of history's experienced particularity is decisive. His own life is perhaps a kind of testimony to this understanding.[41]

VI. Jewish and Christian Convergence

Wycliffe's vision remains, I believe, one of the most potent — and hence dynamic — articulations of the character of Scripture that the Christian tradition has bequeathed us. Yet not only the Christian tradition! For we find here a deep convergence with Jewish thinking, particularly among the rabbis. And the convergence itself is a sign, perhaps, that the figurally enscriptured universe of a Creator God — for this is what we are talking about — is bound to the nature of the Scriptures themselves. That is, the intrinsic character of Scripture *as* Scripture within the canonically given text *tout court* is more important to positing creation as figurally ordered than is any theological inference drawn from specifically Christian claims. Indeed, it is possible that such claims are themselves, at least as they are logically delineated, inferences from the temporal fact *of* the Scriptures (something indicated by Jesus, in e.g. Luke 24:25-27?). In any case, Jewish scriptural reading is founded precisely on the practical effects of a parallel construal of divine time: "there is no 'earlier' or 'later' in the Torah."[42] This hermeneutic "rule," with a complex origin, also had a varied application, and it would be wrong to assign it an extensive

41. See the biography by G. R. Evans, *John Wycliffe* (Oxford: LionHudson, 2005), which does not emphasize this self-understanding, except perhaps late in life, viewed through the lens of something like his *Dialogus*. Evans's *The Language and Logic of the Bible: The Road to Reformation* (Cambridge: Cambridge University Press, 1985), pp. 128-39, which touches on Wycliffe and temporality, does not enter much into the exegetical questions. Distinguishing the rapidly constructed legend about Wycliffe from his own sense of self is not easy.

42. Talmud, *Pesachim* 6b.

metaphysical force.[43] Still, that force was frequently appealed to in an effort to gauge the relationship of Torah to creation. And attempts at characterizing Jewish understandings of temporality that take this rule seriously have recently been made.[44]

Goldberg raises the issue of how time is "reckoned" according to diverse "markers," and argues that in this respect Judaism and Christianity parted ways. The Christian assertion of contrastive times — Old and New — clearly altered how time was to be construed and relatively measured by comparison with Judaism, and we have seen that the duality proved self-consciously central from at least Origen on. Within the medieval Christian imagination, it perhaps even transformed itself into a metaphysic of the *novum* that was to prove profoundly influential in later Protestant and then Enlightenment thinking.[45] And this way of doing so stood and continues to stand in contrast with

43. On the various exegetical applications, which complicate a simple philosophical discussion, see Margarete Schlüter, "The Creative Force of a Hermeneutic Rule: The Principle 'There Is No Earlier and Later in the Torah' in Midrashic and Talmudic Literature," in Rachel Elior and Peter Schäfer, eds., *Creation and Re-Creation in Jewish Thought: Festschrift in Honor of Joseph Dan on the Occasion of His Seventieth Birthday* (Tübingen: Mohr Siebeck, 2005), pp. 59-84. For a wider perspective, see J. D. Levenson, "The Eighth Principle of Judaism and the Literary Simultaneity of Scripture," *Journal of Religion* 68 (1988): 205-25, especially 219-25. Levenson does not in fact deal with the "rule," but rather with the presupposition that the rule lives off of, that is, that the Torah is given by God in its unity, and does not exist as a human artifact in its most basic form. This fact actually permits historical-critical study of the biblical text, according to Levenson; but that is because the temporal aspects of the text's genesis thereby discerned make little difference to the text's religious (divine) meaning, which supervenes upon its historical details. I am more or less in agreement with Levenson here; but I am interested, as he is not, in what this implies about our knowledge of "history" itself.

44. Sacha Stern, *Time and Process in Ancient Judaism* (Oxford: Littman, 2003), has caused a few waves with his claim that Judaism, until the Middle Ages, lacked a "Greek" notion of *chronos* or measurable and extended time continuum, and upheld a more punctiliar and processual understanding of temporality, one that was in fact more amenable to certain scriptural and liturgical claims. Sylvie Anne Goldberg has argued for developing and "plural" Jewish conceptions; see her two-volume treatment of the question, *Clepsydre* (Paris: Albin Michel, 2000 and 2004), vol. I: *Essai sur la pluralité des temps dans le judaïsme*; vol. II: *Temps de Jérusalem, temps de Babylone*. For a more succinct entrée, see her "Questions of Times: Conflicting Time Scales in Historical Perspective," *Jewish History* 14:3 (2000): 267-86.

45. This is an important detail in the history of ideas that lies beyond the scope of my essay. It should be clear as my own argument unfolds that the development of this conceptuality as a cultural lens has not proven beneficial to human flourishing, let alone a proper conception of God's relationship to time. The centrality of the *novum* has often been studied, in Christian contexts, in relation to views of history — millenarianism, and so on. See Carl B. Hoch, Jr., *All Things New: The Significance of Newness for Biblical Theology* (Grand Rapids: Baker, 1995), for a contemporary distillation of still very common foci of Christian novelty. On Christian discussions of newness and "renewal" through the High Middle Ages, see the bibliography by

traditional Jewish reckoning of time. For the latter, by contrast, was marked by liturgical representations — perhaps framed by specific events — and then ordered according to Beginning or Ending (Creation and End).

We can ask how different these two ways of "marking" time really were, in their substance. Both Jews and Christians ended up periodizing time, although in very different ways (cf. the desire by Christians to order all of time exhaustively by patterns of e.g. 6 or 7 "ages," which were linked to progressive perfectionism tied to the incarnation). Still, was the thrust that different in terms of scriptural readings? Certainly, one view — evidenced by Neusner[46] — says, "yes": the uniquely Jewish experience of exile/subjugation and persecution, with the loss of the Temple, "banished history" and led to a "static" view of time that was to reflect eternity in all important respects. The Scriptures — Torah and Tanakh — would, via their interpretation, yield "timeless" referents, rather than temporally-located (and hence particularistic) referents.

Neusner approaches this last claim using the notion of "paradigm": Talmudic time is "paradigmatic," not successive/causal/linear/cyclical. The Torah provides patterns or paradigms, defined in terms of specific scriptural persons and their narrative configurations (e.g. Patriarchs, Moses and Israel, events, etc.) and these "permanent" paradigms instantiate themselves repeatedly in "time." They are "eternal" or "timeless"; and Creation is the place they find their forms. Neusner is adamant that this way of looking at time drives out all sense of sequential or "rational" causality. Indeed, it renders much of "history" "inconsequential": only what can display the scriptural paradigm is of consequence. And the "meaning" of history or time is one of relative clarity with respect to the paradigm's emergence to view ("imperfect" to "perfect").

Giles Constable, in Robert Louis Benson, Giles Constable, Carol Dana Lanham, *Renaissance and Renewal in the Twelfth Century* (Toronto: University of Toronto Press, 1991), pp. 66-67. For medieval and modern trajectories — and only a few limited ones — see Henri de Lubac, *La postérité spirituelle de Joachim de Fiore,* 2 vols. (Paris: Éditions Lethielleux, 1978-80). Pentecostal theology, in our day, has seized on this detail of pneumatic novelty, bound to the moment, in which time itself has no past. The issue of Christian commitment to novelty, at this point, needs to be engaged on the level of the moral life, something whose meaning more touches contemporary thinking, with its individualist emphasis. More broadly, in terms of theory and modernism, see Michael North, *Novelty: A History of the New* (Chicago: University of Chicago Press, 2013). It is a danger of the occasionalist vision, one I readily acknowledge, that it can so easily slip into grim determinism or anarchic novelty. This was part of the argument between Arnauld and Malebranche on divine "intervention" in history and the character of natural "laws" of physical experience. See my discussion in Ephraim Radner, *Spirit and Nature: The Saint-Médard Miracles in 18th-century Jansenism* (New York: Crossroad, 2002), pp. 130-68.

46. Jacob Neusner, *Theology of the Oral Torah* (Montreal/Kingston: McGill-Queens, 1999), pp. 241-320.

Neusner is also adamant that the actual shape of scriptural interpretation in this context is one of "fabrication" for the sake of paradigm-display. But is this the right way of putting it? That is, is the assumption of paradigm-assertion in time not one that demands correspondence, and therefore affirmative of its "discovery" rather than its "fabrication"? This was always the way that Christocentric defenders of typology explained what they were doing. Is the method really any different for Jewish interpreters of "paradigms" of, say, Temple and Exile? Furthermore, is not the very reality either of fabrication or discovery not one of dynamic engagement with one's own time(s)? There is a sense in which Neusner's discussion is governed by the same modernist straight-jacket of temporal conceptualities shared by critics of medieval historiography, by which one is forced to choose between stasis and dynamism as if the spoils of human experience were reduced to such options, in the face of an obscured divine creative manifold.

Neusner in fact identifies four general "models" by which the history of the world — time — is "ordered" according to his paradigmatic scheme: according to "periods" culled from scriptural history; according to paradigms of Israel's relationship to the world; according to patterns perceived within specific scriptural events; and according to the "future" of Israel. And here, returning to our base text from above, the *Genesis Rabbah*, largely bears him out.[47] Likewise, commentators from quite different perspectives, like James Kugel, provide confirming parallels.[48] And precisely here we can see the claims of the midrashic texts regarding the Scripture they comment upon moving in analogous directions to basic Christian exegetical conclusions regarding the relationship of Bible to divine creation.

The opening of the *Genesis Rabbah* (on I.i), for instance, makes use of the classic text of Proverbs 8:30f/8:22, to lay out the paradigmatic premise: The "beginning" is Torah itself. Hence, all things in creation follow its "wisdom" or pattern. As many have noted more broadly, the parallel between Torah and the Christian *Logos* within this interpretation is intimate. The fundamental claim to a primordial pattern is then repeated elsewhere: e.g. in I.iv, on the six things that existed, as it were, "before" Creation: Torah, the Throne, the Patriarchs, Israel, the Temple, the Name of the Messiah, and Repentance.[49]

---

47. Jacob Neusner, trans., *Genesis Rabbah: The Judaic Commentary to the Book of Genesis. A New Translation, Volume I, Parashiyyot One through Thirty-Three on Genesis 1:1 to 8:4* (Atlanta: Scholars Press, 1985).

48. See Kugel's compilation of midrashic texts, in James Kugel, *Traditions of the Bible: A Guide to the Bible as It Was at the Start of the Common Era* (Cambridge, MA: Harvard, 1998), pp. 43-92.

49. See Kugel, *Traditions*, p. 54, for scriptural linkages — that is, figural significations.

These pre-existing paradigms are justified according to the very discussion of the Torah's patterning, using particular biblical cases. They coincide in certain key respects with more mystical versions of the basic idea, perhaps of the same era, like the *Sefer Yezirah*.[50]

So, in II.iii, the discussion of "chaos" at the front end of creation is granted a correspondence to the history of Israel, via Adam's sin, and its subsequent outworking in Cain, and so on. Or, again, the primordial light is displayed in the future Temple (II.v). The actual word usage in the Torah is significant; e.g. "light" is used five times in the creation narrative, and this must stand for the Five Books of the Torah itself. And the history of Israel follows just these kinds of minute details in the text. E.g. III.ix: the "one day" of the first day of Creation given temporal display in the raising of the Tabernacle in Exodus 25:8 and Numbers 7:12. A single mention of a word like "light" has within it the full history of Israel's liturgical life — calendars, festivals, etc. (VI).

These kinds of moves are all familiar from Christian figural practice. A major interpretive question is whether "rabbinic time" is a novel or at least uniquely framed cultural construction. Neusner makes just this historical-critical claim regarding the formation of rabbinic textual interpretation, and it lies behind his (ironically) more modernist concept of some kind of older, more "biblical" conception of dynamic temporality that stands in contrast to the distinctive attitudes of later Judaism. Many of his colleagues are not convinced, indeed wonder if the ontology of time Neusner infers from Mishnah and Midrash is actually more in *continuity* with earlier biblical and perhaps more broadly Mediterranean attitudes.[51] Is it perhaps the case that this way of reading the Bible is *already intrinsic to scriptural discourse* as it imposed itself and was assumed by Jew and early Christian alike? What would it mean to speak of Christian "paradigmatic" time? Is this way of construing matters applicable to Patristic discussion? If not, how does it differ? Or medieval? How is the "paradigmatic" outlook different from Eco's argued "symbolic universe" and its presuppositions of history? Finally, how different is this from Wycliffe himself?[52]

50. On the *Sefer Yezirah* and its enigmatic discussion of creation through the Hebrew letters, see the critical edition and translation by A. Peter Hayman, *Sefer Yesira: Edition, Translation and Text-Critical Commentary* (Tübingen: Mohr Siebeck, 2004). Some of the treatise's problematic elements, e.g. assumptions regarding pre-existing matter, were corrected in the developing recensions of the book, to emphasize *creatio ex nihilo*.

51. See the brazenly hostile critique by John C. Poirier, "Jacob Neusner, the Mishnah, and Ventriloquism," *The Jewish Quarterly Review*, New Series, Vol. 87, No. 1/2 (Jul.-Oct., 1996): 61- 78, esp. pp. 70-78.

52. One area I have not discussed, but that needs to be considered in this context, is the very nature of the "Scripture" that is being referred to: are we referring mainly to written

VII. The Constraints of Early Modernity

These are potentially important questions for Christians, especially, and carry with them implications with respect to Jewish-Christian mutual understanding.[53] In terms of the history of Christian figural reading, however, they have

---

text, or to something else? On this score, we might well study the relation of orality and the literary artifacts that mark the Torah, in this case, as "scripted," and not simply as scripted in some fashion, but as generally communicated in this or that way. I will refer, in passing, to this discussion in Chapter 6, on Athanasius and the lectionary, but it is worth noting perhaps that even Wycliffe's complex understanding of Scripture as only epiphenomenally a written text may be bound up with a context in which the Bible is mostly spoken, heard, remembered, and repeated — rather than written down and read. See my remarks above. On some of the implications of the oral character of the Hebrew Bible's genesis, see Susan Niditch, *Oral World and Written Word: Ancient Israelite Literature* (Louisville: Westminster/John Knox Press, 1996). Martin Jaffee has offered a helpful imaginative exercise in detailing the "ontological" weight that might be discerned in the various levels of "Torah," from its inscribed original, as it were, to the written forms of oral Torah and finally to the embodied discipline of the faithful holy person who follows Torah; it is one that could be applied, *mutatis mutandis* to Christian understandings of the Word's ordering power within the world, especially in conjunction with the kinds of ontological systems someone like Wycliffe proposed. See Martin Jaffee, "A Rabbinic Ontology of the Written and Spoken Word: On Discipleship, Transformative Knowledge, and the Living Texts of Oral Torah," *Journal of the American Academy of Religion* 65:3 (Autumn, 1997): 525-49.

53. It is George Lindbeck who first clearly opened up this line of inquiry, with his proposal for an "Israel-like" ecclesiology, which was in fact based on a common figural standard of self-definition between Jews and Christians. See his "The Church as Israel: Ecclesiology and Ecumenism," in *Jews and Christians: People of God*, ed. Carl E. Braaten and Robert W. Jenson (Grand Rapids: Eerdmans, 2003), pp. 78-94; "The Church," in *Keeping the Faith: Essays to Mark the Centenary of* Lux Mundi, ed. Geoffrey Wainwright (Philadelphia: Fortress Press, 1988), pp. 178-208; and "The Story-Shaped Church: Critical Exegesis and Theological Interpretation," in *Scriptural Authority and Narrative Interpretation: Festschrift Hans W. Frei*, ed. Garrett Green (Philadelphia: Fortress, 1987), pp. 161-78. While I have tried to indicate certain limited ecclesiological reorientations this might generate for Christians (more recently in *Brutal Unity* [Waco, TX: Baylor University Press, 2012]), the actual work of placing Jew and Christian, Jewish Israel and Christian church, within a single figural universe of Scripture has not yet been attempted. It should! Certainly, the project known as "Scriptural Reasoning," which brings together Jews, Christians, and Muslims to read their Scriptures together on the basis of each group's self-understanding is not only necessary in its own right, but also a potential spur to the kind of integrated figural thinking I am suggesting. But it is too soon to know what fruit it will bear on this front. On a Roman Catholic perspective of the latter, which links in with aspects of more recent Catholic approaches to scriptural interpretation, including figuralism, see Kevin L. Hughes, "Deep Reasonings: *Sources Chrétiennes, Ressourcement,* and the Logic of Scripture in the Years Before — and After — Vatican II," *Modern Theology* 29:4 (2013): 32-45. Finally, J. David Dawson's penetrating critique of Daniel Boyarin's rejection of Origenist allegory as inherently supercessionist deserves careful study, insofar as it analyses with great

a more genetic bearing. The intuited convergence of Jewish and Christian scriptural ontologies meant that, once the normal routes for figural reading dried up, it was the marginal path of rediscovered Jewish exegesis, of a peculiar kind, that permitted ongoing Christian figural practice to survive, occasionally even in a creative fashion. On the one hand, Roman Catholic figuralism maintained itself, although with increasing apologetic limitations.[54] On the other, Protestants found themselves pressed into a position in which traditional figural reading was tainted by its Catholic origins, and required new grounds if it were to be creatively re-appropriated. This it did in at least three ways: the first is *Christian Hebraism*; the second, the developing mechanism of *historical self-referentiality*; and the third, *sectarian rationalization*. I can merely summarize them here.

So to the first early modern ground for figural reading. The rejection of Roman Catholic traditionalism in favor of a more scripturally-focused set of exegetical practices tended to remove medieval commentators altogether from the fund of practical interpretive formation and to severely relativize Patristic exemplars.[55] The avenue of Jewish scholarship, however, remained open, at

---

detail some of the figuralist dynamics that properly *tie* Christianity to Israel, both in particular with Paul's self-understanding and more generally with early Christian figuralist exegesis. See John David Dawson, *Christian Figural Reading and the Fashioning of Identity* (Berkeley, CA: University of California Press, 2002).

54. I have outlined some of this in *The End of the Church* (Grand Rapids: Eerdmans, 1999), in discussing various post-Reformation theological contexts in which the anti-Protestant polemic desiccated figural reading on the part of Catholics. Having said this, there remained avenues of continued interest and vitality, not only among self-conscious renewal groups like the Jansenists, with their patristic and Augustinian (and finally millenarian) exegetical revival (See Radner, *Spirit and Nature*, 2002), but among a broad range of other more devotionally-ordered scholars, missionaries, and schools of thought at least into the 18th century. There remains a good deal of historical work to be done in uncovering this story, which has been obscured by the myth of historical-critical progress. Handbooks like Jeronímo Lloret's (Heironymus Lauretus) *Sylva, sue potius Hortus floridus allegoriarum totiius Sacrae Scripturae* (1570) may well testify to the formalized and almost ornamentalized character of such figural reading; but their popularity — which included Protestant readers — also indicates a more vital role for the practice, as does their merging into forms of vernacular preaching, a literary and homiletic area whose shape requires more careful study.

55. Despite a clear opening given to the study of the Fathers by the Reformation — among both Protestants and Catholics — the tendency of Reformed theology was to relativize Patristic authority. An extreme, though highly popular, version of the type was Jean Daillé's *Traicté de l'Employ des Saincts Peres Pour le iugement des differends qui sont aujourd'huy en la Religion* (Geneva: Pierre Aubert, 1632), whose translation into English in 1675 as *Treatise on the Right Use of the Fathers* proved popular well into the 19th century. While some Anglicans felt very differently about this, and turned to the Fathers for constructive and authoritative doctrinal and ecclesiological directives, Patristic exegesis itself was not embraced, although with some

least in the minds of some. And concern to master Hebrew for the proper understanding of the Old Testament led a few to delve more deeply into Jewish exegesis, inevitably bound to rabbinic and often kabbalistic traditions. This was not a line that the majority of Protestant scholars would follow; but enough did as to provide the basis for an influential and subterranean movement that was to carry through into the 18th century.[56] Many students of Hebrew exegesis were in fact religious anti-Semites of one kind or another, although not all.[57] But Christian Hebraism, in its various blendings of Platonism, alchemy, free-church sectarianism, and finally natural science, proved a fertile ground for maintaining figural approaches to the Bible's meaning.[58] And it did so precisely on the basis of a common, if general, grasp after a world of radically relativized temporal order, dependent upon the creative power of God by which reality might be parsed in some kind of synthetic framework. For many, that framework was in fact scriptural, in a way that depended on both a rabbinic and (at least in form) Wycliffite understanding of the relation of Word and material history.

---

exceptions, like Samuel Parker, whose *Bibliotheca Biblica, Being a commentary on all the books of the Old and New Testament* (Oxford: William and John Innys, 1720-35) were remarkable productions of encyclopedic erudition (Parker only managed to get through the Pentateuch in this multi-volume work). Most commentary dipped only sparingly into early Christian writers.

56. Perhaps "movement" implies too focused a set of interests. But the fact that Puritan Anglicans like Andrew Willet could engage in studies of rabbinic (and Patristic) exegesis for the sake of their own Old Testament reading, even as contemporaries like Robert Fludd were pressing the Kabbalistic byways of their physical investigations, each maintaining a clear repudiation of Catholic allegorical pretensions, is indicative of some shared and larger realm of permitted scriptural imagination. Richard Popkin proposed a "Third Force" in 17th-century philosophy, and we might suggest an analogous "force" at work with respect to biblical exegesis and hermeneutics, although at this stage it would only be a theory awaiting greater definition and testing. See Richard Popkin, *The Third Force in Seventeenth-Century Thought* (Leiden: Brill, 1992).

57. On pre-17th-century Christian Hebraism, see the overview by Stephen G. Burnett, "Philosemitism and Christian Hebraism in the Reformation Era (1500-1620)," in *Geliebter Feind Gehasster Freund: Antisemitismus und Philosemitismus in Geschichte und Gegenwart: Festschrift zum 65. Geburtstag von Julius Schoeps*, ed. Irene A. Diekmann and Elke-Vera Kotowski (Berlin: Verlag für Berlin-Brandenburg, 2009), pp. 135-46. More fully, see his book *Christian Hebraism in the Reformation Era (1500-1660)* (Leiden: Brill, 2012). Catholic Hebraists were relatively numerous; but they suffered under greater ecclesial and local control than did Protestants in their work, and, it seems, the lines of creative exegetical influence were less open and, perhaps for structural reasons, less penetrating into the common and devotional life of the church.

58. See the collection edited by Allison P. Coudert and Jeffry S. Shoulson, *Hebraica Veritas? Christian Hebraists and the Study of Judaism in Early Modern Europe* (Philadelphia: University of Pennsylvania Press, 2004).

Francis Mercury van Helmont is perhaps the most well-known of this group, whose interests were to form an explicit scholarly chain into the 19th century.[59] Van Helmont's interests, intersecting with members of the so-called Cambridge Platonist group, Newton, Anne Conway, Leibniz, and others (including, later, even Wesley), were eccentric to modern thinking. In particular, the intense search for an integrated natural theology marks them out, along with those of others in his era, as driven by novel intellectual and cultural pressures, often shaped by hopes for social reconciliation in a divided world. Certainly, from the perspective of traditional exegesis and theology they verged on the heretical. But the conviction that there was an "original language," that it was in fact (an uncorrupted) Hebrew, and that such a language contained (however explained) the creative power of God's ordering of nature and the world, bore an unusual analogue to early Jewish and Christian thinking.[60]

The more explicit forms of this trajectory were restricted — although if we consider the interplay of Quaker, Boehmian, and other outlooks with the established religion in England, perhaps less so than one might suppose. "Normal" preaching and commentary among Protestants instead adopted, at most, a restrained form of typology. The Lutheran Salomon Glassius's *Philologia Sacra* (1623) proved a significant and long-lasting influence, insisting on a *sensus duplex* for the Scripture's single literal meaning, and thereby establishing a tradition of a modest "mystical" reading among certain Lutherans. Herman Witsius, the Dutch federal theologian, laid out in his *De oeconomia foederum Dei cum hominibus* (1677) the basis for a vigorous typology based on historical correspondences. Both figures, along with others like Vitringa,

---

59. See Allison Coudert, *The Impact of the Kabbalah in the Seventeenth Century: The Life and Thought of Francis Mercury Van Helmont (1614-1698)* (Leiden: Brill, 1999). Coudert's scholarship over the past few years has been of especially important note. Her edition, along with Taylor Corse, of van Helmont's 1667 *The Alphabet of Nature* [*Alphabeti vere naturalis hebraici brevissima delineatio*] (Leiden: Brill, 2007) has made available to the larger scholarly community a crucial document. The notes are particularly helpful in opening up avenues of interest to this topic.

60. Van Helmont's vitalism may have proved a problematic theory as applied to a metaphysics of Hebrew letters and vocalizations. But the overriding purpose of understanding Scripture in a way that takes the text as fundamental to the character of God as creator and orderer of the world is consonant with earlier efforts. Cf. *The Alphabet of Nature*, pp. 103, 149-59. On actual exegesis, see his last work, *Quaedam praemeditatae & consideratae Cogitationes super Quatuor priora Capita Libri Primi Mosis, Genesis nominate. Prolate a Francisco Mercurio ab Helmont* (Amsterdam, 1697), which is thought to have the hand of Leibniz behind it. (See *Alphabet of Nature*, pp. xvii-xviii, for a discussion.) It is debatable whether the approach taken here constitutes a "naturalized" figuralism, or a figuralized nature; I tend to read it as the latter. However, more Christocentric followers of this tradition had no trouble disengaging the naturalism, as can be seen especially as the 18th century wore on.

were widely read in England (Witsius himself came and worked as chaplain to the Dutch court in London) through the early 19th century, and provided a basis for both Anglican and dissenting hermeneutics to maintain a responsible, as they saw it, use of various forms of figuralism.[61] Indeed, it was Puritanism that most fully embraced the figural model, explicitly committing itself to an exclusive typological approach, but in practice, often ranging into the area of ontological scripturalism associated with some of the forms of Christian Hebraism noted above. In popular practice this moved, in time, into the realm of historical dispensationalism, which still had resonances with a certain kind of temporal Platonism, embodied most famously, but hardly uniquely, in Jonathan Edwards. Samuel Mather, Benjamin Keach (who borrowed liberally from Glassius), William McEwan, and others all contributed to a literature on figural hermeneutical method that found its apogee in the only now recovered work of Cotton Mather in America.[62] The latter's magisterial biblical commentary

61. Matthias Flacius Illyricus (Matija Vlačić Ilirik), the Croatian who became a central figure in the Lutheran Reform in Germany, is often credited with founding the discipline of Protestant hermeneutics, with his influential *Clavis scripturae sacrae* (1567). The work's anti-Catholic orientation limited figural reading enormously, even while some of his philosophical presuppositions, including the organic and holistic conception of Scripture pneumatically ordered, opened up later reflection in a figural direction. Glassius's and Witsius's work, although inspired from other sources, nonetheless built upon the systematizing commitments of Flacius. Glassius drew from the Pietist well of e.g. Gerhard, while Witsius, a follower of sorts of Cocceius, built his typology upon the unity of the Covenant of Grace between Old and New Testaments. A later translation of Witsius is available as *The Economy of the Covenant Between God and Man*, 2 vols., trans. William Crookshank (Edinburgh: John Turnbull, 1803). The material on typology is laid out systematically in vol. 2, pp. 188-231. On Lutheran pietist "mystical" readings, see Benjamin T. G. Mayes, "The Mystical Sense of Scripture According to Johann Jacob Rambach," *Concordia Theological Quarterly* 72 (2008): 45-70. More broadly, see Johann Anselm Steiger, "The Development of the Reformation Legacy: Hermeneutics and Interpretation of Sacred Scripture in the Age of Orthodoxy," in *Hebrew Bible / Old Testament. The History of Its Interpretation*, vol. 2, ed. Magne Saeboe (Göttingen: Vandenhoek & Ruprecht, 2008), pp. 691-757. There remains much research to be done among these writers and their contemporaries. For instance, no study that I know of has been done on the remarkable work of Johann Heinrich Ursinus, whose *Theologiae Symbolicae, Sive Parabolarum Sacrarum Sylva* (1646) is an elaborate figural treatise that aims at joining Scripture and nature in an arresting detail.

62. See Samuel Mather, *The figures or types of the Old Testament by which Christ and the heavenly things of the Gospel were preached and shadowed to the people of God of old : explained and improved in sundry sermons* (Dublin, 1683); Benjamin Keach, *Tropologia, or A key to open Scripture metaphors* (London: E. Prosser, 1681). Keach also wrote several other works of explicitly figural exegesis, e.g. on the parables of Jesus, not to mention his own extended allegories of the Christian life. The Scots minister William McEwan's handbook *Grace and truth: or, The glory and fulness of the Redeemer displayed*, in an attempt to explain, illustrate,

shows the extent to which Christian Hebraism had penetrated even into this corner of the Protestant wilderness — perhaps not surprising, in the context of our earlier discussion regarding the historical character of "exile" within Christian experience. It was just here that the question both of vocation and theodicy met in a peculiarly compelling way.

By and large, however, this more Protestant current tended to stress, as I said, the dispensationalist historical dynamic at work in the relationship of Old and New Testament, as well as in the meaning of particular scriptural figures. This brings us to a second avenue by which figural reading of the Scriptures was maintained in the developing modern period: that is, through *historical self-referentiality*. For the dispensationalist ordering of types served a particular tropological purpose. Samuel Mather's case is illustrative. Consolation, he writes, is the chief fruit of typological reading: as Christians, we are in the fulfilled "dispensation," the better time, and knowing this through the typological parsing of Scripture provides the fruit of encouragement. This represents a particular historicizing impulse that becomes prominent. (It is one that is, arguably, an ironic reversal of Paul's reasoning in 1 Corinthians 10:6-12, where the "present" is seen as one of greater danger, typologically.) The issue for Mather was one of ordering the historical dispensations correctly. There is a temporal "progress" in this respect, which is tied to knowledge: the referent of the knowledge is always the same, i.e. it is the "gospel." What is at stake is how clearly people see this gospel at various times.

Old Testament typology is founded on a progressive pedagogy — one that can still be applicable to the Christian — in which the "darkness" of the gospel's presentation in the types is gradually lessened, until there is a full enunciation of the gospel. At the same time, those in the Old Testament who were themselves "elect" — e.g. the Patriarchs — did *in fact* see the full gospel of Jesus within the actual "types," that is, in their physical facticity as artifacts

---

and enforce the most remarkable types, figures, and allegories of the Old Testament (n.p., 1764) proved very popular, going through numerous editions in Britain and, in the 19th century, in America as well. Jonathan Edwards left several small writings devoted to figures, in addition to his wider exegetical writings; three of them have been collected in *The Works of Jonathan Edwards*, Vol. 11: *Typological Writings*, ed. Wallace Anderson, Mason Lowance, David Watters (New Haven, CT: Yale University Press, 1993). For an overview, see Thomas M. Davis, "The Exegetical Traditions of Puritan Typology," *Early American Literature* 5 (1970), and Donald R. Dickson, "The Complexities of Biblical Typology in the Seventeenth Century," *Renaissance and Reformation* 23:3 (1987): 253-72. One of the fullest bibliographies in this area, of over 120 pages, is that of Sacvan Bercovitch, in his *Typology and Early American Literature* (Amherst, MA: University of Massachusetts Press, 1972). Cotton Mather's remarkable commentary is just in the process of beginning to be published. See Cotton Mather, *Biblia Americana*, Volume 1: *Genesis*, ed. Reiner Smolinski (Tübingen/Grand Rapids: Mohr Siebeck/Baker Academic, 2010).

that were oriented towards it (e.g. in this or that "ceremony" or in the Temple, or even in their own personal lives, as with Abraham). The progressive character of the typological schemata — their dispensations — means that the flow of knowledge and referent is always unidirectional: the true meaning of any type lies in the future, never the past. Hence, the church in Mather and others transforms herself into an "anti-type" rather than remaining herself a type of something else; and her progressive dispensation means that her form must be more "perfect" than the type referring to her. This obviously breaks down the ability of Old Testament types to "judge" the church.[63] A key evidence of this kind of restrictive/progressive application lies in the excision, and not only in Mather's hands, of Roman Catholicism from anything but condemning types; and a restriction therefore of the typological principles even in clear New Testament cases like Ephesians 5, so that Roman Catholic meanings can be excised (e.g. the "sacramental" character of marriage must be explicitly denied in the text, if the dispensational anti-type of the [Protestant] church is to be maintained).

This more Protestant current tended to dry up by the early 19th century, and in part this was perhaps due to its intrinsic inability to engage historical experience in a more textured way that might open it to scriptural reality broadly. When the squeezing of the Old Testament's applicability becomes more and more acute, and the New Testament church's own typical character becomes increasingly *anti*-typical (i.e. taking the place of Christ), the present is invested with an exclusively consummating element that cannot bear the weight of actual historical life, and the tropological force of Scripture for theodicy breaks down. Instead, attempts to maintain Protestant typology proved anemic and constricted, as can be seen in the brittle, if nonetheless widely read, handbooks of someone like Patrick Fairbairn.[64] By contrast, it was the sectarian experience of beleaguered community, as among the Darbyites or, initially, among the Anglican Tractarians, where a more expansive figuralism was explored, however marginally. This *sectarian rationalization* represents a third form of more popular figuralist development in modernity. John Nelson Darby, for instance, took up the dispensationalist categories of Puritan Protestantism with a vengeance, but he was able to apply it in a non-progressivist fashion. His notion of a "church in ruins" drew upon earlier models of historical declension, and so opened up the Old Testament to a renewed, if

63. Cf. also Mather's use of the criterion of "dissimilarity" which is meant to protect the anti-type from negative details within the type; Samuel Mather, *Figures or Types*, pp. 56-59.

64. Patrick Fairbairn, *Typology of Scripture*, 2 vols. (1845) (Philadelphia: Smith and English, 1854; enlarged edition).

narrow, relevance in explaining the present.[65] The early Tractarians, in a parallel manner, turned to especially Old Testament figuralism as a way of reading the church's life, although in their case with a more flexible typology that was more Christocentric. John Keble, already in his famous "Assize Sermon" of 1833, adopts this approach, reading the Church of England in the 19th century in terms of the types of Israel in the time of monarchy and judgment.[66]

By the time Keble laid out his meandering manifesto for figural exegesis in 1840, the Christocentric character of his interest is more prominent, and his self-conscious apology for "Patristic" exegesis means that he is trading on a range of early church assumptions about divine creation and time. Keble, however, is also a polemicist. And within the stream of Anglican High Church controversy, he continues to fight against "rationalism" and "anti-supernaturalism," much as his 18th-century forebears did.[67] Figural reading is tied to

65. See R. R. Reno's discussion of the ecclesiological import, and problems, associated with Darby's influential work, which contributed to some of the pre-millennial fervor of 20th-century North American evangelicalism, with all of its troubled political consequences. R. R. Reno, *In the Ruins of the Church: Sustaining Faith in an Age of Diminished Christianity* (Grand Rapids: Baker, 2002), pp. 16-22. For a broad overview, see Paul Boyer, *When Time Shall Be No More: Prophecy Belief in Modern American Culture* (Cambridge, MA: Harvard University Press, 1992).

66. The sermon that is traditionally seen as launching the Oxford Movement, more accurately entitled "National Apostasy," can be found in John Keble, *Sermons Academical and Occasional*, 2nd ed. (London: John Henry Parker/Rivington, 1848), as Sermon VI, on p. 127. In 1840 Keble penned the penultimate of the "Tracts for the Times," Number 89, *On the mysticism attributed to the early Fathers of the Church* (London: Rivington's, 1841). This marked the fullest discussion of figural reading by the movement, leaving aside Pusey's unpublished *Lectures on Types and Prophecies of the Old Testament* (manuscript at the Pusey House Library, Oxford), which has recently garnered renewed interest. The most vital actual use of commentary to come out of the group came much later, however, with John Mason Neale's *A Commentary on the Psalms from Primitive and Mediaeval Writers*, 4 volumes (London: Joseph Masters, 1869-74), which was in fact significantly written by Richard Frederick Littledale (whose name was added in later editions).

67. I have left out this story, to be seen either as the root of this third form of modern figuralism, or as an extension of the first, or perhaps as its own fourth identity, born of a mixture of various elements. The pre-Tractarian High Church figuralist movement was bound mostly to a group known as the Hutchinsonians. Once well-known, if hardly always admired, these 18th-century High Church Anglican preachers and theologians were linked in various (often only vague) ways to the eccentric autodidact John Hutchinson. Hutchinson played his part smack in the middle of the nexus of Christian Hebraism and natural science that swirled about the turn of the 17th into the 18th century. His theories about ancient Hebrew and the text of the Pentateuch, along with natural physics, were much discussed at the time. Most of those who were later called "Hutchinsonians" had left behind the particular physical and even historical theories of Hutchinson, but maintained a commitment to the revelatory character of the Hebrew Scriptures in their verbal particularity. Eventually they embraced an often preg-

this particular polemic, as he seeks to open up the created world to those visible windows onto God's eternal being that are grasped otherwise in the Scriptures. His Patristic commitments, nonetheless, keep this larger argument firmly tethered to a Christological center as well as to an ecclesial location, whose lived tradition (vs. e.g. Darby) is viewed as a vehicle of moral transformation in knowledge. Keble himself is no exegete, and his use of figuration in both parsing the Scriptures and the world is wooden. But he insists that the figures of the Bible are meaningful because of the reality of the world's creation "in Christ" and movement "to Christ" and finally joining "with Christ" in the church, whose book Scripture is. Picking up Providence as a key element in making sense of this, he shares the historicizing character of the entire Protestant tradition, although without the strict dispensationalism that came to obtain for most. Finally, Keble's deeply Platonist sympathies, although hardly determinative of his thinking, tended to shape his theological interpretations in general.[68]

Keble's was a road mostly not taken, however, apart from a few isolated theologians like Lionel Thornton.[69] By and large, as the standard histories of interpretation like Frederick Farrar's demonstrate, Keble's interests were dismissed as part and parcel of the obscurantist "fancies" of Origenist subjectivism.[70] It was only with the late 20th century's reappropriation of Patristic

---

nant figuralism, as in the case of the widely-read William Jones of Nayland. Their generally conservative approach to doctrine coincided with their sense of divine creative temporality. Some of their connections with later 19th-century High Church and Tractarian leaders are outlined in Peter B. Nockles, *The Oxford Movement in Context: Anglican High Churchmanship, 1760-1857* (Cambridge: Cambridge University Press, 1996), pp. 13-20, 45-47; and aspects of their writing have begun to be examined by others. But the deeper importance of their ideas and practice in the context of 18th-century British thought is only just being explored. For a recent and important foray into analyzing this literature, see the unpublished dissertation by David Ney, "Divine Oracles and Modern Science: Newtonianism, Hutchinsonianism, and the Old Testament" (2015).

68. Cf. his reading of Hooker, in his famous and beautiful Preface to Hooker's *Laws*, already in the first edition, *The Words of that Learned and Judicous Divine Mr. Richard Hooker*, vol. 1 (1836), pp. lxxxviii-xcvii.

69. Thornton's most extensive engagement with this is his three-volume *The Form of a Servant* (London: Dacre Press, 1950-56). One might also mention the earlier efforts of Richard Chevenix Trench, whose fertile mind took up Patristic exegesis with a non-apologetic hand and simply wove it into his own reading. See, more formally, his *St. Augustine as an Interpreter of Holy Scripture* (London: John W. Parker, 1851).

70. Frederic William Farrar, *History of Interpretation; Eight Lectures (Bampton Lectures of 1885)* (London: Macmillan, 1886). See especially Lecture IV on "Patristic exegesis" (pp. 161-242), but also his denigration of rabbinic interpretation, and general comments throughout. Farrar's judgments were far-reaching in both their influence and expression of ingrained prejudices.

and especially Origenist reading, in the wake of the work of de Lubac and von Balthasar especially,[71] that Farrar's judgments have now begun to be displaced. But these revised judgments are seen still mostly in historical-critical terms, rather than in normative or constructive ones. Despite the flowering of scholarship on the history of interpretation, which now includes major encyclopedic works, there is little sense of what to *do* with this newly granted respectability for earlier forms of exegesis. Discussion remains fixed, mostly, on the level of authorial intention and its basis for proper understanding of a text "on its own terms": how did the authors of the Bible understand the relationship of referents within the texts they either wrote or edited? How were these books intentionally used and read by the early church, within the context of their self-understandings? To this degree, we have got no further than Goppelt's insistence that Paul was "in fact" a typologist, and therefore if one wants to take Paul seriously, one cannot dismiss his outlook.[72] But what is one to do with the outlook more positively? Part of the challenge is simply that, however much one might wish to rail against the coercive historical-critical reduction of scriptural meaning, historicism remains the working metaphysical assumption of most modern readers, including those with respect and affection for Patristic thinking. This is true even of someone like de Lubac.

And the history of figuralism does at least locate one area we must engage if "respect" is somehow to inform understanding and practice. And this understanding and practice are not simply of antiquarian interest: the moral foundation of scriptural reference, if nothing else, has grounded its credibility in the claim, intrinsic it seems to scriptural articulation itself, that God is

71. The story of the *ressourcement* movement has been told numerous times. But the recovery of Origen lies at the center of one aspect of the movement's energy. In 1942 Jean Daniélou and Henri de Lubac, along with Claude Mondésert, launched the ground-breaking series of Patristic texts known as *Sources Chrétiennes* and many of the initial volumes provided some of the first modern editions of Origen's commentaries. Hans Urs von Balthasar had earlier published, in 1938, his anthology of Origen's writings, translated as *Origen: Spirit and Fire. A Thematic Anthology of His Writings*, trans. Brian. Daly (Washington, DC: Catholic University Press 1984). And De Lubac followed, with his lengthy study of Origen's hermeneutics, *Histoire et Esprit: L' intelligence de l'Écriture d'après Origène* (Paris: Le Cerf, 1950), that became the basis for his extensive multi-volume study of medieval exegesis as a practical outworking of a common interpretive theology, continuous with Origen's. See his *Exégèse médiévale: les quatre sens de l'Écriture* (Paris: Aubier, 1959-64), 3 vols. in 4.

72. Leonhard Goppelt, *Typos: The Typological Interpretation of the Old Testament and the New* (1969) (Grand Rapids: Eerdmans, 1982). Goppelt's twin commitment to historical-critical method and Protestant theology allowed his work to be heard by Reformed and evangelical scholars of the university; but it also did little to dislodge the historical presuppositions of biblical interpreters; nor was it meant to!

creator of the very times in which we seek to find our meaning. God, that is, is creator of our temporal framework's experiential contours, which are themselves subordinate to his being in a way that relativizes their formative power in every way. If we are to know God, we will do so through the dissolution of this framework's priority; and within that dissolution, the Scriptures will be rightly heard and our own lives righty ordered. In the chapter that follows I will offer an imaginative construal of such a dissolution, one in which the Scriptures' actual place within the created order can, in some measure, be gauged.

CHAPTER 3

Imagining Figural Time

Time, whatever it is exactly, stands with the creature in relation to the Creator. It is bound up intrinsically with creatureliness. Whether or not *finitum capax infiniti,* the very notion of a "distance" between the two is at best only suggestive, and creaturely "capacity" can only constitute an incomprehensive grace: that is, if a creature can engage its Creator, it is only because of the Creator's completely asymmetrical and unilateral enablement. Scripture is defined within this inexplicable structure of creative relationship. It is worth, then, returning to the central question posed by many early readers of Genesis, Augustine among others: How is it possible for a world to exist "in time" when it comes from "outside" of time in its productive origin, God? And since, strictly speaking, there is no "before" for created time in any case, what are some of the conditions of possibility for temporality, such that we can relate it to God?

Modern philosophers have themselves struggled with this question, from both theistic and non-theistic perspectives. It is not quite enough to say that Scripture's own understanding of time can dispense with the question, for the question itself is posed *by* the Scriptures, and once posed especially with respect to the primary referent of Scripture, God, then Scripture itself is problematized as a history-speaking document. It is not possible to read Genesis 1 with Isaiah 44:6ff. and Revelation 1 and 2 and 22, and to escape the temporally explosive force of Psalm 119:160/Isaiah 40:8/1 Peter 1:25 as it speaks to scriptural discourse: the Word that utters and is uttered stands with God in that place wherein "before and after" do not apply in any fashion we would normally use the terms. Thus, to read a modern analytic philosopher like Jack Meiland discuss the character of

THE HISTORY AND THEOLOGY OF FIGURAL READING

historiographical claims[1] is to enter precincts that sound very familiar to the Genesis-saturated mind of Augustine:[2] whatever creaturely existence's temporal experience may seem to imply, its reality as *creaturely* demands, more profoundly, that its ordered sequential character of past-present-and-future be reconceived from the perspective of its character as *God*-created.

Meiland makes use of what have become well-known alternative frameworks for describing "time." On the one hand, he considers the common assumption that time somehow embraces a set of things that are "in" the "past," which gives them a certain ontological condition, distinct from that of the "present" and "future." This common view mixes up several different notions, however. First, that of time as a kind of spatial relation, in which things "move" from being in future to present to past (although only in this one direction); and, second, time as a condition of being: things in the "past" "don't really exist" and so on, and only the "present is real"; and, third, that things are themselves, in their being, senescent: they come to be and disappear, yet "in between" they change in a certain way and age. Still, in common thinking, things move from unreality to reality and out of reality again, in a certain order, even while we continue to speak of them as *all* real: "the past," "the present," "the future." So when we speak of "knowing the past," *what* exactly do we think we are perceiving? Something "real" or "unreal"? And "where" is it?

Might it not make more sense — and this was Meiland's argument, along with others' — and at least help us to avoid these kinds of metaphysical quandaries, to conceive of reality as "tenseless" in its objective referents? In such a tenseless framework, one "thing" (event, object) stands "in relation" to another thing in some determined (though by whom is another matter) order. To this order we will give the names "before" and "after," yet things in themselves exist wholly *as* themselves just as they are, independent of some absolute temporal container that marks past, present, and future. In a sense, would it not be easier if we simply called time "unreal," as the philosopher

1. Jack W. Meiland, *Scepticism and Historical Knowledge* (New York: Random House, 1965), remains an accessible and still challenging exposition of the conundrum we engage when we attempt to "know the past"; and the constructivist approach to historical knowledge that Meiland embraces as a result shares many similarities, on the flat plane of creaturely existence, to elements I will propose as congruent with, and perhaps implied by Scripture's character as God's own "words" given to creatures.

2. Cf. the problem as stated by Augustine in *De Genesi ad litteram* I.15-17. I will be referring to the translation of Edmund Hill, in Augustine, *On Genesis: A Refutation of the Manichees; Unfinished Literal Commentary on Genesis; The Literal Meaning of Genesis* (Hyde Park, NY: New City Press, 2002), pp. 174-75.

McTaggart famously proposed?[3] Then we could simply get to the business of assessing the *order* of things, and furthermore, of gaining clarity about what exactly we are ordering (people, documents, present memories, hopes, motives, stones, and the rest).

For Augustine, the objects of creation are "ordered" by God for creaturely apprehension with a view to some purpose, yet exist for God as his creatures as a singular whole. God creates all things *simul*, at once, yet, in their inner structure (to which he gave the much discussed name of *rationes seminales*, or "rational seeds") are the divine orderings for their appearance in time. Reality is a kind of single tapestry, all woven together in one piece by God in an instant, each element placed in its relation to other threads and designs; yet it is "unrolled" as it were, within (and along with) the cognizance of creaturely existence. This unrolling of what is a single network of created reality's aspects provides the character of temporal experience, as well as defining what is meant by God's "providence." It is a strange gathering of variegated movements and developments, encounters and contingencies, that, when understood in their entirety, derive from the single act of God given in a way that discloses, from one perspective, an occasionalist power of ever instantaneous divine sustenance. Divine "presentism" — everything ever and all at once for God — is combined with an accommodated divine conservation in relation to creatures:

> And so by his hidden power he sets the whole of his creation in motion, and while it is whirled around with that movement, while angels carry out his orders, while the constellations circle round their courses, while the winds change, while the abyss of waters is stirred by tides and agitated by cyclones and water-spouts even through the air, while green things pullulate and evolve their own seeds, while animals are produced and lead their various lives, each kind according to its bent, while the wicked are permitted to vex the just, he unwinds the ages which he had as it were folded into the universe when it was first set up. These, however, would not go on being unwound along their tracks, if the one who set them going stopped moving them on by his provident regulation.[4]

3. The "container" theory of time, offered an absolute character, is most often associated with Isaac Newton. The "relational" theory of time, with McTaggart. For some introductory presentation of these, and other philosophical frameworks for time, see Philip Turetzky, *Time* (New York: Routledge, 1998).

4. The quote is taken from Augustine, *De Genesi ad litteram* V.41, p. 297. See the larger context in Augustine, *De Genesi* V.40-41. See also *City of God* 10.12. On the divine simultaneity of creation, see IV.53-55; V.27-28. (The oft-repeated notion that Augustine based all this on a

Augustine reaches this complex set of conclusions on the basis of considering together the basic claims of Scripture regarding divine creation, the habits and uncertainties of personal experience, and the specific words of Scripture in their "literal" placement (e.g., not only the statements in Genesis, but other related phrases, as in Psalm 33:9 on God's speaking and immediate act). And it is important to keep the motive for this kind of odd refashioning of reality in mind. For the *specifically* fundamental Creator-creature divide we have already emphasized as scripturally central, properly confirmed by simple, if disorienting, reflection as Augustine (and others) sees it, is eruptive in its explanatory force.

Here we can move into my own reflections, which I will lay out first as a kind of meditation on larger themes, and which I will then present more structurally as a set of imaginative propositions, numbered by heading. As I will explain later, these are not meant to explain in fact how Scripture refers to what we experience as temporal realities; but rather to expose the ineluctable mystery that stands on the threshold of history, and that properly — that is, truthfully — subverts our too-limited temporal frameworks.

---

misunderstanding of the Latin translation of *simul* in Sirach 18:1 is clearly off-base; Books IV and V of *De Genesi* are elaborate reflections that do not depend at all on this single verse.) The relationship of "simultaneous" creation to our creaturely apprehension is discussed in IV.5-55. See also *City of God* 11.16, 21-15. *De Trinitate* III.1-9 contains a long discussion of the relation of the natural order, including miracles, to the "seeds" created *simul* in Genesis, but given their proper "order" in experienced time by God's design. Likewise, *De Gen.* V.9-11, and *City of God* 11.5-6. Related texts can be found in *City of God* 7.30. See the helpful overview on the relation of creation, providence, and, in this case, miracle within this context, in Chris Gousmett, "Creation Order and Miracle According to Augustine," *Evangelical Quarterly* 60:3 (1988): 217-40, 251-54. There are other contexts in which Augustine makes analogous claims — one of which became important in the early 12th-century discussions that gave rise to the term "nominalism": the faith known e.g. by the patriarchs is "the same" as that known by the apostles, even though their apprehensions of it were "tensed" (Abraham knows Christ in the "future," while the aged John knows him in the "past"). God's knowledge of the truth is in fact tenseless. See the discussion by Chenu, in M. D. Chenu, "Contribution à l'histoire du traité de la foi," in *Mélanges Thomistes* (Paris, 1934; imprimatur 1923), pp. 123-40; "Grammaire et théologie aux XIIe et XIIIe siècles," AHDLMA 10 (1935–1936): 5-28; *La Théologie au douzième siècle* (Paris, 1957), pp. 90-107. There were, and are of course, various ways to describe this conceptually. That is part of my argument. On how the Creator/creature distinction can indeed be upheld fruitfully among these different conceptual paths, see the argument that would bring Thomas Aquinas and Barth together on just this front, including notions of time and eternity, in Christopher A. Franks, "The Simplicity of the Living God: Aquinas, Barth, and Some Philosophers," in *Modern Theology* 21:2 (April, 2005): 275-300. Franks engages the question of analogy, for which see Chapter 5 below.

I. Some General Themes

Let me take some of the common themes of Christian figural reading we noted in our last chapter and lay them out more generally. In particular, if we take the elements of the *Creatio ex nihilo* God-creature distinction, and the perceptive *ascesis* of temporal life oriented by the Scriptures to God, we might get something like the following.

The issue is how to conceive of the ordering comprehension of God and the experienced limitations of creatures *together*. After all, it is this "togetherness" that Scripture not only presupposes as a divine speech to human beings, but of which Scripture itself is actually disclosive. Temporality and movement, temporality and distinction, all seem to go together. Yet just because of this, the relationship of God, as the fabricator of this distinctive set of movements that seems to order what we call reality, cannot be one of "ultimate" sequence or sequential existence. This is the Augustinian and analytic conclusion, albeit open-ended. If there are "seven days" of creation, the divine relation to that sequential order cannot be constricted by beginnings and endings that are measurable in creaturely terms. Created reality is "one thing," in its identity in relation to God; and it is so temporally as well, although only God knows this properly. From within the multiple corners of this reality, time and identity are limited relations, perceived as such by creatures, and used as such for the sake of some mysterious divine purpose: we know only what we know and do only what we do — hardly anything! — for a reason that, finally, is God's alone. Yet how does the "one reality" of creation differentiate itself into these divinely purposed individuals whose existence is experienced as non-integrated and discrete entities? And how does God "will" this differentiation if in fact it is all "one reality," however complex? "Let there be light," "let there be creatures," and the other declarations of God in Genesis and throughout Scripture speak to the divine determination; but such declarations also do not clarify how this determination stands vis-à-vis the divine reality of "before the creation of the world," the single "book of life," and so on, or more deeply, the unified and perfectly integrated "mind of God" that Scripture also affirms, and that seems to "murder Time" in its very articulation.[5]

---

5. See the challenging and invigoratingly honest essay by Neil B. MacDonald, *Metaphysics and the God of Israel: Systematic Theology of the Old and New Testaments* (Milton Keynes, Buckinghamshire: Paternoster/Grand Rapids: Baker Academic, 2006). One problem I find with MacDonald's approach is that focusing exclusively on the divine determination, in all of its Gordian-knot-cutting function, seems to render much of Scripture's own articulate discussions of God arbitrary. It is one thing to lift up the divine sovereignty as a singular metaphysical — because, in a sense, supra-metaphysical — defining quality to God's being as Creator. This seems

So, the mysterious togetherness of God and his creatures presses to unravel the exclusive hold of historicist metaphysics on our truth-telling. It is, after all, God who determines what it is to exist in a differentiated manner and also the "what" that will so exist. Not only is the causal character of this differentiation asymmetrical — only God originates it; but so is its apprehension — only creatures sense their differentiation as explanatory of reality. Differentiated existence, that is, presents itself exhaustively from the side of the differentiated, in the sense that what we as creatures experience as our differentiated character seems to define that differentiation — our particularities, our specific scope of understanding and consciousness and so on. But the very positing of our creation by a Creator means that, at least in theory, we know that there is far more to this existence than our own sense about it. Hence, we can say that *our* differentiation as creatures is given in the limitations of our knowledge and experience — our perception — through the ordering of the one creation that is God's to so order. It is the limited apprehension of the "one reality" of God's making that marks differentiated apprehenders, or conscious creatures. We can affirm that we are specific in what we specifically do not know, or in the specific contours of our limited apprehension. Here lies the foundation, in part, of the central virtue of human humility.

All this means that the time and history we experience is, "in itself," a fundamentally obscured category of definition, because bound to the limited character of our apprehension. It is not irrelevant, to be sure; indeed, it is at least inescapable, in a Kantian sense. But time and history are rather linked to, they emerge from, the fact that God has determined to create us as individual beings, and they are bound to the obscurity of our place in the single will of the Father. Time derives from God loving specifically these limited perceptive aspects of his creation, loving specific limitations of the truth. The one thing that is God's creation is granted diversity, through existent limitation, by means of the suffering by God of what is "less than" another thing, and less than all things, and far less than anything that God is as God. Differentiated creation is a condescension by God of a miraculous, because self-limiting, extent. That extent in all of its ramified particularities is in part what we mean by time.

And thus, time must be completely congruent with the loving will of

---

to me right. But it is another to forbid, as it were, the scriptural qualifications of such sovereignty to stand in something more than a divinely conventional relationship to the revelation of God's own self. If there is God before or at least in a way that transcends "beginnings" (cf. Ps. 102:25-27; Isa. 43:10; etc.), then it is right to consider the relation of this divine "beforeness" to the temporal before-and-afterness of creaturely experience. The assertion of God's metaphysical distinction from all metaphysical distinctions is appropriate for grounding our scriptural discussion; but it cannot elaborate that discussion.

God, with its origins, means, and ends. This is its foundational connection to Scripture, which we understand to be a truthful expression of just this loving will. Time *cannot possibly be something in which Scripture happens or in which Scripture locates its described happenings.* Likewise, since it is the foundational and focused character of God's love that allows for individual existence and perception — that is, identity as a creature and thus as a "subject" of a creaturely kind — Scripture's own being is bound up, in a prior way, with the true being of individual creatures, and finally with their perceptions as their limited lives are so defined. Scripture thus exists, as the Christian (and Jewish) tradition has variously claimed, in a relationship of priority to individual creatures; and the reality of these creatures is, conversely, subordinated to the Scriptures. This relationship exists in particular with respect to what we call the temporal existence of creatures.

Let us return to the matter of creaturely reality, of creatures themselves, of things created. In a sense, all creatures are divine artifacts, and as such they represent this reality of God's love. That there *are* creatures is "how" God loves, so as to be creative. That is, distinction is the form of God's creative love insofar as distinction is the form of a limited reception and perception of reality. Time is how eternity is apprehended by creatures, in the long-standing Christian claim that derives, at least, from Plato. Yet the specifically Christian take on this must be that eternity so apprehended is in fact obscured eternity, not Leibniz's monads each of which reflects the whole. To experience time is to experience the less-than-God, in a radical fashion. Yet this too is not enough to say. For more than that, to experience time is to experience the divine self-giving, the ordering of God's own being *pro nobis*, which is indeed eternity truly, but wrapped in its own suffered self-offering. To be a divine artifact is to be loved; and the fact that God loves is to have a world populated with objects, or artifacts — multiple nodes of perceptive relation — that stand as the building blocks of creation and that constitute its being in substantial terms. From a creaturely perspective, *to be is to perceive and be perceived as artifacts of God*, as the patience of God's condescension for the sake of limited existence.[6]

In light of this, we can call Scripture the articulation of this populating creative divine reality of love. "Articulation" by whom? By God himself. Genesis 1, then, speaks truly, and Augustine's reflection in *Confessions* XIII.24 on the relationship of creative "multiplication" and Scripture's multiplied meanings is a mimetic expression of this. Scripture is God's eternal word spoken "in time," and hence its ramifications must be perceived as infinite (cf. XIII.29). But the

---

6. This will sound suspiciously like Berkeley, in an overtly theological guise, and that is not an accident. See below.

truth of Genesis 1 as an expression of divine creation also emphasizes the absolute dependent temporality of objects and creatures upon God's artifactual will. When Augustine writes that the whole creation, simply by its being, is singing out "You have made me!"[7] it is also the case that the Scriptures speak this first, by being that Word which is God's creative act "in the beginning": as if God said through it, "Because I make what is not me, you shall have a time, a life-span whose shape is marked by the limits of your grasp of truth, according to the grace of my design." That this Word, and the design of this Word, is Jesus Christ is the great revelation of what all things are in terms of the gift-giving of God as God's own given self.[8]

On the one hand, we can speak of a certain "epistemic grace" at work within the granted life-span, the limited reality, of creatures.[9] We know anything because of the "grace of nature" — i.e. we trust in the basic framework of our experience, insofar as it is given to us by the very reality of our life as creatures made by God. That does not mean that we trust everything about it! Indeed, much of our lives is shaped by the hard edges of ignorance and experienced deceit (including our own) which we encounter. This issue of sin, and of Original Sin, is not extraneous to our knowing; but it is also not exhaustive of it either. Simply by being alive, we are granted an order to our lives — we are temporal creatures, useful to God — by the grace of God's ordering artifaction.

Much of the common-sense way we approach the world, including aspects of our mechanistic science, is founded on this natural trust we have in our essential usefulness to God. Even so, we can also say that "time" — understood in this "natural" because engraced way — is also "how God loves" and hence creates. Duration — our natural perception — is created love at work. We know ourselves, other things, their identities in ways that are indeed engaging

---

7. Augustine, *Confessions* 10.6.9; *Expositions of the Psalms*, on 148, 10; etc.

8. While I am not drawing any of the ethical or vocational implications, let alone nuances, of Jean-Luc Marion's discussion of "givenness," or being-given-as-gift, his comprehensive phenomenology in terms of such "givenness" in implied theistic terms is partly what I have in mind here. See his *Being Given: Toward a Phenomenology of Givenness*, trans. Jeffrey L. Kosky (Stanford, CA: Stanford University Press, 2002). "What do you have that you have not received?" in Paul's simple but exhaustive summary (1 Cor. 4:7).

9. See Robert J. Fogelin, on "epistemic grace" via Wittgenstein: "This brings us to this passage: *OC*, 505. 'It is always by the grace of nature [*von Gnaden der Natur*] that one knows something.' In making knowledge claims, or at least claims to empirical knowledge, we rely on the grace of nature not to defeat us — at least when we have behaved reasonably well. When so graced, we are said to know. The philosopher, we might say, wants to replace this covenant of grace with a covenant of work." See Robert J. Fogelin's *Pyrrhonian Reflections on Knowledge and Justification* (New York: Oxford University Press, 1994), p. 92.

our own identities and that are "used" in the order of things, because we exist as objects of love. So, duration and artifaction seem to be two aspects of the same creative love.

The order is important: it is not that God "creates distinction and things"; it is that, when God lovingly creates, there are durable artifacts. Hence, durable artifacts are the epistemic visage of the fact that God lovingly creates. They are nothing in themselves, except that they are this. As a result, there is no reason to go beyond the artifactual durability of things to some further metaphysical substratum: "time," "being," or the rest. Rather, the only substratum is God's loving creation of something other than himself. This is the basis of "occasionalism" as a metaphysical claim — which is not so much a claim at all, but an anti-claim: God makes us in love, and lets us be according to that love, which he orders according to that which is not himself, which is creaturely.[10] But what this being is, and what its time constitutes, is irrelevant except insofar as it alerts us to the fact of our being as God's making. And the fact that there is a Scripture that is God's Word means that this Scripture itself precedes all metaphysical substrata as well. If we care to posit them, they are to be understood according to this one grammar of truth that is the Scripture, indeed are themselves the articulation of this one grammar of God's loving creation of that which is not God, within which all created perceptions are but the limited squints and exhausted scannings of perceptive thanksgiving.[11]

10. In what follows, some will see the evident similarities of my thought experiment with Berkeley, although transferring the "immaterialist" perception to an encounter with what I will call a divine artifact, however that is in fact ontologically constituted. I make no apologies for the connection. On issues of Berkeley and time as it relates to his larger metaphysics, see Fred Ablondi, "Berkeley, Archetypes, and Errors," *The Southern Journal of Philosophy* 43 (2005): 493-504. Also Sigmund Bonk, "George Berkeley's Theorie der Zeit: 'A total disaster'?," in *Studia Leibnitiana*, Bd. 29:2 (1997): 198-210, which offers not only an explication of Berkeley's ideas on time, but places them within the context of efforts at articulating an alternative to Newtonian absolute time.

11. There is some resemblance in what I am presenting to Kevin Vanhoozer's base metaphor for a scriptural metaphysics as a "divine drama," with Scripture as the "script" that is being performed, variously, in and by creatures. Vanhoozer's use of the image of a divine "author," with all the difficult yet rich characterizations of intention and creation of a certain cognitive quality, could be readjusted to the present model, and perhaps vice-versa. However, I am deliberately avoiding a "communicative" framework, which the dramatic metaphor implies (and which Vanhoozer draws out in later work) as if this is the basis of a divine-human relationship. I prefer to begin, at any rate, with the more primal aspect of creation proper, irrespective of intended apprehended meaning, except insofar as such meaning is identical with the fact of the Scriptures as they are given. It may be that creation *is* itself an act of divine communication; but if so, it is so peculiar an act as to defy our usual sense of the term, which implies some kind of referent outside itself. If the Scriptures are the Word of God, written or otherwise, it

II. Some Particular Ways of Conceiving Temporal Perception and the Scripture's Reference

We can move more particularly into the realm of scriptural reference now, and of its interpretation. Scripture speaks of the order of that which God creates. It both presents that order and is also, in its perception then, coordinated on this basis with the realities encountered by the human creatures who read it. Creatures encounter the world "according to the Scriptures," which themselves mark out the acts of God's creative differentiation of things. The issue of encounter and perception, then, becomes central to understanding how Scripture presents God's truth.

As I have indicated, a straightforward phenomenological reflection upon temporal experience — even one such as was done by Augustine — unveils the mysterious and confusing character of what we call "time," and the relation of past, to some kind of "present," and to an expected or imagined future. In general, such reflection ends by fastening onto the present alone as the foundation for apprehension, and to the present's logical exhaustive status. The more one thinks about time, as experienced, the more past and future recede from apprehended realities, in favor of a voracious instant of immediacy.

Building blocks for any concept of past and future, then, derive from the momentary encounters of the present, that is, from immediate engagements of subjects and that which is other than, yet apprehended somehow by, subjects in the moment. Whether these moments are themselves temporally "dilated" in experience, so as to contain somehow the intimations of past and future, is contested. But the foundational character of the moment is generally agreed as involving subject and object in conjunction.

We can, then, consider time in terms of just these encountered objects, engaged by a subject.

This is especially the case if we are going to maintain as fundamental the reality of God's creative priority to all things, as I have suggested, based on the Christian tradition's own claims and exegetical practice. One can call each object of reality an "artifact," and the study of artifacts has indeed been central to recent considerations of the construction of "historical" reality, and of the way we gauge the character of the world around us as being temporal.[12] That is,

---

is not clear that they are communicating anything but themselves. "Drama" is itself a "use," to be sure; but first must come the things themselves, in relation to their Maker, the "meaning" of whom is no other than himself.

12. I have been influenced by the work of George Kubler, for instance, in discussing the geographical character of art and its proper understanding. See George Kubler, *The Shape of Time: Remarks on the History of Things* (New Haven, CT: Yale University Press, 1962). Ar-

moments are filled with things, and the way things are organized by subjects, in relation to one another — what I will call "usage" below — represents the character of time. Experiments in sensory deprivation indicate its destructive effect on the perception of time. One might extrapolate that, in a world where there was only a single perceiving subject, yet nothing to perceive, there would be no time. This does not mean there would be no life or subjectivity, however.[13]

chaeologists who have followed him, like Bjørnar Olsen, have quite forcefully moved into the realm of ontological speculation. See his stimulating *In Defence of Things: Archaeology and the Ontology of Objects* (Lanham, MD: AltaMira Press, 2010), which pushes back against discourse theory for understanding the world we live in, and instead presses for a more chastened phenomenological approach to the objects we encounter. It is one that has great implications for how we view both the present world and "the past." But the conceptual field changes radically when this kind of speculation is located within a theistic field of divine creation, as we must do within Christian theology. And it is, of course, such location that will permit notions of "absolute use," which some anti-representationalist archaeologists today frequently question, not only as culturally-specific but as blindingly anthropocentric. Do not "things" have their own integrity apart from the role they play in human life? On the other hand, a strong notion of theistic creation may also achieve that independence for material things people like Olsen advocate: human beings themselves fall into the category of "artifact," in a univocal sense. But these kinds of questions are all to the good! Philosophers like Rudder Baker have argued for closing the gap between "natural" objects and artifacts as human products, as has Dennett in his own way. This is useful for theological considerations, since both kinds of artifacts are now within the context of a divine creator and can be analyzed similarly. L. Rudder Baker, "The Shrinking Difference between Artifacts and Natural Objects," *American Philosophical Association Newsletter for Philosophy and Computers* 7 (2008): 2-5. More recently, see her *The Metaphysics of Everyday Life* (Cambridge: Cambridge University Press, 2007). See D. C. Dennett, *The Intentional Stance* (Cambridge MA: MIT Press, 1987); Eric Margolis and Stephen Laurence, eds., *Creations of the Mind: Theories of Artifacts and Their Representations* (New York and Oxford: Oxford University Press, 2007); Amie L. Thomasson, "Artifacts in Metaphysics," in *Handbook of Philosophy of the Technological Sciences,* ed. Anthonie Meijers (Elsevier Science, 2009): 191-212; P. Simons, *Parts: A Study in Ontology* (Oxford: Clarendon Press, 1987); P. Simons and C. Dement, "Aspects of the Mereology of Artifacts," in *Formal Ontology,* ed. R. Poli and P. Simons (Dordrecht, Boston, London: Kluwer, 1996), pp. 255-76. On the fundamental shift that must take place in understanding things as artifacts, if God is Creator of the world, see Peter McLaughlin, *What Functions Explain: Functional Explanation and Self-Reproducing Systems* (Cambridge: Cambridge University Press, 2000), *passim* but especially Chapter 7, "Artifacts and Organisms," pp. 142-61. McLaughlin has had an interest in the history of science, including Paley and the argument from design, and his more theoretical work here demonstrates, among other things, the hermeneutic stakes at issue in theistic creation as a fundamental commitment.

13. Michel Henry is among those who have most profoundly reflected on the question of the relationship of interiority and the world of encountered objects. His own religious philosophy is founded on this relationship that cannot be pulled apart given the reality of God. See his *The Essence of Manifestation,* trans. Girard Etzkorn (The Hague: Nijhoff, 1973), and his late work *Incarnation: une philosophie de la chair* (Paris: Seuil, 2000). Henry's reflections on time, however, are ones I have not been able to grasp and therefore do not follow.

No time at all? Certainly, there is the prior reality of God, which by definition founds the creaturely subjectivity of any given person, quite apart from other persons. But this fact alone, within the context of the parameters of artifactual time, provides a basis for understanding the fertile relationship of the Scriptures with historical existence.

I have enumerated what follows simply for ease of following my logic, but more importantly, for ease in locating challenging elements that plausibly, I would argue, emerge simply from considering the character of the world as God's own making, one in which the Scriptures, as God's Word, must have a unique place of priority. While only with Section 8 do I broach matters that we have directly dealt with in the previous material, Sections 2-7 are possibly inferred elements related to them, ones that indicate some of the richness of consequence that exploration of this topic must expose. Finally, my schematic approach here is meant to underline the experimental and imaginative aspect of this exercise: every encounter with our existence in time confronts us with a profound mystery. Bound to God, that mystery cannot be sidestepped or overleapt in our reading of Scripture any more than in the encounter with our own births and deaths; but nor can it be fastened down by the insistences of our logics. To use one of the terms below, the "thicker" our immersion in this mystery, which includes the Bible, the truer it must be.

1. Proem

1.1 God is the creator of all things. All things therefore are artifacts of God (that is, things "made" according to a [divine] "art").

1.2 The character of an artifact properly applies to all creation.

1.3 All creatures are artifacts in relation to God.

1.4 Neither materialism nor immaterialism is necessarily implied. The metaphysics in this construal are relational, in the sense that they imply or derive from ways of talking about the divine Creator-created artifactual relationship.

2. Artifacts and Usage

2.1 Artifacts: every reality we encounter is either a surd or an artifact. By "surd," we mean something that has no perceived place within any sensible framework at all.

2.2 A surd, while in fact an artifact in relation to God, has no relationship to anything else in its creaturely apprehension. Surds can become artifacts as they are incorporated into patterns of usage. But surds in themselves, as surds, cannot be expressed by creatures. In order to even be described, a surd enters into the realm of useful analogues at least.

2.3 An artifact, on the other hand, is a reality that is put to use in some fashion. That fashion includes cognitive, physical, imaginative, and emotional use.[14]

2.4 All usage is bound to patterns, by definition: intentional, consequential, and so on.

2.5 All patterns are reducible to common usage, that is, to a context in which multiple persons are engaging realities in similar ways.

2.6 To recognize something as an artifact — rather than encountering it as a surd — is to be engaged in patterns of usage, i.e. with others.

2.7 Recognizability is thus common usage.[15]

2.8 There are multiple forms of usage, which we can call "thick" and "thin." A thick usage is one that involves complex patterns and therefore various levels of recognizability — and perhaps masks various levels of confused recognitions (e.g. the political process); a thin usage is usually one that masks fewer confusions and exists within fewer interlocking patterns (e.g. quenching thirst by drinking water).

2.9 Recognizability presumes relationship and uniformity. Thick usage emerges from longer processes of recognition, and often involves multiplying units of relationship within that process of recognition. Thin usage emerges from more immediate recognitions.

2.10 Usage tends to multiply artifacts around initial artifacts; e.g. artifacts are applied to or engaged with other artifacts.

3. Change

3.1 Change refers to usage, not to artifacts/realities.

3.2 Change constitutes the multiplication of or addition to or subtraction from the usage of an artifact.

---

14. My decision to employ the term "use" and "usage" is not technical. I take it in the sense of the root significance of "meaning" rather than of "performance," although there is an overlap. I am after "intention" (which may be unconscious) understood broadly, in terms of organizing perceptions. And while more complex forms of use are indeed performative in the sense of impinging on the reality of what is perceived in a regularized way (e.g. handling something, hitting it, etc.), use need not imply this, since we can use perceptions to integrate into thought processes only. When it comes to "time," there is a clear cultural constructionism (broadly understood) that I am asserting. See Alfred Gell, *The Anthropology of Time: Cultural Constructions of Temporal Maps and Images* (Oxford: Berg, 1992). Ultimately, however, even thought processes impinge upon other objects, and thus are more externally performative as well. There is also a deliberate resonance here with Augustine's distinction between "use" and "enjoyment," although here it is applicable only when our discussion touches upon God in relation to creatures.

15. All of this is confirmed, in a broad way, by scholarship in the cognitive sciences.

3.3 Selves are artifacts, in relation to perceiving entities.

3.4 What we call "the present" refers to the place wherein artifacts are used — by multiplication or subtraction.

3.5 What we call, for instance, "aging" or "change through time," refers to the use put to a succession of artifacts (that may or may not appear different in their various successions).

3.6 Selves exist only in a given usage.

4. Memories

4.1 Memories constitute the usage of artifacts that are no longer present to the senses. Memories that are not in fact used somehow are only surds, and are not recognizable. They are in fact "forgettings."

4.2 That usage is founded first on the imaginative, but would be meaningless if it were to end there. That is, imaginative memories that are not effective somehow in using further artifacts remain surds and disappear.

4.3 Imagination is therefore an element of usage, rather than an alternative to it.

4.4 Memories, used in certain ways, themselves constitute artifacts.

5. Death

5.1 Death refers to usage, subjective or objective, not to a condition of being.

5.2 Death constitutes a final limitation on (not cessation of) an artifact's usage.

5.3 There is little difference between death and the ongoing disappearance of artifacts (that is, the cessation of their apprehension), except that death refers to a uniform final limitation, one that is recognized by others and that therefore enters into a consistent pattern of usage, rather than an experienced one bound to a single artifact.

5.4 "The dead" are never immediately or wholly dead, as long as they are remembered. But there are degrees of disappearance in this case, thicker and thinner deaths.

5.5 It is possible that the moment of death constitutes an artifactual surd. Given God, however, that is not possible. Death as a surd is a human fantasy.

5.6 Surds, then, including death, are only theoretical. God knows all things, which means that God is "God of the living, not of the dead," and that all things "are alive to God."

6. The Past

6.1 The past refers to a certain kind of usage that we make of either artifacts or of memories (which are a certain kind of artifact).

6.2 Usually, that usage involves engaging artifacts *with* our memories.
Memories are bound to the past, but the past involves more than
memories.

6.3 Hence, the engagement that is the usage of memories also includes
other perceived artifacts: artifacts + memories + other artifacts; e.g
persons + memories + feelings + reactions; or artificats + memories +
documents + memories + books + ideas + actions, etc. Memories are
always part of present usage; and the past is one such present usage.

6.4 There is no "past" that is not remembered and therefore used. I.e. the
"past forgotten" is not the past at all. It is, to the subjective perceptor,
nothing.

6.5 Some forgotten pasts are remembered. We call this "discovery" or
"remembering anew." But this actually refers to the creation, in some
fashion, of an artifact. (I will be asserting that this fashion is God's
own act.)

6.6 There are as many pasts as there are artifacts to be remembered, really
or theoretically, or in conjunction with other artifacts and their uses.

6.7 There are potential moral implications for this, especially when held
in conjunction with "absolute use." See below, 11.10.

7. Continuity of Self

7.1 There is no self without usage, thick or thin — i.e. whether by the
recognitions of complex or immediate patterns (and, hence, whether
by developed human intelligence or by more simple intelligences).

7.2 Human usage presupposes "others," insofar as the forming of patterns
requires multiple artifacts and their various levels of recognizability
require the participation of other users; hence there is no self apart
from other selves existing in a pattern of usage. There is no self in an
empty world, unless we count God as the Other. (We may and must
do this theoretically, but in fact, Scripture indicates that this has never
been the case.)

7.3 The reality of God, therefore, assures all creatures of having an identity, for God is the permanent and immovable "other."

7.4 Since God does not "forget," there is no "past" for God, to be remembered or discovered or created. God may create memories for
individuals, and these may be used as a subject past for them; but they
cannot be past for God.

7.5 If God were to stop using his artifacts, they would, by definition, be annihilated.

7.6 Death is not necessarily annihilation. God is always, vis-à-vis creatures, "the God of the living," although human usage (or lack thereof) may identify them as "dead."

8. Time

8.1 What we call "time" is the set of all usages of artifacts, in their forms of thickness and thinness and disappearance, as the latter is presumed.

8.2 There is no "time" where there is no usage, by someone. Time presumes not only one artifact, but at least two, in relationship one to another.

8.3 While one might speak of "private time" and "public time" in order to distinguish subjective experience from shared experience, the distinction is misleading: all subjective time is bound up with others, and thus with some form of public time. Hence, "conventional time" is the only time there is, although it also varies enormously depending on the web of usage that is involved.

8.4 All time is thus "learned time" of some sort, including the common time by which various common artifactual usages are engaged, and tasks performed with others.

9. Causality

9.1 This argument presumes a Humean approach to causality, both in terms of its character as conventionalized "expectation," and the argument regarding infinite regress in its investigation.

9.2 From a theological perspective, it pleads ignorance on the one hand, and points in the direction of a kind of grand, if obscured, occasionalism on the other, the latter of which is itself a kind of pled ignorance within a theological framework. That is to say, it is not a matter of denying causality, but rather of pleading ignorance about it in absolute terms, except insofar as all causes must somehow be located in God.

9.3 The notion of a "first conserving cause" (cf. Ockham) can serve as an analogue for the kind of pragmatic temporal order that human creatures experience: artifacts are "given" to us, in the sense that they are "conserved" (as we are) simultaneously with our perception of them. The divine origin of all things is the foundation for any discussion of time and of its meaning. But this indicates that time and its meaning are founded upon the divine creative will that orders our mutual encounters of things and persons.

9.4 God's use of his artifacts is absolute, in the sense that it constitutes the ultimate reality of all created things; but creatures can use artifacts themselves, according to limited and diverse frameworks, that may or may not include God perceived. Such human usage is included somehow within divine use.

10. Historical Study

10.1 Artifacts can be used for various purposes, one of which is to order imaginatively their common-sense (i.e. conventionalized and useful) causal network.

10.2 This ordering itself is used: imagination is always applied, in hope or in fact.

10.3 Since the study of history foundationally involves memories of disappeared objects and artifacts, the past it posits is compelling only as it is compellingly put to use.

10.4 But that past is only the use to which a historical construal is put.

10.5 Again, there are thus many pasts and many histories, of varying degrees of compelling interest, tied to the thickness and thinness of their use. While this supports a constructivist view of "history" as historiography, it is one ultimately constrained by divine order and truth.

11. God, Time, and the Scriptures

11.1 God is the one "reality" that is neither artifact nor (theoretical) surd.

11.2 Hence, the relationship of God to God's own self, as it were, is both possible and non-temporal (e.g. Trinitarian life). God is not limited by the characteristics of artifacts.

11.3 God's relationship to creatures — artifacts — is mysterious, in that it presupposes an engagement of that which is not temporal with what is temporal — the real but unusable with the usable but contingent.

11.4 But if God is engaged with creatures, God is therefore engaged with the engagements of creatures, which are by definition temporal; thus at least God is engaged with temporality somehow.

11.5 God therefore, though unusable himself, can be said to "make use" of creatures.

11.6 That usage, however, is *sui generis* — it derives from God's character as both singular artificer, and the one who is not himself an artifact. Augustine's attempt to distinguish "use" from "enjoyment" is perhaps related to this distinction between divine and creaturely "usage."

11.7 Human beings perceive God according to certain uses, and hence according to limited, though ultimately ordered, apprehensions.

11.8 God's usage of creatures is definitive, in that this "usage" is foundational to all the limited use that defines temporal existence. As God uses creatures, in his *sui generis* way, all possible creaturely usages are granted their possibility and effect.

11.9 If there is a definitive time, or absolute time, it is only in relation to God, who because he is timeless, cannot define time in any humanly absolute way; absolute time is thus a meaningless concept in creaturely terms; though we might say that the definitive usage of creatures by God is absolute in this relative comparison.

11.10 God's use defines our ultimate relation to what we know of as "the past," and this will determine notions of guilt, forgiveness, mercy, and so on. That divine use is unlimited by human perceptions and therefore could include the (humanly understood) "disappearance" or "chance" of the past.

11.11 The "unknown time" or "unexpected time" of the final days (cf. Mark 13:32) is a way of speaking of all times that are not humanly usable, but are divinely used: it speaks to the completely asymmetrical relationship of God and creature in the ultimate ordering of artifacts that are temporal.

12. God and the Scriptures

12.1 God's will — that which ultimately "defines" artifacts — is made known to human creatures in the Scriptures, which constitute some instantiation of the mysterious timeless-temporal reality of God, in relation to creatures. Thus Scripture's own time is "unknown," because it straddles the threshold of God's asymmetrical time and creaturely time, and cannot be included within a simple historical frame.

12.2 This is a key point when gauging Scripture's referentiality: it is always "apocalyptic" in the sense of disclosing a reality otherwise and "beforehand" unused. And it is always "creative" insofar as, from a creaturely standpoint, it inserts artifacts into human usage.

12.3 It is therefore appropriate to speak of the Scriptures as God's Word in relation to the Son, who is God and becomes incarnate, because the two stand in a similarly unique relation to creation and creatures.

12.4 Thus, the artifactual character of Scripture must itself be mysterious. Various ways of describing this have been given, all of which are properly and irresolvably allusive. Scripture is not like any other artifact — or book — in the world. It is not doctrine, it is not science, it is not story, it is not a set of rules.

12.5 The Scriptures, that is, somehow indicate that definitive usage that is God's, and thus what absolute (divine) time might be in theological terms — should one care to use this phrase at all.

12.6 Human perception of God is exclusively given according to Scripture, that is, according to God's will, whether understood as such or not by the creature.

12.7 But it is primordial, or divine history, which may or may not be understood as such by human creatures.

We can draw several further conclusions regarding the unique temporal character of the Scriptures in their referential character:

13. Scripture and Its Reception as an Artifact in Time

13.1 Every given word/reading/hearing of Scripture is an artifact. It is bound — used — within the pattern of a whole, known as "the Scriptures," whose artifactual integrity is given in a book, itself used in various contexts (liturgy, study, travel, hope). These artifacts are indeed "bound" to God's single pattern of "Scripture" — the Law and the Prophets, Psalms, the Gospel and Letters. Any given artifact is always *that*. That is its divine "use"; and in this scriptural usage of all things, it is "God's word" to us.

13.2 The textual questions and variations are not unimportant; but they are only important as used within related, not essential, patterns: *responsibility* to the Word, "searching" the Scriptures, care, self-criticism, etc., vis-à-vis the single pattern.

13.3 And, furthermore, textual/transmissional issues are themselves bound up with the limitations of historiography as a discipline of knowledge, whose various uses are clear only in light of their ultimate usage of God.

13.4 Wrong words, manuscript variations, mistranslations, etc. are themselves only retrospectively — that is, within some changed pattern of use — problematic. They do not necessarily problematize the reality of the Scriptures, in their given artifactual character at this or that time, as being the Word of God, of God's will made known and as the divine order given to creation.[16]

---

16. Issues of translation are obviously important, and also tricky. Augustine famously dealt with this in a kind of providential way in *De Doctrina* II.12-15 and, in parallel, III.27. Another way of dealing with this, not altogether of a different kind, but more interested in upholding the ecclesial locus of "the Word of God," is Paul Griffiths' notion of "canon tokens," in terms of authorized translations and "versions." See his "Which Are the Words

14. Scripture as History-making[17]

14.1 Therefore, the time of human creatures is being used by God in a way that conforms to Scripture, insofar as the latter (Scripture) is inclusive of the former (human time).

14.2 Scripture does not "develop" and is not part of a tradition; it orders all experienced developments and the ultimately uncertain usages we describe as traditional.

14.3 Hence, time itself, as the set of all artifactual usages, is conformed to the Scriptures.

14.4 Human usage — temporal existence, including the past, the present, and becoming — is being used by God in conformance with — "according to" — the Scriptures.

14.5 Human beings will experience time as it emerges from, is reflective of, and is being conformed to the Scriptures.

14.6 The link — as the definitive ordering of creaturely artifacts — between past, present, and becoming, then, is Scripture itself.

14.7 Scripture represents the pattern of recognizability by which all things exist. It is the shape of time itself, time at its "thickest."

15. Scriptural Figuration

15.1 Scripture is properly read as the divine artifactual order. That is, every artifact finds its place somehow within the order of Scripture's usage of this artifact.

15.2 Scripture is also intrinsically *about* artifacts, and, in a broad sense, its "genre" is always artifactual, something which corresponds to the traditional notion that the "first sense of Scripture" is always "literal" or "historical," that is, is about and making use of the artifacts of God's ultimate creation.

---

of Scripture?" *Theological Studies* 72 (2011): 703-22, the theory of which he relies upon in his commentary on the (Latin text of) *Song of Songs* (Grand Rapids: Brazos Press, 2011). Wycliffe's levels of reference for "the Word" might also apply.

17. This way of putting things is obviously problematic ecclesially. While it coheres with a certain *sola Scriptura* attitude, it does so without the pneumatological claims often associated with Reformed circles. These are claims that tend to render Scripture as an object requiring apprehensive skill to encounter — with all the humanly subjective transferral of powers and criteria that comes with this — rather than as the subject of that encounter. (See the concluding chapter.) Further, the notion of Scripture itself as "history-making" certainly flies in the face of simple juxtapositions of Scripture and Tradition, whether under some larger umbrella of "revelation" or as elements coordinated in some other way. In my proposal, the inference is that tradition is always plural and malleable; or, if one wishes, it finds its final coherence as coincident with creation's purpose itself. But tradition is not a distinct divinely creative force, however construed.

15.3 We must say, too, that the "literal" meaning of Scripture is always therefore about both "the natural" and the "supernatural," that is, the artifact itself and the fact that it is part of God's creative ordering. (The terms, thus, denote perspectives of conception, not realms of being, the former being more restricted than the latter.)

15.4 Not all artifacts are immediately referred to by indicative nominal signs in Scripture (e.g. Napoleon is not mentioned in Scripture; nor are vaccines for smallpox).

15.5 Therefore, many artifacts are otherwise indicated in the Scriptures, since they are nonetheless included within them.

15.6 **What is called the "figural character" of Scripture refers to the fact that all artifacts are so indicated and included**. This again, constitutes a key claim.[18]

15.7 The figural reading of Scripture is therefore not something opposed to or other than or in addition to the "literal reading" of Scripture; it is rather a way of describing the literalness of Scripture's reference, that is, that all of it is bound up with the created/creative dynamic of time in an originating and inclusively orienting way.

Again, several further consequences can be drawn from this.

15.8 The figural reading of Scripture is that reading of the words of Scripture that uncovers the exhaustive artifactual reference of scriptural language.

15.9 Specifically Christian reading of Scripture identifies the exhaustive reach of God's artifactive character with the being of Christ, "in whom, by whom, and for whom all things are made."

15.10 Scripture therefore names all artifacts in a primary way. Hence, although the name "Napoleon" does not appear in Scripture, the person we call Napoleon is in fact named in the Bible. A figural reading will discover how this is so.

18. A central feature of this discussion is to remove the term "figure" from purely rhetorical or logical categorization, and locate it within a metaphysical context of objective reference. This is an important issue, and is taken up in Chapter 5 in the discussion of the "incarnational synecdoche." I would stress at this point, though, the difference that a committed theological approach makes here. It is possible, for instance, to engage in complex and nuanced non-theistic discussions of figuralist reference that deliberately seek to hold back from questions of objective reference simply because they are logically too difficult to resolve, yet nonetheless hover about the edges of this possibility quite explicitly because a world without such possibility is perhaps too hard to bear. See, for instance, the rich logical discussion by Stephen Yablo, "Go Figure: A Path through Fictionalism," in his collection *Things: Papers on Objects, Events, and Properties* (Oxford: Oxford University Press, 2010), pp. 177-99.

15.11 This includes all of our common-sense temporal referents: they too are figures, bound to divine artifactual usage. Thus, for instance, "old" and "new" are scriptural figures before they are temporal determinants; that is, they refer to divine usage, and only secondarily to some organized temporal sequence, humanly experienced. Just so, the "old" and the "new" can properly refer to artifacts that resist such organized sequence.

15.12 But because these are the artifacts that are God's own creation, they are so named somehow as being "in Christ" and Christian figural reading of Scripture traces these names — that is, all names in Scripture include all artifacts, and all artifacts are named by Christ in a way that fulfills his divine use of them.

15.13 Is there a scriptural "type"? (or better, "antitype"?) Christ Jesus! But Scripture is not "less" of Jesus; it is Christ displayed in this form as antitypical artifact, of which the Scriptures are indeed the type, at any given time, of his very life. Even this is too limited: they *are* Christ among us.

15.14 It is incorrect, then, to say that there is no past, present, or future in Scripture; rather, all these are elements of Scripture's referrals, but in multiple ways that always include exhaustively the use God would put us to, that is, our created lives within his creative life.

15.15 The reading of Scripture in this way is itself a form of change or becoming — an *ascesis*. Such reading uncovers a range of multiplied, added, or subtracted divine uses in which we are located within the set of artifacts that is God's created domain in Christ.

15.16 Time, theologically understood, is the use by which God conforms creatures to the exhaustive referral of the Christian Scriptures.

15.17 Time is scripturally malleable, and its history has a logical and teleological priority to all human historical construals, durationally and physically.

16. Christ Jesus and Time

16.1 The Word stands as the mystery of God which gives rise to the mystery that is the Scriptures. They are his image. Yet they do not partake of artifactual existence in the same way.

16.2 As Jesus, the Word becomes an artifact that is ordered according to the forms of Scripture. He is subject to the same dynamics as a horse or a tree or a pedestrian in Cairo. He is not *less* bound to God's creative will, however: he is given to other creatures to be perceived, recognized, and used.

16.3 But the Word's artifactual reality as Jesus is also creative. Just as it is only God's creative love that originates creatures through a mysterious condescension, so in Jesus, that creative love is at work to an infinite extent: this particular condescension *is* creative love in its fullness.

16.4 Hence, Christ Jesus is the power of God *as* artifactual existence; and the encounter with Jesus as artifact is an encounter with God's creative being.

16.5 To encounter Jesus is to be ordered according to the Scriptures; and such an ordering is itself that encounter.

16.6 That ordering takes place "in time," that is, through the means of usage, thick and thin, that constitutes temporal existence. Jesus can be met, remembered, forgotten, manipulated.

16.7 Yet in this case, all such temporal realities are subject to the truth of God's ordering of time in a direct way: this "time" is always the "time of Christ" insofar as its usage is his own life at work: what Scripture has called the ineluctable character of all Christological encounter as judgment or mercy.

16.8 The temporal particularity of Christ Jesus is capable of being ordered in diverse ways, historically or otherwise. The only true order, which is not subject to temporal usage in any exclusive fashion, is Scripture's. The reign of Tiberius and the governorship of Pontius Pilate are all immovable scriptural realities, and hence divinely created truths, although their "historical" meaning, as perceived by human creatures, is subject to different patterns of usage. God inserts the artifact that is his own Son and self into the encounters of his creation as he chooses, for his purposes; the use made of these is to be judged only according to the Scriptures, and will be disclosed in divine terms "at the end of time."

16.9 There is no privileged temporal "point" in which the insertion of the incarnation is decisive, except that described in the Scriptures on its own terms. Hence, even as an artifact, time is measured by Christ, and not the other way around.

16.10 The relation of church and sacrament to Christ is other than the Scripture's relation to him. The church is a collection of human creatures — divine artifacts. As a created collective entity, it has no creative powers such as does the incarnate Body of Jesus, nor does it directly express the ordering truth of God's will, as do the Scriptures. Yet it marks the one creaturely witness of both scriptural truth and the Son's ultimate mystery of condescension. In the church, the promise of artifactual encounter with Jesus in judgment and mercy is inviolable: here alone with certainty is given the mystery of Christ without forgetfulness (though perhaps with hostility), and this certainty is tied to the artifactual usage we call the sacraments.

16.11 The inviolability of this promise is bound up with the life of the Holy Spirit (another topic). However, it is the complex movement of the Spirit in this process that permits the church to be called "the body of Christ" insofar as the ultimate condescension of God is made known here *as ultimate*, and hence as a complete giving over and becoming one. Temporally speaking, there is no incarnation without the church.

16.12 Scripture and sacrament do not correlate as two equal pillars of the church. They are different in kind, and the first exposes the order of the second, as well as determines the usage of the second as a realm of *ascesis* or becoming in Christ.

III. Limitations on This Discussion

In laying out the above schema, I cannot help but acknowledge its own lacunae, questions begged, and even implied contradictions. Furthermore, it is curiously bloodless, with none of the necessary richness that ought to accompany any Christian discussion of "time," that is, the essential pathos of relational life. At best I have only implied this indirectly, through presenting the presuppositions of use that are bound up with a populated universe.[19] But how could I have avoided such gaping holes? Indeed, there would be something wrong if it all fit together neatly, and if instead of a scheme, I attempted to provide a systematic treatment. The case made in Section 12 for the Scripture's figural meaning is, from my perspective, central and, I hope, consistent with the Christian tradition. But it is expressed in a way that properly *can* engage other elements of temporal order as a created reality for the sake of opening up the boundaries of our preconception, not because this form of engagement is necessarily truer than some other construct. The point is to "thicken" our sense of the created texture of our existences in the light of and with Scripture, not to thin it out. With Augustine I would agree as to the central challenge of any reflection upon Scripture: to constrict the

---

19. One place to see something of the possible directions this might go is Emmanuel Levinas's early, but still profoundly moving, *Le temps et l'autre* (1948), translated by Richard Cohen as *Time and the Other and Additional Essays* (Pittsburgh: Duquesne University Press, 1987).

Scripture's referents is to misunderstand what Scripture is, because one has misunderstood who God is.

In any case, what I have offered above is solely an argument about Scripture, and it is not designed to be a comprehensive description of the nature of "the world," as it is experienced, nor, as must be obvious, of the nature of God as Triune or Christologically revealed.[20]

Nothing said here, furthermore, is meant to undercut the fundamental experiential value of "common sense," which represents, after all, artifactual existence. Hence, past, present, future, becoming, memories, death, and the rest are, in their common sense experience, valid categorizations of existence. Likewise, the inquiries, experiments, hypotheses, and testable conclusions bound to these experiences — including observations and calculations — stand, on their own terms, as reasonable exercises, although the breadth of their explanatory value is highly limited.

Nonetheless, my reflections have also relied on certain basic skeptical frameworks that are designed to indicate the ways in which "common sense" experience depends on profound mysteries whose ultimate ordering is coherent with traditional Christian claims regarding scriptural revelation: the creative life of God and what we call the purposes of God, if they are even only glimpsed at, as they inevitably are as we delve into the shockingly vast and shadowed corridors of our existence — such a possibility even will render the scriptural claims of the Word's priority over experienced time at least plausible. In this way, my reflections are conceived of in analogy with Joseph Butler's program.[21]

The acceptance of this kind of reflection, if not its details, ought therefore to reorient the cultural assumptions that shape "common sense" in ways that will open them to assumptions of other Christian eras and practices. "Past" readings of Scripture such as I outlined in the last chapter, that is, are not "past" at all, but easily and properly disclosive of the character of our world in its relation to God, and are also thus potentially disclosive of the truth of our lives: who we are is given to us in the use God makes of us in relation to our conformance to the Scriptures of Christ. The Scriptures must "reach" that far, if they are indeed the "Word of God."

20. On some of the Christological questions, see below, Chapter 5, on the divine synecdoche.

21. Whereas Joseph Butler, in his famous 18th-century work, could speak of an "analogy" of religion to Nature, in order to lay out the shape of human life in conformity with Christian claims, I might speak here of the "analogy of religion to time" in a more limited and dislocating way. Cf. Joseph Butler, *The Analogy of Religion, Natural and Revealed, to the Constitution and Course of Nature* (London: James, John, and Paul Knapton, 1736).

IV. Exile and History

Let me end by returning to the question of exile in the Scriptures. We earlier raised the issue of the "referent" of the term "exile" in the New Testament, a matter of some debate surrounding the work of N. T. Wright. How do we get at answering this question?

The contemporary historian, confronted by the referring text of Scripture, will usually seek to figure out when the term was originally used, who used it, and the context of that use. She will then perhaps seek to trace the usage of the term through this or that scriptural text, but in doing so will need to order these texts according to a specific chronology and social-contextual outline that can engage the question of "development" and meaning. We used the example of Wright in this case, who then can locate the term "exile" within a specific set of experiences and explanations about God and history that are defined by certain Second Temple outlooks. These are then injected into the meaning of the New Testament scriptural texts, so that Jesus' *own* 1st-century meaning — his "historical" self-understanding — can inform our definition of "exile" and "restoration" as Christian realities.

I myself wondered about whether this method is sufficient to the task of understanding Scripture's referent, in this case "exile," and raised the question in part by pointing to the Christian tradition that in fact read the referent quite differently. The contemporary historian, on the other hand, pursues this method because the use of the historian's work is governed by a set of purposes that determine that there should be a chronological ordering of events as the basis for all referential meaning. This gives us a sense of "time" that is defined by its purpose, as a tool used to order the material of historical research in this way. But how evaluate this purpose? Note that, in light of my outline above, "use" now is our criterion for temporal claims, not a correspondence of "actual" events with "subsequent" human description, whatever that might be. Rather, I have suggested that historians are given artifacts, and order them. To what end? Here we are thrust into the realm of a moral adjudication of historiography. There is no "neutral" use of anything, and therefore modern historians must be judged, at least in part, on what they are doing, and what they are "after," with the constructions, chronological or otherwise, that they provide.

We are familiar with the kinds of questions people ask of chronological historical reference with respect to the Bible. For some, a conclusion that "x didn't happen" seems to end the discussion. But determining that something "didn't happen" still tells one nothing about the "use" of the artifact (written narrative, [mis-]remembered event, and so on). One must first be clear as to why "happening" or "not happening" are key claims for meaning and use. On the other hand, one might claim, as a conclusion, that "*x* did indeed happen." Now what? Even that is not enough to say with respect to Christian meaningfulness, unless this conclusion is joined to a purpose that serves God. Augustine's rule of charity[22] is only one example, but a good one, of the kind of moral criterion by which temporal schemes can be evaluated. But created existence in time — the "did it happen?" framework — is not a privileged one in terms of God's actual creative will: God creates countless artifacts — memories, signs, hopes, and the rest — that are as "real" as anything else, and the "event" aspect of reality is in fact only one form of usage that we make of real artifacts.

We have already argued that the decision by some New Testament and later Christians to use other temporal frameworks for exile served another "use": theodicy and thereby the proper understanding of God's own "use" of our personal existences, and hence the character of God himself. Affirming "continuing" exile, or the exilic character of Christ's own discipling life, and so on, was a means of reconciling experience — what I have called the various encounters of creatures with other creaturely artifacts — to God's love. It might have also been a means of binding oneself to the form of Christ, in acts of attentive response — that is, not just as theodicy but as a form of joyful love in participating in Christ's life. Or, again, the embrace of "continuing exile" despite its purported historical termination in Christ's resurrection, might have been a means of ordering one's own spirit of repentance. All of these constituted "uses" made of the various elements associated with "exile" were bound up with coherent networks of meaning within the Christian churches. *Were these uses God's?*

One might consider these as contested aspects of moral scrutiny, and therefore turn back to the historical question: did Jesus talk about "exile," and if so, what did he mean by "exile" in his time and place? My own suggestion, however, is that such a default position is not only unnecessary but is also insufficient, if taken alone, for engaging the truth of scriptural reference, given the very nature of creaturely existence (and created "time") itself. Rather, the traditional Christian criterion for use is given in the Scripture's own claims: God's purposes are presented in the experienced — temporal — becoming of human creatures into a full conformity with the figures of the divine text. Hence, every scriptural "exile" at every "time" is the actual referent of the text itself, for all these times are in fact the times that Jesus means, given that the whole of the Scriptures in all their parts order existence in a way that Jesus has embraced as his own for the sake of and for sharing with the world. Exile

22. Cf. *De Doctrina* I.35-36; II.7; III.15.

and restoration are both artifacts of Scripture with which we are presented by God, and in Christ; and their "times" will proliferate variously within the experienced lives of individual creatures. In fact, the more they do so, the fuller our scriptural existences — the ultimate order of our lives — will become. The multiple senses of Scripture reflect an aim at this conformity by proposing a kind of schematic of exhaustive use — moral, consummating, historical, and so on — according to which (to use the example) exile, such as is described in the Scriptures, will shape our lives in every conceivable context. As too will our restoration with Israel in the Return and Messianic coming and kingdom. Articulating the outcome to this pressure of reference, internal to the word of Scripture itself, has been a central task of figural interpretation within the history of the church, albeit one that has been pursued in varying and inconsistent ways, often at odds with itself.[23]

One thing, which is all things, has ever happened. It is given in the Scriptures, in all of its parts, and at every time, for all times. This marks the "togetherness" of God's love and creaturely limitation in the ordering subordination of the latter to the former's condescending acts. And it is what we mean when we speak of history as itself the grace of God.

---

23. For a fascinating exploration of this tension of figural engagement see Timothy J. Furry's study of Bede's interpretive approach, in his *Allegorizing History: The Venerable Bede, Figural Exegesis, and Historical Theory* (Eugene, OR: Pickwick/Wipf and Stock, 2013). One of Furry's stimulating moves is to make use of new work in the theory of historiography, including writers like Franklin Ankersmit and Hayden White. Joined to a robust theological set of claims concerning divine reality and agency — but only thus! — this can be a fruitful move.

CHAPTER 4

Creative Omnipotence and the Figures of Scripture

I. Introduction

What essential theological elements uphold a figural reading of the Bible? In my last chapter I laid out a kind of conceptual grid for how the figural apprehension of the Scriptures might make sense of the actual practice of the Christian tradition. This was all *ex post facto*, as it were; and as I insisted, I offered this only in the most imaginative sense: what might be involved in allowing our times to be taken up by certain basic facts which outstrip them? This is what the Scriptures in fact do; but how is not at all evident. So my "grid" was hardly a necessary one. More fundamental, I think, is the simple but central Christian claim regarding the creative power of God, a power exercised over and in relation to all that exists. If God is indeed the creator of all things (and hence we are right to call all things "divine artifacts") and among these things are the Scriptures in a way that is somehow unique vis-à-vis other created artifacts — then Scripture's relation to such artifacts (that is, to all other things) will follow the ordering that God establishes. The specifically figural ordering of Scripture's meaning is a way of expressing that established scriptural relationship to all things; and "figural reading" is the way that relationship is apprehended in its true ordering. It is not a set of meanings, but the encounter with such meanings as God presents them. To read Scripture figurally is to read just this kind of Scripture, and as a Christian to do so in just such a way that this established relationship is that very relationship given by and in Christ.

But is an appeal to God's creative omnipotence with respect to the Scriptures sufficient to disclose this figural relationship that undergirds all creation?

Indeed, one key argument made by some intellectual historians over the past fifty years has been that such an appeal is a specifically *modern* one, and precisely one whose assertion has contributed to the *dismantling* of figural reading of the kind the church has traditionally proposed. There have been various philosophical culprits identified in this purported lapse into constricted divine omnipotence. For instance, there is John Duns Scotus and his debated dismissal of metaphysical analogy in favor of "univocal" notions of being, a philosophical move that somehow reduced the mystery of divine life to a common set of humanly discernible (finally historical) categories. There is William of Ockham and his notion of an inaccessible divine *potentia absoluta* (absolute power), whose arbitrary self-limitation to humanly measurable forms of *potentia ordinata* (ordained power) likewise left the Bible dangling in the sphere of human manipulation. Or there is Luther, who seemed more at ease with the irrationality of the *potentia absoluta*, which only stripped the Bible of coherent comprehension of the world. Even Newton's supreme Governor stands as the Grand Engineer, overseeing but a machine whose cogs Scripture can at best describe or otherwise lapse into irrelevance. Protestants, Peter Harrison has taught us, dealt with the unpredictability of divine omnipotence in relation to human sin by "empiricizing" their studies, and finally reducing the Scriptures to the probabilistic theories of their increasingly positivist imaginations.[1]

---

1. On Harrison, see Peter Harrison, *The Bible, Protestantism, and the Rise of Natural Science* (Cambridge: Cambridge University Press, 2001), a book that, whatever its limitations, has provided fertile provocation to research. On the wider debate regarding late medieval philosophy, see John Milbank in various places, e.g. "Only Theology Overcomes Metaphysics," *New Blackfriars* 76:895 (July, 1995): 325-43, including in the collection *The Word Made Strange: Theology, Language, Culture* (Oxford: Blackwell, 1997). Some of Milbank's arguments were drawn from the application made of Scotus by Gilles Deleuze — though Milbank rejects Deleuze's positive embrace — in the latter's *Difference and Repetition* (1968), trans. Paul Patton (London: Continuum, 2004), pp. 44-48. A good array of discussion on this can be found in *Modern Theology* 21:4 (October, 2005). Readings like Milbank's have been taken to task by Scotus scholars as well as scholars of Reformed theology, whom some have linked with developed late-medieval Scotism and/or nominalism. Despite this, the view of Scotus-as-instigator of a new and malignant metaphysics has been paralleled by a range of significant scholars, from Louis Dupré to Brad Gregory and Hans Boersma. For a good discussion of this, *contra* Milbank et al., with pertinent references, see Richard A. Muller, "Not Scotist: understandings of being, univocity, and analogy in early-modern Reformed thought," *Reformation & Renaissance Review* 14:2 (2012): 127-50. Charges that medieval nominalism was the (negative) cause of Protestantism were not new. They were well-established by English-language scholars in the early 1960s and marked the end of a long tradition of evaluation, parts of which can be traced to the 16th-century Thomist revival, and that were repromulgated influentially by philosophers like Étienne Gilson. See William J. Courtenay, "In Search of Nominalism: Two Centuries of Debate," in his collection *Ockham and Ockhamism: Studies in the Dissemination and Impact of*

Some of these critics have gone further and argued that there is a contradiction, on this score, between a modern metaphysic of divine omnipotence, *tout court*, and the more supple ontological concerns of the ancients and medievals whose re-appropriation *qua* metaphysicians (generally Platonic ones) alone can, as it were, save the Bible.[2]

I am trying to locate figural reading as a kind of common sense, if disruptive, Christian practice. And I want to suggest that divine creative omnipotence — a bedrock Christian belief — is both sufficient to explain and to account for it. In this chapter I will explore this question in the form of a schematic case-study. My purpose is not to question whether and under what conditions and why figural reading of Scripture may be a good thing. I have already indicated why it must be, given the nature of God's life vis-à-vis ours. Instead, I will examine how, if at all, the shift to a new metaphysic in the 14th century — Ockhamist in particular, but nominalist as the term is generally used — affected the possibilities of figural reading of Scripture.[3] I hope thereby to raise some questions about the relationship of metaphysics and our reading of the Bible that can at least make my own basic claim regarding figural common sense more plausible from a historical perspective. And perhaps, thereby, I can assuage some concerns over the possibility of contemporary figural reading, whose cultural context is generally seen as nominalist in some basic way. When it comes to the "what then shall we do?" question, I am arguing for a more fervent and focused witness to the creative sovereignty of God in our world.

In a way, the present exploration may seem a recondite project of intellectual history. But just these kinds of historical arguments have in fact affected influential readings of the Bible, as the reach of someone like Frederic Farrar

---

His Thought (Leiden: Brill, 2008), pp. 1-19. The larger Christian goals of some of these writers are not all the same, and, in the case of Milbank, Gregory, Boersma, and Dupré, I share many of them. Here, however, I am after a more basic foundation for figural reading of Scripture, which I believe is sufficient for the purpose; and it is one that ought to be more ecumenically acceptable furthermore, at least on a descriptive level. Andrew Louth has himself pointed here to this more basic reality, in stressing the foundational importance of the Christian doctrine of *creatio ex nihilo* (see his *Origins of the Christian Mystical Tradition: From Plato to Denys*, 2nd ed. [Oxford: Oxford University Press, 2007], pp. 73-79), whose ability to ground figural reading, as I argue here, need not require a Platonic metaphysics (athough it might certainly adopt one).

2. Among those associated with the Radical Orthodoxy movement named above, cf. recently Adrian Pabst, *Metaphysics: The Creation of Hierarchy* (Grand Rapids: Eerdmans, 2012).

3. I am well aware that the category of "nominalism" has been challenged, and probably rightly so, as even an adequate, let alone fair, description of the interests and commitments of various late-medieval thinkers. But it remains a standard category, with a number of standard elements, however fuzzily applied to actual individuals. See Courtenay, above.

in the 19th century indicates. So before proceeding further, I need to offer some explanations for my method as well as some disclaimers with regard to its adequacy. In the first place, why approach the issue in terms of the 14th century? In the main, I suggest we do this because of the relative consensus that just this period marks some kind of fundamental alteration of world-conception in Western Europe that affects, among other things, Bible reading. A foremost and early advocate of the return to figural reading — he called it more broadly "allegory" — Andrew Louth himself pointed to Ockham and the theological/philosophical movements influenced by him as the seminal origin of the more lurid changes in attitude towards the Bible that finally did away with the possibility of figural readings in the Enlightenment.[4] And I will be using Louth's well-received thesis as an entry point into this discussion. Ockhamism itself is generally regarded as a force for considerable change, if by no means sudden or alone, in breaking up what many scholars still like to think of as a "medieval synthesis" of reflection and practical attitude towards the world. Oberman, Leff, Ozment, Funkenstein, Sylla, Smalley, and others in an earlier era, in their different ways and with regard to different elements, all make this kind of point, and their views, albeit in a variety of forms, continue to be replicated by others.[5]

But the exact relation, if any, between the changes in metaphysical conception that Ockhamism brought about and biblical interpretation has not been explored. Epistemology and natural theology have, instead and on the whole, constituted the main areas where nominalism's creative (or destructive) influence has been examined. And there are probably good reasons why this is so, at least superficially. Ockham himself, who did not achieve the rank of "master" or "doctor," never officially commented on Scripture. He has left us no system-

4. Louth, *Discerning the Mystery: An Essay on the Nature of Theology* (Oxford: Clarendon Press, 1989), p. 6.

5. Heiko Oberman, "Some Notes on the Theology of Nominalism with Attention to Its Relation to the Renaissance," *Harvard Theological Review* 53 (Jan., 1960): 47-96; Gordon Leff, *The Dissolution of the Medieval Outlook: An Essay on Intellectual and Spiritual Change in the Fourteenth Century* (New York: Harper and Row, 1976); Steven Ozment, *The Age of Reform 1250–1550: An Intellectual and Religious History of Late Medieval and Reformation Europe* (New Haven: Yale University Press, 1980); Amos Funkenstein, *Theology and the Scientific Imagination from the Middle Ages to the Seventeenth Century* (Princeton: Princeton University Press, 1986); Edith Dudley Sylla, "Autonomous and Handmaiden Science: St.Thomas Aquinas and William of Ockham on the Physics of the Eucharist," in *The Cultural Context of Medieval Learning: Proceedings of the First International Colloquium on Philosophy, Science, and Theology in the Middle Ages — September 1973*, ed. John Emery Murdoch and Edith Dudley Sylla (Dordrecht: D. Reidel, 1973); Beryl Smalley, "Problems of Exegesis in the Fourteenth Century," in *Antike und Orient im Mittelalter*, ed. Paul Wilpert (Berlin: Walter de Gruyter & Co., 1962).

atic evidence as to how his metaphysical innovations might have affected his hermeneutic.[6] The second part of his career, in any case, was wholly given over to polemical concerns with the papacy, dealing with the issues of Franciscan poverty and the relationship of temporal and spiritual powers. While some of his writings from this period do afford us with glimpses of his scriptural method, they probably ought not to be taken as anything close to theoretical exposition of what "holy Scripture" means and how it means for the church.

There were, of course, other Ockhamist theologians who have left biblical commentaries.[7] But they have not been studied in any detail (and I am, alas, not equipped to do so now). So we are left somewhat in a bind. While someone like Smalley is sure that the 14th century (and into the 15th century) demonstrates a radical decline in exegetical dynamism, and that this is, in part at least, linked to shifts in theological and philosophical outlook, we have no real evidence with which to judge how exactly this could be the case.[8]

6. How logical and philosophical questions might both derive from and inform the reading of Scripture more generally is outlined in G. R. Evans, *The Language and Logic of the Bible: The Road to Reformation* (Cambridge: Cambridge University Press, 1985), p. 108. But, as she notes, modern scholars are only on the front end of even examining these questions historically, and therefore conclusions should probably be avoided.

7. One might mention Robert Holcot's famous commentary on Wisdom, *Super libros sapientiae* (repr. Frankfurt/Main: Minerva, 1974). The kind of figuralism Holcot maintains, as it turns out, is hardly free-flowing, and he tends to approach the book in terms of a moral scholastic. Still, the figural presuppositions are always in play. Among Franciscans who shared aspects of Ockham's ecclesiology, there was Peter Olivi, who preceded him by a generation, yet whose influence on Ockham is evident. Olivi's prophetic readings of the Bible, like Joachim of Fiore's, are noteworthy, but nonetheless emerge from a traditional figuralist framework. See Petri Iohannis Olivi, *Lectura super Lamentationes Hieremie*, in M. Bartoli, *La Caduta di Gerusalemme. Il commento al Libro delle Lamentazioni di Pietro di Giovanni Olivi* (Roma, 1991); *Peter of John Olivi on the Bible*, ed. D. Flood & G. Gál (St. Bonaventure, NY: Franciscan Institute, 1997); D. Burr, *Olivi's Peaceable Kingdom. A Reading of the Apocalypse Commentary* (Philadelphia: University of Pennsylvania Press, 1993); S. Piron, "La critique de l'Église chez les Spirituels languedociens," in *L'anticléricalisme en France méridionale, milieu xii*- *début xiv*ᵉ *siècle*, Cahiers de Fanjeaux, 38 (Toulouse: Privat, 2003), pp. 77-109.

8. Cf. Smalley, "Problems of Exegesis in the Fourteenth Century." While she doesn't refer to Ockhamism or nominalism directly, she wonders, on p. 274, "whether a theologian who shared the current tendencies towards scepticism and fideism would have felt happy about turning his talents to account in commenting on the sacred text." Holcot, in particular, is singled out for her scorn (p. 271). Of course, Smalley adheres to the view that equates the advance of literal exegesis with the progress of biblical commentary in general. In her own negative way, as we shall point out later, she underlines the 14th century's continued dominance by figural interpretation. It should also be pointed out that Louth quite deliberately sets himself up against the kind of exegetical values Smalley promotes (see esp. his chapter 5). Although with such an opposition, we are faced by a contradiction: for Smalley, the 14th century is bad

My own sense, indicated in Chapter 2, is that any shifts which did take place had less to do with metaphysics than with intra-Christian ecclesial implosion. Other dynamics, in any case, including university structures and demographic changes, played a role.[9] Indeed, if we look simply at the exegetical handbooks that continued to be printed well into the 16th century among Catholics (and they were often read by Protestants too, who in turn wrote their own versions), figural readings — whether called "spiritual" or "mystical" or divided into various levels of meaning — continued to be standard fodder for study, as I have noted.[10]

What I propose to do, then, is to try to get at the possible relationship between Ockhamist metaphysics and a figural biblical hermeneutic indirectly. Rather than concentrating on purely theological aspects of figuration — that is, those dealing with Christological typology, for instance — I will confine myself, by and large, to the question of the symbolization, or lack thereof, of the natural world. By this, I mean only the kind of "symbolizing mentality" that someone like Chenu attributes to the 12th century, applied across the board, not only to Scripture, but to an understanding of the cosmos as a whole. As I pointed out, this is the general way medieval conceptualities about the natural world are still defined.[11] Turning to the possible figuration of the natural world does have the advantage of allowing us a clearer view of the role of metaphysics in sustaining figural mentalities in general. And this, after all, is not subsidiary to our main concern. In addition, it allows us entrance into one particular field of indirect pertinence to the purported Ockhamist metaphysical shift, and that is the place of properly Franciscan attitudes in the development of his ontology. Again, while I have not found any serious attempt to trace the influence of a Franciscan context on Ockham, the context and its influence have been alluded to by several prominent scholars.[12] And that Ockham un-

---

because it can't advance the creative use of the *sensus literalis*; for Louth, the 14th century is equally denigrated, but for laying the groundwork that undercuts the *sensus spiritualis*.

9. See the discussion by William J. Courtenay, "The Bible in the Fourteenth Century: Some Observations," *Church History* 54:2 (1985): 176-87.

10. E.g. Jeronimo Lloret et al., whom I mentioned in my second chapter. Not that we cannot see an attenuation of this standard fare, and real shifts in interest by many. But the search for change has, I would guess, overshadowed the reality of continuity.

11. Chenu, *Nature, Man, and Society: Essays on New Theological Perspectives in the Latin West*, ed. and trans. Jerome Taylor and Lester Little (Chicago: University of Chicago Press, 1968), chapter 4. It is now a standard view.

12. Heiko Oberman, "Fourteenth-Century Religious Thought," *Speculum* 53:1 (1978): 84-86, 89ff., speaks of the "Franciscan hegemony" in theological and philosophical discourse, without, however, trying to articulate what is particularly "Franciscan" about the problems that gripped people, except their evident connection with the Friars Minor. Funkenstein, *Theology*

derstood himself as a Franciscan, and not simply as a thinker who happened to be a friar, is clear from his subsequent career and his overriding personal commitment to the issue of religious poverty.

The revolutionary role Francis's own person and interests played in the latter 13th and 14th centuries in contributing to a social and imaginative shift seems to parallel at least the metaphysical shift associated with the Ockhamists.[13] While I certainly wish to make no historical claims about any supposed "Franciscan" metaphysic, nonetheless, it might be instructive to see how a purportedly Franciscan attitude toward nature, which only parallels an Ockhamist philosophy of nature, to be sure, might bear on the issue of natural figuration. Are there any connections?

A third avenue of indirect approach to our question of figuration, opened up by an examination of the natural order in general during this period, is that of the representational arts. There are some interesting claims made by, for instance, Umberto Eco, about the relation of Ockhamism and aesthetic form that need at least to be raised, particularly in comparison with earlier, more explicitly symbolizing natural representations in the 12th century and beyond.

After exploring these three areas (and not necessarily in the order given above), we can return more deliberately to the question of figural readings of

---

and the Scientific Imagination, p. 139, refers to twin Franciscan genealogies for Ockham's ontology of individuals, but again, he doesn't hazard any guess as to why these interests should be particularly linked to the followers of St. Francis.

13. We refer, most recently, to literary historians like Fleming, Jeffrey, and Sorrell, as well as art historians like Stubblebine. See John Fleming, *An Introduction to the Franciscan Literature of the Middle Ages* (Chicago: Franciscan Herald Press, 1977); David L. Jeffrey, "Franciscan Spirituality and the Growth of Vernacular Culture," in *By Things Seen: Reference and Recognition in Medieval Thought*, ed. David L. Jeffrey (Ottawa: University of Ottawa Press, 1979); Roger Sorrell, *St. Francis of Assisi and Nature: Tradition and Innovation in Western Christian Attitudes toward the Environment* (New York: Oxford University Press, 1988); James H. Stubblebine, *Assisi and the Rise of Vernacular Art* (New York: Harper & Row, 1985). One attempt, somewhat strained, to build a connection between a medieval "Franciscan metaphysics" and a particular grasp of reality and life that is, in fact, bound to the *vita evangelica* of Francis, is Kenan Osborne, OFM, *The Franciscan Intellectual Tradition: Tracing Its Origins and Identifying Its Central Components* (St. Bonaventure, NY: Franciscan Institute Publications, St. Bonaventure University, 2003); more pointedly, see his "A Scotistic Foundation for Christian Spirituality," *Franciscan Studies* 64 (2006): 363-405. More abstractly, and without any real historical grounding, the social philosopher Agamben has lifted up a supposed Franciscan "ontology," which he has, interestingly, linked to peculiar (messianic) Christian notions of time and history. See Giorgio Agamben, *The Time That Remains: A Commentary on the Letter to the Romans*, trans. Patricia Dailey (Stanford: Stanford University Press, 2005), pp. 23-27. See also Alain Badiou, *Logics of Worlds: Being and Event*, volume 2, trans. by Alberto Toscano (New York: Continuum, 2009), pp. 558-59.

the Bible in particular, and try to assess the ways in which metaphysics may or may not sustain such readings in the 14th century.

Perhaps in part because of the indirect modes of approach to which I am confined in investigating the question, my answer regarding the need for a special figural metaphysics will ultimately be negative, and that in two ways. First, I will conclude that there seems to be little relation between the supposed 14th-century metaphysical shift and the conditions for the possibility of figural readings of the Bible. But this will raise the question, then, as to whether any kind of metaphysical foundation for such readings is necessary. And an answer to this question will lead me to claim that, while no *particular* foundation may be required, a foundation of some sort is. In Ockham's case, I shall claim that it is a fairly traditional Augustinian commitment to divine purposive omnipotence. And, negatively again, it would appear that, if there is a place where Christian theology and common sense are obliged to look more responsibly, it is to the question of whether such general foundations are available to us today.

II. The Shape of the Natural World in the Ockhamist Shift

As a contrast to the kind of world-conception Ockham and his direct predecessors are purported to have ushered in, let us outline briefly the general Platonic scheme of nature that prevailed, in various forms, in the 12th century. As a nominalist, even one defined by "realistic conceptualism," in Boehner's phrase,[14] Ockham is notorious for having rejected *in toto* the real ontological status, not only of all categories except substance and quality, but also of all categories independent of their instantiation in individuals, including substance and quality. Hence, the Ockhamist denial of universals as real entities apart from the mind's conceptual abstraction, seems to mark a complete reversal of the standard Platonic ordering of reality. But what did such standard Platonic ordering suggest as to the shape of the world? I will follow Chenu's description of this in *Nature, Man, and Society*.[15]

Chenu identifies at least three main Platonic strands informing 12th-century Christian thought: the Augustinian, the Timaean/Boethian, and the Dionysian. While he admits that they are frequently hard to disentangle in individual cases, he feels confident in at least affirming their original theoret-

---

14. Cf. Philotheus Boehner, *Collected Articles on Ockham*, ed. Eligius Buytaert (St. Bonaventure, NY: The Franciscan Institute, 1958), pp. 156-74.

15. Chenu, *Nature, Man, and Society*, Chapter 2 (titled "The Platonisms of the Twelfth Century").

ical distinctiveness, and their continued ability to inform the thinking about nature and symbolization in different ways. Although "incompatible" with each other in several elements, the three types also share a common "Platonic" core: an ontological commitment to intelligibles over sensibles, a sense of dialectic between divine transcendence and immanence, the notion of human divinization as our progressive end, and a universe without intermediaries between grades of being. From a Christian point of view, the basic metaphysical elements informing the universe were God, form, and matter.

Apart from these common elements, the three types of Christian Platonism Chenu identified are distinguished by the following: 1) Augustinian Platonism: characterized by a sense of order (*ordo*) among beings, rather than by a hierarchy, as in Dionysius; by antinomies of body and soul (world and spirit, man and God, nature, grace, etc.) rather than by gradations and participations; by a search for immediacy in the human/ divine relationship; and by a devaluation of history and secondary causes as a result. 2) Timaean Platonism: derived from a renewed study of Plato's dialogue *Timaeus*. Especially among the scholars at the school of Chartres, this kind of Platonism emphasized the cosmological dimensions of natural interrelations. Given that this was the *Timaeus* read through Chalcidius's Stoicizing commentary, there was a focus on the organic ontological wholeness of the universe (*universitas*). Its almost homogeneous common vitality (*anima mundi*), and its part/whole ontological mirroring (*microcosmos/macrocosmos*), provided a natural order wherein universal order was more directly tied to divine immanence than to the structure of being. (This was Boethius's contribution to the scheme.) 3) Dionysian Platonism: after the rapid diffusion of the Dionysian corpus in the latter part of the century, the notion of participatory hierarchy of being in the universe was introduced. God was seen as present directly in a graded order of being to all parts of the cosmos, which related to each other by a kind of "sympathy"; humanity's relationship to God was progressive and ascending, through the hierarchy, now understood as symbolic, not in a semiotic sense, but in the metaphysical sense of continuous participation and movement ("metaphor" in the strong sense, as an ontological "transferal").

In and of itself, this typology seems helpful. Where it becomes somewhat misleading, perhaps, is when it is applied specifically to the understanding of symbolization that different 12th-century thinkers employed. Chenu will want to contrast an Augustinian, semiotic, literalist attitude among the Victorine exegetes, for instance, with a Dionysian, "realist," spiritualizing attitude among other biblical exegetes of the period.[16] Here we have the first instance where it

---

16. Chenu, *Nature, Man, and Society,* Chapter 3, e.g. pp. 126ff.

is not at all clear in what way an alternative metaphysic will attenuate figural readings.[17]

For there is no question that the Dionysian or the Timaean universe will be one in which reality is best approached on a symbolic level. Objects, whether animate or inanimate, exist within an interrelated network of being, of forms, or of spirit; each reveals the other in some fashion, and all objects reveal their origin or their end, or even their inhabitant to some degree, which is God.[18] But is there any logical reason why a merely ordered universe of beings, whose interrelationships derive from the orderer and not from the intrinsic traces, within each being, of the orderer, cannot also be equally susceptible to figural apprehension? We shall leave this question to the last section, but it should be clear already that the Augustinian Platonic alternative — which, by the way, is generally the strand that predominates later in the 13th and 14th centuries, even among Franciscans — need not *a priori* be considered inimical to figuration (as Louth's own ideas seem to indicate). Further, the cleavages between orders — and hence between things in many instances — that Chenu applies to Augustinian Platonism in particular, including that between nature and grace, bears enough compatibility with later nominalist metaphysical interests, e.g. of Gregory of Rimini, that we must be alert to the way in which its capacity to comprehend a figural universe might well be parallel to the Ockhamist dismantling of the Platonic framework. I shall point this out in the case of the "Irish" Augustine of *De Mirabilibus Sacrae Scripturae* in a moment.

There can be no question, however, but that Ockham's natural world is of another order than that of, say, Alain of Lille or William of Conches (not to mention the Victorines):

> The universe is an animal. . . . From the life of the divine mind, from the world soul, from the growth principle of created life, the eternity of the universe has its rise. . . . The universe is a continuum, a chain in which nothing

17. As with Smalley, we must be aware of Chenu's own biases in his treatment of figuration. For all his celebration of the 12th century's creative symbolization of the world as a whole, his sympathies are clearly with the Augustinian attenuation of ontological symbolism. The Victorines, lying more firmly in this tradition of attenuation, temper the Platonic tendency to "rob things of their independent ontological value" (p. 131) by founding their scriptural apprehension on the literal sense. Not only must we ask if this is really the case for the Victorines (with the exception perhaps of Andrew), but whether assumptions like "Augustinian" literalism do not lead us into misconceptions about the character of "realism" with regard to natural representation and its ontological basis. (Cf. Chenu's comment on p. 134, that "realistic painting" of nature had to wait until the advent of Aristotelianism in the 13th and 14th centuries, and the demise of a Platonist world view.)

18. Chenu, *Nature, Man, and Society*, pp. 126, 127.

is out of order or broken off. Thus roundness, the perfect form, determines its shape. And so, that complex faculty or spirit which is present in the universe never permits the hostile force to overflow its bounds.[19]

Here, nature and God mutually refer to one another through an ontological interpenetration. With Ockham, we are given this kind of summary:

In addition to the relation of grace to merit, the ramifications of God's absolute power extend from intuitive knowledge of non-existants to his revelation of future contingents, the creation of infinite worlds and souls, of a better world, of the world and beings from eternity, of matter without pre-existing form and form without matter, the separation of accidents from substances, attributes from subject, cause from effect and absolutes from one another, by not creating one without the other, or by annihilation or conservation of one without the other, through God's direct supercession of a second cause.[20]

We shall have the chance to see that positing the *potentia Dei absoluta* and all that it might accomplish — and here Leff merely strings together many of these possibilities mentioned by Ockham in various texts — need not demand an existing universe that is any different *visibly* and *experientially* from Bernard's. But that is not the point. It is certainly hard to see how a universe where virtually all things are possible through God's intervention, even what is now unnatural, could be one where inter-reference of an ontological kind could make sense. For in this case there could not be ontological lines along which metaphor, in the strong sense, could occur. Objects cannot carry us; words certainly, in themselves, cannot; only God, absolutely, can effectuate *translatio*.

Funkenstein provides us with a lucid, albeit complex, entry into the shape of the Ockhamist shift with regard to the natural world. In a staggeringly erudite attempt to trace the coincidence of a number of disparate "ideals" — many of them theological — into the forms of 17th-century science, he lays out several areas where Ockham moved away sharply from earlier medieval conceptions of the universe. According to Funkenstein, the rise of a 17th-century science formed around a conception of infinite Euclidean space was made possible by the fusion of four ideals in particular: linguistic univocity,

19. Bernard Silvestris, *The Cosmographia of Bernardus Silvestris*, trans., intro., and notes Winthrop Wetherbee (New York: Columbia University Press, 1973), ch. 4.

20. Gordon Leff, *William of Ockham: The Metamorphosis of Scholastic Discourse* (Manchester: Manchester University Press, 1975), p. 456.

cosmic homogeneity, mathematization of space and movement, and mechanization of being.[21]

It was Ockham, and his immediate predecessors, so Funkenstein argues, who made possible the decisive conceptual break with earlier notions of a non-homogeneous universe of discrete forms and entities. And this was done, in large measure, by reviving a notion of univocal language used in reference to being and to beings in the world. Funkenstein explores this development under the category of "God's Body," a suggestive heading designed to encompass in particular the different ways various thinkers and epochs envisaged the nature of God's presence (and omnipresence in the Christian traditions) in the extended cosmos.[22]

While Anselm's ontological proof depends on a univocal notion of being, it was largely ignored or outright rejected in the Middle Ages precisely because the Platonic metaphysical framework that ruled until the latter part of the 13th century conceived of the universe in distinctly equivocal terms. It was only the 17th century, finally, with its drive for a single, unequivocal language for all reality, that demonstrated the gulf between a homogeneous universe of things ordered according to similarity and difference[23] (the Enlightenment) and a non-homogeneous Nature characterized by "intrinsic meanings" that exist within a "coherent interlocking system" of symbols and allegories (the 12th and 13th centuries).[24]

Funkenstein is not altogether persuasive about all this, however, and for reasons similar (if from the opposite direction) to those that may bedevil Chenu's linkage of Augustine to literalist tendencies in exegesis: what is the relationship, if any, between ontological distinctions among objects — e.g. between creatures and between creatures and God — and ontological metaphor, the movement of being or understanding from one object to another? It could be argued, for instance, that the equivocal language demanded by, say, a Dionysian apophaticism could really serve the articulation of an *ontologically* homogeneous universe. It is hard to find more homogeneity than a universe animated by a World Soul, like William of Conches postulated. Likewise, it is not at all clear that the revived Platonism of many 17th-century scientists (e.g. Henry More and Malebranche) was inimical to the positing of a symbolizing universe, for all its mechanistic character.

21. Funkenstein, *Theology and the Scientific Imagination*, p. 30.

22. Funkenstein, *Theology and the Scientific Imagination*, p. 24.

23. This was Michel Foucault's overall thesis regarding the "epistemic" mentality of the 17th and 18th centuries, and has gained wide currency. See his *The Order of Things: An Archaeology of the Human Sciences* (New York: Pantheon, 1970).

24. Funkenstein, *Theology and the Scientific Imagination*, pp. 28ff.

Be this as it may, there is no doubt but that Ockham, and his Franciscan predecessors Scotus and Aureole, formulated a move from equivocation to univocity in our speech about God in particular (but the emphasis on "speech" is important) that was to mark a new way of conceiving of God's presence in the universe. And it was this perhaps — so goes Funkenstein's argument — that then linked up with the Stoic aspects of the Renaissance Neoplatonism to provide 17th-century philosophers with their "clear and distinct" language about a perfectly ordered and extended world of nature.[25]

From Funkenstein's account, however, it would seem inevitable that the move to univocity means a move away from symbolization towards literalism in the exegetical parsing of texts as well as of the world. Pure equivocation, as in Dionysian Platonism, demands that knowledge of God as well as God's presence to the world be had only through symbols ("strong," that is, ontological, metaphors). Thomas Aquinas attenuates such equivocation through his theory of the *analogia entis*, which straddles to some degree the seemingly unresolved tension between the Dionysian notions of participation (through the similitudes of perfection in beings) and of apophatic signification.[26] Pure univocal signification, however, is advanced by Thomas, according to Funkenstein, through his adherence to the primacy of the literal sense in exegesis, which allows for spiritual readings, not of nature itself, but of things, events, and people depicted in the Bible only.[27] Thus, slowly, we see the movement away from a symbolized universe, where God cannot be present except through the apprehension of what he is not, towards a universe where the presence and apprehension of God in the world becomes standard and uniform.

This is achieved most fully by Ockham's formulation of the univocal application of "being" to God and creatures, and by his definition of God's omnipresence in terms of "definitive" location (vs. Thomas's "nondimensional" omnipresence of God). According to Ockham, particularly in his treatment of the presence of Christ in the Eucharistic host as well as in heaven, God is present wholly and in all parts at once and in such a way as to be corporeally subsistent. This he calls "definitive" presence — the whole and all its parts in every part of a place — and he can assert it because his ontology rejects quantity as a category independent of quality or substance (to which quantity refers connotatively): to have dimension is only an accident (thus water can "contract" into air and still be water, although now "rarefied water") and to

---

25. Funkenstein, *Theology and the Scientific Imagination*, pp. 57-72.
26. We shall revisit Thomas in the next chapter.
27. Funkenstein, *Theology and the Scientific Imagination*, pp. 55-56.

lack quantity in no way mitigates the integrity of the whole substance and all of its other accidental qualities.[28]

If we grant the significance of these moves by Ockham, we must still ask what role they play in founding or unseating a symbolizing universe. Does the univocity of being and the definitive omnipresence of God necessarily move us towards the further underlining of the *sensus literalis* applied to the world at large? It is hard to see how this might be so.

In the first place, Ockham's unequivocal language about God has been amplified conceptually by Funkenstein well beyond the bounds of Ockham's own use.[29] For Ockham, as I understand him, univocity in our language about God exists at a purely conceptual level. Our concepts of God are always composites of features abstracted from concepts of creatures. They do not derive from intuitive cognition of God, the way our concepts of creatures must ultimately do. They are univocal in that they do refer to God and to creatures with a common term. But they are not univocal in their ontological reference. There is no "being" in reality that exists in common among creatures and God. There is only a concept that is commonly (though properly) used for both and separate "beings" who exist separately.[30]

28. For Ockham and Thomas on the physics of the Eucharist, cf. Sylla, "Autonomous and Handmaiden Science," pp. 361-72.

29. See footnote 1 above on others of this critical tradition, and on retorts of their reading of Scotus in particular.

30. Ockham, *Reportatio* III, Q. viii, translated in Boehner, *Ockham: Philosophical Writings*, pp. 118, 125; cf. also Boehner's introduction to that volume, pp. xl ff.; cf. also Marilyn McCord Adams, *William of Ockham*, 2 vols. (South Bend, IN: University of Notre Dame Press, 1987), pp. 950-54; cf. also Leff, *William of Ockham*, p. 381. Even Duns Scotus's press for the univocity of being is less ontological than it is semantic: if the concept of being is univocal, it is because the verbal sign for that concept — *ens* — refers to that to which "to be" is not repugnant. *In IV Sententiarum* d.9, q.1, n.2 (ed. Vivès, in *Opera Omnia*, Vol. XVII [Paris, 1894], p. 7b). See the discussion in Olivier Boulnois, "Duns Scot, Théoricien de l'Analogie de l'Être," in Ludger Honnefelder, Rega Wood, Mechthild Dreyer, eds., *John Duns Scotus* (Leiden: Brill, 1996), pp. 293-315. (It should be said that Boulnois has his own theological purpose in all this, one that accepts the Scotist "rupture" but that sees "modernity's" genealogical tie to this rupture as far more obscure than do some critics. See his "Reading Duns Scotus: From History to Philosophy," *Modern Theology* 21:4 [October, 2005]: 603-8). With respect to Ockham, the focus on conceptualization and hence discourse as the realm of problematics, rather than "ontology" in a modern sense, is obscured, it seems to me, by Jenny Pelletier's otherwise painstakingly thorough treatment of Ockham's "metaphysics," when she simply allows univocity of linguistic reference to stand for some kind of common ontological entity that she thinks, in itself, can support an "onto-theology." See Jenney Pelletier, *William Ockham on Metaphysics: The Science of Being and God* (Leiden: Brill, 2013), p. 205. But she herself provides a sufficiently subtle description of Ockham's theological qualifications to all this, in her final chapter, as to render the Scotus-Ockham ontotheological genealogy unilluminating. I have been more helped in the

This being the case, it is hard to see how unequivocation, although Ockham claims it (as against Thomistic analogical speech), is anything more than an insistence on a single frame of discourse when referring to God and to creatures. It has no implications beyond the act of talking and certainly carries with it no entailments about the actual ontological relationship between referents. To be fair, Funkenstein does point out that the unequivocal notions of being when applied to God can either lead us to claim no knowledge about God *sola ratione* or to claim a great deal of such knowledge, and that the nominalists chose the former course and 17th-century philosophers the latter.[31] Yet he still wants us to link nominalist univocal speech about God with a literalizing tendency across the board. Metaphysical agnosticism with respect to the relation between God and creatures, however, is as compatible with symbolization of the universe as it is with literal construals of its shape. It could be argued that Pseudo-Dionysius, from within a different vocabulary, claims as little metaphysically as does Ockham from his post-Aristotelian vantage point.

As for Ockham's "definitive" account of God's omnipresence, it seems just as possible that the means by which Funkenstein accounts for its possibility — an overriding emphasis on God's presence through his *potentia* — could just as easily undergird a network of ontological intersymbolizations within the natural and biblical universe as it could demand such a network's disappearance. This is, after all, what Augustine does to some degree, as I shall argue later.

But this brings us to the second major element of change that Funkenstein claims is brought into the medieval's natural metaphysic by the nominalists: the reflective emphasis placed on the distinction between God's ordained power (*potentia Dei ordinata*) and God's absolute power (*potentia Dei absoluta*), independent of his (real) commitment towards the natural order that he has established by fiat. It is the Ockhamist play on this distinction that nearly every commentator on the period underlines as perhaps the most critical feature of the nominalist philosophical theology.[32]

---

murky waters of arguments over "ontotheology" by the recent article of Guus H. Labooy, "Duns Scotus' univocity: applied to the debate on phenomenological theology," *International Journal of Philosophy* 76 (2014): 53-73, which centers on the problem of how to speak of a Creator-God who is also Jesus. I am suggesting that one does so simply and starkly via scriptural figure. Not that this "solves" philosophical problems, only that it properly and finally exhaustively expresses them within the world.

31. Funkenstein, *Theology and the Scientific Imagination*, pp. 24-25.

32. Funkenstein, *Theology and the Scientific Imagination*, pp. 124-52; Sylla, "Autonomous and Handmaiden Science," pp. 369ff.; Leff, *The Dissolution of the Medieval Outlook*, pp. 62ff.; Oberman, "Some Notes," passim; Eldridge, passim; etc.

The practical significance of the distinction is perhaps overdrawn, however. Origen himself had already noted that God could be considered under two aspects, the manner of his action according to his theoretical power (*agere per potentiam*) and the manner of his actual deeds according to the order of his willed character of justice (*agere per iustitiam*).[33] What was brought into relief by these two aspects was not a tension within God's being, but the fact of his omnipotence exercised in a particularly ordered fashion. For all the discussion about the manner in which the Ockhamists drove a wedge between the two aspects, in reality they remained, on the whole, faithful to Origen's own understanding.

Clearly, Ockham did use the distinction to point to a number of contingent aspects about our relationship with God: indeed, all of our relationship with God is contingent, insofar as he is our creator and continual conserver. Thus, we have Ockham pointing out how God, *de potentia absoluta*, could save someone who was not in a state of grace; how God could, given his omnipotence, cause someone to have intuitive cognition of some non-existent or non-present object; in short, how God could cause directly *anything* that normally takes place through secondary causes. Pushed to the most detailed of ontological compositions, this meant that God could cause matter to exist without form, qualities without substance (and vice-versa), and so on. Cosmologically, it meant that God might have created different, more, and better worlds than the one now in existence. Historically, it meant that God could have chosen other means for human salvation, if he chose to accomplish salvation at all, than those he did choose (with some of Ockham's followers speaking, for instance, of the possibility of God becoming incarnate in a stone or in an ass). The list could be lengthened easily.

But absolute power is only theoretical; ordained power is what is actual in God's life. There was nothing radical in pointing it out. It is true that the actual terminology of the two powers, while not new, was employed with a new vigor in Ockham's day and thereafter. The truth embodied in the distinction was well-worn already, perhaps.[34] But granted that, though the principles were not new, the stress on their enunciation was. From the point of view of a vision of the natural world, did this Ockhamist stress on divine omnipotence and the theoretical possibility of God's acting in ways other than those to

---

33. Funkenstein, *Theology and the Scientific Imagination*, p. 126.

34. Cf. Thomas Aquinas's frequently used distinction between absolute and consequent necessity in God (in his discussion of topics like predestination and the incarnation), which amounts to saying the same thing from another perspective: God is wholly free in theory, but having made certain choices, he is "consequently" bound to them.

which he committed himself in the cosmos as given, offer a radically new set of perspectives and understandings of the character of reality?

The curious thing is that contemporary scholars give quite opposing assessments about the possible impact of this emphasis. In large measure, where one comes down on the matter depends on how seriously one is willing to restrict the import of the "theoretical" nature of the *potentia Dei absoluta*. Sylla[35] claims that the distinction itself between the two powers allowed for Ockham to conceive of a natural science that was theoretically independent of theology.[36] By explaining the presence of Christ in the Eucharistic host in complete and deliberate *disregard* for natural physical norms, although never denying the legitimacy of those norms in the natural order, Ockham ignores any need to bring the two orders into a single and coherent conceptual frame. This preserves the conceptual integrity of both the physical and the supernatural realms. Sylla likens his way of relating theology and science with the modern pragmatism of James Conant, "who advocates using our separate conceptual schemes in the areas where they have proved successful without trying to combine them in 'world hypothesis' of doubtful validity."[37] The *potentia absoluta*, then, is confined to theory only when we are dealing with non-theological realities.

Funkenstein can claim a similar conclusion from a slightly different construal of the *potentia absoluta*'s reach.[38] In his view, the theoretical positing of the divine omnipotence over and against any prior or concomitant divine ordering has a very *non*-theoretical implication in the realm of the natural sciences: there is no inherent order, in Ockham's eyes, to be gleaned from the investigation of nature.[39] God creates only singular things, not orders of things, and each of them exists in immediate relation to God, not through their locus within a larger created framework. By relentlessly applying the "principle of annihilation," by which God can *de potentia absoluta* conserve one element while destroying its "natural" composite or cause, Ockham redirects our at-

---

35. Sylla, "Autonomous and Handmaiden Science," pp. 357-61, 372-75.

36. This is in contrast to Aquinas, "whose philosophy is often sublimated' to the special demands of theological doctrine with little attempt to preserve the conclusions of normal, natural, non-theological philosophy to reconcile what is said in the theological context with what might be said in a purely natural context" (Sylla, "Autonomous and Handmaiden Science," p. 372).

37. Sylla, "Autonomous and Handmaiden Science," p. 374.

38. Funkenstein, *Theology and the Scientific Imagination*, pp. 134-36.

39. Again, this characterization of Ockham is made in contrast to Aquinas, for whom "order" in terms of metaphysical context, even if admitted as contingent, is prior to individual things (Funkenstein, *Theology and the Scientific Imagination*, p. 135).

tentions from the intrinsic order of the world to the "aggregate" nature of the world as "brute fact." This means, in short, that Ockham leaves us with a desacralized physical world, whose dry structure has meaning only according to the conceptual order we bring to it. The "physical" laws of nature are now only that: purely physical.[40]

Edward Grant sees a theoretical bonanza for science as a result of the Tempier condemnations in Paris in the 1260s and '70s.[41] Aimed against the scientific conclusions of the day — e.g. the adoption of Aristotelian notions of the eternity of the world — the seemingly regressive ecclesiastical censorship of this material actually opened up a number of important new scientific venues by stressing God's free omnipotence — the *potentia Dei absoluta*. Instead of articulating the "necessities" under which God must act in the natural world, the stress on omnipotence gave an impulse to the theoretical conceptualization of, until then, natural and physical impossibilities. Ockham was one among many thinkers (including, among others, Ripa, Bradwardine, Buridan, Oresme) who now could entertain notions such as the multiplicity of worlds or the existence of an inter-cosmic void. While these were devised under the rubric of God's omnipotence, their very possibility as associated with the divine capacity led to an almost hyposticization of their (still only theoretical) reality. Infinite, indivisible space became identified by the 15th century with "God's immensity," and "except for extension, the divinization of space in Scholastic thought produced virtually all the properties that would be attributed to space during the course of the Scientific Revolution."[42] The curious implication of this kind of reading of nominalism is that it demonstrates how natural physics and theology need not in any manner be separated in order for each to be articulated according to what is later judged the appropriate canon. That is, Sylla's Ockhamist "separation" of natural and theological science is, in Grant's view, really their complete identification from the perspective of divinity.

Finally, we should note how Oberman takes Grant's identification and casts it in terms of the naturalization of the world.[43] Arguing that for Ockham and for most of the nominalists, the *potentia Dei absoluta* was *purely* theoretical, and without practical status except perhaps as a devotional guard, Oberman conceives of the nominalist natural world as one ordered solely by the *potentia ordinata*, the clear and predictable ways of God to which he

---

40. Funkenstein, *Theology and the Scientific Imagination*, pp. 144-45.

41. Edward Grant, "Science and Theology in the Middle Ages," in David Lindberg and Ronald Numbers, eds., *God and Nature: Historical Essays on the Encounter between Christianity and Science* (Berkeley: University of California Press, 1986), esp. pp. 54-57.

42. Grant, "Science and Theology," p. 57.

43. Oberman, "Some Notes," and Oberman's response to Sylla, pp. 395-96.

committed himself in creation.[44] Oberman proposes an image now famous for the description of the nominalist vision: humanity inhabits a "domed" world, within which the laws of nature and God's promises operate ineluctably, while above which the hidden, mysterious, and wholly inaccessible power of God's absolute freedom hovers, without ever breaking in.[45] Life within the "dome" of God's ordained power — the natural world as it is — is "lonely" and ultimately pursued in an autonomous fashion. Although human salvation is granted solely on the basis of God's acceptance of a person, irrespective of their character and being, God has so ordained it that no one is accepted without grace and merit. Thus, we live in a world according to well-established rules, the following of which is linked — if only by divine will — to specific ends. Free actions within this universe are simply "more praiseworthy" than others. Even Adams, who is eminently and fairly sympathetic to Ockham, must admit that the "pelagian" implications of this kind of understanding of the world are fairly clear to see.[46]

In general, all these views concerning the Ockhamist natural world and how it is conceptually related to God in metaphysical terms seem to me overly concerned to identify some fragmenting force within the nominalist scheme vis-à-vis an earlier medieval "synthetic" religious understanding of nature. From the point of view of our particular topic, natural symbolization, Sylla's understanding of Ockham might imply a breakdown of the metaphoric nexus between the natural world and theological meaning.

Funkenstein's understanding implies a demise of an ordered network within the natural world, certainly one fundamental to 12th-century figural naturalism; Grant's account of an unconscious nominalist appropriation of the divine theoretical to the physico-divine actual indicates, if not the breakdown of symbolizing possibilities, at least their transference into a naturalistic realm; finally, Oberman's "dome" thesis seems suitable only for a universe drained of metaphysical connections, as well as spiritually vital conventional ones. In all cases, the inevitable march towards the literalistic reading of the natural world appears demanded by the Ockhamist metaphysical shift.

And such a conclusion seems intuitively attractive. Still, I think we should resist it, and for at least two reasons. The first is a purely historical observation;

---

44. To Sylla, Oberman rightly notes that Ockham never conceived of the Eucharist, or of any other element of the Christian experience, as a locus of God's exercise of *potentia absoluta*. Sylla herself is inconsistent in the way she describes Ockham's metaphysical appeal to definitive omnipresence: sometimes she calls it "a kind of second order ordained power" ("Some Notes," p. 361), at other times she simply labels it "absolute."

45. Oberman, "Some Notes," pp. 63-65.

46. Adams, *William of Ockham*, pp. 1286-1290.

that is, that scientific pointillism — the separation of objects and events into discrete units of investigation and even explanation — seems to have coexisted easily with a world whose meaning was construed, even metaphysically, in a symbolic or figural fashion. We should, for instance, take seriously Chenu's assertion that already in the 12th century a remarkable efflorescence of scientific investigation and discovery seemed to have little bearing on the symbolic signification of things. All that counted, in the end, was the degree to which the things themselves, even if segregated from a system for the sake of analysis, stood in relation to their creator. For Platonists, this might mean that things stood in an immediate relationship of being with God, God being "the chief inhabitant of the earth," to use Chenu's phrase.[47]

But it was just as possible to construe the relationship in terms of will or love or power or cause, and retain a balance between a universe of segregated items that, nonetheless, stands in such an essential continuity with God's life that the apprehension of one implies that of the other. We shall see that this was the case, quite explicitly, well into the 17th century, in the remarkable example of Nicolaus Steno. That the equivocal language of the 12th-century Platonists could express the univocity of being, while the univocal language of the Ockhamists served to express the equivocal nature of beings, only shows that these aspects of expression are not themselves tied to their meanings in any necessary fashion. Something else must come into play.

A second reason I think we should be careful about stressing the fragmenting implications for the conceptualization of the natural world that the Ockhamist metaphysics may have provided is that, quite simply, Ockham himself does not stress it, nor do many of his followers. Here I believe that the distinction between the two divine powers has led us astray into thinking, despite ourselves, that the two are really separate, and that God's practical action must be in either one or the other sphere, but never in a unitary fashion.

It is not simply the case that Ockham asserts that there is only one power in God, of which the *potentia absoluta* is, as it were, the unwilled divine capacity. This is only to stress, all over again, the distinction between theoretical and practical possibilities. Rather, the emphasis, for Ockham, lies on what God wills, not on what corresponds to some notion of the "ordinate and the inordinate," the ordinary and the extraordinary.[48] All that God wills is ordinary. And the point is, there is no *a priori* limit on such willing, at least insofar as

47. Chenu, *Nature, Man, and Society,* p. 129.

48. Ockham, *Quodlibet* VI, q. 1, in William of Ockham, *Quodlibetal Questions: Quodlibets 5-7,* trans. and ed. Alfred J. Freddoso and Francis E. Kelley (New Haven, CT: Yale University Press, 1998); cf. Leff, *William of Ockham,* p. 16.

such a limit might be defined apart from God's actual willing — e.g. by some standard that might provide an external measure to God's character and use as a criterion for what God might allow himself to will.

In this sense, the *potentia Dei absoluta* is purely theoretical, at least when understood as a set of divine capacities. But there is no such set. There is only the pure freedom of God's willing. And hence, the *potentia absoluta* itself defines the character of God's actual decisions, the *potentia Dei ordinata*. They are divinely willed — whatever they are — simply because God wills them.

This touches on the question of "time" in an Ockhamist metaphysic, and it is one that obviously parallels aspects of my own notion of "time as use," rather than absolute, in a divinely artifactual universe: God simply orders the "instants" of our experienced life according to his own will, love, character, purpose, or being.[49] It would be wrong to insist that Ockham himself is not inconsistent in all that he says on this subject. What is clear, however, is that the natural world, governed as it is according to some conventional process[50] that is perhaps accessible to some probable degree of conceptual clarity, is nonetheless open to the reach of God's unfettered will to act. This openness does not make the world an "arbitrary" place, as critics of Ockham's supposed skepticism claim. It simply means that it is the kind of world where God can be expected to act efficaciously according to his purposes. Such a world is "ordinary."

Hence, miracles are not examples, in Ockham's universe, of God's switch over into the realm of the *potentia absoluta*. Miracles are ordinary; they can be expected in the sense of falling within God's known and unknown purposes, because the ordained power of God is informed by his absolute freedom. Yet what is willed is not extraordinary. It is consistently God who is willing, and to be taken as part of the consistency that is God's relationship to the world.

I think that it may be just this point that brings confusion into Sylla's discussion of the Eucharistic presence of Christ. For Christ to be definitively present in the host (and elsewhere) may well demand that God accomplish directly what usually is accomplished by secondary causes. But this is not to say that God has abrogated ordinary ways of doing things when he accomplishes Christ's presence in the host, acting any way he pleases, as long as he doesn't involve himself in a logical contradiction. God's ways in the Eucharist

---

49. See Herman Shapiro, *Motion, Time, and Place According to William Ockham* (St. Bonaventure, NY: Franciscan Institute, 1957), pp. 91-106; see Adams, *William of Ockham*, pp. 858-60.

50. We should realize, however, that generally Ockham is dealing with theological, not physical, matters — e.g. the order of grace when he speaks of the realm of God's "ordained" power. In this sense, all he is saying is that revelation and the authority of the church are trustworthy.

are quite ordinary; they are miraculous only insofar as God's way of working in the Eucharist is by way of this specific kind of miracle.

Perhaps it is our post-Enlightenment presuppositions that make it difficult for us to imagine the miraculous in ordinary terms. But this is just what Ockham wishes us to do. In general, it is thought that in part Ockham's principle of parsimony required him to do away with miracles as unnecessary ways of construing events otherwise susceptible to naturalistic explanations. But Ockham does not do this. Indeed, in many instances, he claims that miracles proliferate, when few will do, simply because God so wills it. "God accomplishes many things through multiplied means which He might have accomplished through fewer means. And this He does as He wishes, appropriately and pertinently."[51]

Ockham goes on to say that it is "otherwise" with "natural" causes. It might seem that he is setting up a contrast between what takes place according to "nature" and what takes place according to "will," but this is only an apparent antithesis when we view the whole of the universe as ordered according to the divine will.[52] *Causae naturales*, while always structured according to the divine convention, nonetheless are always open to some new divine construal, which, by definition, will be (divinely) conventional. It is God's usage that counts, not its parsing into this or that sphere of power.

It is *because* Ockham believes in an omnipotent God that he can entertain the existence of a cohesive universe that has room both for the (humanly) predictable and the unpredictable "ordinaries" of life. Keith Ward captures Ockham's point of view well, I think, in an article defending the traditional Christian reliance on miracles and testimony against modern Humean attack:

51. Ockham, *Ordinatio*, 1, d. 14, q.2, on whether the Holy Spirit is ever given without his gifts (answer: yes); cited in Leff, *William of Ockham*, p. 477. I have also consulted the critical edition, *Venerabilis inceptoris Guillelmi de Ockham Scriptum in librum primum Sententiarum ordinatio*, ed. Stephen Brown, Girard J. Etzkorn, Gedeon Gál, Francis E. Kelley (St. Bonaventure, NY: Franciscan Institute, 1967-79).

52. Cf. Francesco Corvino, "Il Significato del Termine *Natura* nelle opere filosofiche di Occam," in *La Filosofia della Natura nel Medioevo. Atti del 3. Congresso internazionale di filosofia medioevale, Passo della Mendola (Trento) 31 agosto-5 settembre 1964* (Milano: Società Editrice Vita e Pensiero, 1966), pp. 613-14. Corvino's analysis of Ockham's semantic use of "nature" and "natural" indicates that, despite some inconsistencies, Ockham tended to confine the "natural" to the non-contingent, non-voluntary, and determined orders of the world (including non-rational animals); the realm of contingency, however, is defined by Ockham in terms of that sphere into which free-will extends. But since human action not only has a broad reach within the world, but the whole cosmos, humanity included, depends on God's free-will, the world as a whole comprehends a complex interrelation between different orders of contingency. Simply calling the natural "that which is determined," as if it were an independent order of purely predictable laws of causality, won't do in Ockham's case.

If someone believes that there exists an omnipotent God, who created the universe for a purpose, then there is an antecedent *probability* that he will act within the universe to accomplish his purpose. . . . But if he acts in the world, then it must be true that something distinct from the natural order as a whole intrudes into it. And that . . . is counted as a miracle, an interference with the natural order. So, if there is a God, there is a very high antecedent probability that miracles will occur. . . . Of course, there is a double peculiarity in speaking of miracles in this way. It is odd to speak of any causal influence which brings about some event which would not have happened if everything had been solely determined by some finite and specifiable set of laws of physics, as a 'violation' of those laws. And it is odd to speak of every event so caused as a miracle. . . . In Biblical times, there was no concept of laws of nature in the post-Newtonian sense. Events were caused by many different agencies. . . . Regularities would undoubtedly have been observed in nature; and there would be a fair idea of the natural, proper or ordinary powers of things to act in certain ways. But the world was full of spirit causes [as well]. . . . The main Biblical miracles do not show that some god exists. They do demonstrate the power of Jahweh, the God of Israel, over nature, history and the spiritual powers. . . . [They are presented] as the natural and proper things to expect.[53]

This is a far cry, I think, from Sylla's notion of two conceptual spheres, the natural and the theological, to be related only "pragmatically." Indeed, although one can distinguish between the two, it is only up to a point that one can do so. Ultimately, there is only one sphere, and that is the one governed by the one Creator God.

And that such a comprehensive sphere, in which the natural and the miraculous are both ordinary in terms of God's omnipresent power, can sustain the metaphorical translation of meaning or even participation between objects and between events in time seems obvious. It is precisely the ordinariness of God's relating will, bringing all these elements into an efficacious whole of meaning, which thereby allows for the symbolization of the universe on a level that is beyond the merely semiotic, in the human sense. They are all rooted in the comprehensive, single purpose of God. If there are signs in the natural world that lead us to a deeper life in and knowledge of God, they are so because God himself uses them immediately. They are divine symbols.

One of the more noteworthy examples within the Christian tradition of this way of construing the significance of the natural world in relation to God

---

53. Keith Ward, "Miracles and Testimony," *Religious Studies* 21 (June, 1985): 131-45; p. 135.

can be found in the pseudo-Augustinian treatise *De Mirabilibus Sacrae Scripturae*.[54] The work was known to Thomas (although rejected as Augustine's), and even if written as early as the 6th or 7th century, represents a way of understanding the relationship between naturalism and symbolization that did not become current until the nominalists.[55] I see it as expressive, in its own terms, of just what Ockham might have thought (and hence, in a way, the not-so-revolutionary notions of the latter in any case).

The author's main purpose is to offer a naturalistic explanation for an array of the main biblical miracles, from both the Old and the New Testaments. The crossing of the Red Sea is explained through the possible freezing of the waters (as is the case for Jesus' walking on the waters along with Peter's brief attempt — but then, so is high salinity given as an option); Jesus' forty-day fast, like that of Moses earlier, explained in terms of the nutrient properties available in the atmosphere; and so on.

It would be quite wrong, however, to see the treatise as motivated by a systematic physical reductionism, in the manner of certain 19th- and 20th-century biblical rationalists (in this sense, Funkenstein misses the mark). Rather, the monk writes out of a profound desire to offer a plausible reading of the relationship between nature and its divine significance, which he forcefully continues to maintain in its figural shape (much in the manner of Thomas Aquinas). In his opening Preface, he explains his method:

> In all that seems to occur extraordinarily with regard to the administration (*administratio*) of things, God does not create a new nature, but demonstrates the same nature by which He governs the world.[56]

This might seem to indicate the existence of "laws" of nature that cannot be superseded, even by God. What the author refers to by the divine *administratio*, however, and much like Ockham, is a set of expected metaphysical composites of nature that are, nonetheless, open to the work of God in an unusual way: the naturally extraordinary occurs in the divinely ordinary. Miracles *are*

54. Cf. Gerard MacGinty, "The Irish Augustine: *De Mirabilibus Sacrae Scripturae*," in *Irland und die Christenheit: Bibelstudien und Mission*, ed. P. Ní Chatháin and M. Richter (Stuttgart: Klett-Cotta, 1987), pp. 70-83, for a discussion of the work's probable origin.

55. Copies of the work continued to circulate under Augustine's name well into the 16th century. Cf. Funkenstein's comment on the work, *Theology and the Scientific Imagination*, pp. 126-27; he finds the tone of the writer to be closer to 19th-century liberal Protestantism!

56. The text is found in *Patrologia Latina* vol. 35, col. 2149-2200. A French translation alongside the Latin can be found in the Peronne edition of Augustine's *Oeuvres Complètes*, vol. XI (Paris: Louis Vivès, 1871), pp. 122-94.

interventions by God, if you will. But they are always "natural" insofar as they occur in God's world with God's creatures. Augustine himself said as much.

Our monk explains it this way: the "natural administration of things" is determined by two *rationes*, one that is "inferior" and another that is "superior." The former occurrences are "quotidian," while the latter are "miracles." Yet both are "natural" in that God is truly doing his work within the natural realm, using "natural means" in one case "over time," in another, *in momento*.[57]

Hence, we read that Balaam's ass spoke, not because he was suddenly endowed with a new rational nature and a new physiological structure capable of human speech. Rather, God directly moved the ass's tongue and manipulated the air waves in order to create a meaningful set of verbal sounds. In Ockham's terms, God accomplished directly what would otherwise have required (unnatural) secondary causes.

Yet just because it is *God* who is really acting in the world, directly and immediately, these "natural" events are divinely revelatory, and not in a purely conventional semiotic sense, of his will and presence. While the writer has told us at the beginning of his treatise that he will eschew figural readings of the events, since others have already provided them, nonetheless, he cannot help along the way but offer a variety of such spiritual senses. Many of the Old and New Testament miracles, for instance (e.g. water from the rock, wedding at Cana, etc.), once given a naturalistic explanation, are then analyzed in terms of their real *virtus* as referring to the church or the Christ or the Christian life.[58] Despite the almost apologetic tone employed, the entire treatise is firmly rooted in the figural and moralizing universe of the era. There is no contradiction here, however, because this universe hangs from the unitary impinging power of a living God.

I believe, then, that it is important to stress not only the possibility of natural science coexisting with a figural understanding of its own findings, but to accept this as the very case, even given the philosophical framework of Ockham.[59] With

---

57. Ibid., 3:9-10.

58. Cf. ibid., 1:3.

59. As noted earlier, this coexistence extended well into the 17th century, and even beyond in a few cases. One of the most remarkable cases where this can be seen is in the work of Nicolaus Steno. Steno was a brilliant Danish anatomist who subsequently went on to lay what most historians of the topic concede to be the foundation of modern geological science, working in the field in Italy. In mid-life he converted to Catholicism (supposedly after seeing a public procession of the Sacrament in Florence), and was later made a missionary bishop to the regions around his homeland, all the while keeping up his scientific investigations. One of his last works, written in the early 1670s for the crown-prince Ferdinand of Florence, concerns the character of natural symbolic signification, *Ornamenta: monumenta, signa, argumenta*. In this short treatise, Steno elaborates a moralizing schema for the material universe, whose

this claim in place, we can move to the question of a 14th-century "Ockhamist" figuralism itself.

III. Franciscan Piety, Realism, and Symbolic Moralization

It is at Ockham's Franciscan context that we must first take a glance, if only to *dispel* the assumption that Franciscanism, as an evangelical commitment, implies a metaphysic.[60] And it is in the study of Francis himself, initially, that we encounter just the sort of automatic derivation of metaphysics from formal attitude, and the reverse, that seems to me so incoherent and untenable until this point.[61] Two important interpretations of Francis and Franciscan thought

---

elements, as apprehended and used by human beings, act, through God's providence, as signs of three orders: of the Curse of the Fall; of the inner-ornaments of the soul; of future beatitude. But the moralizing figures Steno uses are not mere pedagogic devices. Steno believes that God, in fact, has so ordered the material universe as to form a coherent language, which escapes us only because our minds are too small, wicked, and ignorant to grasp its syntax and vocabulary. We tend to admire the things of the world in the same way as illiterates admire the artistry of a fine illuminated letter, although they cannot read the text in which it is placed. Only through revelation, and that in a limited way, are we able to learn some small portion of the vast discourse God has enunciated. Grant sees Steno not as an aberration, but as illustrative of the balance Catholic scientists could indeed maintain between careful observational investigation of discrete objects and their causes and effects, and a committed belief to God's ordering omnipotence which brings these elements into a meaningful relationship one with another. See Nicolaus Steno, *Ornamenta: monumenta, signa, argumenta*, in *Steno: Geological Papers*, ed. Gustav Scherz, trans. Alex J. Pollock (Odense, Denmark: Odense University Press, 1969).

60. Though, of course, many have so claimed. Cf. so profound a scholar as Eugenio Garin: "Ockham in opposition to Aristotelianism, wants to reaffirm outside of all abstract schemes, the vital terms of Christianity. This is why, like Bonaventure, Bacon, and Scotus, Ockham is a follower of Saint Francis. Attached to concreteness, Ockham wants to bring humanity back to the genuine originality of experience, to the listening to the language of the world and of the divine scriptures; he wants to move away from the constructions and fictitious justifications of the Schools." The paradox, for Garin, is that this ontology, which strips everything down to *vox* and *res*, ends by providing a humanistic world of "letters" that finally undercuts Christian values themselves. See his *History of Italian Philosophy*, trans. and ed. Giorgio Pinton, Vol. 1 (Amsterdam/New York: Rodopi), p. 136. Garin's vast knowledge of medieval and Renaissance thought, however, has an odd tin ear for Christian pitch. Kenan Osborne, OFM, on the other hand, will make similar claims, and tie them to a very specific Christian agenda, that is, that there is a metaphysic that upholds a particular kind of "spirituality" (Francis's). See his *The Franciscan Intellectual Tradition: Tracing Its Origins and Identifying Its Central Components* (St. Bonaventure, NY: Franciscan Institute Publications, St. Bonaventure University, 2003).

61. A separate study could be done on the character of visual representations, in particular of Francis himself, from the 13th to the 16th centuries. Could one in fact derive clear meta-

deserve attention here. The first, put forward by Ewert Cousins, is an attempt to argue for a Franciscan reformation of Neoplatonist mysticism. The second, espoused by Roger Sorrell, sees just this subsequent Neoplatonist appropriation of Francis as his betrayal by his followers. Both argue, however, in their way, that the formal attitudes adopted by Francis toward the world around him have metaphysical implications that move away from traditional (and we might add, 12th-century) Platonist symbolization.

Cousins's essay is a proposal for a specific category of mystical experience, typified by Francis, which he calls "the mysticism of the historical event": "in this type of consciousness, one recalls a significant event in the past, enters into its drama and draws from it spiritual energy, eventually moving beyond the event towards union with God."[62] While this kind of mysticism has always been operative in Christianity (and Judaism for that matter) — Cousins

---

physical clues from this, that might impact the character of symbolic religious form in these cases? This seems unlikely. Claims, e.g., of a "rediscovery of nature" have been made for the Renaissance (and actually for the 12th century as well) in standard art histories. By "standard," I mean those embodied in such deservedly respected volumes like H.W. Janson's *History of Art: A Survey of the Major Visual Arts from the Dawn of History to the Present Day* (New York: Abrams, 1962), reedited and revised several times since, or Frederick Hartt's massive *History of Italian Renaissance Art* (New York: Abrams, 1969), again variously reedited, which shaped several generations of young art historians, and are still in use today. Charles Taylor, in his *Sources of the Self* (Cambridge: Cambridge University Press, 1989), pp. 200-203, makes use of this account, in his meditation on historical causality. But what is a "natural" form? How does one "see" it and depict it as a result in such a way that one can speak of "discovering" nature? It was only in the mid-19th century, however, that this idea was first voiced with respect to the Renaissance, perhaps by Edgar Quinet in his *Les Révolutions d'Italie*. On the origins, and struggles, of this standard account, focused mainly on the literary scene, rather than the visual arts, see J. B. Bullen, *The Myth of the Renaissance in Nineteenth-Century Writing* (Oxford: The Clarendon Press, 1994). In any case, the current standing of the Sapir-Whorf Hypothesis with respect to language's reflection of world-perception (and influence upon it) is not currently high. Yet it continues to act as a kind of presupposition in many areas of thought. "Ways of seeing" (cf. John Berger's popular book, from the 1972 television series of that name) have always been attached to "world views" in the standard accounts, something that has overlapped with certain Marxist ideas; but do we really know what this means? My point is not to dismiss the question, but to question any certainty about current responses to it. Something like Alfred Cosby's engrossing *The Measure of Reality: Quantification and Western Society, 1250-1600* (Cambridge: Cambridge University Press, 1997) offers one set of answers, based on the development of certain technologies of measurement in Western Europe, which other historians simply contradict. How to get to the bottom of these kinds of nebulously vast hypotheses?

62. Ewert H. Cousins, "Francis of Assisi: Christian Mysticism at the Crossroads," in *Mysticism and Religious Traditions*, ed. Steven T. Katz (Oxford: Oxford University Press, 1983), pp. 166-75; p. 166.

points to the power of the pilgrimage to places where holy history was enacted — Francis was innovative in bringing this attitude explicitly to the center of Christian devotion.

Cousins draws the logical parallel between the mysticism of the historical event — where one enters into the energy and life of the past event and moves towards God — with the mysticism of nature, where one experiences a similar movement, only in this case through space and natural object, rather than through time. That Francis was an innovator in both realms is to be expected. And that both stood in contrast with the dominant mystical traditions of the age is also obvious:

> With a disarming sense of immediacy, he felt himself part of the family of creation, rejoicing in the least significant creature — in an earthworm or a cricket — and seeing God's reflection everywhere. As is the case with the mysticism of the historical event, this is a far cry from Neoplatonic speculative mysticism, which focuses on an abstract cosmological structure and which turns quickly from the material world and its individual creatures to scale the metaphysical ladder to the spiritual and divine realms by means of universal concepts.[63]

But Cousins wants to claim that this mysticism of history and nature, centered on the visual contemplation of Christ (crucified), actually transformed the Neoplatonist modalities then dominant, and, through the work of Bonaventure, created a new and wholly coherent form of Christ-centered mystical system, quite congruent with Francis's own original impulses.[64] Tracing the development of Bonaventure's mystical thought from the purely emanationist *Soul's Journey*, through the more Christ-centered, but still figural *Tree of Life* mediations, Cousins argues that in his last major work, the *Collations on the Hexameron*, Bonaventure achieved a complete reorientation of metaphysics on the person of Christ, "the center of all the sciences."[65] "The Neoplatonic universe has been Franciscanized, by placing the incarnate Christ at the center of the cosmos, of history, of the soul, and of the spiritual journey."[66]

Sorrell finds just this Neoplatonic appropriation of Francis, however much it influenced its host from its own side, inimical to Francis's own attitudes towards creation in particular. He spends some time demonstrating how Cel-

---

63. Cousins, "Francis of Assisi," p. 168.
64. Cousins, "Francis of Assisi," pp. 172-75.
65. Cousins, "Francis of Assisi," pp. 186-89.
66. Cousins, "Francis of Assisi," p. 187.

ano's and Bonaventure's biographies of the saint consistently reinterpret and deform Francis's "direct" and "emotional"[67] responses to nature into traditional categories of Augustinian Platonism.[68]

The "real" Francis, according to Sorrell, can be gleaned from literary and textual analysis of some of the early biographies and narratives, and, of course, from the few writings left from the saint's own hand. And these reveal a set of attitudes, nurtured originally by twin ascetic and evangelical ideals of the age, and fashioned into something unique by a nature mysticism of immediacy, not of ascent, interiorization, or even metaphysical cosmology. This analysis allows Sorrell, despite his frequently made exhortations to keep Francis moored to the traditional Christianity of his day, to present an attitudinal picture of the saint wholly in keeping with contemporary construals of what an "environmentally-conscious" theology might resemble: intrinsic worth, mutual service, and interdependence. "Creatures, each having autonomous worth and beauty, are yet brothers and sisters to each other, aiding each other, gladly performing their divinely allotted functions."[69]

In different and sometimes contradictory ways both Cousins and Sorrell see Franciscanism in terms of a movement towards the literal immediacy of relation. In Cousins's eyes, Francis's influence "purges" Bonaventure's Neoplatonism of its symbolic complexity (even if it leaves the general system intact) by directing attention to bare events and objects; Sorrell sees Francis as taking an opposing turn away from Neoplatonic sensibilities altogether, and one towards the "spontaneity" of relation between individual creatures. Both

---

67. Roger Sorrell, *St. Francis of Assisi and Nature: Tradition and Innovation in Western Christian Attitudes toward the Environment* (New York: Oxford University Press, 1988), p. 96.

68. "Francis had not been trained as an intellectual in his youth, and . . . had never absorbed the Christian Neoplatonic attitude toward creation — one which led to careful categorization of the levels of creation, their different significances, and the intellectualization and internalization of the mystical experience. It is ironic that both Celano and Bonaventure make use of their Christian Neoplatonic intellectual training to attempt to explain Francis' nature mystical experience. They ignore the fact that their mystical outlook and training had nothing to do with the natural environment catalyzing a mystical experience in a direct manner . . ." (Sorrell, *St. Francis of Assisi*, p. 90).

69. Sorrell, *St. Francis of Assisi*, p. 137. Cf. the section on Francis in Paul H. Santmire, *The Travail of Nature: The Ambiguous Ecological Promise of Christian Theology* (Philadelphia: Fortress Press, 1985), pp. 106-20, and Paul Weigand, "Escape from the Birdbath: A Reinterpretation of St. Francis as a Model for the Ecological Movement," in *Cry for the Environment: Rebuilding the Christian Creation Tradition*, ed. Philip N. Joranson and Ken Butigan (Santa Fe: Bear & Company, 1984), pp. 148-57, where the fit between similar ecological concerns and theological motifs or attitudes is made explicit. Both Santmire and Weigand rightly point out the "cruciform" and "penitential" aspects of Francis's relationship with creation, but neither of them seems to let this fact inform their application of ecological concerns.

agree, along with many others, that Francis's example, and the work and spirit communicated by his followers, enabled a retrieval of the world of "things" — natural and human — for the evolving culture of the late Middle Ages.[70] This was a world increasingly stripped of symbolical associations, in favor of intrinsic differences and discrete characters.

None of the elements any of these commentators point out as peculiarly Franciscan are mistakenly identified. Where the picture presented goes awry, I think, is in its insistent emphasis on the inner incompatibility of Francis's attitudes with the traditional Christian symbolizing practices of the day.[71] But this traditional outlook is a fact that should significantly inform our perceptions of Francis's and Franciscan attitudes toward nature and Scripture as a whole. Both creation and the biblical text were structured around a common order, formed by God's hand and will, and shared by the Son of God in humility and exaltation. If the Franciscan "vernacularization" of culture means anything, it is that the coherence of this realm included — symbolically as much as anything else — aspects of popular experience that had heretofore not been expressed within the same purview of spiritual discourse. The sacralizing of the vernacular is as accurate a way of describing the evolving relationship set in motion by Francis.

Three well-known passages from the early biographies of Francis, which are not overlaid with external allegorical or moralizing commentary like many other episodes, begin to illustrate the point:

Francis abounded in the spirit of charity; he was filled with compassion not only toward men in need, but even toward dumb animals, reptiles, birds, and other creatures sensible and insensible. But, among all the various kinds of animals, he loved little lambs with a special predilection and more ready affection, because in the sacred scriptures the humility of our Lord Jesus Christ is more frequently likened to that of the lamb and best illustrated by

70. Cf. Jeffrey, "Franciscan Spirituality," who calls the "incarnational" focus of Franciscan spirituality the real motor for this retrieval, which comprised, in his survey, everything from science, graphic arts, literature, and linguistic practice. Jeffrey makes much of Bonanventure's positive use of the physical senses in the progress of divine illumination (pp. 149-50). Of course, Bonaventure's incarnational warrant is not simply for the value of sense perception, but is a justification for the *symbolical* import of created things. In this regard, his purposes are hardly divergent from the traditional Neoplatonism of the 12th century, which Jeffrey claims as antithetical.

71. Cf. Sorrell, *St. Francis of Assisi*, p. 48, on Francis's scriptural symbolism applied to natural objects and creatures, and p. 127, on the links between this kind of conceptualization of the natural world with popular depictions of animals in the bestiaries of the age.

the simile of a lamb. So, all things, especially those in which some allegorical similarity to the Son of God could be found, he would embrace more fondly and look upon more willingly.[72]

There follows one of the many stories about Francis and lambs or sheep with which accounts of his life abound. Without a doubt, there is a concentration here on the figure of Christ, as Cousins points out, but the very fact that the figure inserts itself into the creatures of the world is what calls for attention. It is not Celano who imports the notion of " simile" and" allegory"; Francis himself, as he made clear over and over, understood compassion and charity in terms of a response to Christ. And his relationship of compassion towards other creatures was understood in a primary way, not as some spontaneous impulse of affection towards all creation, *pace* Sorrell, but as that same form of affection kindled by the vision of Christ imaged in all things. In this respect, Francis was certainly no different from many strands of traditional (even Neoplatonic) conceptualizations of the cosmos.

To be sure, this is just as often expressed in terms of simple "glorification" by the creation of God, for the pure goodness and blessing of his formative power, and without explicit reference to Christ at all. Yet even in these cases, from time to time, we see the scriptural symbolizations to which Francis was given as being the very conveyances of that glory's signification:

> Indeed, he was very often filled with a wonderful and ineffable joy from this consideration while he looked upon the sun, while he beheld the moon, and while he gazed upon the stars and the firmament. O simple piety and pious simplicity! Toward little worms even he glowed with a very great love, for he had read this saying about the Savior: 'I am a worm, not a man'. Therefore he picked them up from the road and placed them in a safe place, lest they be crushed by the feet of the passersby.[73]

Celano goes on in the same passage to add his own figural connectives: the flowers remind us of the "tree of Jesse," Francis's "fraternization" with the elements, based on a vision of their "hidden" reality, reminds us of the "free-

72. Celano, *Vita Prima*, 28:77. The image applied, as Bonaventure rightly understood, to the whole cosmos, beginning with the human creature, who Francis continually reminded his followers, wore the Son's "noble image" (cf. Celano, *Vita Prima*, 28:76). Translations and citations on Francis, here, in the *Speculum Perfectionis* and in Bonaventure's biography are from Marion Habig, ed., *St. Francis of Assisi. Writings and Early Biographies: English Omnibus of the Sources for the Life of St. Francis* (Chicago: Franciscan Herald Press, 1983).

73. Celano, 29:80.

dom of the glory of the sons of God" and thus of the resurrection, and so on. But far from being "intellectualizations" of Francis, as Sorrell thinks, these kinds of scriptural linkages fit in all too easily with the kind of universe the saint inhabited, one strung together with an inter-signification drawn into the cosmic knot of Jesus' life and glory, and explained in terms of the vast store of memorized scriptural forms.

And that this kind of referral of being to Christ was carried by the deployment of God's power, functioning along a moral and historical network of relating but wholly subordinate creatures, is shown in the many thaumaturgic stories associated with Francis. The place that symbolizing miracle plays in Francis's life, then, cannot be confined to the shadow of his ecological sensibilities:

> While he was staying at the monastery of San Verecundo in the diocese of Gubbio one time, a lamb was born there during the night. It was attacked immediately by a vicious sow which had no mercy on the innocent creature and killed it with one hungry bite. When he heard about it, the saint was deeply moved as he remembered the immaculate Lamb of God and he mourned for the death of the lamb before them all saying, Brother Lamb, innocent creature, you represented Christ in the eyes of men. A curse on the wicked beast which killed you. May no human being or any animal ever eat of it. There and then the vicious sow fell sick and after suffering for three days it eventually expiated its crime by death. The carcass was thrown into the monastery moat where it lay for a long time and became as hard as a board, so that even the hungriest animal refused to eat it.[74]

Sows evidently did not merit the same kind of compassion as lambs, in Francis's view. But in this case, there were reasons — much as Jesus' cursing of the fig tree is recalled — and these lay in the figural replaying within the natural order of the passion and of the curse of the Cross a hortatory call to right living and penitence.

It is just this attitude that undergirds Francis's Canticle. The second half of Sorrell's book deals persuasively and at great length with many aspects of this poem. But because he seems so intent on maintaining the ideological purity and originality of Francis's thought, Sorrell loses sight of the poem's function as scripturalizing the natural world. As Sorrell points out, all the accounts agree that the Canticle was composed, late during Francis's illness,

---

74. Cf., among many other texts, the *Speculum Perfectionis*, in Habig, *St. Francis of Assisi,* p. 118.

to offer a performative expression of human repentance for the ingratitude with which we ignore God's care for us through other creatures.[75] The work, in short, has a kind of moral message, that we praise God "because of" (as given in the Umbrian dialect used) the "most useful" tasks creatures perform on our behalf.[76]

Not only is the anthropocentric and instrumental nature of the poem brought into relief through this interpretation — the glory of creatures lies in large part in their gratuitously given usefulness, quoting or paraphrasing from Psalm 148 or the Canticle of the Three Young Men, or alluding to texts from Genesis. In addition, as both the early Francis narratives and Sorrell point out, the various natural elements described in the poem exist as symbolic exemplars of the Christian life — the Sun and the Lord of Justice, the connection between the waters and Baptism, vegetation and Christ symbolism, and so on. The song's end quite explicitly lays out the penitential and homiletic framework, in which the rest of the piece is located:

Praise to Thee, my Lord, for our Sister bodily Death
From whom no man living may escape:
Woe to those who die in mortal sin.
Blessed are they who are found in Thy most holy will,
For the second death cannot harm them.
Praise and bless my Lord,
Thank Him and serve Him
With great humility!

When natural creatures are celebrated in this way for their role in explicating human duty and destiny in scriptural terms, it seems anachronistic to understand their being in terms of some new and liberating ecological or cultural metaphysic. Instead, we are confronted by the poem with a coherent universe of beings subordinated to the salvific will of their creator, whose call for a life of service and praise is embodied in the flesh of Christ. The history of salvation, clearly anthropocentric in its scriptural enunciation, becomes the signifying framework in which all creatures move.

The Canticle, then, is closer to the symbolic world of the medieval bestiaries and the lapidaries than many would like to admit.[77] These widely diffused,

75. Sorrell, *St. Francis of Assisi*, pp. 118ff.
76. Bonaventure, *Legenda Major*, 8:6.
77. Sorrell, again in passing, acknowledges this possibility; Sorrell, *St. Francis of Assisi*, pp. 48, 127.

popular and scholarly compilations of lore about animals and rocks have been called by contemporary students of the genre anything from "childish myths"[78] to "natural history."[79] They display a combination of learned description and history, accounts of miraculous animations, avuncularly helpful tips and explanations of the creature's relationships with the human world. Many entries are capped with a symbolic lesson, usually of practical religious import — what White and others call the stock "moralization." The wild ass signifies the devil, and brays when night and day are equal, that is, when the children of light and darkness are of the same number — thus should we beware; the raven teaches us to love our children, and the duty of family; and so on.

The encyclopaedic element and attraction is obvious. But the bestiary functions as a whole, as well, much like Francis's Canticle. Its catalogue of diverse wisdom, clothed in the flesh of beasts and birds and fishes and their habitats, is designed to envelop the reader within a fabric of godly providence, working variously within the world, but drawing its diverse skeins into a single cloth, marked with the figures of the scripturalized universe of the natural order. So clothed, we are exhorted to a life of devoted and obedient openness to the God of creation, moving towards our salvation and making use of creation's gifts with thankfulness.

Most bestiaries contain one specific, extended, and self-contained "moralization," whose relation to the whole must remain baffling unless we read the whole itself in relation to this overriding religious exhortation. In the bestiary translated by White, the *quocienscumque peccator* ("whensoever the sinner . . .") is inserted between the entries for "dog" and "sheep." In itself, it makes no specific reference to the animals surrounding it. Rather, it links the way of the Christian *viator* through this world to the road extending from Adam's fall to humanity's final restoration. This offers the writer a brief opportunity to describe the naming and categorization of the animals in Eden:

> Whensoever the sinner wishes to please his Maker, it is useful and necessary that he should look for three Spiritual Guides. [. . .]. The first Guide is Weeping of the Heart, the second True Confession, the third Real Penitence.

78. Chenu, *Nature, Man, and Society,* pp. 115, 133.

79. T. H. White, trans. and ed., *The Book of Beasts: Being a Translation from a Latin Bestiary of the Twelfth Century* (New York: G. P. Putnam's Sons, 1954), p. 231; White's bibliography, though dated, still guides us to the central development and study of the bestiary genre. White's book retains its value, and has been republished by the Parallel Press of the University of Wisconsin (2002). For more recent work, see Willene B. Clark and Meradith T. McMunn, eds., *Beasts and Birds of the Middle Ages: The Bestiary and Its Legacy* (Philadelphia: University of Pennsylvania Press, 1989), and Michel Pastoureau, *Bestiaires du Moyen Âge* (Paris: Seuil, 2011).

Their Governors are Love of God, Right Intentions, and Good Deeds. The Spiritual gifts are Cleanness of Body and soul, Chaste Speech and Perseverance in Good Work. These appear before the Trinity [. . .]. It is then, indeed, that, with such clothes, together with the three Guides, the soul can decently be introduced into the heavenly kingdom, where it will be rewarded with that beatitude which the angels enjoy. It was to obtain this that God created Man. [. . .] If Man had stuck to these things, the heavenly kingdom would not have turned him away, but, because he did not stick to them, he has let slip his inheritance. It was ADAM who first gave names to animals, calling each and all of them something or other, according to the sort of nature which each of them had. Moreover, people addressed these animals in the First of Languages, [etc.].[80]

Does the biblically informed simplicity and vernacular of the Canticle render its meaning so wholly different from this labored and heavy bestiary homily? I think not. Particularly as we locate this latter's penitential call within a larger, popularly entertaining and informative — if not exactly ecstatic — survey of the created order to which the moralization gives only, in comparison, the lightest, one might even say, most delicate of hues. That the bestiary, and more sophisticated developments of the genre, became Franciscan literary specialties is not surprising.[81] The firmly established scriptural context of Paradise lost and the difficult road back to God's arms through a good, if bewildering, creation is the common soil not only for the popular piety of the era, but for Francis's most ardent Christocentric spiritual advice.[82]

If we can then speak, in Francis's case, of a symbolic moralization of the natural world, we can make better sense of the way his figuration of creatures and objects works in relation to Scripture. Wallace-Hadrill ends his illuminating study of *The Greek Patristic View of Nature* by drawing a parallel between Francis and these earlier Fathers of the East. It is a similarity few are prepared (or are perhaps knowledgeable enough) to make, yet it is probably apt just in regard to the question of moralization.[83]

In his last chapter, Wallace-Hadrill treats especially the practice by the Fa-

---

80. White, *Book of Beasts*, pp. 68-70.

81. Cf. John Fleming, *An Introduction to the Franciscan Literature of the Middle Ages* (Chicago: Franciscan Herald Press, 1977), pp. 159-63; but passim in ch. 4.

82. Cf. Francis's *Admonitions*, in Habig, anchored in the description of the fall, in #2, and ending with a hymn to the personified Virtues, to a get a flavor of this fundamental aspect of Francis's conceptual formulations of Christian vocation within the world.

83. D. S. Wallace-Hadrill, *The Greek Patristic View of Nature* (Manchester: Manchester University Press, 1968), p. 130.

thers of construing nature figurally in the context of scriptural teaching.[84] He sketches a wide variety of methods employed, from scriptural similes to a vast array of personal, idiosyncratic, and literary allegories, where certain animals stand for specific virtues or sinful characters, or where Christian or pagan attitudes are likened to various natural phenomena. In addition, the early Fathers employed conventional as well as creative historical typologies of the events or event-related objects within Scripture. Finally, a kind of naturalistic typological figuration can be consistently observed, where elements and phenomena of nature metaphysically, in some usually unspecified manner, transport the contemplative human mind to spiritual realities linked with them (e.g. the seasonal growth and flourishing of vegetation with the Resurrection, the play and extent of sunlight). All these figurating methods, however, are employed unsystematically and interchangeably. It is difficult to make the distinctions between purely literary, mnemonic, conventional, providential-typological, and metaphysical figuration.

More important for us is to realize that the strongest form of figuration — wherever it is that we claim to see it used — is understood as what I have called "strong metaphor," or *anagoge* in the Greek. Anagogy here is not to be confused with the more technical significance it held in Western medieval exegesis. It is a broadly inclusive term, referring to the power, indeed, the nature of an object or event or even simple conventional sign, to lead the mind into a realm of spiritual reality where the soul is more fully nourished by God. Anagogical figuration is first of all a form of divine pedagogy or guidance, only secondarily a comment on the nature of figurating objects themselves. It is a form of godly moralization that depends on an understanding of the subsuming creative omnipotence of a God able to order the elements of the world into a signifying framework of elucidating passage. There is a paradox here at work. In a real sense, the introduction of the Christian notion of *creatio ex nihilo* undercut the ability of a variety of antique metaphysical systems to sustain such a comprehensive figural natural universe; yet it is just this notion's core formulation of divine omnipotence that allowed for such a natural universe to continue to act figurally.[85]

Francis's "moralization" of the world is little different from this inherently unsystematic method of anagogy practiced by the Fathers. And drawing such

84. This, we may remember, was one of Keble's great emphases in his *Tract 89* on the "Mysticism of the Fathers."

85. This has been pointed out by many historians of doctrine. For one clear and brief exposition of the way this fact influenced mystical theology among the Greek Fathers, cf. Louth, *The Origins of the Christian Mystical Tradition* (Oxford: Oxford University Press, 1981), pp. 75-90.

a connection helps us avoid demoting the religious significance of medieval moralizing figuration to the rank of mere moralistic discourse. For Francis, as for his tradition, it is the created shape of the world itself that forms the human person for the salvation offered in Christ Jesus — a formative impetus that is not only congruent with the realities of Scripture, but stands as Scripture's material element kneaded in God's hands. A lamb, a worm, a rock, fire, death itself — each can lead us further towards God as we read it — and thus "use" it — rightly. God, by his very will, has placed all these objects in a symmetry of signification, and holds them there.[86]

IV. Augustine and the Signification of Omnipotence

This too, it seems to me, ought to be the general framework within which we view the Augustinian approach to figuration, so influential in the later Middle Ages. Chenu was right, in some sense, to distinguish Augustine's more purely "semiotic" Platonism from Dionysius's ontologism. But his emphasis on the conventional basis (as opposed to the ontological basis) of signification should not blind us to the real and divine power of signs to act as metaphors for the truth. This is a capacity granted them by God, much in the way that I am claiming the Greek Fathers and Francis understand anagogy or moralization.

As early as the *De Magistro*, Augustine puts forward his theory of language as a system of signs conventionally constructed to signify prior knowledge gained through experience. Words have meaning for us only because we know already the things to which they point: "We learn the force of a word when we come to know the object signified by the word. Then only do we perceive that the word was a sign conveying that meaning."[87] And since the world is thus known independently of language, the instrumentality of language seems limited in itself; language is useful only within the realm of an already formed knowledge, and taken as a system of signs alone; it is "ontologically" without substance.

In addition, Augustine stresses both in the *De Magistro* and elsewhere

---

86. We begin here, I think, to touch on aspects of what Louth, in *Discerning the Mystery*, is pointing to when he speaks of the formative nature of Christian tradition, ruled by the Spirit. What is being brought out here, however, is that a particular conception of God's relationship with the world is being presupposed, even for the more specifically ecclesiastical character of "tradition."

87. Augustine, *De Magistro* ("The Teacher") 10:34. The citations follow those in John H. S. Burleigh, ed., *The Early Augustine* [Library of Christian Classics, Vol. VI] (London: SCM Press, 1953).

that language is, taken in itself, deceptive as to both its referent and the truth of that referent.[88] There stands between words and their accurate and effective signification a host of obstacles, ranging from simple and willful deceit to the incomprehensible mystery of Christ's life that religious language in particular is designed to express. Not only, then, is language (and Augustine makes little distinction between spoken and written language) an empty tool in and of itself — conventional signs — it is also frail and liable to break in the hands of frail and frequently wicked human beings.

Yet Augustine does have the deepest regard for the power of Scripture (and language in general, for that matter) to communicate God's truth, in ways that are both trustworthy and effective. Bearing in mind that the world of truth is independent of language, and that the right use of language is dependent on the spiritual health of the persons using it, Augustine argues, in *De Doctrina Christiana*, for a theory of language — particularly scriptural language — based on the operation of divine grace. Not only do conventional signs — the words of Scripture — communicate effectively through the power of grace, but they themselves fulfill their signifying purpose when they communicate the power of grace itself, the building up of the hearer in faith, hope, and charity.

The first book of *De Doctrina* sets forth this theoretical framework clearly. As the work progresses, and Augustine lays out various rules for the interpretation and study of Scripture, these might seem, taken on their own, indicative of the lineaments of an independent semiotic system, unless we frame their formulation in terms of the larger anagogic purpose: Scripture speaks by grace, and its truth is revealed in grace. Augustine begins the treatise by describing how someone can learn to read by the miracle of prayer and how the word "God" can refer meaningfully only through the divine "condescension." He carries through the last book of the treatise — which is devoted in large measure to figuration — with the application of the "rule of faith": Scripture is to be interpreted, whether literally or figurally, according to the manner in which it "builds up the reign of love."[89]

Augustine warns his readers not to depend on the extraordinary miracle of the Holy Spirit's intervention in order to understand Scripture. Diligent

---

88. E.g. *De Vera Religione* ("Of True Religion"), where the complicated way ideas are impressed upon the mind causes many difficulties and deceptions (in the Burleigh edition); or in *De Catechizandis Rudibus* ("On Catechizing the Uninstructed"), where the gap between the marvelous divine truths only inchoately grasped by the teacher in his imagination and the articulated words used to describe these truths is a cause for linguistic misunderstanding. (For the *De Doctrina*, and *De Civitate Dei* below, see *Select Library of the Nicene and Post-Nicene Fathers of the Christian Church*, vols. 2 and 3 [Grand Rapids: Eerdmans, 1954]).

89. Augustine, *De Doctrina Christiana* ("Christian Doctrine"), III:10; cf. III:2.

and self-disciplined study of the text is necessary. Nonetheless, it is because the meaning of the text, the effective meaning of its language, is carried on the back of God, as it were, by the Holy Spirit who "sheds love abroad in our hearts," that we can be led by Scripture more deeply into the life of Christ. Scripture as a whole is a moralizing, anagogic gift; literal and figural understandings of its meaning are demanded and limited only by this larger gracious scheme of spiritual metaphor.[90]

If Hugh of St. Victor, for instance, exemplifies the Augustinian tradition with respect to symbolic exegesis, as Chenu suggests, it is not because he has some greater proclivity, thereby, to a literal exegesis vs. the more Dionysian interpreters of his era. *The Didascalion*, it is true, makes many of the same distinctions between signs and ideas and the things ideas signify that Augustine makes. In so doing, he seems to accept the largely skeptical view of the ontological basis of language that Augustine propounded. But Hugh, like Augustine, understands that the spiritual meaning of Scripture — the rule of faith, "faith" itself — is Scripture's point. And the literal sense, though described as the first foundation of the interpretive "building" (Hugh even uses an allegory to picture the process of interpretation) is only "rough," and sustains what is the truer and more vital "second foundation" — the spiritual sense of the whole, upon which are based the wide range of more particular elements of figural meaning which reveal the truths of the faith. That Scripture can do this at all, is the work of God's dispersal of Wisdom into the world, bringing diverse objects into relation with one another for the use of the inquiring spirit.[91]

The confusing mix of exegetical strategies employed by commentators and preachers of the later Middle Ages, then, even while they lead Smalley to decry their failure to advance "serious" exegetical study of the Bible, derive from a coherent, if general, understanding of the moralizing nature of the universe as graciously explicated through the power of God, something Scripture itself somehow unveils and manifests. Francis was no innovator or revolutionary with respect to this general tradition. He affectively emphasized certain areas of regard, but his hermeneutic, if we care to use such a term, was consistent with his milieu, one stretching both backwards and forwards for some distance.

---

90. And this explains why, in any case and despite his low ontological estimation of language, Augustine can still emphasize the fact that "spiritual" exegesis is more noble than literal interpretation. Indeed, it is because divine grace is the meaning and vehicle of Scripture together, and words are in themselves empty, that he can call literal reading of the Bible a kind of "miserable slavery," even while he is careful to provide limits to spiritual reading; cf. *De Doctrina Christiana* 111:5.

91. Hugh of St. Victor, *The Didascalion of Hugh of Saint Victor*, trans. by Jerome Taylor (New York: Columbia University Press, 1991), V:3 and VI:4 (pp. 121-22 and 139-44).

And it is important to see that the "realism," the "vernacularism," and the "literalisms" that are identified with the Franciscan tradition of scriptural exegesis did in fact, and necessarily so, coexist with the most prolific use of figurating approaches to the Bible. The consistently interchangeable use of *exemplum, narratio, fabula*, and *figura* by mendicant preachers and commentators could demand a range of theoretical justifications, some metaphysical, some naturalistic and scientific, some purely ethical.[92] But in no case (and perhaps to the chagrin of modern scholars tied to a notion of exegetical progress) was this diverse and inconsistently-argued-for use of method seen as problematic. This was so precisely because, given the "Augustinian" attitude toward language and towards God's graceful imposition of its use in the world, literalism and figuration both stood within the reach of his purposive might. Moralization of Scripture, in its many levels of realism and abstraction, reflected the experience of divine omnipotence and proximity within the world as a whole, ordering the possibility of salvation through knowledge and practice.

V. Ockham's Figural Exegesis

Coming back to Ockham in particular, I think it is crucial to bear in mind the figural flexibility afforded by the Augustinian theory of signs. The latter's semiotic framework for understanding language makes little sense without its being informed by the power of grace that makes divine use of what is otherwise a merely conventional system of signs set within a human culture.

And more than anything else, Ockham's theory of signification is Augus-

---

92. For a good overview of the variegated wealth of this kind of exposition, see G. R. Owst, *Literature and Pulpit in Medieval England: A neglected chapter in the history of English letters and of the English people* (Oxford: Basil Blackwell, 1961), pp. 2-5 (vernacular "renaissance" linked to the Friars), 22 (Neoplatonic metaphysics of figuration), 24 (mendicant mixing of mystical and scientific figures), 37-41 (Franciscan "realism"), 48 (Platonic presuppositions), 56-59 (scriptural figures in general), 99 (the longevity of the figural style into the 17th century), 151-54 (*exempla* in general), 190-93 (moralization of the natural world, including the use of bestiaries). For fuller translations, see Siegfried Wenzel, *Preaching in the Age of Chaucer: Selected Sermons in Translation* (Washington, DC: Catholic University of America Press, 2008). The most engaging English anthology remains J. M. Neale's *Mediaeval Preachers and Mediaeval Preaching: A Series of Extracts* (London: J. & C. Mozley, 1856), whose Introduction is also worth reading in the context of discussions of figuralism in our final chapter especially. On some summary discussions of English preaching in this regard, from the later 14th century, see Siegfried Wenzel, *Latin Sermon Collections from Later Medieval England: Orthodox Preaching in the Age of Wyclif* (Cambridge: Cambridge University Press, 2005), pp. 318-22.

tinian.[93] As with Augustine, Ockham understands spoken and written language in terms of conventional signs, instituted *ad placitum*, that is, arbitrarily in terms of form, but by common agreement. These signs can signify meaningfully only what is already known through experience, and thus operate "recordatively," through the intervening signification of remembered concepts of things. And while "mental" language — concepts — is also a system of signs, and is even seen to be a system structured like a language, its signs are "natural," in that they follow the immediate intuition of objects.

It is true that Ockham is, in many ways, less skeptical than Augustine about the trustworthiness of the original conceptual cognitions that form the basis of linguistic signification. He has little room in his system for Augustine's indwelling Wisdom, the illuminating Teacher who is Christ and who thereby legitimates and confirms the basis of our otherwise dubious apprehension of the truth by providing us inwardly with the self-evident universal bases for our knowledge. For Ockham, as we have noted, our immediate cognition, the concepts that embody this, are of the things themselves, and constitute evident knowledge. But because our communicative language is a system of conventional signs, it becomes crucial to clarify at all times the exact referents for our words, that is, what concepts (and via concepts, what objects) words stand for, or supposit. Ockham's logic, which is relentlessly based on the principle that language functions through supposition — signs standing for concepts or things — is thus driven by the fuel of stripping away signs to get at their supposits. Given his metaphysics, such supposits or ultimate referents can only be individual beings in specific contexts.

It is this non-illuminist Augustinianism on the subject of signs that has perhaps encouraged us to think of Ockham as pressing towards a thoroughly literalist hermeneutic. But this is to confuse issues of ontological causation in language with signification proper. It is true that, in discussing certain texts from Scripture or from the "saints," Ockham will frequently take care to distinguish how an author might use words to signify connotatively — e.g. using the figure of a stone to supposit for the concept "God" — and the (mistakenly) perceived metaphysical basis that might seem necessitated were one to take the phrase literally.[94] This is not to say that the language of *figura* is improper, insignificant, or unnecessary. Ockham reduces the manner of its effective sig-

93. Cf. Boehner's articles "Ockham's Theory of Signification" and "Ockham's Theory of Truth," in his *Collected Articles on Ockham*, ed. Eligius Buytaer (St. Bonaventure, NY: The Franciscan Institute, 1958), pp. 201-32 and 174-200 respectively.

94. Cf. e.g. the *Ordinatio* 36:1, where Ockham cites Augustine's *De Trinitate* 5:8 on metaphorical and proper significations of God in order to prevent ascribing the literal signification of signs like "rock" or "lion" to the essence of God.

nification to conventional supposition. But that it signifies effectively, he never questions.[95]

Since, as I have noted earlier, Ockham did not himself comment on Scripture, and his philosophical, logical, and theological works are themselves little oriented towards Scripture, we are left with indirect avenues towards assessing his hermeneutic. What is clear, however, is that even in these areas of non-scriptural investigation, Ockham had an unvarying sense of the authority of Scripture to signify the truth, on whatever level of supposition one determines that this is done. Hence, the recurring standard by which one adjudicates a contested opinion in matters, usually theology, is formulated by Ockham in a scale of decreasing importance as follows: Scripture and what can be inferred from Scripture, the authority of the church, the authority of the saints, and, sometimes, experience or evident reason.[96] That the authority of Scripture is thus granted the supreme status as arbiter derives, quite simply, from its supernatural status — from the fact that it is revealed by God.[97] And if revealed by God, wholly trustworthy in all of its significations.

It is true that Ockham clearly distinguishes what is thus known supernaturally by faith from knowledge proper, considered as science which is derived from evident principles. And since the truths of Scripture are accepted on faith, they do not constitute evident knowledge, in the way that even the witness, grasped intuitively, of a miracle might constitute knowledge of some event (although not necessarily of the event's cause). But the distinction between faith and knowledge is not crucial here. Scripture is authoritative even over individually intuited knowledge from experience. It reflects, as surely as anything does, the activity of God's power exercised for human salvation.

As such, and just as for Augustine and Francis, the figuring capacity of Scripture is sustained through grace, and it is a capacity deployed not only within the closed system of biblical signs; it extends into the world of human

---

95. See William J. Courtenay, "Force of Words and Figures of Speech: The Crisis over *Virtus sermonis* in the Fourteenth Century," in William J. Courtenay, *Ockham and Ockhamism: Studies in the Dissemination and Impact of His Thought* (Leiden and Boston: Brill, 2008), pp. 209-28, for a helpful explication of why Ockham was *not* a restricted literalist when it came to linguistic signification.

96. A glance through the indices of the *Ordinatio* under the heading "Sacra Scriptura" will lead one to many instances of the refrain; cf. also Sylla, "Autonomous and Handmaiden Science," p. 374 and note 109, where she refers, for some reason, to a doubtful work of Ockham to make the same point.

97. For the relation between theology and knowledge, see Leff, *William of Ockham*, pp. 335-49, and the citations, mainly from the *Ordinatio*, which he gives.

relations and the created order as a whole. To see this at work in Ockham, however, we must move away from the theoretical work for which he is most famous and enter into some of the writings of his last phase, the controversy over Franciscan poverty and the power of the papacy.

It is, in any case, in works from this polemical period that scholars have attempted to cull Ockham's mature views on scriptural authority. Without entering into the debate concerning Ockham's actual position on the matter, it would seem that the general order of authority by which he operated in his earlier theological works remains intact.[98] Scripture's explicit teachings have foremost authority, followed by its implicit teachings (logically inferred under the authority of the church), followed by the universally accepted authority of the church (dissent by definition undercutting such authority), followed only last of all by individual reason and experience.

It is in his *Breviloquium de Principatu Tyrannico* that Ockham expresses some of his clearest strictures on the interpretation of Scripture. Written sometime in the decade before his death (that is, sometime around 1340), the work gives a good precis of the Franciscan's own thinking on the issues of poverty, and the relationship between the secular and spiritual powers. By this time, Ockham himself had fled Pope John XXII's court in Avignon for the safety of Louis of Bavaria. He had already made his study, at the request of his superior Michael of Cesena, of the question of Franciscan poverty and the rulings of previous popes, and he had reached the conclusion that the current pope's rulings against the principle of poverty were heretical. In the *Breviloquium*,

98. Part of the problem of deciphering clearly Ockham's views on the matter is that the fullest treatment he gives to the question of scriptural authority, especially as it relates to various traditions of the church, is in a work (the *Dialogus de Imperio et Pontifica Potestate*) presented as a dialogue between two opposing views, neither one of which is ever identified with Ockham's. Oberman discusses two influential interpretations, that of de Vooght and of Tavard, in *The Harvest of Medieval Theology*, pp. 361-65. Cf. also Leff, *William of Ockham*, pp. 641-42. At issue is the degree to which Ockham was willing to subordinate ecclesiastical tradition to Scripture. My guess is that de Vooght's view (versus Leff's, for instance) is the most accurate, that is, that Ockham wavers somewhat between a statement of unequivocal superiority for Scripture and one that accepts the interpretive framework, and in some instances even the independent authority, of certain church traditions (all inspired by the Holy Spirit) as long as they are consistent in some measure with Scripture (Paul de Vooght, *Les Sources de la Doctrine Chrétienne d'après les Théologiens du XIVe siècle et du Début du XVe* [n.p.: Desclée de Brouwer, 1954], pp. 161-67). Although with a smaller focus in view, I. J. Minnis will come to conclusions similar to my own about Ockham's exegesis and its relation to his "nominalism," in "Material Swords and Literal Lights: The Status of Allegory in William of Ockham's *Breviloquium* on Papal Power," in Jane Dummen McAuliffe, Barry D. Walfish, Joseph W. Goering, eds., *With Reverence for the Word: Medieval Scriptural Exegesis in Judaism, Christianity, and Islam* (New York: Oxford University Press, 2010), pp. 292-308.

then, what is at issue scripturally is the capacity of biblical texts, under certain circumstances of interpretation, to act as legislative justifications.[99]

On a broad scale, Ockham seeks to curtail the use of biblical passages as proof-texts for papal supremacy over the sphere of the secular powers, as well as for supreme papal authority in the interpretation of Scripture in general (as e.g. on the topic of religious poverty). The fifth book provides the most extended series of instances where this problem is discussed. Ockham begins by attacking the notion that Christ conferred upon the papacy power over the Roman emperor, a claim that had been buttressed by various New Testament texts such as Jesus' giving to Peter the power of the keys, Peter as the Rock, and so on — all perhaps indicating the Petrine office as standing vicariously for Christ's rule.

In 5:2, Ockham then lists a number of texts used by the pope to prove that, as vicar of Christ, the power he held included a temporal jurisdiction: e.g. Matthew 11:27 ("All things have been delivered to me by my Father") and Matthew 28:18 ("All authority in heaven and on earth has been given to me"), as well as numerous others. Ockham replies that this plenitude of power that was evidently Christ's is to be understood as referring "spiritually" to his divinity, as well as to his power in "spiritual things," and continues to apply to him only with reference to his glorification post-Resurrection.

This has two implications: first, if it is spiritual, it does not refer to secular power; second, if it derives from his divinity, then the pope cannot claim it, otherwise we would expect the pope, like Jesus, to heal the sick, perform miracles, dispense, as necessary, with the laws of nature and of custom. This the pope cannot do, and therefore the pope never received this power. We may notice here, simply, that a divine "spiritual" referent is adduced by Ockham in the effort to limit the verses' practical human applications.

In 5:3, Ockham explains the basic principle to be followed when interpreting biblical texts practically, that is, in the sphere of ecclesiastical law. Seizing on two other favorite passages used by the pope to uphold the two-fold powers given him, the famous "two swords" verse from Luke 22:38 and the "two lights" verse of Genesis 1:16, Ockham launches into his attack on arbitrary use of "allegory" to sustain authoritative rulings: "The mystical sense of Scripture, which is not contrary to the truth, can be used for edification and exhortation, but never for the proof or the confirmation of doubtful or disputed positions,

99. See Hamman's introduction to the work, pp. 1-25, for a discussion of its political and literary context; pp. 26-31 on Ockham's view of Scripture as evidenced in the treatise, in P. Adalbert Hamman, *La Doctrine de l'Église et de l'État chez Occam* (Paris: Editions Franciscaines, 1942).

unless that very mystical sense is expressed in the divine Scripture itself or in what precedes it."[100]

As Hamman points out, this is to apply to all figural readings something of Jerome's principle for the use of the deuterocanonical scriptures. Nonetheless, Ockham immediately softens his criteria: not only can a figural reading be authoritative if it is found in Scripture itself, but it may also carry weight if it is supported by evident reason (*vel racioni evidenti innititur*). Moments later he adds a third circumstance that might support the authoritative use of a figural reading: citing Augustine (*Epistola* 93:8), he mentions *testimonia manifesta* as that which might corroborate such a reading. Yet despite these three possibilities, Ockham repeats over and over again that mystical or allegorical readings of Scripture have no role to play in the adjudication of disputed questions among Christians.

But how can Ockham sustain these limitations on the application of figural exegesis when the saints before him have used it for just such juridical purposes? In 5:4, Ockham answers this reply by citing the example of Augustine's use of the phrase from Luke 14:23 — *compelle intrare* — to justify the coerced restoration of schismatics into the Catholic church. Do not suppose that such a figural use of the words from Jesus' parable itself was sufficient to legitimate the recapture of heretics for the faith. Rather, only if the truth of the strategy were first clearly established from within Scripture and from evident reason could this text be subsequently applied in any comprehensible fashion. And in fact, Augustine provides us with a rule of sorts, for Ockham: figural readings are always only secondary, in matters of law, to some other more potent "authority" — whether Scripture itself, universally accepted tradition, or clear reason; at which point, the mystical sense of texts can be brought forward in order to strengthen or "delight" those who have accepted the authoritative meaning in question already.[101]

In subsequent chapters in the fifth book, Ockham gives several examples of how equally plausible mystical readings of certain texts used by the pope could lead to positions contrary to his; that is, figural readings tend to be somewhat arbitrary outside some larger frame of reference and meaning that limits and directs their signification. But exactly what the contours are of such a larger framework of authority Ockham leaves, as we have seen, somewhat unclear. At times he can say that those best equipped to judge the pope's orthodoxy are those most well-versed in Scripture, i.e. the theologians (cf. 1:8,

---

100. Translation in William of Ockham, *A Short Discourse on Tyrannical Government*, ed. A. S. McGrade, trans. John Kilcullen (Cambridge: Cambridge University Press, 1992), pp. 133-34.

101. Cf. Augustine, *De Doctrina Christiana* 11:6, on the mystical "delight" figural interpretation of Scripture affords one who is already advanced in understanding.

vs. the canonists). But there are times, in this latter part of the treatise, e.g. 5:4, where it seems that any person gifted with reason and the ability to read Scripture clearly and located firmly within the bounds of the church is capable of determining if the pope errs.

Clearly something larger is being assumed by Ockham as the context within which scriptural significations are both effective and appropriate. And this context is neither a rule for literalism nor simply a set system of hermeneutic devices following certain rules. Thus, despite Ockham's delimitation of mystical interpretations in Book Five of the *Breviloquium*, it must be noticed that much of the larger argument about the extent of temporal powers, possessions, and voluntary poverty takes place under an encompassing figure — by no means universally accepted in Ockham's narrower sense — of Paradise and the Fall.

Students of the intricacies of the debate over Franciscan poverty in the 13th and 14th centuries agree that Ockham did little to advance the main principles in favor of religious poverty, except through his reinterpretation of the relationship of supra- and sublapsarian Adam to property and to the rights of possession. John XXII had sought to counter the Franciscan claim that Jesus had lived a life of absolute poverty while in the flesh and had invited others to follow him in this — a call the Franciscans saw themselves as fulfilling. One way in which John hoped to undercut the assertion of Christ's absolute poverty was to move the discussion back to the Old Testament, and to Genesis in particular. Since Adam was given dominion over the earth before his fall, John argued that human beings had been given an inalienable legal right to lordship over all creation. Although after the fall, this extended dominion was restricted to personal property, the continuity of legal ownership was both unbroken and divinely instituted. Christ and his disciples held possessions (including the disputed "bag" kept by Judas) and Franciscans were countering the divinely given vocation of Adam in denying this.

Ockham, following Michael of Cesena, countered the pope by reappropriating a venerable Patristic position that identified the introduction of all private property with the fall. Before the fall, according to Ockham, Adam had enjoyed "dominion" over the earth, not in the sense of possession, but in the sense of free enjoyment or use of the earth's fruits, in peaceable conjunction with the animals. This state of "possessionless" use constituted, in Ockham's view, the divinely given law of liberty offered the "entire human race"; as divine, it was also "natural," and it was just this state of freedom in the condition of innocence that Christ (and subsequently Francis following him) came to restore through their lives.[102]

---

102. For the history of the controversy, see Leff, *Heresy in the Later Middle Ages*, vol. 1;

That human positive law legitimately upheld the right to private property was the case only after the fall, and existed only given the still imperfect state of the fallen world; and such human law was independent of the original divine set of rights given in the Garden. If Franciscans, then, chose to give up their human right to property, this was to conform them to the divine law, which human law had no power to contravene. Natural right superseded human positive law. On the other hand, to locate dominion, even understood in the constricted manner of Ockham, in the natural and divine law, and to recognize rights over property in the legitimate, though limited, human positive law was to grant to human beings as a whole powers and rights over property that were not tied to the church. Secular rulers, then — even infidel rulers — had legitimate claims to authority.

In the *Breviloquium*, it is in 3:7 and following that Ockham outlines this argument, one that he had already used in earlier works. What is interesting, given the warnings he will use later about applying certain figures of Scripture across dispensational bounds (e.g. what pertains to Christ in the flesh or spiritually in glorification, or what pertains to Israel in the flesh as opposed to the spiritual and moral Israel), is that Ockham seems to take for granted that the figure of Adam and Eve, of the Garden, of the fall, of the skins given them by God, of Judas's bag much later — all of these biblical stories or objects nonetheless retain for him authoritative and universal significance, quite beyond their literal signification. In the case of Adam, of course, he is following scriptural precedent itself in applying him as figure for all of humanity; but what of his garden fruit or his skins (although, in the tradition, these elements of the story are likewise symbolized)? What of Judas's bag? Is it permitted by Scripture itself to take this single object as exemplary of the relationship Christians should or should not have with private property? (Of course, both sides of the controversy, not Ockham alone, sought to explain the significance of this element for the elaboration of an ethic of property.)

There is no point trying to find a consistent framework for explaining Ockham's legal appeal to these texts, when he has rejected such appeal for others. He is certainly not beyond using opposing arguments as may best suit his purposes. But beyond this, the fact is that Ockham's universe of signs is as anagogically oriented as those of most of his contemporaries. Scripture in particular is, for him as for so many others, the gift of an omnipotent God who has so construed the world and ordered the words of the Bible, that the

---

for a brief review of the arguments from Scripture involved, see Gordon Leff, "The Bible and Rights in the Franciscan Disputes over Poverty," in *The Bible in the Medieval World: Essays in Memory of Beryl Smalley*, ed. Katherine Walsh and Diana Wood (Oxford: Basil Blackwell, 1985).

latter may function broadly in an inter-signifying role to navigate through the former in the direction of salvation's grasp.

We are not familiar with Ockham the preacher; but even in the drily argumentative prose of the *Breviloquium* he intimates his own sense of ease with the moralizing temper of his contemporaries. In 4:7, for instance, he once again attempts to formulate the ways in which figural readings of the Old Testament can make legitimate sense. In this context he must evidently eschew pure legislative literalism; what the Old Testament Israelites practiced as a constituted and politically organized theocratic nation is not to be a model for the church. Ockham's distinction is wholly unoriginal: the ceremonial law, the judicial law, and the sacraments of the Old Testament are not be imitated, only the "moral" acts and works of the Jews. Then Ockham cites Romans 15:4 as his rule of figuration: "For whatever was written in former days was written for our instruction, that by steadfastness and by the encouragement of the scriptures we might have hope."

In the manner of Augustine's *regula fidei* of love, Ockham invokes the *regula* of moral encouragement, construed in its more narrowly anagogic function: the building up of hope for the future of salvation. It is no accident that Ockham chose as his proof-text the Romans verse, whose scriptural context deals with the submission of the strong to the weak, following the example of Christ. For it is just Ockham's argument here that the Old Testament "kingly" priests cannot be taken as a model by the papacy, whose own power is more properly grounded in the example of Jesus' "service" to others, rather than his rule over them.[103]

The final chapters of the treatise methodically demonstrate the spiritual disaster that comes from reading the Old Testament's theocratic institutions as types whose literal features are to be carried through into the common mores of the newer covenant. If these texts are to speak to Christians today, Ockham implies, it is through the power of their formative influence on the Christian virtues of hopeful discipleship of Jesus. But these meanings are imbedded in the larger purposes of God. They are accessible neither to rules that govern literal exegesis nor to rules that govern figural exegesis. Instead, they are disclosed through submission to the larger figure of the created order — the movement from Paradise to its restoration in Christ — imposed by the power of the creative God. Within this universe, figured in this way, the words of Scripture are meaningfully effective in a host of signifying functions.

---

103. Cf. the *Breviloquium* 2:5 and 2:6 for Ockham's earlier elucidation of this theme. I have consulted the text in William of Ockham, *Breviloquium de Potestate Papae*, ed. L. Baudry (Paris: Librairie Philosophique J.Vrin, 1937), as well as the English translation of William of Ockham, *A Short Discourse on Tyrannical Government*, ed. McGrade, trans. Kilcullen.

Indeed, Ockham's worries about the right application of the *sensus mysti-cus* are precisely that: worries about application, not about the meaningfulness of the sense itself. And these concerns of application center on the legislative role that this might, inappropriately, play. But here it is really a question of determining what stands as the governing *figura*, not whether figuration itself is to be permitted adjudicatory weight. Within the larger scheme of the movement from Paradise, through fall, and restoration in Christ, what Ockham clearly takes as his governing figure is the shape bequeathed him by his Order. While I have found no direct descriptions in his work of "Poverty," symbolized, it is her presence, even in the quasi-juridical language of rights employed by Ockham, that is hovering over his discussion. This "gospel within a gospel," to use a modern formulation, is not simply an abstract rule for limiting figural application; rather, it is a rule because in itself it represents the figure of human relationship with the world established by God, and therefore signified in the words of Scripture and the creatures of the cosmos.[104]

VI. Conclusion

If this conclusion is brief, it is largely because its main points have emerged repetitively in the course of what has preceded. The purpose of this chapter, to remind the reader, has been to determine to what degree figural readings are

104. To see how this might be the case more clearly, we need only look at that most popular of devotional works of the later Middle Ages, the *Meditations on the Life of Christ*; see Isa Ragusa and Rosalie Green, eds., *Meditations on the Life of Christ* (Princeton: Princeton University Press, 1961). Written by a Franciscan monk for a Franciscan sister, the book is frequently cited as a prime example of just the literalizing and vernacularizing tendencies of Franciscan piety (cf. Jeffrey, "Franciscan Spirituality," p. 148). And while the homely sentimentality of the retelling of the gospel stories is undeniable and especially winning to modern ears, we would be missing what seems to me one of the main goals of this work if we were to ignore the way in which these meditations are framed within the larger figure of restorative *Paupertas*. The author's frequent digressions into the realm of moralization over virtues and vices based on the *exempla* of the stories, very quickly slips into a tangible symbolization of the characters themselves, extended into the realms of heaven. In particular *Domina Paupertas* is revealed to be the Virgin Mary herself, whose historical role becomes easily blurred with her function as anagogic force within the Christian's life of pilgrimage towards heaven. And Poverty herself is ordered under a larger scheme, allegorically articulated: the heavenly dispute between Truth and Mercy, Justice and Peace, that opens the book, although explicitly identified as "figure" (taken, like much else in the book, from Bernard), states clearly the way cosmic realities like the fall and the incarnation are to be the motivating referents of the succeeding historical events and persons, whose figuration, however, will be moored in the incarnational virtue of religious poverty.

necessarily sustained by broader metaphysical or philosophical frameworks. In doing this, I chose one particular period where scholars have claimed to identify a momentous conceptual shift with regard to the "symbolizing mentality." This period was the 14th century, with an emphasis on William of Ockham.

We approached the period from several fronts: metaphysics and natural science, representational form, Franciscan piety, and some of Ockham's own exegetical remarks. In each case it seemed clear that, whatever significant changes were effected by thinkers of the period, and by Ockham in particular in these areas, the notion and effective practice of figuration was neither simply dislodged nor particularly weakened.

There are differences connected with the Ockhamist shift that emerge, to be sure. The "singularism" associated with his metaphysics, or with Franciscan piety, is undeniable, and stands in definite contrast to the Neoplatonic metaphysics of participation that was espoused, in differing ways, by some thinkers of the 12th century and beyond. Nor would it make much sense to deny the fact that an evolving notion of what science demanded in terms of observation and method altered, to some degree, the relationship that could be claimed to hold between objects and between their significatory roles in various conceptual frameworks. But there is no evidence that Ockhamism in itself necessitated these changes, nor that the changes themselves necessarily undercut the possibility for a religiously motivated figuration of world and Scripture.

I have suggested, however, that while a Neoplatonic metaphysics may not be necessary for the possibility of figuration, there was certainly an alternative conceptual support for maintaining figuration as a meaningful practice that was in play, not only for Ockham, but within the religious tradition of which he was a part.

Whether we want to identify this conceptual support in terms of an Augustinian sense of the comprehensive dynamic of divine grace, or more theoretically, in terms of the Ockhamist notion of God's ordained and absolute powers, we are dealing with a clear and subsuming category of purposive and, with respect to the world, creative omnipotence. And this alone, adapted to an Augustinian theory, to a Franciscan devotion, or to a science of natural history, provides the basis for claiming the revelatory inter-signification of creatures and words, bound to the scriptural text in a fundamental way, in which figuration consists.

What these conclusions do not tell us is whether the metaphysics of participation or of omnipotence are the only possible supports for a figural practice. Nor do they tell us whether the practice itself needs any kind of conceptual support at all. We might, for instance, wish to claim that there was a demise, perhaps associated with the Enlightenment, in the intelligibility of divine omnipotence, and that this is what lies, in part, behind the demise of allegory, picking up Louth's historical worry. But even this, while perhaps true for certain individual and influential thinkers, is doubtful. It has been shown that moralizing figuration, which for all its inconsistencies was still firmly rooted in a vision of divine omnipotence, continued as a widespread practice well into the 17th century, both popularly in preaching and on the level of academic science.[105] We have only just begun to explore this reality, however, and even more tentatively, for the 18th century. In addition, a reexamination of the place of miracle in popular and church-centered theology and piety might well provide a picture that goes counter to the science-vs.-superstition-triumph-of-rationalism view of what developed during this period. Historical attention has too often focused on one strand of the intellectual genealogy of modernity.[106] It is not really the case that Pentecostalism arose out of nowhere at the beginning of the 20th century; its roots were in a well-nourished and multifaceted Christian terrain that itself was already spread around the globe in the form of vital and traditional — and figurally oriented — Christian communities. What is specific to modernity is *not* that these communities disappeared — indeed, from one perspective, they flourished — but that they were attacked by the culture which they themselves had nurtured.

There is no question in my mind, however, that explicitly Platonic versions of figuration, like Louth's, involve prominent roles for the Holy Spirit's dynamic guidance and the strong metaphoric character of words and traditional discourses. And since these are understood through naturalistic images of force, their entire conception depends more primarily on a high view of omnipotence, rather than on ontological participation or indeed any other

105. Cf. Owst, pp. 98-102, which refers, among others things, to the continuity of figural practice that lies behind Bunyan's work; cf. also our earlier remarks concerning Nicolaus Steno. But I have indicated, in Chapter 2, other lines of continued figural engagement.

106. If I have one major historical criticism of Frei's masterful *The Eclipse of Biblical Narrative: A Study in Eighteenth and Nineteenth Century Hermeneutics* (New Haven: Yale University Press, 1974), it is that the work can easily leave us with the impression that a certain group of academic commentators on the sense of Scripture from the 18th century on represents a movement of interpretation that was and is indicative of the evolving churches as a whole. Indeed, one would almost never know, from his book, that there were churches in which the Scripture was heard, discussed, and prayed over, and that there were intellectually competent and aware commentators committed to this fact, all of whose experience was barely regulated by the hermeneutic debates Frei discusses. It is the relationship between these groups that needs exploration. The historical question, furthermore, touches on the much-charged debates over the "genealogy of modernity" that, as we have indicated, lie behind some of the current interest in the late medieval thinkers.

philosophical framework.[107] And if, in fact, it is an acceptance of such omnipotence that has been attenuated in the modern world, then the common sense of scriptural figuration will have at least begun to dissolve.

This could be problematic for any attempt to renew scriptural reading in our day. Unless, as I will suggest later, the Bible creates its own possibility for reception, literally or figurally; that is, unless it has been endowed with or is governed by a divine power beyond itself or through itself. In which case, while it may not be necessary to claim such power prior to encountering the text, it will be incumbent upon us at some time, as communities or as individuals, to acknowledge, observe, contemplate, commend, and celebrate this power. Even the latter occupations are not common among our theologians today. But the common sense of the church may be deeper than we recognize. Certainly, it is founded on the reality of a divine being whose reach goes beyond the sharing of words, but includes the use of his own self within speech. To that we now turn.

107. This includes, in Louth's case, a sociological hermeneutic that might equally derive from the emphases of Gadamer and Polanyi, and that sees "tradition" exclusively in terms of communal practice.

CHAPTER 5

Figural Speech and the Incarnational Synecdoche

I. Where Is Christ in the Scriptures?

Does creative omnipotence, undergirding the figural web of Scripture, pre-
clude ontological claims regarding Scripture's reality as it relates to human
ontology more broadly? One of the critiques of Ockhamist-styled nominalism is that it rendered impotent such an ontological relationship, one often
construed in "participationist" terms.[1] The critique is frequently framed in
terms of a historical narrative that moves from nominalism to Protestantism
to the "autonomous" realm of scientific reasoning to the secular state.[2] One
of the things I have been arguing for is, in a way, an *expansion* of common
sense to include figural reference within the Scripture's normal semantic range,
rather than fixating its possibility within some clearly defined metaphysical
framework. "Common sense" here is akin to the *consensus fidelium* of common Scripture reading within the broad range of the church's life from her
inception until the present — a practice of reading that has always and often
unreflectively included figural reading. But if I am right, it is important to test
whether such an expanded common sense can also include other elements
that are rightly embedded within the Christian tradition. One of these central

1. See Matthew Levering, "Participation and Exegesis: Response to Catherine Pickstock,"
Modern Theology 21:4 (October, 2005): 587-601. More broadly, see his *Participatory Biblical
Exegesis: A Theology of Biblical Interpretation* (Notre Dame, IN: University of Notre Dame
Press, 2008).
2. This is part of the basic narrative explicated by Brad Gregory's *The Unintended Ref-
ormation: How a Religious Revolution Secularized Society* (Cambridge, MA: Belknap Press of
Harvard University, 2012).

elements is precisely the Christological center that has always governed the Christian reading of a two-testament Bible. While creative omnipotence can rightly ground figural reading as a simple metaphysical baseline, and one that escapes most contested metaphysical details, it is only one aspect of a baseline that has always been shaped by the central claims of a gospel regarding God's self-giving. From one perspective such a gospel is itself a scriptural articulation; but it is also one that allows the Scripture its Christian articulation from the start.

In order to see what this might mean, and how "normal reading" presses the figural ordering of Scripture in a particular Christ-centered way, let us consider what has often been explained in, for instance, Platonic terms, but that is more basic than such a specifically philosophical construal. What I have in mind is the incarnational aspect of creative omnipotence that must place Scripture's figural import within a specific aspect of referential usage that is Christ-directed in some fundamental fashion. One approach to this aspect is to engage the question of Scripture's "particular" language as contrasted with other religious languages, including especially other non-Christian religious languages.

Indeed, it is with the nature of Christian language about God, in this case specifically scriptural language, that we are concerned. But we can examine how this language might work by noting the way this language pushes us towards a peculiar and collisive posture with regards to alternative languages — the languages of the nations, as it were. It is in this encounter of languages, one in which scriptural language exerts an overwhelming force, as being the language of the omnipotent creator, that the figural center of the text begins to show itself, and to show itself as Christ-referring. If all things are given us by God, including the language of God's own creative self-reference with creatures, then this language will *ipso facto* be uniquely configurated, and uniquely reflective of God's very self. As I suggested in Chapter 3, the language of Scripture, *qua* language, if in fact it is the language of the omnipotent God of creation, however divinely invented, orders the world according to its Christ-reference; and the world finds its form only because of this. Can this possibly make sense?

It is not a retrogressive question. It has, in fact, been broached with some contemporary practical relevance within the field of inter-religious dialogue, but it could easily be extended to the realm of all non-scriptural forms of discourse. Within the inter-religious field, Christian language is often viewed as referential in such a way that some object is indicated — an artifact beyond language — which can then itself be examined in religious terms, for the sake of identifying difference or identity between religions. Particularist Christian claims, as they might be called, are so only because their referents cannot be located except within the particular orderings or usage of Christian faith and life; broader, perhaps universal claims can be so identified insofar as their referents can be located in larger sets of religious or more generally human usage.[3] But this is only one way, a very modern way perhaps, of understanding the encounter of religious languages. If, as George Lindbeck famously maintains (using an Austinian category), doctrinal propositions are really "performative utterances," insofar at least as they are true, then we must allow that the "logical" space occupied by such utterances in the Christian religion is not exhausted by a description of their referents.[4] They also require some description of the "work" they do. I will be returning at greater length to this question in Chapter 6. Here I wish to consider a way in which scriptural figuration emerges logically from the character of Scripture simply as being "God's" own words — words which, from a non-Christian perspective, seem to have a "life of their own," even while, from within the apprehending Christian life, they are bound to "the life of the world" which is the Word's own life.

I will not, as it turns out, be adopting Lindbeck's own cultural-linguistic framework for locating an utterance's "work." I will not do so largely because it does not sufficiently emphasize (and for some readers, it even obscures) the comparative potency of the scriptural linguistic (and, by indirection, cultural) system. Post-liberal theology has, quite deliberately, sought to mark off the precincts of specific linguistic, and hence religious, cultures; but it has not found a way, according to its pluralistic logic, to rearticulate the frankly hegemonic center of scriptural speech. Instead, I will locate the Scripture's "work" in an objective ontological and historical framework, determined by Scripture's own discourse, that is, by the incarnation. Be that as it may, once we extend the logic of a scriptural claim to the sense of its words in some fashion, to the work it does, the space it occupies will look very different *with respect* to competing claims. And this is a crucial point to underline: scriptural language, if it is God's, "works," not only within a self-contained sphere of its own self-reference, but it works "outwards," towards and into the (non-Christian, as it were) world. The obviousness of this observation is recognizable, however, only if we also recognize Christian speech as being in some essential fashion not simply the "language of Zion," in Lindbeck's felicitously repeated formulation, but also the language of Zion's king.

3. Cf. the terms of discussion offered by Joseph DiNoia, *The Diversity of Religions: A Christian Perspective* (Washington, DC: Catholic University Press, 1992), whose important book I will use as a conversation partner here.

4. Cf. George Lindbeck, *The Nature of Doctrine* (Philadelphia: Westminster Press, 1984), p. 65.

II. Blasphemy, Pain, and Religious Reference

Let me turn to a well-known story about the monk Serapion, taken from Cassian's *Conferences*.[5] The features operative in this account will serve our purposes later on, so we can acquaint ourselves with the story here, if only to enter into the discussion broached above. Serapion was famous as an Egyptian ascetic in the fourth century. His purity of life and devotion to Christ in prayer were legendary, and brought him many disciples. Cassian himself reports several conferences delivered by the abbot Serapion, and in general presents him as a sage working on the level of commendable wisdom.

However, by the time Serapion was an old man, word got back to the bishop in Alexandria that the famous monk had fallen prey to disturbingly erroneous views about the nature of God. These views were later attacked as "anthropomorphite" in the ensuing battle with Origenism waged among the Egyptian monks at the end of the fourth century. Georges Florovsky argues, probably rightly, that the real issue with Serapion centered on his Christological imaging in prayer.[6] Cassian, however, indicates that Serapion's anthropomorphism extended to his devotional picturing of the uncreated Godhead in human form. (And perhaps Florovsky is too quick to dismiss this possibility, one made real for just the Christological considerations he advances.) As Cassian repeatedly emphasizes throughout his *Conferences*, prayers should aim at the total evacuation of all images and *historia* from the mind and spirit, but most especially any images of the Godhead *"which it is a sin even to mention."*[7] Serapion himself was an influential master, and his teachings and practices were no doubt infecting hosts of disciples. An alarmed hierarchy back in the city dispatched a deacon, a theological point-man, to Serapion's wilderness monastery, to set the abbot straight. Finding the old monk, he argued with him forcefully, "on the basis of Scripture and hard reason." And

5. X, 2nd Conference of Abbot Isaac, ch. 3; see Cassian, *Conferences*, in *Select Library of the Nicene and Post-Nicene Fathers of the Christian Church*, Series 2, Vol. XI, trans. Edgar C. S. Gibson (Grand Rapids: Eerdmans, 1964), p. 402.

6. Georges Florovsky, "The Anthropomorphites in the Egyptian Desert, Parts 1 and 2," in *Aspects of Church History* [Coll. wks. vol. 4] (Belmont, MA: Nordland, 1975), pp. 89-96. A recent detailed study by Paul A. Patterson argues that Florovsky was wrong to interpret the anthropomorphites as focused on the "incarnate Christ" while branding Cassian as a deformed "Origenist"; rather, the anthropomorphites actually *did* seek to image the uncreated Godhead in their prayers, and this is precisely where they overstepped the line. See Paul A. Patterson, *Visions of Christ: The Anthropomorphite Controversy of 399 CE* (Tübingen: Mohr Siebeck, 2012). On anthropomorphic language about God more broadly, see Edward L. Schoen, "Anthropomorphic Concepts of God," *Religious Studies* 26:1 (March, 1990): 123-39.

7. Cf. Florovsky, *Aspects of Church History*, p. 92.

eventually the deacon succeeded, we are told, in decisively demonstrating that no form resembling a human body could ever be attributed "to that infinite and incomprehensible glory [. . .] whose nature is incorporeal and uncompounded and simple and can neither be apprehended by the eyes nor conceived by the mind." At length the old abbot was "shaken by the numerous and very weighty assertions of this most learned" deacon, and he agreed to submit to the church's ruling that he give up his practices of imagistically anthropomorphite prayer.

That done, Serapion excused himself, and retired to his cell for prayer — a new kind of prayer! But soon after, those outside overheard him as he burst into a "flood of bitter tears and continual sobs. He cast himself down on the ground and exclaimed with strong groanings: 'Alas! wretched man that I am! They have taken away my God from me, and I have now none to lay hold of, and whom to worship and address I know not!'"

It is a rather pathetic story, and one that, in different guises, has been played out repeatedly in the church's history, even in our own day. But at this stage of our reflection, we need note only four points about Serapion's sad disciplining. First, rather evidently, the dispute involved Christian language — how we speak about God, what words we use, mentally or aloud. Second, this question of language is, in particular, a controversy over *reference*, not practice alone. How one prays, how one *ought* to pray is Cassian's concern, to be sure. But this concern is enclosed in a debate over what the linguistic practice embodies referentially: who is God? *does* God have a face, or hands, or eyes, or arms? Third, the referential aspect of the conflict is fraught with force, is played under the shadows of divine power and energy — that is, how one refers to God is of importance because the practice of naming and the names we use press us into the realm of the holy, of God's own self, such as it is. The authorities are worried about sin, the sin of even mentioning certain names or of speaking in a certain way. In short, the discussion over Serapion's devotional talk touches the realm of *blasphemy*. Finally, Serapion's own response to the outcome of his discipline suggests, to elaborate on our third point, that the practice of naming God and the names one uses are bound to the actual condition of our spirit — joy, or in his case when forced to give up his form of speech and thought, bitter despair. They are enmeshed in the order of our total lives.

The referential concern of scriptural language is inevitable, and the questions it raises inescapable, as points one and two suggest. But they are not enough; and indeed, their significance alters as they are raised and answered within the context of points three and four. That is, any logical space that is to be descriptively non-reductive about Christian claims must be able to comprehend that aspect of Christian scriptural speech that carries the weight of blasphemy (or its opposite, glorification) and pain (or its opposite, delight). These are central "working" aspects of Christian language. When such language is used, it may, in other words, evince any of these characteristics; it probably *must* evince some of them. When I speak of God, I either praise God in my words, or blaspheme God; I either wrench my soul, or I am deeply lifted up in spirit.

But where are we to locate the possibility our speech has of either glorifying or blaspheming God? I would suggest that, whatever we do, we must move away from locating the blaspheming/glorifying aspects of Christian speech in anything other than the reality of God's own creative power, God's self in relation to the world as his creature(s). While figural readings have found justification in a form of literary understanding or linguistic order,[8] neither of these, though undoubtedly true in a way, properly express the relationship of divine word to all else. Blasphemy is not, in Serapion's case, a possibility because of a narrative disunity or an intrasystematic incoherence in his practice, failing to hold together the narrative relationships of Old and New, or failing to do what is implied within the faith of the community by what he says. In Serapion's case, it is just the opposite: Serapion is a *saint*! Blasphemy arises as a possibility because of the strange nature of how reference, in and of itself, works: how a simple word, uttered in faith, can nonetheless, all on its own, touch or combust in its divine reception.

My assertion, to reiterate, is that both points one and two, regarding speaking and reference, must be held together in any attempt to explicate the comparative scope of Christian claims. To separate the two sides is to limit our description of Christian language to either a neutrally linguistic or a practical functionalism, in which all we describe are the roles language *plays* in the Christian system, but not, in fact, the effective work language does. This limitation, as I will argue later, is apparent in the over-enthusiastic espousal of analogical predication for God. It is also, I think, apparent in attempts to construe the nature of Christian language in terms of symbolic or semiotic intrasystematic coherence — something that figural reading, in its derivation from God's Christological ordering of all creation in time, is *not*. The result, in either case, does nothing to go beyond the kind of intra-communal stasis that seems ultimately to be the outcome of strictly particularist understandings

---

8. So, for instance, Frei lodged the figural within the framework of "narrative unity," while Lindbeck saw one of its central powers as deriving from Scripture's (and the Christian faith it sustained) "intrasystematic" coherence, which depends on "intratextual reading" of the kind figuralism embodies. See Frei, *The Eclipse of Biblical Narrative* (New Haven: Yale University Press, 1974), pp. 1-9, 31-40; Lindbeck, *Nature of Doctrine*, pp. 116-23.

of religion that have come to describe most post-liberal appropriations of a figural Scripture.

This is where interreligious discussions can bring into profile the specific character of Christian scriptural language. In that intrasystematic function-alist construals of religion are consciously non-foundationalist, the inter-religious attitudes they must necessarily suggest are neutrally self-protective (if such construals are not, that is, to embrace a deliberate irrationalism). In such non-foundationalist self-understandings, a religion is a particular construal of the world, bound only to its own inner coherence and neither seeking nor depending upon some common feature with other religions. A religious pluralist like John Hick rightly wonders about this kind of logi-cally sensitive though truncated particularism: to the degree that they lead to non-intrusive and mutual tolerance on the basis of a partial- and rela-tive-truth theory, such particular construals of religion are being true to their own presuppositions. But to the degree that they continue to insist on their own truth and another religion's falsity, if only on the basis of intrasystematic descriptive and logical coherence, they are avoiding the logical outcome of their own the non-foundationalist axioms.[9] Hick was here responding to an essay by the Christian philosopher William Alston, whose own interest lay in the rationality of Christians' adhering to a particularist faith, even when confronted with the non-foundationally adjudicatable diversity of religions. Alston knows that the Christian practice of forming beliefs about God makes sense only within the Christian system itself, in a circularly demonstrable way.[10] While this does not mean that a Christian "is free to set herself up within the boundaries of her own community and ignore the rest of the world," it does lead to the suspicion that "it is only in God's good time that a more thorough insight into the truth behind these divergent perspectives [of different religions] will be revealed to us." Although we cannot demonstrate it now, nothing forbids, on this account, the Christian religion from turning out to be exclusively true, while the others turn out to be false.

This outcome would resemble the Nestorian Patriarch Timothy's well-known Parable of the Pearl: in the midst of a world darkened by ignorance, God has placed the pearl of true faith, as in a night-time chamber. Many grasp after this pearl on the floor, but only one can hold it, while the others have picked out pieces of glass or stone that the gloom enshrouds. Yet in the

9. John Hick, "A Concluding Comment," *Faith and Philosophy* 5:4 (Oct. 1988): 449-55; see p. 455.

10. Cf. William Alston, "Religious Diversity and Perceptual Knowledge of God," *Faith and Philosophy* 5:4 (Oct. 1988): 433-48; see p. 437.

darkness, no one can know for sure who *does* have the pearl. And only when the dawn breaks will the truth be seen.[11] Hick appropriately wonders how rational it might be to continue standing in this darkness, convinced that one is holding the pearl when there is no real reason to believe one is. Why even assume there is a single pearl?

But Hick's criticism holds good for any particularist construal of religion that limits referential usage to intrasystematic functionalism, either of a logical or practical kind. It is *God's* use of his artifacts that is at issue, and that finally grounds the figures of Scripture, not the usage of apprehending created subjects. Unless the work Christian language does is tied up with its referential objects, unless, that is, there is a connection between the objective referents and language's *divine* effectiveness as opposed to a connection merely between *ways* of referring and linguistic function within the realm of human apprehension — then there is no way out of the non-foundationalist dilemma over relativism, and not only in inter-religious discussions. And confronted with such diversity of religious claims, the particularist will necessarily be forced to attenuate or limit practice that initially fell within the descriptive bounds of the system, but that now must be sacrificed to maintain the peace of *inter*-systematic agnosticism. That blasphemy and pain are potentially intrinsic to Christian language, however, points us in another direction. Let us follow in that way.

III. Divine Glory: Describing the Presence of Holiness

We turn to Sacred Scripture at this point. Is this allowed? While appeals to the authority of revelation cannot, from a non-foundationalist point of view, adjudicate competing religious claims from a neutral perspective, they are absolutely required from a particularist position, insofar as such appeals constitute, descriptively, the functioning of Christian linguistic practice: this is what Christians do, and how they use their Scripture. We should be clear, however, that such appeals, while descriptively necessary for the particularist, might also be capable of adjudicating competing claims, even if such adjudication is unacceptable or unconvincing to non-Christians. Appeals to revelation may adjudicate precisely because the revelation is true, is in fact from God. How one becomes convinced of its truth is thus secondary to the reality of its truth, or to the implications of its truth. When we secure the logical space for Chris-

11. Cf. "Timothy's Apology for Christianity," ed. and trans. A. Mingana, in *Woodbrooke Studies*, vol. 2 (Cambridge: W. Heffer and Sons Ltd., 1928), pp. 1-162; see especially the conclusion on pp. 88-90.

tian claims, then, it is not first of all to the manner of being convinced of these claims that we turn, but to the reality and implications of the claims, taken to be true in themselves. The reality of blasphemy and pain, holiness and delight that is bound up with Christian language, is similarly accessible to us insofar as we accept the reality of the revelation we assert we live by.

When we open ourselves to the vision Isaiah received at the time of his call (Isa. 6:1-7), we therefore do so as to a vision of which we are a part, and the referents of the images the prophet outlines are to us, as to him, objectively constituted, quite apart from the question of the significance of the actual shapes adopted by the vision. That is, even if we decide that God does not sit on a throne, as Isaiah claims to see him doing, we must at least accept the fact that the vision is from God, and the ostensive referents given in the vision are intrinsically a part of the vision God gives. Whatever their significance, they are not only subjectively interpretive of the vision received. This, at least, I take to be a descriptively accurate claim of Christian particularist self-understanding, as opposed to one made according to a pluralist epistemology of revelation advocated by someone like Hick. But if this is so, then we already have an opening into a comprehension of what kind of vision and world someone like Isaiah receives, an understanding that goes far towards resolving even the issue of the ontological reality of the visionary referents.

> In the year that King Uzziah died I saw the Lord sitting upon a throne, high and lifted up; and his train filled the temple. Above him stood the seraphim; each had six wings: with two he covered his face, and with two he covered his feet, and with two he flew. And one called to another and said: "Holy, holy, holy is the LORD of hosts; the whole earth is full of his glory." And the foundations of the thresholds shook at the voice of him who called, and the house was filled with smoke. And I said: "Woe is me! For I am lost; for I am a man of unclean lips, and I dwell in the midst of a people of unclean lips; for my eyes have seen the King, the LORD of hosts!" Then flew one of the seraphim to me, having in his hand a burning coal which he had taken with tongs from the altar. And he touched my mouth and said: "Behold, this has touched your lips; your guilt is taken away, and your sin forgiven." (RSV)

There are at least three elements to this vision that provide for a glimpse of the nature of God's revelatory speech. First, Isaiah delineates the nature of the vision as one that unfolds in the *presence* of God. Not only is Isaiah given a set of images of God, but they are images whose power presupposes the *proximity* of their referent: e.g. the seraphim of the vision actually leave the plane of the image and descend into physical contact with Isaiah, touching his lips with a burning coal taken from the pictured altar. The images of the vision, then, impart more than cognitive or symbolic meaning; they embody in themselves the presence of God and of God's own "space," as it were (his throne room and spiritual servants).

Second — and this is the most obvious given the visionary nature of the event — this presence is *describable*: the images render not only similitudinous conditions, but actually provide what we might call a material narrative. Not simply is a kind of story told, but the events are bounded and specified by the objective shapes that function, in normal usage, as material descriptors. The clear contrast to this kind of describable presence would be one whose reality must be mediated by the marginal circularities of experiential self-reference — attempts to capture feeling, sensibility, and ineffability, leading to evident metaphoric language. In Isaiah's case, instead, the divine presence is not clearly mediated by subjective linguistic rendition; rather, the language attempts to render unmediated objectivity in formal shapes. The presence of God is describable.

Third, this describable presence of God, revealed in the vision, is holy. Without entering into word-studies, it is enough to consider that the central claim of the visionary context is the angelic description of God as "holy." Even more important, however, is the stated effect of this initial part of the vision on Isaiah himself: "Woe is me! for I am lost; for I am a man of unclean lips, and I dwell in the midst of a people of unclean lips; for my eyes have seen the King, the LORD of hosts!" The describable presence of God, which is called "holy," is also experienced as such by Isaiah, who is terrorized by the probability of succumbing, in his reception of this presence, to the consuming nature of the holiness itself. He must flee; he must hide; he must, if the vision is as it purports to be, surely die. The describable presence of God is revealed as holy precisely insofar as it relentlessly threatens the survival of unholy participants.

This vision of Isaiah, I think, is a good example of the character of biblical language to make possible the reality of blasphemy and pain in its handling. We are not yet at the point in our discussion where we can claim that the biblical language *itself* embodies these possibilities, but here they surely point at least to this language's ties to such potential. Blasphemy, of course, is a form of speech, and it is crucial to recognize that the holiness of God's describable presence is confronted, in this vision, exactly on the level of verbalization. Not only does Isaiah retell the vision — this much is uninteresting — but he grasps the nature of God's presence in his recognition of having "unclean lips," and dwelling among "a people of unclean lips." Sin, and its subsequent removal or covering in forgiveness, is located on the level of speech, of "the lips." Isaiah's commission, further, is to enact this encounter with holiness on the level of speech — to prophesy to the people of Israel, to disseminate descriptively the severe play of divine description. His language is to refer to holiness, even as he is driven headlong into the dying stench of consumed profanity — "until cities lie waste without inhabitant," etc. (6:11).

If we are to take sufficient stock of the logical space of our language, then, we must attend to just this destructive potential and its faithful counterpart. Both, I suggest, are founded on the filiation of revelatory speech from the describable presence of God's holiness. Indeed, we must struggle with the possibility that such speech is referentially tied to such holiness, to such description, to such pressures of proximity. Blasphemy, as speech that transgresses the bounds of holiness, and pain that suffers the judgment of that ghastly intrusion — both derive from the fact that words can be and usually are embodiments or at least expressive garments of God's presence, touching the character of God's holiness, and capable of such cosmic engagement because of God's referential describability. If scriptural words are themselves divine artifacts, something about the peculiar character of their origin has bridged the divide of difference between them and their creator. Certainly, holiness has been scrutinized as central to our understanding of the Old Testament God, and has, although less often of late, been seen as expressive in some measure of God's presence. But holiness's link to descriptive referentiality has rarely been emphasized. Yet this is what we must do.

A long and wearying list could easily be unfolded here, so only a few examples will suffice:

- Genesis 32:30. When Jacob crosses the Jabbok river on his way back to Palestine, he meets, we are told, a "man," who wrestles with him all the night. We know the story well. Is it an angel only? We should like an answer here — but what are angels, anyway? When Jacob releases him, and the man blesses him in return, Jacob exclaims: I have seen *God* face to face, and yet my life is spared!
- Exodus 33:10. Moses, we read, goes into the Tent of Meeting on a regular basis and speaks with God. "Thus the Lord used to speak to Moses face to face," we read, "as one speaks to a friend."
- Exodus 33:23. Only a few verses later, however, Moses asks to see God's glory, and the Lord replies to him, "You cannot see my face; for no one shall see me and live. But I will place you on a rock. And when my glory passes by I will put you in a cleft of the rock, and I will cover you with my hand until I have passed by; then I will take away my hand, and you shall see my back." And so Moses sees only the "back" of God. But a back he sees.

- Exodus 24:12. There are the many passages where we read of people seeing God in the heavenly throne room. On Sinai, for instance, "Moses and Aaron, Nadab and Abihu, and seventy of the elders of Israel went up, and they saw the God of Israel. Under his feet there was something like a pavement of sapphire stone. And they beheld God and they ate and drank."
- Isaiah 6, Ezekiel 1. Prophets like Isaiah, as we have seen, and Ezekiel see God on his throne as well; they see his feet, and his train of light, and Ezekiel says, "something like a human form" of bronze, with legs and loins, sitting on the throne.

There are some tensions here, to which we shall return presently. But there is also a constant motif joining the themes of holiness to describability in all these cases, a descriptiveness here applied to God that is specifically anthropomorphic. The poles of fear for survival in this describable presence and abundant delight in its refulgent shadow each point to the characteristic force driving God's presence into visibility. It is a force not only to be reckoned with, but it is also graciously imposing in its consuming or enlivening embrace. In this context, the circumspection of Ezekiel's similitudes at several removes — "a likeness as it were of a human form" — is less an expression of inexact representation as it is of careful and humble articulation, a verbal grasp of something whose vigor escapes control and whose movement threatens to overwhelm. But the danger, threatening entry into the potential of blasphemy and pain, is made possible by the reality of that verbal grasp, not by its inadequacy.

This last is an important point, because it stands in contrast to a common view that divine holiness reveals its threatening character insofar as it outstrips describability, as it judges the arrogant efforts at verbal control, and as it presses into ineffability. But this normal view is, I believe, off the mark. Describability is not the human subject's prideful manipulation of a divine and impenetrable datum, but the very form of gracious presence itself. If this were not the case, holiness could never cause the pain or joy of *recognition* that it does. To be sure, ineffability seems to be a direction in which description of God does often tend, and the anthropomorphic specificity of many Old Testament relations of God's presence drift, it might be argued, towards an entrapment of scattered figurations more suggestive than shapely or probative.

Take the case of Habakkuk's vision of God (3:3ff.) where the anthropomorphic elements of the prophecy — hands, gaze, posture — appear as metaphoric boundaries to more concrete naturalisms like earthquake, light, plague, and flood. In this context, *all* the specificities might seem to slip into the realm of evocation. Or again, there is Job's striking case. At the end of his long agony of misfortune and complaint, Job is confronted by a vision of the vast panoply of nature's extraordinary form: sun, stars, waters, mountain snows, hail, rain, fields of wheat, seas and fish, birds, goats in the hills, the wild ass, the ostrich and the lion, rivers, the crocodile. Job sees it all as God "answers" him out of the whirlwind with these realities. Then Job claps his hand to his mouth and says, "I know that you can do all things, and that no purpose of yours can be thwarted. . . . Therefore I have uttered what I did not understand, things too wonderful for me, which I did not know. . . . I had heard of you, by the hearing of the ear. But now my eye sees you! Therefore I despise myself, and repent in dust and ashes" (42:2-6). Can we imagine that the catalogue of natural wonders here, now completely devoid of anthropomorphic detail, actually constitutes the "seeing" of God in anything other than a metaphoric or highly asymptotic fashion? If so, the dissolution of anthropomorphic language might indicate the context of holiness as one of ineffability.

But this would get, I believe, the whole relationship between holiness and speech backwards. Ineffability is the consequence of sin, of unbelief, and it comes into play only because holiness *is* made present in tangible terms. The natural specifics of Habakkuk and Job *are* in fact integral elements of the visual experience, they *are* divine descriptors, otherwise their power to condition human response even in the negative form of divine consumption — judgment — would be nothing more than figurative. This is not yet the place to attempt an explication of the method of description they do offer. It is enough to emphasize that the descriptions are still tied to referential presence. If we are to maintain the affirmation of revelatory holiness, we cannot insist that the self-disclosures of the Israelite God are identically shaped as the figments of the "groping" searches of pagans mentioned in, say, Acts 17:27. The move to ineffability — the "unknown" God — is instead predicated on a prior self-constitution by God into describability, much as Adam and Eve's hiding from the "presence" of the Lord is grounded in his intimate proximity to an otherwise pure heart (Gen. 3:8; cf. Matt. 5:8).

This relationship is best seen in the Bible's presentation of the reality of divine "glory," a reality which can rightly be taken as the summary and encompassing reference to God's describable holiness. While "glory" is frequently used in the Old Testament as a synonym for God's very presence, it denotes that presence always as a tangible holiness. In most of the texts which we have already noted above, the assertions of anthropomorphic or naturalist particularity in reference to God are made in conjunction with the qualifying terms of "glory" — the glory of God's visage, the glory of his power, the glory of his might, the glory of his throne room, the glory of his presence, of his coming and his going. None of this is formless, to be sure; as if to reassert, God *has* a face. But grasping that the face is "glorious," is glory itself, and it floods the form with the holiness that *does* in fact drive the features of that face into human ineffability, features of such beauty, of such purity, of such a brilliance and expanded shining as to undercut our very "seeing" itself. God's obscurity, in this light, is really a function of God's hyper-formliness.

Ezekiel's visions, which instance a drift into ineffability, mark that tension between sight and obscurity in just the terms of tangible glory that are scripturally normative. God's movement from, away, and back to the Temple in chapters 1, 10-11, and 43, although initially cast in bounded similitudes, becomes by the end clearly one of describable presence in encounter with human sin — glory within the world — that manifests its weight and substance, its form, as it embodies a relationship of personal judgment and grace towards Israel. The expressions of judgment and grace are predicated on the reality of God's glory as physical presence, however, and not the reverse.

This too is the implication of a text like Deuteronomy 4:15-24, which climaxes in the verse taken over in Hebrews 12:29 — "our God is a consuming fire" — but begins with the claim that the Israelites "saw no form" on Horeb when God spoke to them. The formlessness of God in our encounters with God depends on the "devouring" quality of God's presence, which is in fact the form of Glory in relationship with the unholy. To behold the form of God is to be judged. If this is so, formlessness is a kind of gift, a reprieve, a veiling of a form we cannot bear. Formlessness is a gift, but only secondarily so. The judgment itself presupposes a more fundamental formliness behind this grace.

This kind of negative grace is well-illustrated in a story recounted by Metropolitan Anthony Bloom in his short classic *Beginning to Pray*.[12]

> Many years ago a man came to see me. He asked me to show him God. I told him I could not, but I added that even if I could, he would not be able to see Him, because I thought — and I do think, — that, to meet God one must have something in common with Him, something that gives you eyes to see, perceptiveness to perceive.
>
> He asked me then why I thought as I did, and I suggested that he should think a few moments and tell me whether there was any passage in the Gospel that moved him particularly, to see what was the connection between him and God. He said, "Yes, in that chapter of the Gospel of John, the passage about the woman taken in adultery." I said, "Good, this is one of the most beautiful and moving passages. Now sit back and ask yourself,

---

12. Anthony Bloom, *Beginning to Pray* (New York: Paulist Press, 1970), pp. 3-4.

who are you in this scene from the Gospel? Are you the Lord, or at least on His side, full of mercy, of understanding and full of faith in this woman who can repent and become a new creature? Are you the woman taken in adultery? Are you one of the older men who walk out at once because they are aware of their own sins, or one of the young ones who wait?" He thought for a few minutes then said "No, I feel I am the only Jew who would not have walked out but who would have stoned the woman." I said "Thank God that He does not allow you to meet Him face to face."

Meeting God, looking at God, describing God as present is something on one level we *cannot* do, if our very being, mixed, distorted, unholy as it is, is not to wither in the shadow of the holy glory that marks the frame of our Maker. For to see God, to do what on a more basic level we *are* called to do — to love God even — is to have the very fibers of our existence, the very weave that holds together life as we know it and hold on to it, the inner fabric that we call "ourselves," turn in a flash to ash. The grace of obscurity and its concomitant ineffability is true grace, in this respect. But it is also an unfulfilled grace, existing as it does within the realm of the divine "forbearance," and not yet that of the divine manifestation of glory (cf. 2 Pet. 3:9).

Ineffability and formlessness, then, must be construed as a compromised adjustment to blasphemy and pain, their gracious accompaniment, but not their antidote or their alternative consummation. Lurking behind this entire sphere of human interaction with God lies the pulsating formliness of the divine life, intruding, holy, and describable for those with eyes to see. If God inserts within our apprehension his artifacts for our use, and ultimately for his, it seems as if God also inserts himself, somehow bound to the forms of artifactuality. And the impulsive presence of this formliness, comprehending as it does the failures of human vision, provides also its destiny, determines the outcome of human form, of human speech, and of the human receipt of grace. What is prior must also be what is ultimate (Rev. 1:8), even as it defines what now is. Thus, in securing the logical space of Christian claims within a dialogical framework, this encompassing formliness of glory must be affirmed and explicated, even as, in the Deuteronomic text to which we referred earlier, the formlessness of God was asserted within an interreligious framework decrying imagistic idolatry (cf. Deut. 4:19). But whereas the latter text speaks of a situation of limited grace — that is, historically, from within a dispensation of forbearance, still leading to fulfillment — the Christian claims are made with reference to the dynamic of fulfillment itself, of expansive and intrusive grace, of the outbreak of glory into its inherent self-disclosiveness of tangible presence.

IV. The Incarnation and Words of Glory

In fact, the central claim of Christianity is radically focused on just this consummating and enclosing appearance of glory, shaped by the conclusive grace that pushes forbearance into recreation. The opening of John's Gospel tells us that "no one has ever seen God" (1:18), a remark that questions the Old Testament anthropomorphic and particularist visions of God "face to face." But it is only a fundamental questioning if we ignore the purely circumstantial stretch aimed at by John's comment. (The phrase "no one shall see me and live" in Exodus 33:20 is likewise a statement explaining a circumstantial and dispensationally limited reality. It cannot, as we have seen, be understood to buttress the notion of prior ineffability.) The "fullness of time" (Gal. 4:4), which signals the assertion of the encompassing realm of glory, reaches into the world, instead, with the disruptive exposition of what was only typically evidenced in the Old Testament visions we examined: "God the Son, who is in the bosom of the Father, he has made God known" (John 1:18).

Two points about the incarnational redefinition of divine knowability need to be stressed here. First, the "knowing" to which John draws attention is explicitly the knowing of "description" (Greek: *exegesato*). John is probably echoing Sirach 43:31, where the author actually *questions* the possibility of "seeing" and "knowing" God. But to Sirach's question, John provides a resounding affirmative. The "knowing" of God to which he refers is not a cognitive understanding, but a literally descriptive retelling, based on vision, the recounting of what one has seen and touched. The Son, then, is the one who describes God and outlines the divine form and shape itself.

But second, the Son is also the one who is, in himself, preeminently divine describability in itself. He is divine embodiedness, which accurately posits the encompassing glory of God to human vision. "And the World became flesh, and dwelt among us, full of grace and truth, and we have beheld his glory, glory as of the only Son from the Father" (John 1:14). The describer is the described, inserting himself into the realm of human apprehension that is otherwise littered with the divine offerings of differentiated artifacts.

Before touching on the importance of this last equation, we must be clear on what level this descriptive identity is being asserted. Describability alone can exist within either sphere of limited and fulfilled dispensations, as we have seen. But in John's prologue and elsewhere in the New Testament, this describability is, just as in the Old Testament, linked to divine glory, and thus to the full presence of holiness itself. The very divine quality that undergirds necessary *judgment* also underlies the fact of the incarnation. They are one and the same holiness, the same glory, the same beginning and end of God. But they have, in the incarnation, dispensationally achieved a peak of visionary specificity.

"Behold, he is coming with the clouds and every eye will see him, every one who pierced him; and all tribes of the earth will wail on account of him. Even so. Amen" (Rev. 1:7). It is not so much that the glory in Christ will be revealed only in the future — and thus that the judgment of holiness is as yet unfinished — as it is the case that the glory that Christ has already been present and revealed and will consummate the judgment its proximity has already presumed (cf. John 3:19; cf. 12:31). That the world "knew him not" (John 1:10) is here not an affirmation of either unknowability or ineffability, but of their opposite, thrust into the midst of intransigent sin. The glory that lies as God's own being is who Christ is, historically enacted. This means that even the body of God will inhabit that space and be so clothed as to render the same movement of relation towards the wicked and the righteous as is described in, say, Psalm 97, when speaking of the transcendent God: God dwells in "darkness," yet is both fire to evil and light to the upright. The paradox of a blatant revelation in *chiaroscuro* is affirmed in the very historical reality that "all the peoples behold his glory" (Ps. 97:6). He *was* in the world — a historical moment in the incarnation that brings to the temporal top the fragrant cream suffused throughout the *eternal* comprehension of the world by God. Ineffability and invisibility is only the spitting out of such insistent and permanent richness, the flipside of historical particularism as it tastes of sin.

My loose use of the terms "ineffability" and "invisibility" up to now gains some new precision in the light of these observations, especially as they are read in conjunction with the Christian equation noted earlier between describer and described. That God's ineffability might depend on God's visibility, as a matter of logical priority, need not be an innovative or even insightful comment until cast in terms of the incarnational equation just mentioned. At such a point, the mere logical priority receives the weight and direction of an ontological dynamic. God is, historically, a speaker and is spoken of, because God does have a human body, if in a comprehensive fashion, one that bears the visible contours of the glory that moves to effulgence. Ineffability, on the other hand, can only be the reaction of resistance to such a dynamic of visible expression; invisibility can only be the blindness of willful revolt to such outpouring of tangible holiness; and human sin can only be the practical and explicit denial of particularistically divine corporeality. To say, as John does, that "the Word became flesh," "full of glory," which "we beheld" is to reformulate the notion of human speech about God into the shape of manifesting reference: in speaking God is visibly present. To be effable is to be seen; to speak is to make seen, and hence to enter into the dangerous realm of holiness. Within the realm of an unimpeded creaturely apprehension, all the senses are joined.

This, I believe, is an implication worth noting. It is made more explicit in John's first letter (1:1-4). Hearing, seeing, and touching the "word of life," the "eternal life which was with the Father and was made manifest," are all part of the one human response to receiving God's glory as the incarnate Lord Jesus. But this reception of a divine advent, initiated from above as it were, is only the first stage of what is meant by the incarnation. For if reception alone marked the terminus of the incarnation, then subsequent human speech about God could be judged according to criteria of *accuracy* in ostensive description only. It would be possible, then, to lay out the boundaries to the logical space of Christian speech about God only in terms of the *way* language refers, without embodying the form and character of the reference itself in the course of such explanation, and so too without touching upon the precincts where the war between God's holiness and creaturely profanity is waged. Christian speech, in such a case, could be uttered "neutrally," even safely.

But human reception does not, linguistically, mark the terminus of the incarnation of God. John tells us, instead, that "that which we have seen and heard we *proclaim* also to you (Greek: *epaggelomen*; cf. "we testify to it" — *martyroumen*, in verse 2), so that you may have fellowship (*koinonia*) with us; and our fellowship is with the Father and with his Son Jesus Christ. And we are writing this that our joy may be complete" (1 John 1:3-4). Reception here gives rise to proclamation and testimony about the visible word of God in Christ, life itself. And this event has as its goal the creation of *koinonia* — fellowship and union — between speaker and hearer. It constitutes the expansion of the union established between God and the believer into a joyful fulfillment that can include even the now unbelieving hearers. The incarnation has as its human terminus, linguistically, the embodiment of a divine mission, and the dynamic glorification of God in Christ through the widening envelopment of delight — all this, accomplished in the act of Christian speech itself. The talking itself is infused with the divine mission into the world.

The incarnation comprehends the glorification of God in the testimony of human speaking: to speak of God *delightfully*, as opposed to painfully and blasphemously, as opposed to destructively and consumingly, as opposed to ineffably and invisibly, is to launch out into the particularist motion of proclaiming witness, the glorifying pull towards fellowship and union, the descriptive apprehension of manifesting reference, the transformation of *ecce homo* into *ave verum corpus Dei*.

The intertwining destinies of delightful and glorifying speech together with objective anthropomorphic referential talk about God is critical according to this understanding of revelation. It is made historically and dynamically inevitable through the reality of the incarnation of God in the human flesh of the one person Jesus, the Christ. And that these two aspects of speech — glory and anthropomorphism — *are* intertwined historically, and in a comprehensive and not merely dispensational and developmental fashion, is also made inevitable by the incarnation of an eternal and transcendent God. For this God, the historical particularities of historical experience in Jesus are subsumed eternally and transcendentally by the positing of his glory. The momentary nature of the incarnation in history — its artifactual insertion — reflects the eternal nature of the incarnation, its identity as God's own creative being. In the incarnation, the specificity of divine glory reaches from "beyond" history into it, so that the artificer becomes the artifact itself: divine glory is specifically formly, as we saw, and its form is Jesus the Christ. The "body" of God in Christ, then, is God's body, and is thus prior to its historical or temporal apprehension in Jesus. "[You were ransomed] with the precious blood of Christ, in the fashion of a lamb without blemish or spot, apprehended in advance [RSV "destined"] before the foundation of the world, but made manifest at the end of time for your sake" (1 Pet. 1:19-20; cf. 2 Tim. 1:9; Rev. 13:5).

Some sense of the amazing scope of this twin destiny, in eternity, of language and the human form of God, is given in the opening chapters of the Letter to the Hebrews. The first two verses of the letter present the historical inequalities of speech about God as comprehended and surpassed by the human speech of Jesus: "In many and various ways God spoke of old to our fathers by the prophets; but in these last days he has spoken to us by a Son, whom he appointed the heir of all things." But the variety of the past, surpassed by the present of Christ's teaching, is more than an evolving progression over a graduated incline; it is more even than a leap from historical adequacy in partial revelation to some fuller disclosure. For the talk of Jesus is the talk of God from the beginning, just as the form of the incarnated Son is even God's form of glory: the Son, "by whom he also created the world[,] . . . reflects the glory of God and bears the very stamp of his nature." While the prophets described God, as they saw God, the Son describes God as the One who knows himself, whose words are the words of glory, that is, the very form of holiness manifested in presence. Yet, in this, the prophets describe God with the words of the Son himself.

And so, for the writer of the Hebrews, anthropocentrism becomes a form of theo-centrism. Most unexpectedly, in describing God's mission, the author leaps over the entire mediating realm of angels that might traditionally have been thought to lie, creatively, in between God and humanity.[13] Human salvation, for instance, is lifted up in contrast to the grave consequences of ignoring the "message" of the Son, the speech of the Incarnate One (2:1-4). But in doing this, the author reduces all the spiritual beings between God and humanity to the role of "deacons" to this humanitarian terminus. The glorious speech of God is human speech, not the angelic tongues referred to by Paul; its sphere of power is exclusively "salvific" in human terms — outside this sphere lies only a "just retribution"; and its enunciation is the very expression of God in the world's history as it unfolds for the establishment of an order beyond this material cosmos. The human speech of God encompasses the transcendent goal of history, then, even as humanity and its form is continuous, at least in visible and practical terms, with the shape of God as creative agent. "For surely it is not with angels that he is concerned, but with the descendants of Abraham" (2:16). "For it was not to angels that God subjected the world to come, of which we are speaking" (2:5). The form of humanity appears to be the very final cause of creation's ordering: "It has been testified somewhere, 'What is man that thou art mindful of him, or the son of man, that thou carest for him? Thou didst make him for a little while lower than the angels, thou hast crowned him with glory and honor, putting everything in subjection under his feet.' Now in putting everything in subjection to him, he left nothing outside his control" (2:6-8; RSV).

Of course, teleological anthropocentrism, within the realm of God's creative agency, is a claim well-nigh anathema to most modern theological concerns. But the principle here outlined gains its force not so much because of some human presumption to divine favor, but through a reviewing of God's purpose from this side of the incarnation. "As it is, we do not yet see everything in subjection to him. But we see Jesus, who for a little while was made lower than the angels, crowned with glory and honor because of the suffering of death, so that by the grace of God he might taste death for everyone" (vv. 8-9). "Having one origin" with human beings, "sharing" in their "flesh and blood," "partaking" of the "same nature" — that is, being in the *koinonia* to which John refers as the terminus of Christian speech — Jesus Christ has revealed humanity to be the comprehended form of God's movement through history into eternity. And the glory that is Christ's form glistens as the advancing reformulation of human constitution — by grace, through suffering, in this earth. Not only do we "see Jesus," but we "consider Jesus," as the "apostle and high priest of our confession" (3:1; cf. 4:14; 10:23),

---

13. Gregory Palamas will make the same kind of move in transforming Pseudo-Dionysius.

182

the one who projectively establishes our speech about God within the space of holiness, within the embrace of glory, within the manifested survival of expanding fellowship between God and humankind, living in the visionary presence of God.

This extended walk through some of the New Testament witnesses to the incarnation points us clearly, I think, in the direction I laid out earlier, as we considered the aspects of glorification and blasphemy in human speech about God from a Christian perspective. All of our talk, from the Old Testament through to the New Testament and the Christian church, is transferred from the dominion of darkness (invisibility and ineffability) into the kingdom of God's beloved Son, because of the full indwelling of God in Christ Jesus, before, in, and to the end of creation (cf. Col. 1:13-20). This movement of transferal is at the core of God's life, and because of it revelation is possible — the *vision* of God is possible — and the visionary glory of the spoken word about God is rendered truthful in holiness and effective in enunciation. Georges Florovsky sums this up in a passage from his compactly illuminating essay on "The Holy Spirit in Revelation":

> God descends to man, shows His Face to man, speaks to him. And man sees God, is lost in the vision of God, and describes what he has seen and heard, becoming witness to what has been revealed to him. Therein lies the significance of the Old Testament Divine visions, of the Old Testament Revelation. In them there is a certain essential anthropomorphism, and this is not so much because of the weakness of human understanding, or from a sense of "adaptability," but as a foretaste of the coming incarnation. It is already in the Old Testament that the Divine Word becomes human, is incarnated in the human tongue. . . .
>
> What is human is not suppressed or swept away by Divine inspiration; it is only transfigured. . . . Now *too* the Word of God is to be heard in the Bible, and now through this eternal, eternally living book, God's Revelation *continues* coming down to us. It is therein that the mystery of the Bible consists; this is the mystery of the inspired, transfigured, transubstantiated word.[14]

This is the world seen in its divine usage, "according to the Scriptures." And this Christian word is always alive, always witnessing, always descriptive of the glorious presence of God's features in the world, struck into the

---

14. Georges Florovsky, "The Holy Spirit in Revelation," *The Christian East* 13:2 (1932): 49-64; 51, 54.

flesh by Jesus, and rendered into a vital light by the transformative power of holiness.

V. Metaphor, Analogy, and the Linguistic Veiling of Glory

Anyone familiar with Thomas Aquinas's views on anthropomorphic language about God would readily note the antithesis Florovsky's definition above proposes. And here we can take up our concern over the more recent turn to Thomistic analogical predication as an appropriate means of securing the logical space of Christian claims in our more pluralistic and sometimes dialogical framework.[15] It is a turn clearly attractive to particularist apologists for the Christian faith because of the promise it provides for buttressing universal claims within a larger agnostic universe, one in which dialogical relationships with other religions or even with non-theists must thereby seem normative rather than peculiarly motivated. Universal claims, under this set of rubrics, are permissible, but they cannot be insistently applied since they are always only vaguely bounded. Analogical speech is a way of talking particularistically, even within a universal reach, that is always non-threatening. The turn to analogical predication allows for this since it is founded on the conviction that the true being of God is beyond worldly, let alone purely material, apprehension. And this would include especially images based on corporeal reference. What David Burrell calls "the Distinction" (borrowing from Robert Sokolowski's phrase "the Christian distinction"), the unconnectedness between the transcendent God and creation, a divide across which human understanding, let alone speech, cannot pass with lively certainty, demands that any verbal reference we make to God be formulated in ways that are not univocal to their

15. This is the approach, for instance, that DiNoia takes. But it is followed by many others, e.g Gregory Rocca, *Speaking the Incomprehensible God*, whose extensive treatment of Thomas owes a great deal to David Burrell (see below), and to the earlier work of Ralph McInerny, i.e. his seminal *The Logic of Analogy: An Interpretation of St. Thomas* (The Hague: Martinus Nijhoff, 1961). The topic itself forms a central part of the debate over the "turn" in theological metaphysics in the 14th century, referred to in the last chapter. The question of whether Thomas himself held to a notion of analogy that involved participatory causality from God's side is debated. For this debate, pro and con, see the contributions to Thomas Joseph White, *The Analogy of Being: Invention of the Antichrist Or the Wisdom of God?* (Grand Rapids: Eerdmans, 2011). On more recent scholarly discussions, see E. J. Ashworth, *Les théories de l'analogie du XIIe au XVIe siècle* (Paris: Vrin, 2008). A clear outline of some of the implications of this approach is given by Robert Masson, "The Force of Analogy," *Anglican Theological Review* 87:3 (Summer 2005): 471-86, who presents the analogy as a metaphoric enterprise in a strong sense of opening up "new fields of meaning" across the divide of equivocal semantics.

normal usage in human interaction. Metaphor, and analogy as, arguably, a particular form of metaphor, is the manner in which Thomas and modern followers of Thomas seek to speak meaningfully about a God who stands on the other side of created and composite being, yet with which we have to do, and indeed with whom we are in a fundamental relation.

What is a metaphor and how does it differ from analogy as we use each figure to speak of God? In 1:9 of his *Summa Theologiae*, Thomas gives at least three particular reasons why the Holy Scriptures might employ "bodily" figures or metaphors for divine referents. The first reason is based on the "distinction" noted above: "God provides for all things according to the kind of things they are. Now we are of the kind to reach the world of intelligence through the world of sense." He quotes Dionysius here, who writes that "the divine rays cannot enlighten us except wrapped up in many sacred veils."[16] The limitations of human reason and experience, then, demand that the intelligibility of divine communication be operative in corporeal, material form. But these are only *figures*, "adapted" to our incapacities, in Florovsky's negative formulation.

The second reason given for corporeal figures of speech in the Bible is that this figurative "disguise" to God's objective referentiality, as Thomas calls it, is in its very evident incongruity a sign to us of God's transcendence, of the gap between God and creaturely speech and understanding. "For in this life what [God] is not is clearer to us than what he is; and therefore from the likeness of things farthest removed from him we can more fairly estimate how far above our speech and thought he is" (ad 3). The "crudeness" of anthropomorphic or corporeal figures for God is in itself a warning to us that we *cannot* describe God accurately, that we *cannot* understand or apprehend his features or his form — or even think such qualitative aspects are attributable to him absolutely.

There is a third reason Thomas gives for the legitimate and non-literal use of bodily metaphor in our language about God, and this is perhaps the most striking. Drawing on the kind of apophatic distancing and mystagogical layering employed by Dionysius, Thomas tells us that figurative speech is a kind of sacred *protective* shield for divine realities from the unholy gaze of profaners. It is "a defense against unbelievers ready to ridicule — to these the text refers, 'Give not that which is holy to the dogs' (Matt. 7:6)." When figurative speech is so used, "divine matters are more effectively screened against those unworthy of them" (ad 3). Here, more even than in the two reasons given above, Thomas shows how his own understanding of anthropomorphism, or

16. All references to Thomas's *Summa Theologiae* are taken from *Summa Theologiae Ia qq. 1-13*, ed. T. Gilby (Garden City, NY: Image-Doubleday, 1969).

linguistic formalism as a kind of indirect reference, goes counter to the incarnational centering of Christian speech as we elaborated it above. Tangible reference, for Thomas — metaphor — is a check *against* blasphemy and pain, rather than their potential opening through making glory present, through being the living embodiment of glory's propinquity.

What of analogy itself? If analogy is in fact a form of metaphor, as Thomas uses the term generally, then it will be clear how a contemporary particularist scheme of analogical predication like DiNoia's lies on the same protective, as opposed to disclosive and visionary, foundation as we have just noted in Thomas's treatment of anthropomorphic or figurative language. On the one hand, Thomas's discussion of metaphor in relation to the name "God" (Ia 13:9, especially response and ad 3) might lead us to assume that analogy is indeed dependent on the figurative structure and purpose of signification. "Divine" or "godly," like "wise" or "good," says Thomas, are applied to creatures analogically or metaphorically, in a way that seems to suggest that these two terms be equated. On the other hand, in 13:6 Thomas distinguishes between a metaphorical and an analogical use of certain predicates for God. Metaphorical expressions, he says, "apply primarily to creatures and secondarily to God," while for analogical expressions the order is reversed: they apply primarily to God and only secondarily to creatures. This is the case, for instance, in the use of perfective attributes for God, which are only secondarily and derivatively applied to creatures, according to a quasi-Neoplatonic metaphysic of participation. Can we resolve these two ways of relating metaphor and analogy by Thomas? My own feeling is that, while distinguishing the two is important for Thomas in that it helps rule out the primary application of anthropomorphic attributes to God, for instance, the distinction between metaphor and analogy in itself carries no effective cognitive weight. Whether divine attributions are understood metaphorically or analogically, our actual ability to know what the attributes *mean* when applied to God is nullified in either case by the divine transcendence. It is simply impossible to render God's simplicity in language.

DiNoia, for his part, is correct to distinguish Thomistic analogy from metaphor understood as "non-discursive" or "evocative" symbolization.[17] But this is not Thomas's understanding of metaphor. My point is to emphasize that, in Thomas's own terms, "metaphoric" language (which includes anthropomorphic reference) is functionally a larger category between univocal and equivocal reference that is comparable to his general description of analogy in these terms (cf. 13:5). DiNoia is also correct to stress the fact that Thomas's view of analogy attempts to secure a "straightforward reading of utterances which

---

17. DiNoia, *Diversity of Religions*, p. 196.

have the form of affirmative predications."[18] But my point is to emphasize that the limitations Thomas places on the "literal" reading demanded by analogical predication, which purport to be in contrast to "metaphorical" predication (cf. 13:3), are really such as to render *both* forms of predication similarly restrictive of cognitive and objective content.

Another way of getting at this problem is to examine the celebrated distinction Thomas makes between the *res significata* and the *modus significandi* in our predications of God.[19] In 13:3, respectively, Thomas writes about analogical predications of perfections applied to God as follows:

> We understand such perfections, however, as we find them in creatures, and as we understand them so we use words to speak of them. We have to consider two things, therefore, in the words we use to attribute perfections to God, firstly the perfections themselves that are signified [i.e. the *res significatae*] — goodness, life, and the like — and secondly the way in which they are signified [i.e. the *modus significandi*]. So far as the perfections signified are concerned, the words are used literally of God, and in fact more appropriately than they are used of creatures, for these perfections belong primarily to God and only secondarily to others. But so far as the way of signifying these perfections is concerned, the words are used inappropriately, for they have a way of signifying that is appropriate to creatures.

Is not Burrell accurate in summarizing Thomas' protective intentions here, by really *inverting* the distinction between the appropriateness of applying the predicate to God, and the inappropriateness of the way we apply it? "We can then use such an [analogous] expression of God without pretending to grasp his manner of realizing it. For we can appreciate that we do not understand what it is [i.e. the *res significata*] as God realizes it."[20] Thomas wants to assure us that we know what "it" is, since we know it as applied to creatures. But if we cannot know the *manner* of applying "it" to God, do we really know what "it" is at all? In fact, the method of analogical predication is much clearer on the issue of this "manner" of application than it is on the "what" that is actually applied to God: the *modus significandi* based on the negative reformulations of creaturely attributes governed by ontological divine traits like God's simplicity. The philosopher Frederick Ferré draws a similar conclusion about the "logic

18. DiNoia, *Diversity of Religions*, p. 201.

19. Cf. DiNoia's explication of the usefulness of this distinction on p. 198; also Burrell, in *Exercises in Religious Understanding* (Notre Dame, IN: University of Notre Dame, 1974), pp. 129-31.

20. Burrell, *Exercises*, p. 133.

of analogy" in our language about God: rather than providing clear referents in its use, analogy functions "by explicating *rules* limiting the use of words drawn from ordinary non-theological contexts in formulae containing the word 'God' (where 'God' entails such words as 'infinite' and 'transcendent')."[21]

Just here, contemporary particularists may be right in thinking that a scheme of predication whose objective content is more a set of "rules" for talking than a vision of God, is appropriate to an interreligious dialogical context. They may be right, however, for reasons opposite to those that purportedly motivate our modern concerns for dialogue in the first place. Protective strategies, like Thomistic analogy are, as I have indicated, designed to *shield* "divine matters" — the objective referents of Christian religious talk — from unholy or "unworthy" apprehension. And this may indeed be required in a religiously pluralistic or secular cultre. It is not, however, what most Christian apologists, dialogists, or just plain evangelists claim for what they do. It is rather hard to see, I would imagine, what kind of "knowledge" may be gained about Christian claims when they are cloaked in such protective garments.

It may even be misleading to think that Thomistic analogy goes further in its referential claims than comparable attempts to map our predicational logic for talk about God among Jewish and Muslim thinkers.[22] In fact, Muslim traditionalists like Ibn Hanbal and later disciples like Al Ash'ari made similar use of the *res significata* and *modus significandi* distinction in efforts to apply "literal" predications to God.[23] This theological similarity has been obscured in the past by the crude assumption that Muslim traditionalists employed "anthropomorphic" predications to God in a literal fashion that Thomas could never do. In reality, when features like "face" or "hand" are applied to God "literally" as Ibn Hanbal insisted they be (since they were so applied in the Qur'an), the objective meaning of such predication was immediately undercut and obscured when, again as the Hanbalites and Asharites insisted, it was emphasized that we could never know the *modus significandi* of their application, the "how" (Arabic: *bila kaifa*). Islamic anthropomorphism, on closer view, is perfectly congruent with the logic of analogy, and can even occupy quite nicely

21. Frederick Ferré, *Language, Logic, and God* (Chicago: University of Chicago Press, 1961), p. 76.

22. Cf. Burrell's treatment of Maimonides, Avicenna, and Aquinas on this score, in *Knowing the Unknowable God: Ibn-Sina, Maimonides, Aquinas* (Notre Dame, IN: University of Notre Dame Press, 1987), especially c. 4.

23. Cf. Michel Allard, *Le Problème des attributs divins dans la doctrine d'al-As'ari de ses premiers grands disciples* (Beyrouth: Imprimerie Catholique, 1965), cc. 2-3; A. J. Wesninck, *The Muslim Creed: Its Genesis and Historical Development* (Cambridge: Cambridge University Press, 1932), c. 8.

the same logical space as most Christian claims about God made within the bounds Christian analogical particularists uphold.

The crucial aspect, therefore, of Christian distinctiveness in language about God is, as I have been arguing, to be found in the incarnational reality that undergirds all Christian speech, the words themselves, their very possibility, their effective force. And it is just this incarnational context and foundation that Thomist analogists often leave out from the picture. Thomas *does* differentiate the status of the purely philosophical logic of God and that of the logic of belief — *sacra doctrina* — but his treatment of analogy is not defined by this contrast. The "rules" for our use of language about God apply with equal force whether we are working our way through the "preambles" of the faith on the basis of natural reason, or whether we are analyzing the witness of Sacred Scripture. Similarly, someone like DiNoia presents his exposition of the way to secure logical space for Christian claims on the basis of a method — Thomas's — that makes no reference to the incarnation as the source of *all* Christian language about God. And without such an incarnational basis, the Christian "space" for speech can provide little that contradicts, for example, either Jewish or Muslim affirmations limiting the objective meaningfulness of anthropomorphic language. The consequence of this inability is precisely to render any subsequent affirmation of the incarnational reference nonsensical and impossible.[24]

VI. The Incarnational Synecdoche

If we were to attempt an alternative characterization of Christian language, it must begin with the incarnational presence permeating its affirmations. Drawing on a schema made current by the critic Kenneth Burke, we would have to claim for Christian language a broadly *synecdochic* character, as opposed to a metaphorical one.[25] Synecdoche is normally understood as a linguistic figure wherein the part stands for the whole, or where the whole is represented in some part which it comprehends. In the Christian context of which Burke speaks, and which I would adopt, it is the verbal expression of what the incarnation of God in human flesh manifests ontologically in apprehended history. Analogy as a limiting protective trope that properly describes the figural

24. This has been pointed out, for instance, by David Shapiro, in *"Possibile Deus-Homo?"* *Judaism* 32:3 (Summer, 1983): 358-65.

25. Cf. Kenneth Burke, "Four Master Tropes," in *A Grammar of Motives* (New York: Prentice-Hall, 1945), especially pp. 507-11.

character of concrete descriptions of God would be ruled out in this scheme, because it simply does not say enough, and indeed fails to say what should be said about the words of Scripture.[26] I have in fact used the term "synecdoche" in Chapter 2 as an indicator of a traditional Patristic approach — Basil in particular — to human descriptors of God in Scripture.[27] The human body of God in Christ, eternally expressive of God's glorious being, makes of our anthropomorphic and bodily language about God the "two-way" or "reversible" path of continuous inter-reference that Burke identifies as peculiar to synecdoche: the language of the human body *is* the language of God. Christian language is a "representation" of God (and "representation" is Burke's definition of synecdochic function). Christian language is an embodiment of the glory of the embodied Word who is Jesus. This synecdochic character of Christian language, as indeed of all Christian representation, has as its center the truth of the incarnation, which establishes Christian communication as a necessary and objectifying — glorifying — witness in every aspect of its enunciation.

The synecdoche of microcosm/macrocosm, which Burke calls the "noblest synecdoche, the perfect paradigm or prototype for all lesser usages," is, as it turns out, the image used by Christian thinkers who have pursued the synecdochic nature of Christian speech most persistently, especially in the Eastern Orthodox tradition deriving from Irenaeus and Gregory of Nyssa.[28] It is one, furthermore, that depends on reconceptualizing temporality itself in some fashion, as we indicated in Chapter 3, so that the incarnation itself is no longer exhaustively explained in terms of a single insertion point in time.[29] What Lars

26. The *analogia entis*, however, might possibly be construed in synecdochic terms.

27. Luther made explicit use of the term, in ways that moved beyond the rhetorical, in trying to describe the referential meaning of the Lord's Supper, with respect to the relation of "this is my body/blood" and the elements themselves, the latter of which stand as a "synecdoche" of the former. See, for example, his *Confession Concerning Christ's Supper* (1528), in *Luther's Works* (American Edition), vol. 37, ed. Hilton C. Oswald and Helmut T. Lehman (St. Louis: Concordia, 1976), pp. 301-3, 330. Calvin, by contrast, was self-consciously cautious in refusing to make this kind of connection. His own reliance on a theology of "analogy," instead, was deeply protective in its motive. See Randall C. Zachmann, *John Calvin as Teacher, Pastor, and Theologian: The Shape of His Writings and Thought* (Grand Rapids: Baker Academic, 2006), pp. 209-29.

28. Cf. Pelikan, *Imago Dei: The Byzantine Apologia for Icons* (Princeton, NJ: Princeton University Press, 1990), pp. 172-74.

29. Maintaining a temporal scheme of exclusive serial insertion points or instants obviously creates all kinds of difficulty for outlining the divine implications of the Chalcedonian definition. Cf., as an example, the Puritan Thomas Goodwin's remarkable treatise on "The Heart of Christ in Heaven," which, on the one hand, seeks a way to engage Jesus' dispositions of affection and compassion for sinners as a divine and eternal character, yet on the other must in some way make it seem as if God, at a certain point in time, *became* compassionate

Thunberg calls the "theandric universe" of Maximus the Confessor, for example, is an instance of the application of incarnational metaphysics to the question of Christian speech (among other things). Maximus's thought proceeds from a grasp of the anthropomorphic expression of God's being centered in the unifying and creative dynamic of the God-Man, who holds together the universe according to Colossians 1:17.[30] As we saw in our examination of the Letter to the Hebrews, the assertion of some special place for humanity in the created universe, one which overleaps even the mediating realm of angels, is less the product of a prior anthropocentrism as it is the derivation of an incarnational articulation of God's glory in the Son. Incarnational synecdoche for Maximus means primarily that the cosmos is ordered in terms of glory, structured always (barring the impediments of sin) according to God's will "to effect the mystery of his embodiment [Gr. *ensomatosis*] in the world."[31]

Moving outwards from this foundational dynamic of embodiment, apprehended in the historical incarnation in Jesus, Maximus distinguishes a triple *ensomatosis* in creation, Scripture, and human form (via the *imago Dei*), in a manner reminiscent of Origen. The Word (*Logos*) is embodied as the enlivening principle of being (the *logoi*) for members of each of these three spheres, manifesting visibly the power of God coming forth to be met. Not only do the words of Scripture, then, refer in a purely semiotic fashion to the divine objects, but their referents are actually present in their form as apprehended meaning. The Word is present as Life within the words, for the Word is the Word as it is the enfleshed Word.

According to this perspective, the incarnational origin and motor of linguistic symbolization in Christian speech remains paramount. The symbols have no inherent power in themselves, or in some constituted human cognitive apparatus of reception, to convey the presence of God *except* insofar as the Incarnate One, Jesus Christ, is present as the one speaking and receiving his

---

in this way in contrast to his previous form of mercy. That is, Goodwin inadvertently raises up an Old Testament-New Testament contrast in God's character that is explicitly analyzed in terms of two different kinds of scriptural linguistic signification: in the Old Testament, divine attributes are explained "metaphorically," in the New Testament, because of the incarnation, they now apply "really." See Thomas Goodwin, *Christ set forth in his death, resurrection, ascension, sitting at Gods right hand, intercession, as the cause of justification. Object of justifying faith. Upon Rom. 8. ver. 34. Together with a treatise discovering the affectionate tendernesse of Christs heart now in heaven, unto sinners on earth* (London: Robert Dawlman, 1642), pp. 111-33 of the second treatise.

30. Cf. Lars Thunberg, *Man and the Cosmos: The Vision of St. Maximus the Confessor* (Crestwood, NY: St. Vladimir's Seminary Press, 1985), c. 4.

31. Thunberg, *Man and the Cosmos*, p. 75.

word in us.[32] As Florovsky points out in his treatment of the Egyptian anthropomorphites with which we began this discussion, the theological conflict surrounding their referential speech was not so much over the use of words in themselves, as over the reach of the incarnation's glorious manifestation in creation, in particular in the Image of God.[33] If the incarnation of the Word is prior and creatively synecdochic, then divine form is apprehended even in human form today, in flesh and word.

To be sure, the issue of the incarnate character of Christ, which holds together both human and divine "natures," cannot be easily resolved in this framework, and it constitutes one of the nagging problems of the anthropomorphite controversy: is the "actual" uncreated divine nature describable? Eastern Orthodoxy after Maximus certainly continued to struggle with the synecdochic nature of Christian language in just these terms. The character of the incarnational basis of all divine synecdoche, for instance, was brought to a new clarity in the fight against iconoclasm. But Dionysian apophatism, and the protective strategies of linguistic veiling it entailed, continued to bedevil efforts, as in the West, to gain a clearer notion of how our language can and does refer to God in the church's use.[34] Only with Gregory Palamas was a sufficiently cogent formulation given of God's glory as embodied presence, even in symbolic shape. To be sure, Gregory himself seems to have given little attention to the specific problem of linguistic reference, and it would not be fair to attribute to him the specific view of synecdochic reference I am presenting here. But the implications of his vision of "natural" symbolization and the uncreated divine energies can, I think, be reasonably extrapolated so as to give warrant for my perspective.

Gregory's thought remains bound to the Dionysian tradition to the extent

32. This certainly differs in focus from claims that would posit some kind of fundamental created bridge to the symbolic apprehension of God, although it need not do so in theory, if one grants creation's location as a logical outcome of God's incarnation in Christ. Cf. Louis Dupré's contention that the human mind is constitutively and selectively symbolic "by nature," and that universal — i.e. non-particularistically Christian — symbols can convey the presence of God universally, in "Negative Theology and Affirmation of the Finite," in *Experience, Reason, and God*, ed. Eugene T. Long (Washington, DC: The Catholic University Press, 1980), pp. 156-57.

33. Florovsky, *Aspects of Church History*, pp. 95-96, 126.

34. Cf. John of Damascus's surprisingly narrow treatment of linguistic symbols in his *Third Oration on Images*, c. 21 (see *P. G.*, vol. 94, col. 1342; see the translation in John of Damascus, *On the Divine Images: Three Apologies Against Those Who Attack the Divine Images*, trans. D. Anderson (Crestwood, NY: St. Vladimir's Seminary Press, 1980); cf. too Pelikan's contradictory review of this material in *Imago Dei*, pp. 179ff., where an unworkable attempt is made to bring verbal images into similitude with visual icons on the basis of iconodule theology.

that he will still err on the side of caution when it comes to discussing the *manner* of God's visible apprehension. In his debate with even more radical Dionysians like Barlaam, he sought to claim the Areopagite's mantle for his beleaguered hesychast brethren, by stressing the non-corporeal nature of God's describability: "intelligible," but "invisible," he insists; "spiritually" perceived, but never "sensible."[35] It might seem that the kind of "spiritual" apprehension of God to which Gregory refers is as poorly ostensive and objective as any ana-logical referent. But, in fact, Gregory pushes apophatism, quite legitimately, to a level of negation that allows for the true manifestation of God in "antinomy," a disclosive paradox.[36] While God may be "beyond all affirmation," he writes, God is *also* "beyond all negation." The "more-than-divine" (Gk. *Hypertheos*) that is God, in relation to the human mind's logical conception of God, can and does come to human beings, as a "light," says Gregory, which "the saints themselves say — for they know by experience — exists. This existence is not symbolic, as if caused by some passing fancy. Rather, this light is the imma-terial and divine effulgence, the invisibly visible and incomprehensibly com-prehended grace grasped by the spirit."[37]

The use of these deliberately paradoxical, or even antinomic expressions — "invisibly visible," "incomprehensibly comprehended" — is obviously meant to distinguish the kind of apprehension of God that is possible and real for the Christian from the apprehension of created artifacts. And the stress upon the Creator-creature distinction can rightly, in some circumstances, be couched in apophatic terms. The distinction, finally, between figural appre-hension of Scripture's meaning is also rightly given in the same way, since it is an expression of the same reality: the unseen God makes himself seen; the God beyond speech speaks and is heard. The miraculous character of this is grasped as a figure. Figural readings, applied to God's own being, are given precisely because, by miraculous grace, God shows himself to us in Christ; and this showing, though beyond all showings, is yet real, such that the words that describe these disclosures describe them directly and truly, *insofar as they are indeed God's words*, doing the work of God as God would have it done; that is, insofar as they are Scripture. At the same time, the "spiritual" meaning of Scripture, given to those who are spiritual only by the Spirit (cf. 1

35. Gregory of Palamas, *Triads*, 11:3-8. I will use the enumeration of Gregory's *Triads* given in *Grégoire Palamas, Défense des saints hésychastes* [Triads], trans. in French by Jean Meyendorff (Louvain: Peeters, 1959), 2 volumes.

36. We will return to the question of antinomy in our next chapter.

37. Gregory, *Triads*, 11:3-8. John of Damascus, in fact, says something similar when he discusses what exactly it is that the writers of Scripture "saw" or understood of God as they used the expressions they did; see Oration III. C. 21.

Cor. 2:14-16; 2 Cor. 3:16-18), expresses the distance and humanly ungraspable character of this reading, its divine origins and humanly unordered form, whose use can only be enjoyed as a gift from him who first uses. That is its "apophatic" nature, in that it does not derive from a human speaking, but from a divine source of utterance.

It is no more than common sense to admit that God's objective presence is not the same as a tree's. But having admitted this, one has learned little, and forfeited much, if one somehow concludes therefore that God's presence is *less* immediate and objective than the tree's. It can only be *more* so, and in this sense, its presence comprehends the immediacy of physical proximity, even as it surpasses it, and transforms it. In the paragraph immediately following the one quoted above, Gregory goes on to point out how the non-symbolic light that is God can be present to individuals, bodily identified, in different ways: by bringing them, as it were, *out* of their physical space (e.g. Paul's Third Heaven experiences), by transforming their bodies themselves into a light (e.g. Moses, coming down from the mountain, and Stephen at his stoning), even by "becoming accessible to corporeal vision" and "hearing." Quoting Gregory Nazianzus, he describes how the "invisible and impenetrable" energy of light that is God comes into the world and "becomes, to a certain degree, penetrable by created nature." It is important to see that here he goes far beyond the protective framework of figural speech, and rather tries to appropriate such speech as something concretely epiphanic of the truth, even more so than simple material referentiality.

We might linger here on Gregory's notorious "real distinction" between God's essence and God's energies, the former of which remains inaccessible to us, the latter of which is the "penetrated" nature of God, but both of which are wholly and unreservedly God.[38] For our purposes, however, all that we need to

---

38. On the "innovating" — taken negatively — character of this Palamite distinction, in contrast with Thomism and even other Eastern theologies, cf. Journet, "Palamisme et Thomisme," *Revue Thomiste* 60 (1960): 446. But this judgment has been challenged, rightly or wrongly. See the work of Anna Williams, *Ground of Union: Deification in Aquinas and Palamas* (Oxford: Oxford University Press, 1999); and Édouard Divry, *La transfiguration selon l'orient et l'occident: Grégoire Palamas, Thomas d'Aquin: vers un dénoument oecuménique* (Paris: Téqui, 2009). A treatment of deification in its own right would engage Maximus far more centrally, but that is not my concern; I only wish to indicate possible ways of construing scriptural language within the contextual continuity of East and West. But see Norman Russell, *The Doctrine of Deification in the Greek Patristic Tradition* (Oxford: Oxford University Press, 2005). Making use of Maximus, rather than Gregory, Antoine Lévy has argued for a much closer convergence between East and West, articulated from distinct vantage points regarding God's relation to the creature; see his *Le crée et l'incrée. Maxime le Confesseur et Thomas d'Aquin* (Paris: Vrin, 2006). The issue for Lévy has to do with broader ontological questions than my

gauge is how the antinomically objective presence of God, even to corporeal apprehension, is really, for Gregory, a way of drawing the ontologically historical conclusion of the reality of the incarnation. The notion of manifested divine energy, distinct from hidden essence yet still wholly God, and the notion of the incarnation of Christ Jesus in time — a person handled and seen — are synecdochically related in a metaphysical fashion. Furthermore, the subsuming outflow of glory on which both claims are founded, encompasses our own human activities of apprehension — we see what God gives us to see, and as we take hold of this sight we use it — we are drawn into the Scripture-ordering reality of God's own temporal usage, which constitutes the "world" that God has created, and in which we live. The noteworthy text from the *Triads* deserves quotation in full here, insofar as it understands "spiritual" apprehension to be comprehensive, synecdochically, of corporeal apprehension:[39]

> Since the Son of God, in his incomparable love for men, did not only unite his divine hypostasis to our nature by putting on an animated body and a soul endowed with intelligence, in order to appear on earth and live among men, but since he also united himself to the human hypostases themselves, in mingling himself with each faithful by communion with his holy body, and since he becomes one body with us [*syssomos hemin ginetai*] and makes us a temple of the whole divinity — for in the very body of Christ "dwells corporately all the fullness of the divinity" (Col 2:9) — how should he not illuminate those who worthily communicate with the divine ray of his body which is within us, lightening their soul, as he illumined the very bodies of the disciples on Thabor? For then that body, source of the light of grace, was not yet united to our bodies; it illumined from without those who worthily approached it and sent the illumination to the soul by the intermediary of the eyes of the senses; but today it is mingled with us and exists in us, it illuminates the soul from within.

The con-corporeality (*syssomosis*) that God creates with human beings in the body of Christ is that synecdochic link through which the apprehension and communication of the divine glory is made — this *is* God's glory as it does its work in the world. Insofar as this link exists, established in the incarnation of God in Jesus Christ, human symbolization of divine describability is radi-

---

own; and in fact, it is perhaps only by moving in this direction that some of the differences on the matter of linguistic signification seem to fade; but that may actually mask some of the issues I am trying to engage.

39. *Triads* I:3:38; the English translation is given in Meyendorff, *Christ in Eastern Christian Thought* (Washington, DC: Corpus Books, 1969), p. 159.

cally transformed. Gregory stands within an Eastern tradition of biblical exegesis for which the "spiritual" sense of Scripture tended to be prominent, if not preeminent. But as Meyendorff has shown, even as he respectfully endorses such metaphorical reading, Gregory drastically reorients the interpretive project towards trenchantly realist exegesis: the figure is not a reminder of or indicative of the truth, it is the form of God's creating power itself.[40] It is that power drawn close, the distance shrunk. And this he does solely on the basis of the incarnational presence. "The body of Christ is truly the Body of God and not a symbol," Gregory writes; and although Christ himself can be seen as a "symbol, he is so only to the degree that he manifests himself" (i.e. to the degree that he is a symbol of himself, as a literal and self-presenting sign). Elsewhere in Scripture, metaphorical readings are allowed only by "homonym," that is, by direct transferal of meaning according to the application of the same name (e.g. "God is a consuming fire" could be read as the "fire of judgment" against sinners, as long as "fire" is taken literally in each case). This is itself a form of realism, which limits more loosely evocative interpretation. And even here, homonymic metaphor always presumes the objective and historical-temporal referents of the original names.

When it comes to particular referents, however, like the Thaboric light, Gregory presses into use a notion of "natural symbol" in which the sign not only "stands for" something, but is synecdochically linked to the *presence* of this referent. The "light" on Thabor seen by the apostles at the Transfiguration is the glory of God, not a scriptural sign given to us merely for a cognitive understanding of that glory's promise in the eschaton. More than this, although Gregory's view of the realist and naturalist symbolization functions mainly to defend the objective referent of the Thaboric light grasped by the hesychast at prayer, it is defensible to push his synecdochic incarnationalism into the broad range of Christian speech in the same way he applies it in a limited fashion to liturgical speech in the Eucharist. This is just the direction the Palamite theology, as it spread through the modern Orthodox tradition, will take it. Florovsky develops his ideas about Christian revelation, Scripture, and theology — about Christian speech as a whole — in this current, as do many others. And it accounts for the vitalist character such speech seems to have for the tradition. Florovsky, long before the phrase became popular, describes the Gospels as "verbal icons"; they are "narrative" or "historical images," which present the contours of the face of the living God "through the demonstration of the spirit and of power"; they contain and give rise to witness and to the building up of

---

40. Meyendorff, *Introduction à l'étude de Grégoire Palamas* (Paris: Éditions du Seuil, 1959), pt. 2, c. 4, especially pp. 266-73.

the church, to the spreading of God's vision and body, to the glorification of God's being in the world.[41] We should be clear that there is no claim being made here that God has a "material" body in some kind of way that is univocal to our own material forms. The logical concerns of some theologians of analogy are rightly brought to bear here. But just this discontinuous "distinction" between the Creator and his creatures permits the incomprehensible self-giving of God in a material form that is in fact "true" to take place, "in accordance with the Scriptures" and only in such accordance.[42] Permeated by the word, history is held together, given its impetus and direction, by the synecdochic web of utterable divine features to which Christian speech gives voice in mimetic fashion.

VII. The Evangelical Context of Delightful Speech

If the incarnational synecdoche of glory is indeed accepted as the "logical space" for Christian claims, then it seems to me that attempts to maintain dialogical particularity in a non-exclusivist tenor must founder. That is part of the practical linkage between figural reading and, as it were, the shape of the world we live in as diverse human beings. For not only will the Christian in dialogue be making particularist claims of universal scope, but the very character of the language she or he uses in so doing embodies the glory of the Lord, the witness of Christ. Holiness suffuses speech, kindling praise, combusting disclosures, or consuming contradictories. To be sure, there is nothing intrinsic to Christian speech that precludes the enunciation of Christian claims in a context of mutual learning among people of differing religious commitments. The question is whether such enunciation can be done without inevitably unleashing from protective, and hence inherently partial, linguistic confines the glorious summons of God in Christ Jesus. And if such an opening to glory is indeed inevitable, or even likely, then speaking of Christ in the words of Scripture sets in motion, within the free arena of human interaction, the holy disclosure of God's presence, a presence that can only engender delight or pain, but nothing so mild as to be between the two, except if that be also a form of mercy and judgment itself.

The implication for Christian speakers, of any kind and in any place, is that we can either be evangelical or blasphemous, one or the other. That is one

41. Cf. Florovsky, "The Holy Spirit in Revelation," p. 57.

42. Hence, there is nothing in this proposal about the character of Scripture itself to demand claims about God's eternal Christological "materiality" like Stephen Webb's fascinating suggestion in his *Jesus Christ, Eternal God: Heavenly Flesh and the Metaphysics of Matter* (New York: Oxford University Press, 2011).

of the foundational practical choices upon which a figural understanding of God's speech in Scripture depends. For God's glory is not a neutral presence. In the same way, those who hear can delight in the word or be thrust into the darkness of rejection. And while the divine forbearance may indeed grant each one of us, in any given situation whether we speak or hear, a providential space of shielding shadow, we can neither presume upon such mercy nor revel in it apart from the cost of its offer paid upon the Cross. It is in this sense that Christian speech, whether in dialogue, pulpit, classroom or the floor of Parliament, can only be particularist if it is also exclusivist — willing to speak in the place where dwell the sharp alternatives disclosed by the incoming of God's presence in glory. The figures of the Scripture are actually shaping the world into the forms with and within which we live. They literally *compel* us, in Jesus' phrase (Luke 14:23).

The concern expressed by Paul in 1 Corinthians 10:14ff. on the topic of eating food once offered in sacrifice to idols is a good example of what is at stake, not only in the material ingestion of meat and drink, but in the sharing of the Word of Christ Jesus, the Word made flesh. The sharing of Eucharistic food is a "participation" in the body of Christ synecdochically represented. And although, from a certain perspective of faithful participation in this body, no ingestion of other food can cause a diminution of that communion with the Lord, nonetheless the exclusive nature of this communion determines that any ambivalence of faith will result in an alternative participation, with demons:

> What do I imply then? That food offered to idols is anything, or that an idol is anything? No, I imply that what pagans sacrifice they offer to demons and not to God. I do not want you to be partakers with demons. You cannot drink the cup of the Lord and the cup of demons. You cannot partake of the table of the Lord and the table of demons. Shall we provoke the Lord to jealousy? Are we stronger than he?

The dynamic of Christian speech is no different. Apart from evangelical enunciation, all Christian talk threatens to dissolve into the realm of what is not God, what is not holy, what confronts glory only as shadow — demons, powers, dominions, whose only future is subjugation to God, not free expression. Hence, we can understand the advice of Paul in 2 Corinthians 6:14–7:1, where *separation* from unholiness, from unbelievers, from consort with Belial becomes the *general* character of the Christian vocation.

This really brings us to the heart of the question hovering over scriptural speech for Christians. Realist objectification is what the movement of God as glorious is about. What lies outside the incarnational movement of Christian speech, outside the confessing, delighting, witnessing speech that makes explicit the principle and terminus of incarnational language — what lies outside *this* kind of Christian talk encounters its words only under the canopy of judgment. Christian speech itself is uttered in the same space. And what encounters this speech and fails to apprehend, in a literal way, the object synecdochically represented therein is inevitably thrust into the sphere of consuming dissipation. Such is the exclusive character of the divine glory — exclusive because holiness subsumes, and it is a glory that *is* embodied in Christian speech. Any conversation, discussion, dialogue, sermon, or acclamation whose evangelical dynamic from the Christian side is impeded is a speech flirting with God's destructive outbreak in the present, and assured of his fire in a future whose reality is bound to the moment.

The opening chapter to 2 Thessalonians is still the paradigmatic statement of the effective workings of Christian language in this regard:

> those who do not obey the gospel of our Lord Jesus, [they] shall suffer the punishment of eternal destruction and exclusion from the presence of the Lord and from the glory of his might, when he comes on that day to be glorified in his saints, and to be marveled at in all who have believed, because our testimony to you was believed. (1:8-10)

The testimony of Christian speech is the Word itself — or rather, "himself" — whose coming is the advent of God's judgment because it is also the advent of God's holy glory, verbally embodied, and because the describer is the described whose own flesh constitutes the description uttered.

Contemporary proponents of innocuous Christian speech must surely bristle at this vision. And, frankly, the historicization of scriptural language, which is itself a kind of conscious metaphorization, only tethered to one temporal-semantic level — has aimed at presenting the Scriptures' own words as innocuous in themselves. How then should we read and speak? Is it all a matter of eternal destiny? This may be the case. But it may not be the case as well. Uttering the holy may be a motivation among Christians, it is true, for either self-important trumpeting or for great reticence. But it need not necessarily lead to such officiousness or to such buttoning of the lips, even in contexts where the immediate goal of communication between people of different religions is purely informational.

One thinks of the early Tractarians of the 19th-century Church of England, whose espousal of a notion of Christian speech similar to the one presented here neither led them, ultimately at least, to the arrogance of coercive imposition of their faith on others, nor reduced them to fretful silence in the face of unbelievers or their own personal fears. All "communication of religious knowledge," in the phrase of Tract 80, was to be carefully ordered, indeed ordered according to "reserve," but also expansively motivated by the incarnational missionary impulse.[43] At the core of their attitude, however, was the same sense that, in Owen Chadwick's elegant description of Keble's attitude, "religious truth was an awful judgment, to be approached like a burning bush, with shoes from off the feet, to be approached with wonder and fear, not with the axe of the critical intellect."[44] Wonder and fear provide both strength to speak and freedom from self-assurance and from pride.

But what this example underlines as well is that Christian speech, and more importantly, scriptural speech itself, cannot be voiced, from a Christian point of view, outside a missionary context, outside the incarnational context of bringing to speech the descriptive witness of God's presence, which is even there pressing towards communion in holiness. The words of the Bible *are* the Word of God doing its work, fulfilling its purpose in the world, by making the world as God makes it, fulfilling its artifactual destiny (cf. Isa. 55:10-11). The form and practice embodied in such missionary talking is surely varied, flexible, circumstantial, determined by the character of the love it holds in itself if it is to survive at all in God's presence. But whatever its practice, such talking must tread linguistically a way towards the upper reaches of delight, or one towards the deeper valleys of pain. There is no middle path of waiting in between. To speak the truth of Christ, even to the wind, is to disclose the pattern of the speaker's ultimate destiny. "Go to, go to," Lear tells the plain-speaking, descriptively objective, effably concrete Cordelia, "mend your speech a little, lest it mar your fortunes." And so her speaking does, and not hers alone, however true her words may be. For the truth is hard; it moves, expands, and works within the world into which it has been inserted, thrust, hurled; a world perhaps without the strength to handle its spinning body. It is one reason why Pentecostal reading of the Scripture, however narrow, is also the only consistently figural form of speech still practiced among Christians: it grasps, at least in theory, the fundamentally divine and divinely creative character of biblical speech.[45]

---

43. Isaac Williams was the author of the Tract, entitled "On Reserve in Communicating Religious Knowledge," found in John Henry Newman et al., *Tracts for the Times*, Vol. IV [Tracts 78-82], New Edition (London: J. G. F. & J. Rivington, 1840).

44. Owen Chadwick, *The Mind of the Oxford Movement* (Stanford, CA: Stanford University Press, 1969), p. 36.

45. Pentecostal figuralism is central to the movement's hermeneutics. It is based on a fundamental historical dispensationalism that has merged the particular present of the Holy Spirit's new work in history with the past of the New Testament, giving rise to the phrase "this

My guess, though, is that all this — with its investigation of medieval scholastics and ancient monks — represents the kinds of intuitions that most Christians in fact shared about their Bible for centuries: Scripture's words are powerful, because they are God's; but they are God's in the sense that they engage the power of his life in Christ, formatively, in creating, converting, and renewing by the Spirit. Just because of this, the figural character of Scripture — even as the term connotes a kind of shaping of form — has also always been intuitively reasonable, and wonderful. The character of Scripture's figural speech, then, just because of its creatively omnipotent inventor, is a word in motion, creating even as it moves, and creating new life — for this is the artifactive power of its purpose — within the spaces of its apprehension and beyond. God is the God who saves, we proclaim: as such God's words bring his own self, Christ Jesus, to the place where he joins maker and creature, artificer and artifact in a new thing: his creative speech is made the speech of the world. Figural readings proliferate, as Augustine suggested, for this reason; they cannot be tied down, except to the forms of God's own self, in Christ. For this is his life as it takes the world as his own.

---

is that," taken from Peter's sermon on the original Pentecost in Acts 2:16: "But this is that which was spoken by the prophet Joel. . . ." Specific prophetic fulfillment or restorationism, however, moved into a broader biblical "presentism," so that the principle of "this is that" was frequently applied to the entire Scriptures in a manner that exploded a strictly dispensationalist framework. The Pentecostal theologian Ralph Macchia, thus, speaks of the "'present-tenseness' to the events and words of the Bible, so that what happened then, happens now"; see Ralph Macchia, "Theology, Pentecostal," in *The New International Dictionary of the Pentecostal and Charismatic Movements*, ed. Stanley M. Burgess and assoc. ed. Eduard M. van der Mass (Grand Rapids: Zondervan, 2002), p. 1122. On the geographic and cultural breadth of this particular kind of figural approach, see Paul Gifford, "The Bible in Africa: a novel usage in Africa's new churches," *Bulletin of the SOAS [School of Oriental and African Studies]* 71:2 (2008): 203-19, for which the term "novel" may in fact be in error. It was Aimee Semple McPherson who provided a classic Pentecostal synthesis in her autobiographical collection actually entitled *This Is That: Personal Experiences, Sermons and Writings* (Los Angeles: The Bridal Call Publishing House, 1919). The book's more doctrinal dispensationalism is frequently deployed, complete with charts. But in fact, the book's descriptive narrative, from personal stories to sermons to teachings, is a relatively thick figural textual application of Scripture in which the historical lines have blurred or melted altogether. Instead, it is a rich typological and allegorical discussion, which at one point (cf. p. 531) is bound to an explicit *exitus-reditus* Trinitarian image.

PART 2

FIGURAL READING IN PRACTICE

CHAPTER 6

Juxtapositional Reading
and the Force of the Lectionary

I. Figural Reading and the Difference It Makes

In this chapter I want to move beyond what have been to this point, frankly, mostly theoretical questions about figural reading. Now I want to address some of the ways in which the Bible's text, enfigurated as it is, actually shapes our understanding of the truth. The theory which has preceded has had its own truth-value, to be sure. And on this level I have wanted to stress two things in particular:

1. The first is the deep power of Scripture as the word of the creating God, who in fact creates us "in Christ," through the Spirit. To say that Scripture is the word of *this* God is to open up a world that is often invisible to us, obscured or simply closed to our apprehensions. There are reasons for this obscurity — themselves figurally inscribed in the world! (See Rom. 1.) But there is also enormous, indeed incomparable wonder and joy at having light break through this obscurity (See 2 Cor. 2.) Time, the universe, our ties to other creatures, our relation to God and God's nature are opened up here simply in considering and being drawn into this fact of the figured Scripture. And the shape of theology, needless to say, is deeply implicated in this.

2. The second thing I wanted to emphasize is the more prosaic side of this reality. That is, if this kind of God with this kind of Scripture *is* a reality, then the seeming strangeness of the claims is perhaps not so strange at all. We should not be surprised to find the world differently ordered than we are usually taught within the realm of limited experience. Some of the heavy-lifting of my historical sketches has been aimed at this side of

things, that is, at "normalizing" the figural character of Scripture and thus of our world and lives. This is part of a scholarly and cultural argument, I suppose: an apologia for traditional Christian ways of looking at the world, that churches themselves, not to mention the larger secular society, have turned away from in incredulity or even in sometimes outright disdain. I recall a well-known Yale professor's dismissal of the project of figural reading: "this isn't theology, let alone history; it is prophecy!" One might well have responded, "would that all God's people were prophets," but that would have been to miss the mark in this case. For there is a responsible and rigorous theology and historical scrutiny that flows from the figural character of Scripture, and the church has known it for centuries, despite misplaced efforts at its repression.

But my apologia is also pastoral. I am not only arguing to the incredulous that "the world is stranger than you seem ready to admit." More than this, if you admitted it, and I as well, certain realities that you and I face, often in bewilderment and anger — realities of conflict and violence, failure, frustration, ugliness and loss, death itself — would be more open to finding their place within the tightly woven beauty of the world. (And such is what the world must be if this world is God's, and this God is as the Scriptures present him and orders us towards.) If this is our *normal* life — this life of Genesis through Revelation, this life of Numbers, Ruth, and Job, of the Psalms and Paul, of the four distinct Gospels taken together — if this is life as it is in fact *being* lived, within the contours of the "planets in their courses," then we are indeed *not* without hope in the world, and self-pity is a thing of the twisted imagination.

There are, thus, duties here, because there are gifts. And this goes back to our opening chapter on exile: to understand the character of an enfigured and figurating Scripture is to have our own lives properly clarified from a moral angle as well: what is happening to us, and why? What do the actions of others amount to in the eyes of God? How indeed is God shaping us and to what end? Calvin's discussion of exile, just as Augustine's before him, involved articulating the judgment and mercy of God in very concrete ways — the acts of politicians, of leaders, of empires and invaders, of churches, of friends and enemies. (These kinds of questions were, as I mentioned in the Introduction, one of the very prods to my own engagement with this entire issue.)

So the theory I have led us through has had a deeper purpose that goes beyond methodological "throat clearing."[1] Theory is a way of seeing the truth,

---

1. The phrase is Jeffrey Stout's, *Ethics After Babel* (Cambridge: James Clarke & Co., 1990), p. 163.

in ancient Patristic conceptuality: a gazing at the truth, describing its contours, so as to be taken in by it and shaped by it.[2] What we call "theory" today can at least approach this if we allow it to act as such an access to passive (in the sense of being the object of something greater) engagement. But what do we find, then, as we are so taken in? This is what I want to explore in the next three chapters. And here I will begin with some basic questions about doctrine: how does a figural reading of the Scriptures tell us something true about God? And what are the means by which this happens? I am not at all sure that "doctrine" is the most important consequence of reading the Bible, and I am not assuming that here. Nor am I assuming even some common understanding of what doctrine is or is meant to do. But virtually all Christians recognize the key force of certain claims about God that *are* viewed as necessarily ordering other claims and actions. Some of these claims have done this universally, as it were, and are known and celebrated as having done so. Some are even seen as continuing in this role. I will begin by speaking about doctrine only in such general terms, and want to suggest that figural reading of Scripture can and in fact *has* been an important means of discerning such doctrine.

In this chapter, then, I want to suggest that this is one of the things we discover as Scripture takes us in through its figural order: a universally recognized truth, in Christian terms, about who God is. The central example I will use, however — the equal divinity of the Son with the Father — is one that, of course, has been contested. Is it, then, even right for me to claim it as a "universal" fruit of figural reading? An implicit aspect of this argument will therefore also be that only a figural reading makes it so; and that the claim's contestability is linked to a forgetting of the Scripture's figured reality. Although I will not trace that argument historically, I think it can be done — not only with Arius in this case, but through the various geneses and permutations of subordinationist and Arian-like Christologies that, into our own time, have beset our churches: they derive from a lack of figural imagination, in the profoundest of senses. They are too literal, too historicist, too thin. And as such, they are less than scriptural.

As I move into this section on the practice of figural reading, I will reiterate afresh what the figural reading of Scripture is "about," what reality it engages. I will then move on to look at, as I have mentioned, some dogmatic fruit of such figural reading. In this case, I will make use of the example of Proverbs 8:22-30 in the Trinitarian exegesis of Athanasius. But my points here will be

2. Most famously stressed recently by Pierre Hadot. See, for example, his *Philosophy as a Way of Life: Spiritual Exercises from Socrates to Foucault*, ed. Arnold I. Davidson, trans. Michael Chase (Oxford: Blackwell, 1995), p. 29, but more broadly throughout the book. For a nuanced discussion of *theoria* or *contemplatio* among the Fathers, see A. N. Williams, *The Divine Sense: The Intellect in Patristic Theology* (Cambridge: Cambridge University Press, 2007).

very general. Finally, I want to raise some practical questions that, I believe, are directly tied to figural reading and its dogmatic fruit. These have to do with the Lectionary and its use in our daily and weekly common prayer. But this use is itself a lens through which to grasp how the figural reading of Scripture yields its treasures, how it opens up the times which the Scriptures themselves are shaping. Part of the normalized character of figural reading depends on accepting the fact that one predominant and more modern use of God's artifacts has been tied to sequential and thereby sequentially non-contradictory orderings of their reality. But figural reading, as I have argued, stands as a more inclusive use, divinely initiated, of these artifacts. The dogmatic claims about the Son of God as a Trinitarian person rely on this more inclusive usage. They come to us initially as scriptural "contradiction," but just there open us to the wider reach of God's truth. I will turn to the Lectionary just here, in order to press this point as concretely as possible. In the next chapter, I will look more directly at the way scriptural juxtaposition of texts discloses the inclusive shaping of God's creation.

II. Figure

Let me turn to a scriptural text that has been centrally linked to a dogmatic claim, Proverbs 8. It is only the Scripture's figural character that has permitted this dogmatic claim to emerge. The Christological and Trinitarian readings of Proverbs 8 are, to be sure, "figural" only in a general way. Still, I think that generality is worth reflecting on. In a wonderful article from 1987, the Jewish critic David Stern cited a rabbinic text on the meaning of contradictory explications of the Torah, indeed on contradictory texts themselves:

> [Rabbi Eleazar ben Azarish] recited this proem: 'The words of the wise are like goads; like nails well-planted are the words of masters of assemblies; they were given by one shepherd' (Eccl. 12:11). Why are the words of the Torah likened to a goad? 'To drive us from the path of death to life, like the goad directs the ox that pulls the plough for planting'. But who are the 'masters of assemblies?' These are the scholars who sit together interpreting the Torah, but doing so diversely and often in contradiction one to another: it means this; no, it means that — 'clean' and 'unclean' are the various interpretations. So one asks, 'how then shall I learn Torah?' Therefore Scripture says: All of them 'were given from one shepherd.' One God gave them, one leader (i.e. Moses) proclaimed them from the mouth of the Lord of all creation, blessed be He, as it is written, 'And God spoke *all* these words' (Exod. 20:1).

Therefore make your ear like the hopper and acquire a perceptive heart to understand the words of those who pronounce unclean and the words of those who pronounce clean, the words of those who prohibit and the words of those who permit . . . (B. Hagigah 3a-b)[3]

This story is applied by the tradition, and by Stern, not simply to the interpretations of readers, but to the very words of God themselves. What do we make of this as Christians? My first point is a simple assertion: what our tradition has called "figural reading" of the Bible is, in part, a natural expression of the reality of this "allness" of Scripture mentioned by Rabbi Eleazar — all Scripture's words are God's. This has to do with the Scripture's creative priority to all of created reality, which I have spoken about. From a Christian perspective, they are "all" thus, not in themselves, but as bound to the God who gives himself "in Christ" to the world. The Word has its "allness" expressed, *given* to us in a figurated way; or rather, the fact that it is all given means that it is figurated.

Now this definition is not enough: the self-expression of the Word is given in the "allness" of Scripture, in the fact that this "allness" is *apprehended* by human listeners. I have stressed this in terms of human "usage." Within our own temporal context, this allness is given, practically, in the juxtaposition of texts that are heard or read. That is the root meaning of the term "parable" — *paraballo*: something that is "juxtaposed" so as to provide the form of a singular truth through the contiguity of seemingly disparate entities. And such juxtaposition is the practical reality — neither prior nor subsequent, but the historical embodiment — of this allness: the texts of Scripture must "all" be given to our apprehension in their challenging multiplicity, something grasped via juxtaposition, one text laid beside another and another and another. This fact constitutes the Scripture's own initiating character, which finally supervenes upon our own human usage of its texts, and imposes its own divine creative and comprehensive order on our world. To say "this is God's, and this, and this," and to say it of the God who is "in Christ reconciling the world," is to speak figurally once it is explained. I have already given various other definitions of figural reading or the figural character of Scripture; and I have insisted as well that there must be varied ones, if they are to be faithful to the actual comprehensive and exhaustive reality that *is* Scripture's creative priority vis-à-vis the world. In any case, let me offer in this context another

3. David Stern, "Midrash and Indeterminacy," *Critical Inquiry* 15:1 (Autumn, 1988): 132-61. The quote is taken from pp. 137-38. As will become clear, the issue here is not "indeterminacy" at all, but comprehensiveness.

provisional definition of figural reading for the purposes of this particular discussion: figural reading is the temporal explication, through the juxtaposition of her multiple texts, of Scripture's divine "allness."

III. Proverbs 8:22-31 and Juxtapostional Exegesis

a. Proverbs and Athanasius

Let me try to demonstrate this through a historical example of exegesis that has had enormous import for the Christian church: Athanasius and the interpretation of Proverbs 8:22-31.

The issue with Proverbs 8 seems to be one simply of "reference." Contemporary readers see the referent as historically singular, and, from an authorial intention view, limited to the concepts cognitively apprehended within the time of the purported author. There are important issues of "original" Hebrew vs. Greek words and their meaning, but I will stick to the general here. Proverbs 8 cannot refer to the Son, the "authorial" view claims, because there was no Trinitarian adumbration available to the author of Proverbs. "Wisdom" could mean this or that, but certainly *not* the Son of God who became incarnate in Jesus of Nazareth. Writing a piece on sermon preparation for the text, the patristic scholar Daniel H. Williams notes: "As far as the editor [that is, the "intentional author"] of Proverbs 1–9 was concerned, the philosophical question about whether Wisdom was a hypostasis of Yahweh would have been either irrelevant or far exceeded by the practical issues that were at stake in chapter 8 . . . a hypostasized Wisdom is unnecessary, and misses the point."[4] This is a widely shared contemporary assessment.

Fourth-century Arians, on the other hand, did indeed accept the referent of Proverbs 8:22 as being the "Son of God." And this they shared with the tradition of interpretation that goes back to the Apostolic Fathers, like Justin.[5] It is

4. Daniel H. Williams, "Between Text and Sermon: Proverbs 8:22-31," *Interpretation* 48:3 (July, 1994): 275.
5. On the background scholarship up to the time of writing, as well as a careful exposition of Athanasius's arguments on Proverbs 8:22-31 against the Arians, see Allen Lee Clayton's dissertation "The Orthodox Recovery of a Heretical Proof-Text: Athanasius of Alexandria's Interpretation of Proverbs 8:22-30 in Conflict with the Arians," Southern Methodist University, 1988. On aspects of Athanasius's "hermeneutical" theory below, see James D. Ernest, *The Bible in Athanasius of Alexandria* (Boston/Leiden: Brill, 2004), and his earlier article "Athanasius of Alexandria: The Scope of Scripture in Polemical and Pastoral Context," *Vigiliae christianae* 47 (1993): 341-62.

certainly possible to call this interpretation a "figural" one, precisely insofar as it is bound to a referent that lies outside of the historical context of the purported human author's apprehension. But this would be a too general characterization, and does not get at the Arian-Athanasian debate. The issue between them, of course, was ultimately not *who* did the text refer to, but *how* did it in fact refer to the Son — something that, of course, would shape the nature of the "who" as understood, but not the referent's particularity itself. It was a debate that, as scholars have insisted, was primarily "exegetical." In what way?

What I want to suggest is that the primary difference here between the Arians and Athanasius lay simply in the juxtapositional foundation that Athanasius insists upon, and that seems mitigated by Arian exegesis. To be sure, we don't have access to Arian exegetical discussions in their discursive breadth. But what evidence we have seems to indicate that this was not their way of arguing, preferring instead to engage scriptural texts and their relationship more in terms of a certain logic. I will come back in a moment to the question of logic. But for now, simply look at how Athanasius argues: by the accumulated piling up of texts side by side, and then the demand that their coexistence determine the definition the interpreter must give to their referent.

There is, to be sure, a range of possibilities when one does this, and in particular with respect to Proverbs 8.[6] While hardly novel in this regard, Athanasius dwells more deeply on this juxapositional reading than many others; and the result is a clearer two-nature result in his conclusions regarding the Son: he is *both* divine and human in a full way. As I will note in a moment, the exegetical conclusion results in a definitional "antinomy" with respect to the Son, because of his insistence on holding seemingly contrary texts together.

Arians seem to use scriptural juxtaposition as well, because they want to nuance their claims about the Son, presumably based on the fact that certain Scriptures — like Hebrews 1 or Colossians 1 — place the Son in a position vis-à-vis other creatures that is unique. So, they will say, for instance, that the Son is a creature (based on Prov. 8:22), but "not among the creatures."[7] Certainly, this is a way of dealing with contrasting texts. I would argue, however, that it is a peculiar way, one aimed at resolving tensions based on identifying distinctions bound to a prior claim regarding, in this case, the *monas* or singular unity of God. It will lead to a thinning of figural reading inevitably, because it begins with a clear fencing off of divine reference: only *some* texts can refer

6. Clayton discuses e.g. Eustathius and Marcellus of Ancyra.

7. *Orationes Contra Arianos* (CA), or "Against the Arians," 2:19. I will be citing here the edition in translation in *A Select Library of the Nicene and Post-Nicene Fathers of the Christian Church* (Grand Rapids: Eerdmans, 1957), vol. IV. For the Greek, I have made use of the text in the *Patrologia Graeca*, vol. 26.

to God. With respect to Stern's quote: it cannot "all" be God's, but only some directly; the rest must be organized in a way that protects this exclusive realm of divine reference.

By contrast, Athansasius is profligate in this comparative textual discussion. His main interest lies in 8:22, the most controverted verse. So, for instance, he brings up Genesis 1 on "Creation" (CA 2:19-20): This text, he argues, recounts the sequence of created being, from light to human beings, including now angels and thrones and authorities. There is no word in this and related texts that would permit the Word to stand "with" the creatures but be somehow "not of them"; either he is among the creatures as a creature, or he is among the creators, of whom there is only God. The Arian "line" that surrounds God from creation is too artificial, he claims, and demands that the scriptural text be contorted to maintain it.

Next, Athanasius assembles Psalm 19, John 14:6 (the way, truth, and life), and Proverbs 8:30 to show how "creator," "word," "truth," and the act of "working" hang together in their referent, which is always drawn towards God himself. Thus, it is in a way that cannot be attributed to a creature (CA 2:20).

What about "knowing" or "seeing" God? Is this something a creature can do? Athanasius looks at John 14:9 and 10; and John 6:46 (CA 2:22). Or what of "worship"? Can that be offered to a creature? Yet what of Revelation 22:9; or John 20:28 (CA 2:23), he asks.

The Arians see the Son as a created intermediary between Creator and all other creatures, something somehow necessary for the governance of the world which could not depend so directly upon the infinite otherness of God. But what then, as Athanasius argues, are we to make of Matthew 10:29 and 6:25-30, where God knows the sparrows and each of our hairs individually, and clothes the lilies and feeds the birds (CA 2:26)?

Is not the creation of the creature something that takes place directly from the divine hand? Hence, "wisdom" or the Word cannot be an "intermediary" but a way of naming that very directness, its *own* divine directness as it were: so he quotes Psalm 104:24 or 33:6; 1 Corinthians 8:6 (CA 2:31).

In 2:28 (Section 32), Athanasius provides one of his most florid catena of texts, as he discusses Wisdom as God's very essence: Proverbs 8:25; Matthew 17:5; Psalms 36:9; 104:24 again; Hebrews 1:3; 1 Corinthians 1:24; Jeremiah 2:1; John 1:1; Luke 1:2; Psalm 107:20. Let me simply quote these verses, as Athanasius does, to get a sense of the current here:

- He was still speaking, when lo, a bright cloud overshadowed them, and a voice from the cloud said, "This is my beloved Son, with whom I am well pleased; listen to him." (Matt. 17:5)

- Before all the mountains, he begat me. (Prov. 8:25, LXX)
- For with thee is the fountain of life; in thy light do we see light. (Ps. 36:9)
- Lord, how manifold are thy works! In wisdom hast thou made them all; the earth is full of thy creatures. (Ps. 104:24)
- He reflects the glory of God and bears the very stamp of his nature, upholding the universe by his word of power. (Heb. 1:3)
- Christ the power of God and the wisdom of God. (1 Cor. 1:24)
- The word of the Lord came to me. (Jer. 2:1)
- In the beginning was the Word, and the Word was with God, and the Word was God. (John 1:1)
- They were delivered to us by those who from the beginning were eyewitnesses and ministers of the word. (Luke 1:2)
- He sent forth his word, and healed them. (Ps. 107:20)

The combustion of terms here is not punctiliar; it leads to a wide array of cascading connections and resonances that reestablish the original juxtaposition. As Jeff Bingham has put it, they are part of a "chain reaction," all of whose simultaneous referring is disclosive of God's reality. They must *all* refer correctly.

There is a theological substratum to this disclosure. Theologically, the issue for Athanasius is one of the relationship of Creator and creature: the latter exists in awe and fear of the former, dependent, worshipping, and turning towards (or away, with horrible consequence). This is the *true* shape of being. It is one, I would add, that is consistent with what we have seen of the figural readers of Scripture as a group. The Arian approach seems, at least to Athanasius, to demand some mediation vis-à-vis God, and hence obscures the proper creaturely posture of praise and graciously received salvation. God is shaded by the sub-divine version of the Son the Arians have concocted, so that the directness of God's standing is muted. God creates *directly*, Athanasius insists, from the hairs on our head to the sparrows of the air and flowers of the fields (Matt. 6:25-30), and therefore if the Son is involved, he is involved as God, not as a delegate. Only thus can the absolute care of God and absolute dependence of the creature upon God make any sense (CA 2:17, section 25).

If we are saved or redeemed, then, it is *by God*, not by another. The soteriological stakes are given here, but they derive from the reality of God as our creator: only he can redeem. If there is a *regula* in which Scripture works here for Athanasius, it is this: everything must be given within the framework of a creative renovation from God. That is, the words of Scripture refer to God, as being directly given by God, and hence are divinely significant in an unmediated fashion. Since "all" of Scripture is God's, the simple juxtaposition of

Scripture to Scripture as each divinely referring, will provide, of itself, knowledge of God. Arians are "Manicheans," Athanasius asserts — why? Because their figural impoverishment has a dogmatic trajectory: when the Scriptures refer less and less to God, and more and more to a creation infinitely distant from God, the actual hope of redemption as a powerful reality is sucked dry. (Cf. CA 2:39-41, etc.) To the degree that the Scriptures are not *all* about God, their promises become more impotent. I think this a crucial point.[8]

Athanasian hermeneutics is often explained in terms of his discussion of Scripture's "scope." That is, that a portion of Scripture is properly to be understood only according to the general "scope" of the text. *Skopos* here has been variously translated as "drift," "purpose," "intention" and so on; and in fact Athanasius uses other synonyms for it. Determining the "scope" of a text, he argues, one must determine other matters, like the person referred to, the time, and so on. This leads Athanasius to his famous "economic" approach to OT texts especially: Prov. 8:22 refers to the Son, but to the "time," or "economy" of his incarnation, his "humanity."[9]

What I would like to stress, however, is that one of the keys to any discussion of Scripture's "scope" in these terms — as the whole narrative shape of a passage, in this case perhaps the goal of the human race's redemptive transformation in the Son — requires a *range* of texts in order to assert itself. It is not given within the passage itself, but only as elements within the passage are placed beside other texts from outside of it. Likewise with respect to the smaller elements of Athanasius's theory: to identify the "person" of a text demands that a range of diverse referents be provided as comparative and connected identities. And the identification of the "economy," within the text's

8. While the analogy is not perfect, we may think of the "performative" aspect of scriptural preaching that has been noted by some students of Pentecostal preaching. See, once again, Paul Gifford, "The Bible in Africa: a novel usage in Africa's new churches," *Bulletin of the School of Oriental and African Studies* 71:2 (2008): 203-19.

9. The meaning of *skopos* has been debated, and Athanasius evidently uses varying words interchangeably here — *dianoia*, "character," even "canon." As noted, within the "scope," Athanasius adumbrated three elements necessary to identify for a text's interpretation: its "time" (*kairos*) of reference, the "person" referred to (*prosopon*), and the "subject matter" (*pragma*), all of which are often ordered by Athanasius in "economic" terms. Thus, in Prov. 8, he can identify the time and person in terms of the "incarnate" economy of the Son where words referring to "createdness" are used; but the pre-incarnate economy orders the scope of those texts, like 8:30, that speak to an eternal relationship of Father and Son. Or again, in the context of this discussion, Athanasius turns to Isaiah 49:5 — "he formed me from the womb . . ." — and asks "why?" To gather the scattered tribes. This is the *aetia* or "cause"/purpose, and it points to the "person," that is the one through whom the tribes are gathered, that is Christ the Incarnate Son; hence the *kairos* is also specified. See CA 2:51-53 for an example.

contextual intention or "scope," represents the attempt to order a plurality of lections according to the fundamental faith in a Creator who redeems fallen humanity.[10] On one level, we are not dealing with hermeneutic rules at all, but rather with the inherent power of multiple texts, as God-given and somehow God-referring, to order themselves according to their mutually posited truths. The human reader must sort this out according to the perceived semantic pressures of these texts, but always maintaining their God-referring claims somehow.

The Arian tendency is to allow texts to cancel each other out, according to, it would appear, a given principle of divine ontology. Hence, in Alexander of Alexandria's words, the Arians "ignorantly affirm that one of two things must necessarily be said, either that He [the Son] is from things which are not, or that there are two unbegottens." The Arians insist, then, that a choice must be made, and the Son was created from "things which are not," like all creatures. But Alexander goes on to argue that the orthodox are able to hold the two together, as it were. For "between which two, as holding the middle place, the only begotten nature of God, the Word by which the Father formed all things out of nothing, was begotten of the true Father Himself. As in a certain place the Lord Himself testified, saying, 'Every one that loveth Him that begat, loveth Him also that is begotten of Him.'" The Scriptures, that is, provide us both with a Wisdom or Word that "is" God, and one that is "begotten," hence both are true of the one true God.[11]

b. Antinomial Exegesis

Is this form of juxtapositional meaning simply a way of permitting contradictory texts to refer to a single referent, God? Is that, in the end, the form of a "figure"? The answer, in part, is "yes," and there is a long tradition behind this affirmation.[12] Applying contradictory affirmations to God was a well-known

10. See CA 2:51-52.

11. Alexander of Alexandria's Letter to Alexander of Constantinople (*Ante-Nicene Fathers* [Grand Rapids: Eerdmans, 1957], vol. 6, pp. 291-96).

12. Are all juxtapositions "contradictions" or, as we will put it in a moment, antinomies? No: cf. CA 39, on God's Word and God's words (Commandments). (This is a similar issue to Wisdom as divine attribute, and many wisdoms, of which the Son is one.) Juxtaposed, we see their distinction. But only through a range of juxtapositions! The "words," after all, *are* connected to the Word. And the distinction itself is specified more in terms of the issue of multiplicity (there are many "words," and the Son is one of them) vs. identity. In fact, the relation of words to the Word is *not* resolved here; but the issue of multiplicity is.

aspect of the Dionysian tradition. Nicolas of Cusa, in his 1440 *Of Learned Ignorance*, had famously taken up the notion of a "coincidence of opposites" in God (and its Christological center).[13] The notion of a divine "antinomy," or truthful contradiction, is given explicit religious form in the 17th century, as the term's jurisprudential meaning — two authoritative yet contradictory laws — migrated into the theological sphere. For Pascal, the key term is simply "contradiction," and he is eager to lay out the "contradictory" texts of Scripture that pertain, for his famous argument, to humanity's "greatness" and "wretchedness" both: "What sort of a freak is man!" "There are in faith two equally constant truths," he writes, turning to the scriptural contractions. "My delights were with the sons of men" (which, by the way, is from Proverbs 8:31); "I will pour out my spirit upon all flesh" (Joel 2:28); "Ye are gods" (Ps. 82:6); that's on the one hand. And on the other there is this: "all flesh is grass" (Isa. 40:6), and "Man is like the beasts that perish" (Ps. 49:12).[14] The "resolution" of these contradictions is simply divine "grace," and such grace is, as it were, embodied within the world precisely in the form of contradiction. Vladimir Lossky takes up this early modern theological notion, given philosophical celebrity through Kant's antinomies,[15] and traces it back to Dionysius's dialectic of cataphatic and apophatic assertion,[16] something we alluded to in Chapter 5. Lossky places it at the foundation of Orthodox theology, particularly in its Trinitarian worship.[17] The "one" God who is always named concretely as "Father, Son, and Holy Ghost" is, as he puts it, a "given" in its incomprehensible juxtaposition of referring names. And then Lossky refers to Pavel Florensky, writing "there is no other way in which human thought may find perfect stability save that of accepting the Trinitarian antinomy."[18]

In fact, it is Florensky who had earlier most fully reflected on this matter, from the point of Christian logic, in a chapter from his great *Pillar and Ground of the Truth* entitled "Contradiction." Florensky offers a complex argument, utilizing symbolic logic, in a method that anticipates the extensive work of philos-

13. See the modern translation, along with the introduction by Lawrence Bond, in Nicholas of Cusa, *Selected Spiritual Writings* (Mahwah, NJ: Paulist Press, 1997).

14. Pascal, *Pensées*, 131; see 119-31 (Lafuma numeration); see the English version in Blaise Pascal, *Pensées*, trans. A. J. Krailsheimer (London: Penguin, 1995), p. 36.

15. Kant's lengthy discussion is given in his *Critique of Pure Reason* I, pt. 2, Div. II, Book II, chapter II; see the Norman Kemp Smith translation of 1929 (New York: St. Martin's Press, 1965), pp. 384-484.

16. Vladimir Lossky, *The Mystical Theology of the Eastern Church* (Crestwood, NY: St. Vladimir's Seminary Press, 1976), pp. 23-43.

17. Lossky, *Mystical Theology*, pp. 44-90.

18. Lossky, *Mystical Theology*, pp. 65-66.

ophers of logic in what is called "paraconsistency" theory, the claim, ultimately, that the "law" of non-contradiction is in fact untrue.[19] But Lossky's purpose is to explain Christian faith assertions, and in ways that are close to Lossky's later ascetical and Dionysian purposes.[20] "The mysteries of religion are not secrets that one must not reveal. They are . . . inexpressible, unutterable, indescribable *experiences* which cannot be put into words except in the form of contradictions . . . Contradiction! It is always a mystery of the soul, a mystery of prayer and love. The closer one is to God, the more distinct are the contradictions."[21]

More to our point, Florensky argues, the Scriptures themselves are built upon antinomies, are full of them. "Antinomies stand side by side, sometimes in a single verse. They are found in the most powerful passages, where they shake the soul of a believer like the rushing wind and strike the high places of the mind like lightning. Only genuine religious experience apprehends antinomies and sees how their reconciliation is possible" (p. 120). Job is the epitome of a scriptural book of antinomy — works, righteousness, wisdom, and blessing, held together with nothingness, unlimited omnipotence, and inscrutability. There is the tension of the truth that is driven into the deepest layers of reality here that, in Florensky's version, sounds much like Pascal on grace (one of his favorite authors). "But for direct perception these virgin blocks of 'yes' and 'no' that are piled on top of one another reveal a higher religious unity, a unity that is capable of achieving its culmination in the Holy Spirit. What inner insensitivity . . . to reduce all these . . . to a single plane."[22]

Florensky ends his chapter with a list of examples of antinomies (pp. 121-23): consubstantial/trihypostatic; unmerged and separate natures/indivisible and inseparable nature (Christ). These are all scripturally related. But more explicitly on the latter, he notes: retribution to all according to works/free forgiveness; universal restoration and bliss/double end and perdition; "run so that you might obtain" the prize (1 Cor. 9:24)/"so then it is not of him that willeth, nor of him that runneth, but of God that sheweth mercy" (Rom. 9:16); abiding in Christ one does not sin/whoever says they have no sin, has not

19. Pavel Florensky, *The Pillar and Ground of the Truth*, trans. Boris Jakim (Princeton, NJ: Princeton University Press, 1997), pp. 106-23. Florensky offers an extensive note (n. 209) on some of his parallel interlocutors on "antinomism" (p. 488). On contemporary research and discussion, the most prominent scholar is the philosopher Graham Priest. See his *In Contradiction: A Study of the Transconsistent*, 2nd expanded edition (Oxford: Clarendon Press, 2006) and a collection of essays written since the former volume's first edition in 1987, *Doubt Truth to Be a Liar* (Oxford: Clarendon Press, 2006).

20. Florensky in fact indicates Heraclitus and Cusanus before him on this matter.

21. Florensky, *Pillar*, 117.

22. Florensky, *Pillar*, 120.

the truth; I came to judge the world/I did not come to judge the world (John 9:39/12:47). Thus, "truth is a self-contradictory judgment," he writes; "truth is an antinomy, and it cannot fail to be such" (p. 109).

Is Florensky, one of the most astounding Christian intellects of his generation, verging into hermeneutical tendentiousness? One must be careful of anachronism here. Almost all the Fathers were wary of affirming that Scripture had within itself real "contradictions," a charge associated with the enemies of Scripture. And much effort was made to explain the presence of such *apparent* tensions in the text. In general, however, we need to recognize that this effort was of a very different kind from the heretical response of "resolution-by-subtraction." From Origen on, the assumption was that texts in tension be *preserved* and held together by some other means: deeper meanings, or spiritual referents that coexisted with their historical indications and whose engagement *as such* would lead to a deeper knowledge of the "mysteries" of God.[23] Athanasius follows in this line, seeing the figural referent as that which

23. Cf the famous passage in Origen, *De Principiis ("First Principles")* IV.15 (ANF, vol. 4, p. 364), on the "stumbling blocks" and "impossibilities" that Scripture has divinely implanted in its discourse, taken in its literal sense, that press the wiser interpreter upwards towards its spiritual meaning. Cf. also his *Commentary on John*, 10.10-36 (Origen, *Commentaire sur Saint Jean, Tome II (Livres VI et X)*, ed. and trans. Cécile Blanc, Sources Chrétiennes 157 [Paris: Éditions du Cerf, 1970], pp. 387-407). Basil, e.g. in *De Baptismo* II.Q. 4, discusses scriptural "contradictions" at length (using the more technical term *enantion* or *enantiosis*). Once again, the issue is the higher truth of divine Wisdom that unspiritually advanced persons cannot penetrate, and that is founded on the created unity of God's Word. Practical obedience to the clear command is his more immediate concern. (See *Basile de Césarée, Sur le baptême*, ed. U. Neri, trans. Jeanne Ducatillon, Sources Chrétiennes 357 [Paris: Éditions du Cerf, 1989], pp. 218-27). Gregory of Nyssa, on the other hand, involves himself in the logic of contradiction (*antikeimena*) in his Trinitarian discussions, but uses it to undermine the strict application of human categories to divine life, moving in a direction closer to Lossky (as the latter indeed argues). Scripture becomes the linguistic receptacle of this divine "beyondness," and Gregory will uphold tensions in verbal reference, without admitting to actual logical "contradiction" itself. Cf. his *Against Eunomius*, I.39-42 (NPNF, Second Series [Grand Rapids: Eerdmans, nd], Vol. 5, pp. 93-100). Augustine's interest in Scripture's apparent contradictions is well known. In terms of practical commands or morals, contradictions could not be tolerated (cf. *De Doctrina* III.14-34), and careful appeal is made to the ascending layers of figural reference to resolve tensions (Augustine preferred to speak here of an *obscuritas*, or *ambiguitas*, than of outright "contradictions" — something that touches perception rather than simple logicality; cf. *De Doctrina* II.6 and passim). The exposition of Tyconius' "rules" at the end of *De Doctrina* III serves this end, although it also widens the issue to more doctrinal concerns. In general, though, it is better, he says, to avoid such difficulties by seeking the *unambiguous* texts. (I have used the Latin text of *De Doctrina* in *Corpus Christianorum*, Series Latina, XXXII [Turnhout: Brepols, 1962]). Though he affirms a multiplicity of meanings in many texts, and clearly is open to such possibilities, he is

resolves discrepant commands and the like, such as those regarding sacrifice. These are meanings granted to the faithful by God.[24] The seeds of antinomial thinking, I would argue, indeed lay here, precisely because the assumption was that God's own creative power properly provided and referentially confirmed the resolution of seemingly contradictory texts within the power of the Spirit's work within the reader and church.[25] Most important was that Scripture not be somehow "at war" with itself — a phrase and its cognates that is common to Athanasius and his translators when discussing these matters.[26] Or, in the words of Anglican Articles (20), one may not "expound one place of Scripture" — God's Word written — "that it be repugnant to another." Among the many casualities of intra-Christian division and warfare, not only among Catholics and Protestants but among Orthodox and Catholics, has been the loss of such antinomial thinking, even when acknowledged as "truthful"; and correlated with this is the withering of figural reading as well. While it is not enough to say that debates over justification by faith, for instance, or the *Filioque* are to be reduced to such a loss and withering, their intractably rooted hostilities are certainly related to them.

---

loath to order doctrinal claims on such variety (cf. *De anima et eius origine* 2.14.20-16.22; in *Patrologia Latina*, vol. 44, cols. 507-10). Dogmatically, however, Augustine is drawn to antinomial thinking in terms of his most central claim regarding Christ as Mediator, the God-Man who reconciles "contraries" (see the remarkable passage in *Harmony of the Gospels* [*De consensu evangelistarum*] I.35; in NPNF, First Series [Grand Rapids: Eerdmans, 1956], Vol. 6, p. 100; *Patrologia Latina*, vol. 34, cols. 1069-70). Although pressing the singular literal and "harmonious" sense among the evangelists, he intimates here his larger notion, that the truth of God in Christ is inclusive of the diversity of his members in their accurate witness. (See Carol Harrison, "'Not Words but Things:' Harmonious Diversity in the Four Gospels," in Frederick Van Fleteren and Joseph C. Schnaubelt, OSA, eds., *Augustine: Biblical Exegete* [New York: Peter Lang, 2001], pp. 157-73.)

24. See his *Festal Letter* 19.3, for the year 347, in NPNF, Second Series, vol. 4, pp. 545-46.

25. It is possible to see certain parallels with modern orthodox Jewish hermeneutics, associated with someone like R. Mordechai Breuer. Breuer sought to appropriate historical-critical claims regarding the diversity of Torah authorship to notions of the divine origin of the Torah, referring them to the various "aspects" of divine Truth that God, prior to human receipt of the Torah, orders for the sake of a more complete sharing of what would be an otherwise deformed revelation. The differences and contrasts between these diverse aspects, which one might well correlate with diverse human contexts of origin, are in fact due to the broadly variegated aspects of God's comprehensive truth. The reader of Scripture rightly pursues, often with struggle and collusive effort, to work through these diversities, not so much to resolve them, as to discover God's truth within their difference. See Shalom Carmy, ed., *Modern Scholarship in the Study of Torah: Contributions and Limitations*, Orthodox Forum Series (Lanham, MD: Jason Aronson/Rowman & Littlefield, 1996).

26. Cf. *Letter 59 to Epictetus* 9; or *De Synodis* 45.

IV. Lectionary

The antinomial character of scriptural juxtaposition may well have a theological foundation in this particular, if broad, conviction regarding the nature of the scriptural words: that is, that they derive from a sovereign creator conceived of in a specific redemptive form. But the practical *work* of such scriptural juxtaposition — that is, as it touches the human auditor and reforms his or her creaturely apprehension — takes place through the process of its temporal encounter. Scripture must be heard over time in terms of its juxtapositional "allness"; it is "all" God's. Obviously, there are many ways this can happen and has happened: the constant reading and hearing of Scripture in its breadth; its memorization; its repetition in instruction and so on, such that the cognitive catchment of the Scriptures expands and is populated by increasing numbers of texts. For those times and persons when the Scriptures were memorized, the field of scriptural juxtaposition becomes simply the mind and heart of the Christian, and the Bible's figural press naturally emerges as from the primal soup of the soul. One can see this in much of the church's tradition until recently, epitomized in someone like St. Bernard's sermons on the Song of Songs, where every verse and word is reset by an almost unleashed juxtapositional chain of orderings, with their combustive meanings manifesting themselves of their own power.

To some extent, this is no different in kind from Athanasius's more argumentative ordering of the Scriptures' antinomial meaning. But it is worth pondering on the lived structures that uphold such practices. We can only speculate in Athanasius's case: these structures involved a Christian culture of learned expertise based on memorization in general, and perhaps in his specific life, more pointedly rooted in the varied monastic disciplines of liturgical, meditative, and ascetic memorization of the Scriptures. It was this ascetic culture that, some have argued, encouraged the development of portable Bibles in codex form and that also demanded the repetitive immersion in scriptural retention, of the Psalter in particular.[27] While many monks could say the Psalter by heart, many could also retain large portions of the Gospels and the Old Testament as well. And these texts were corporately ordered in

---

27. See Douglas Burton-Christie, *The Word in the Desert: Scripture and the Quest for Holiness in Early Christian Monasticism* (New York: Oxford University Press, 1993), pp. 43-48, 107-33. The larger question of oral vocalization of the Scripture and its hearing and memorization, not just among illiterate monks, which founds the Bible's working role as Scripture in the earlier Christian tradition — earlier than the recent modern period! — is forcefully explored in William A. Graham, *Beyond the Written Word: Oral Aspects of Scripture in the History of Religion* (Cambridge: Cambridge University Press, 1987; 2nd ed., 1993), especially his later chapters on the Christian and monastic experience, pp. 119-40.

their regular liturgical gatherings. It was here especially where we get our first detailed evidence of juxtapositional lectionary readings that coordinate Old Testament and New Testament texts in extensive fashion.[28]

I will take up the question of the two-testament character of figural reading in the next chapter, but we should note here how central this aspect is to the actual dogmatic disclosures the church in fact received. So, while we don't know the texts used specifically in these early lectionary orderings, it is certainly reasonable to assume that Proverbs, and particularly Proverbs 8, would be a part of such juxtapostional readings — that is, a part of the monastic and perhaps cathedral lectionaries. And even if they were not so ordered, they would be read and heard otherwise within such a dynamic. It is likely, I believe, that Athanasius himself engages his Arian opponents on the basis of just such corporately rendered and memorized "lections," a sometimes technical term to which he refers.[29]

The lectionary, in fact, becomes one of the primary repositories of juxtapostional reading (or hearing!), one that carries its practice consistently through the centuries. It is also, therefore, a key to the ongoing strengthening of the foundations of the apprehension of Scripture's figural meaning and thereby its antinomial dogmatic and imaginative fruit.[30] The basic notion that simply having texts from the whole of Scripture read and heard beside one another might be a place where God did his "work" in Christ was long-held. It lies behind some of the more vigorous defenses of lectionary usage in the church, based on the "public reading" of the Scriptures, particularly in the Church of England. The peculiar juxtapositional character of lectionary read-

28. On Egypt, see Robert Taft, S.J., *The Liturgy of the Hours in East and West: The Origins of the Divine Office and Its Meaning for Today* (Collegeville, MN: Liturgical Press, 1986), pp. 57-91. See also S. G. Engberg, "The Greek Old Testament Lectionary as a Liturgical Book," in *Cahiers de l'institut du Moyen-Âge Grec et Latin* 54 (1986): 39-48.

29. Of course, one cannot really know. But Athanasius does use a sometimes technical term for "lection" (*anagnosma*) on numerous occasions as he quotes a scriptural text, including key texts in his Proverbs 8 debate with the Arians. Cf. CA I 36.3; 55.1; II 8; 51; 56.5; III. 19.4; 42; 4. The *Life of Anthony* 2, to be sure, gives the most celebrated example of a "lection" being read in church that changed the course of history.

30. See Daniel Sheerin, "Interpreting Scripture in and through Liturgy: Exegesis of Mass Propers in the Middle Ages," in Natalie B. Dohrmann and David Stern, eds., *Jewish Biblical Interpretation and Cultural Exchange: Comparative Exegesis in Context* (Philadelphia: University of Pennsylvania Press, 2008), pp. 161-81, who demonstrates the hermeneutical continuity between early medieval lectionary ("Propers") interpretation and earlier Patristic exegetical methods, which rely on juxtapositional provocations. Whether this amounts, as he argues, to a kind of re-writing or re-organizing of the Bible is another matter. Sheerin's essay is replete with helpful references to both primary and secondary literature, as well as useful translated examples of such interpretation.

ing, it must be admitted, is not itself stressed by such Anglican writers. But it is interesting to see how they clearly aimed at uncovering some of the key elements we have been discussing here. Unlike other Christians, Anglicans explicitly reflected on the practice of using a lectionary. They also represent a certain fading of the tradition as well.

Apologias for a lectionary were something Anglicans were prodded into offering, not simply by the fact of the original Prayer Book reform of Cranmer, but by opposition to it on the part of what became Puritan and dissenting groups within Britain. Cranmer himself made the use of the lectionary — known as the "calendar" or "table" of "lessons" for use in Morning and Evening Prayer, as well as on Sundays — a central platform of his liturgical reform in the mid-16th century. His goal, as he explains it in his Preface to the first 1549 Prayer Book, is to make Scripture once again both central to public worship, and so ordered in its reading that the "whole" of it can be easily heard in the course of regular church attendance.[31] It is this "wholeness" or allness of the Scripture that he stresses, and the fact that people need to be exposed to it thoroughly for their Christian lives. The course of readings that mark his lectionary was itself not revolutionary. What was practically radical in his time was that he moved this exposure from the monastery to the parish church, and so simplified the division of the Bible for public reading that its common priests and people could follow this comprehensive lectionary without trouble.

Fifty years and a good bit of political turmoil after Cranmer, Richard Hooker took up the task of defending the "bare reading" of Scripture in the English churches, as something of equal value to preaching, an equivalence

---

31. Cranmer takes the "ancient fathers" as his example to be restored: "For they so ordred the matter, that all the whole Bible (or the greatest parte thereof) should be read over once in the yeare, intendyng thereby, that the Cleargie, and specially suche as were Ministers of the congregacion, should (by often readyng and meditacion of Gods worde) be stirred up to god-lines themselfes, and be more able also to exhorte other by wholsome doctrine, and to confute them that were adversaries to the trueth. And further, that the people (by daily hearyng of holy scripture read in the church) should continuallye profite more and more in the knowledge of God, and bee the more inflamed with the love of his true religion. But these many yeares passed this Godly and decent ordre of the auncient fathers, hath bee so altered, broken, and neglected, by planting in uncertein stories, Legendes, Respondes, Verses, vaine repeticions, Commemaracions, and Synodalles, that commonly when any boke of the Bible was began: before three or foure Chapiters were read out, all the rest were unread. And in this sorte the boke of Esaie was begon in Advent, and the booke of Genesis in Septuagesima: but they were onely begon, and never read thorow. After a like sorte wer other bokes of holy scripture used." Facsimile images and formatted texts of this and a wide range of historical Book of Common Prayer editions can be found at the excellent site http://justus.anglican.org/resources/bcp/1549/ BCP_1549.htm., from which the above quotation was taken.

his opponents had attacked. Simply hearing the Scriptures read in church, Puritans like Thomas Cartwright argued, was of little value, and perhaps even deleterious, without the kinds of careful and extended explications in sermon form for which they had become celebrated. As in many of his particular responses, Hooker goes after what he argues are the inherently human-centered practices of the Puritans: their reliance on personal choice of Scripture text, their tailoring of the Bible to meet their homiletic needs, and of course, their very reliance on human explication of Scripture as the center of their worship. In an extended section of his famous *Laws*, indeed, containing one of his longest chapters in the entire work, Hooker lays out his argument.[32]

The church "preaches" in two ways, Hooker writes, only one of which is what we now normally call delivery of sermons. The first and primary way that the church preaches is by publicly reading the Scriptures, thereby offering "testimony" in that act itself to the fact that God speaks and that the Scripture is God's own uttered truth. Although Hooker claims that he is not trying to denigrate preaching, and indeed holds it as equally important as reading the Scripture, he ends by doing just that. After all, what should we trust more fully: the actual word of God heard or the word of a human preacher about such a divine word? The question Hooker raises in this context is whether the "bare" or "simple reading" of Scripture could be considered an "ordinary means of grace" "unto salvation," or whether such a means could only be had in hearing sermons. He claims that his opponents consider the simple hearing of the Bible "ordinarily" to be without necessary salvific effect, and thus, in such rare events where such effect might follow, its power could only be dubbed "miraculous." It is in his response here that he sketches out what can only be seen as an almost theurgic conception of Scripture reading: miraculous? Yes, but a normal miracle, as Augustine might have put it.

Hooker had already noted the central feature of lectionary reading, that is, that Old and New Testament texts be read one after the other. His explanation of this is rather subdued, and consists of quoting Augustine (along with the *Glossa ordinaria*), and providing the well-worn tropes with a rather cognitive framework in which the Scripture is a vehicle by which the truths of God are communicated and appropriated:

> The cause of their reading first the Old Testament, then the New, and always somewhat out of both, is most likely to have been that which Justin Martyr

---

32. I have drawn from *The Works of that Learned and Judicious Divine Mr. Richard Hooker*, ed. John Keble, rev. R. W. Church and F. Paget, seventh edition (Oxford: Clarendon Press, 1888), V:19 and 21-22, the last of which is drawn out at great length.

and St. Augustin observe in comparing the two Testaments. "The Apostles," saith the one, "have taught us as themselves did learn, first the precepts of the Law, and then the Gospels. For what else is the Law but the Gospel foreshewed? What other the Gospel, than the Law fulfilled?" In like sort the other, "What the Old Testament hath, the very same the New containeth; but that which lieth there as under a shadow is here brought forth into the open sun. Things there prefigured are here performed." Again, "In the Old Testament there is a close comprehension of the New, in the New an open discovery of the Old." To be short, the method of their public readings either purposely did tend or at the leastwise doth fitly serve, "That from smaller things the mind of the hearers may go forward to the knowledge of greater, and by degrees climb up from the lowest to the highest things."[33]

Yet as Hooker moves on, he stresses the "power" of the Word more than its cognitive apprehension.[34] That is the way he explains the Scripture's "inspiration." Pneumatic "virtue" is what is at issue: "necessity," "efficacy," "force," and "conversion." "Bare reading" is a pneumatic encounter. And it is such because this is, in fact, the word that God has chosen and instituted as such for the goal of engaging the human creature. There is an inherent power in hearing the "whole book of God" read in a year, over and against the torturous and limited explorations of human preaching. If one is interested in "saving souls," as the Puritans are, why not follow the example of King Josiah? Driven by the simple words of the Law being read to him (there being no sermons at the time!), he tears his clothes in agonized repentance in the face of God. And if not this sudden "effectual" encounter, there is the directive of Deuteronomy 31:13, whereby the "fear of God" is taught, through hearing, by "degrees" over time.[35]

For Hooker, then, the center of lectionary reading was the literally forcible engagement of the hearer by God's Word, in its "bare" confrontation. The actual character of the texts read were less important than *that* they were read and read in their entirety over time. For the ever-reasonable Hooker, the fact that this had little purchase on systematic theological programs as its rationale is somewhat surprising. But his view was shared by others after him. So Thomas Comber, in his very popular Prayer Book commentary, *A Companion to the Temple* , where he discusses the lectionary lessons: "Let us receive it [the Scripture read] as being truly his (1 Thess. Ii.13) and it will work as effectually as if it came with the terrors of Mount *Sinah*, or were delivered in Thunder

---

33. Hooker, *Laws*, V.20.6, pp. 77-79. Quote on p. 79.
34. This is the burden of the entire lengthy Chapter 22.
35. Hooker, *Laws*, V.22.4, p. 91.

from the battlements of Heaven. And the better to affect your heart, behold the evident demonstrations that God is in and with them."[36] Comber is not without worry over parcelling the Scripture out in bits without making "connections." Like gold, whose very "filings" are precious, the scattered pieces of Scripture are each of enormous value, and demand some kind of synthesis. This, however, takes place in the hearer's memory, as the whole Scripture, received in the course of lectionary reading, is stored up and entered into by the Christian. What the lectionary provides is precisely this comprehensive breadth of hearing over time. After all, God has "dispersed" the "necessary" truths throughout the Scriptures "that some of them are to be found everywhere; so that every part thereof is useful, and none of it must be neglected, much less contemned."[37] Hence, the breadth of apprehension the lectionary provides is essential.

Comber's detailed advice on hearing the Old Testament in particular in this way makes use of a number of limited methods of application that are hardly novel (e.g. note the difference between the ceremonial vs. the moral law, and so on). On this basis, there are parts of the Old Testament that, once grasped, are of uncertain continued value. Or are they? For even here Comber is eager to encourage reading the Old Testament as a whole, however difficult, and urges the use of typology and figural reading in a way that, among other commentators, is already going out of fashion. So, for instance, he suggests that we hear Israel as figuring the church and her Christian people and so on, in warning and promise both, something only Puritans, especially in New England, were still willing to do.[38] The sense of punctiliar, yet synthetically expansive power that the lections both contain and set loose upon the hearers is a consistent refrain among Anglicans: indeed, why else would each Scripture lesson be followed by a hymn of praise — from Scripture no less — except that God actually *does* something in that reading, each and every time?[39]

Having noted these Anglican defenses of the lectionary, we can also observe that they remain somewhat general, as if the practice is only vaguely understood

---

36. Thomas Comber, *A Companion to the Temple: or, A Help to Devotion in the Daily use of the Common-Prayer* Part I (London: Andrew Clark for Henry Brome, 1676), p. 235.

37. Comber, *Companion to the Temple*, p. 230.

38. Comber, *Companion to the Temple*, p. 241.

39. This argument is made by Charles Wheatly, in his own popular *A Rational Illustration of the Book of Common Prayer of the Church of England* [1710, as *The Church of England Man's Companion* . . .] (London: Bohn, 1848), Ch. III, sec. 12.III, pp. 145-46. It is interesting already to see, in a work that deliberately seeks to be a compendium of previous writers on the Prayer Book, that Hooker's name and even direct quotes from his writing continue to appear, just in this area of discussion.

as to its theological dynamics.[40] We are already seeing a drift into devotional individualism, where the hearer is increasingly interested in gathering mostly personal value from hearing Scripture, and where the truths of God and world are slowly fading as the gifts of disclosive figural reading. Indeed, one need hardly trace the history of the lectionary's diverse developments to recognize, therefore, how tenuous a hold these meanings and their fruit will have on the church's understanding, as the culture of scriptural memorization has almost entirely wilted and the "bare" lectionary, unsupported by other skills, practices, and communal understandings, has become the sole means of maintaining juxtapositional scriptural apprehension.[41] Even Cartwright, Hooker's opponent, seemingly admits that the *concept* of a comprehensive lectionary hearing of the Word could make sense; the problem is that it is practically unachievable.[42] This is especially so if the lectionary's powers of extensive juxtaposition are themselves attenuated, through minimization of contrastive content, excision of contrary divine references (e.g. the imprecatory Psalms[43]), or simple disuse. Still, it

40. With respect to Anglican understandings of the lectionary's explicitly *theological* purpose, one can cite, again, Cranmer's simple desire that the "whole" Bible have a means of being presented to the people for their upbuilding in the knowledge of God. While he favored "continual course" lections ("without breaking one piece thereof from another"), the purpose of both — the "whole" and the "in course" — was clearly to preserve and present the "allness" of the scriptural texts. (See his Preface to the 1549 BCP.) Later explicators of the BCP tended to emphasize "harmonization" of the lections as the goal of their juxtaposition. What they meant by this, hermeneutically, is less clear, other than, once again, an emphasis upon the divine origin of Scripture's allness as apprehended somehow. See Anthony Sparrow, whose discussion of the angelic teaching of the lectionary usage underscores this divinely given breadth of reading (*A Rationale upon the Book of Common Prayer of the Church of England* [1672], in the 1840 edition of J. H. Parker [Oxford], pp. 33-40). Other Anglican commentators follow suit: e.g. Charles Wheatly, Henry Hobart, et al.

41. See below, at the end of this chapter.

42. Cf. Hooker, *Laws*, V.22.18, p. 111.

43. Cf. the interesting discussion among the Presbyterians at the turn into the 20th century in the *Expository Times* 17:7 (Jan. 1906): 310-15, where the use of a lectionary is debated, and the Church of England's use of the "entire" Psalter is roundly rejected by some because of its debasement of true "Christian piety" in certain individual psalms. The early church's notion of "verbal inspiration" is seen as undergirding lectionaries aimed at the "whole" Bible, and are labeled as, in any event, "Rabbinic" in their attitudes. By World War I this had become a greater problem, it seemed, and texts dealing with sexual and physical violence especially were seen as problematic: "The modern conscience is increasingly aware of the distress caused to many hearers by these narratives," wrote one commentator on then-efforts to revise the Church of England's lectionary by cutting bits out and rearranging things more thematically. See F. E. Hutchinson, "Revision of the Lectionary," *Journal of Theological Studies* 19 (Oct. 1917): 81-83. See also Diane Thompson, "The Attitude of the Church of England to WW I," McGill University MA thesis, 1968, pp. 80-83.

is worth exploring a moment how figural reading and the lectionary are in fact essentially intersecting enterprises, however diminished in our era.

If we look at the fate of Proverbs 8:22-31 within the lectionary as an example, we see its susceptibility to a segregated reading, apart from its juxapositional potential. Obviously, for as long as the Sunday Propers did not contain an Old Testament reading at all — much of the Anglican tradition's history, as it turns out, along with other churches as well, particularly after the 16th century — the very issue is moot, something I will return to. On the other hand, with the reestablishment of regular Old Testament Sunday readings as part of the lectionary, we can observe Proverbs 8's move back to its traditional and central place, at least in figural terms, insofar as it is currently appointed in the Revised Common Lectionary (RCL) and the Roman Catholic lectionary to be read on Trinity Sunday, every third year (Year C). Here are the appointed Propers:

RCL:
Proverbs 8:1-4, 22-31 (Catholic: vv. 22-31 only)
Psalm 8 (Catholic: vv. 4-9 only)
Romans 5:1-5
John 16:12-15

According to this lectionary order, the readings that accompany Proverbs 8 are not themselves explicit in their connections. Psalm 8 speaks of God's marvelous creation and of the creation of "man" in a special place; Romans 5:1-5 begins with the redemptive act of Christ, moves through the process of the faithful Christian's transformed experience of life, and ends with an affirmation of the gift of the Holy Spirit within the Christian's heart. The Gospel of John 16:12-15, which, in Jesus' words, speaks of the Spirit's coming, also goes on to discuss how that coming arises out of the Son and the Father's intimate communication shared with his followers. What are we to make of this gathering of texts? How are they heard, simply by being drawn together?

One could say that the feast day that is Trinity Sunday itself, of course, provides the governing dogmatic affirmation that preconceives the connections. But in fact that affirmation is made — traditionally and rightly — out of the juxtapositional expression of the appointed Scriptures themselves. The Trinitarian trajectory of the gospel especially is obvious. But the other texts are rather ones that lay out the forms of God's work creatively and redemptively. "Wisdom" in this case is simply allowed to find its place in this interplay, drawn into the psalm's claim regarding the exalted place of "the man" that is laid over against the Son's sacrificial form in Romans. On its own terms, this kind of arrangement does not stand as a contradiction of Arian claims, for instance. But the interplay itself acts, just as it did for Athanasius, as an opening up of possibilities, the power of which constructs just those incomprehensible claims of antinomial truth that emerged for him as for many others.

This lectionary construal is, however, a thin exemplar if taken alone. And in fact, Proverbs 8:22-31 does not appear in any other Sunday set of Propers in these lectionaries. And in the Episcopal Church's lectionary, it is not even a part of the Trinity Sunday selection at all nor of any other Sunday's. Most Christians, then, in these modern lectionary traditions, will either never hear Proverbs 8 read in church or will only hear it once a year in its most challenging position.

So we must face a central challenge: the fact is that the Sunday lectionary in our day is, as the only remaining popular access to juxapostional reading and its antinomial fruit, a weak read. Perhaps this has always been the case. It is the *daily* lectionary, after all, deriving from the monastic order, that provides the ongoing root of such reading. The daily and repeated in-course reading of the Scriptures has, historically, borne the burden of juxtapositional immersion.[44] It was this daily lectionary, after all, that Hooker and the Anglican apologists were generally defending. And in these daily lectionaries, as opposed to the Sunday Propers, we see a range of orderings in various traditions. Taking the Anglican Prayer Book as an example, its successive editions have placed Proverbs 8:22-31 in shifting positions with respect to New Testament texts, based solely on the demands of ordering the entire course of the Scriptures to be covered throughout the year.

Thus, the 1549 daily lectionary has it read in July at evening prayer, along with the 4th chapter of Colossians, preceded by Psalms 41–43. In the 1662 revision, it appears in the same season, but now is paired with Matthew 10:1-24, preceded by that favorite Athanasian psalm, 104. It is optional for the Sunday evensong of 5th Epiphany. In the 1928 American BCP, it is paired with Philippians 1:1-11. Finally, in the contemporary 1979 edition, which divides up three readings as desired between MP and EP, it is given with 3 John, Matthew 12:15-21, and Psalms 20 and 21 (whose latter verses are optional). The rationale for these kinds of textual linkages in the daily lectionary have to do with ordering in-course readings, not preconceived typological connections. They are, from a

---

44. Actual evidence of its ability to shape the church is difficult to gauge. One might note the scholarly derision that greeted L. J. Morrissey's attempt to argue that Swift had based the intricate dates in *Gulliver's Travels* on the Book of Common Prayer's Daily Lectionary and its readings: why would anybody suppose that people would have recognized *this*? And if they had, why didn't they say so? See Morrissey's *Gulliver's Progress* (Hamden, CT: Archon, 1978).

liturgical point of view, "artibrary." But what of their consequence? The textual encounters, as it turns out, are manifold and rich.

If one were to listen to these encounters, in the 1662 lections, one would hear the following order (abbreviated):

[Psalm 104]
Praise the Lord, O my soul: O Lord my God, thou art become exceeding glorious; thou art clothed with majesty and honour. Thou deckest thyself with light as it were with a garment: and spreadest out the heavens like a curtain. Who layeth the beams of his chambers in the waters: and maketh the clouds his chariot, and walketh upon the wings of the wind [. . .] He laid the foundations of the earth: that it never should move at any time. [. . .] O Lord, how manifold are thy works: in wisdom hast thou made them all; the earth is full of thy riches [. . .] These wait all upon thee: that thou mayest give them meat in due season when thou takest away their breath they die, and are turned again to their dust. [. . .] When thou lettest thy breath go forth they shall be made: and thou shalt renew the face of the earth. The glorious majesty of the Lord shall endure for ever: the Lord shall rejoice in his works. [. . .] I will sing unto the Lord as long as I live: I will praise my God while I have my being. And so shall my words please him: my joy shall be in the Lord. As for sinners, they shall be consumed out of the earth, and the ungodly shall come to an end: praise thou the Lord, O my soul, praise the Lord. [Coverdale translation, as found in the Book of Common Prayer]

Proverbs 8:22-31 (AV)
The LORD possessed me in the beginning of his way, before his works of
    old.
I was set up from everlasting, from the beginning, or ever the earth was.
When [there were] no depths, I was brought forth; when [there were]
    no fountains abounding with water.
Before the mountains were settled, before the hills was I brought forth:
While as yet he had not made the earth, nor the fields, nor the highest
    part of the dust of the world.
When he prepared the heavens, I [was] there: when he set a compass
    upon the face of the depth:
When he established the clouds above: when he strengthened the foun-
    tains of the deep:
When he gave to the sea his decree, that the waters should not pass his
    commandment: when he appointed the foundations of the earth:

Then I was by him, [as] one brought up [with him]: and I was daily
    [his] delight, rejoicing always before him;
Rejoicing in the habitable part of his earth; and my delights [were] with
    the sons of men.

Matthew 10:1, 5-20 (AV)

And when he had called unto [him] his twelve disciples, he gave them
power [against] unclean spirits, to cast them out, and to heal all manner of
sickness and all manner of disease . . .

    These twelve Jesus sent forth, and commanded them, saying, Go not into
the way of the Gentiles, and into [any] city of the Samaritans enter ye not:

    But go rather to the lost sheep of the house of Israel.

    And as ye go, preach, saying, The kingdom of heaven is at hand.

    Heal the sick, cleanse the lepers, raise the dead, cast out devils: freely
ye have received, freely give.

    Provide neither gold, nor silver, nor brass in your purses,

    Nor scrip for [your] journey, neither two coats, neither shoes, nor yet
staves: for the workman is worthy of his meat.

    And into whatsoever city or town ye shall enter, enquire who in it is
worthy; and there abide till ye go thence.

    And when ye come into an house, salute it.

    And if the house be worthy, let your peace come upon it: but if it be not
worthy, let your peace return to you.

    And whosoever shall not receive you, nor hear your words, when ye
depart out of that house or city, shake off the dust of your feet.

    Verily I say unto you, It shall be more tolerable for the land of Sodom
and Gomorrha in the day of judgment, than for that city.

    Behold, I send you forth as sheep in the midst of wolves: be ye therefore
wise as serpents, and harmless as doves.

    But beware of men: for they will deliver you up to the councils, and
they will scourge you in their synagogues;

    And ye shall be brought before governors and kings for my sake, for a
testimony against them and the Gentiles.

    But when they deliver you up, take no thought how or what ye shall
speak: for it shall be given you in that same hour what ye shall speak.

    For it is not ye that speak, but the Spirit of your Father which speaketh
in you.

    The movement in these three readings, taken as a group, is from divine
sovereignty, creative fruitfulness, and judgment, to wisdom's light, and then

its culmination in the mission of Jesus, bound up in its self-giving with the Father's Spirit. To say the least, this constitutes an imperative of astounding generosity: God the Creator, through his own infinite wisdom, gives himself up on the Cross, and draws in human creatures as partakers of this divine gift, centered in Christ Jesus. It turns out to be a profound combustion of evangelical proclamation. Indeed, all these lectionary linkages, as it turns out, are ripe with an Athanasian figural potential that, if engaged, would place the listener in the midst of the Scripture's own intrinsic antinomial power and revelation. The fact that they are given through in-course lectionary structures, rather than constructed pairings, like the Sunday readings, is probably irrelevant and perhaps even helpful. Indeed, one can see that the Sunday lectionary's own ability to deliver the figural treasures of Scripture is necessarily limited, simply by the paucity of available dates, and the over-thematizing of readings that has increasingly become the norm in lectionary revision.[45]

Maintaining the breadth of an Athanasian focus, if you will, probably depends then on the foundational framework of daily lectionary practice in any case, or at least on the resources of the listener's memorization of the Bible. That we are, however, no longer a culture that memorizes texts, like Scripture, is obvious. Educational theory has rejected the notion, and that rejection has taken on a clear political cachet, as can be seen in something like Paolo Freire's influential *Pedagogy of the Oppressed*, which so famously critiqued the "banking" concept of knowledge, with all of its socio-economic connotations.[46] And the almost immeasurable information explosion led by digital storage and internet access has obviously fundamentally altered what it means to "know" or "gain knowledge" about many things. Sugata Mitra's challenge on this score — education by cloud-access rather than by personal knowledge "storage" — is compelling. Mitra, a physical-chemist who branched

---

45. Lectionary reformers increasingly want to use the coordination of readings to make some kind of theological "point," or to gather them according to some theological theme. Cf. the (misplaced, in my view) lament of H. Boone Porter on how late this thematizing came in "Day of the Lord: Day of Mystery," in *Between Memory and Hope: Readings on the Liturgical Year*, ed. Maxwell E. Johnson (Collegeville, MN: Liturgical Press), pp. 50-54. That a fundamental and necessary kind of "memory" *is* both granted and richly so through thematized lectionaries is a point well-argued by Fritz West's *Scripture and Memory: The Ecumenical Hermeneutic of the Three-Year Lectionaries* (Collegeville, MN: Liturgical Press, 1997). But, granted a basic liturgical calendar, I wonder if most of our churches are well past the practical habits that would make it useful to juggle any longer the nuances of lectionary reform, which increasingly devolve to the peculiarly sensitized imaginations of individual scholars, rather than the mind of the faithful as a whole.

46. Paolo Freire, *Pedagogy of the Oppressed* (New York: Continuum, 1993); see especially Chapter 2.

out into cognitive science, has argued for a shift towards computer-generated learning, even among the most socially disadvantaged children, and his work has gained international attention.[47] Not only is it no longer "necessary" to memorize information that is, in any case, available elsewhere; but such demanded memorization (still predominant in many non-Western educational contexts) is actually an obstacle to the kind of learning we now need to do, one that involves ferreting through the clues and links of cyber-traces.

But that is not to say that the culture, in this regard, may well be inadvertently dismantling *necessary Christian* habits, as Hooker's reference to Deuteronomy's pedagogical commands illustrates. The subversion of memorization is relatively recent. In fact, memorizing the Bible had been central to Christian concepts of basic scriptural meaning since before Augustine. For the latter, allowing the Scriptures to enter the memory (*mandare memoriae*) was foundational for their understanding. What we would call "knowing the contents" of the biblical books — commandments, stories, and so on — was primary and essential; indeed, without such simple knowledge, no theory or rules of understanding Scripture would be of any use to an individual, he insisted (*In qua re memoria valet plurimum, quae si defuerit, non potest his praeceptis dari*). But the purpose of this storing of content was to allow the various pieces of Scripture to inform one another by comparison, contrast, and mutual illumination, the more "obscure" being clarified by the less, and so on. Augustine uses terms like "familiarity" with the "divine language" and "opening up" meaning and truth as its consequence, with the result that the human understanding becomes literally more "capacious" (*intelligentia capacior*).[48]

Mary Carruthers, in her important work on the place of memory in medieval culture, shows how this fundamental approach of Augustine became explicitly comprehensive of how the Christian grasps the world as a whole, though always tethered to scriptural figures themselves. The human mind perceives images, according to medieval theory, given by the senses and, in Scripture, by the spoken word first (which is then read); these images are constructed by the mind, rightly or wrongly, and become the basis for understanding the world and time itself. The scriptural words, in particular, become, within the interior life of the reader or hearer, living "pictures" that become the present life of God's truth itself, given over to the believer. But at the back of this process is the simple reality of "stored" impressions, memorized scriptural forms, whose power within the mind is what grants

---

47. See his site http://www.hole-in-the-wall.com/.
48. On this, see his *De Doctrina* 2.9.

knowledge of divine truth. ". . . reading, as we have seen, is a complex activity involving both an oral phase, that of *lectio*, and a silent one, of *meditatio*, committing the substance of the text to memory in mental images that enable one to mull it over and make it one's own . . . learning it to familiarize and domesticate it, in that fully internalized, even physiological way that medieval reading required."[49]

The problem of course is that the memorization of Scripture is itself a widely abandoned discipline for most Christians today. Whether or not it is in fact a precondition to the figural reading of Scripture is something I cannot say; but it is certainly something that has been historically necessary to its pursuit. And on this, arguments regarding the lectionary's ordering are becoming increasingly irrelevant to Christian wisdom, except as vestigial signs. There are rear-guard adjustments that one can make, of course: the Christian teacher can deliberately seek to deploy the lectionary's juxtapositional demands in a regular fashion, in sermon, catechesis, and discourse. Where else might one begin? But it is only a beginning. Obviously, what is optimal for scriptural apprehension is the integrated practice of memorized Scripture, calendrically and liturgically ordered regular readings of key portions of Scripture, and preaching that engages, over and over again, the combustive encounter of disparate texts within this continually informed vision. But the optimal has fast ceded place to the incapable, as each plank in such scriptural life has been reduced or withdrawn.

I am not offering a solution to any of this. My purpose has simply been to show something of what is at stake in the challenge. Athanasius's debate with the Arians was a lectionary-based discussion, if not explicitly, a least in a very practical way: it had to do with how the full range of the Scriptures in their apprehended juxtaposition disclosed the truth of God. I believe that Athanasius's discussion is, on that basis, more credible than the Arians', because it is more comprehensive of the texts of the Scripture as they are made to perdure side by side. In our own day, it is such contiguity in temporal extent that has drastically shrunk. To that degree, the triumph of Arianism lies in the thinning out of the figural word, and thereby the dropping out of texts as divinely referring in their meaning and power. Heresy is the deliberated withering, far more even than the purported contradicting, of the Scriptures. But if this is so, at least we know the direction we are being called; at least we know the promise. In the next chapter I want to pursue this promise with greater textual focus. It is, after all,

---

49. Mary Carruthers has been one of the foremost scholarly investigators of this element in classical Christian culture. See *The Book of Memory: A Study of Memory in Medieval Culture* (1990) (Cambridge: Cambridge University Press, 2008). Quotations from p. 276.

a promise that is given, not abstractly, but in the actual gift of the Scriptures, in their actual work. Moving from this general case of juxtapositional reading, let us see up close, if you will, how the church as scriptural alchemist can watch God's truth emerge from the word's reading.

CHAPTER 7

Trinitarian Love Means Two Testaments

Part of this "up close" look at scriptural texts that are brought together is the discovery that the bringing is a divine act itself. That is the nature of Scripture, that it belongs to God and not to human beings; God deploys, human beings recognize. And this being the case, perhaps the promise of figural reading as disclosive of the divine truth of the world is less something to be sought after so much as it is something to be confidently received. Might we not say, for instance, that it is just such receiving from the hand of God that marks the characteristic shape of the Christian Scriptures themselves, as a two-testament Bible? If the Law came through Moses — received by him as God's own gift — so too that same gift, grace, and truth come through Jesus (John 1:17), whose standing with Moses and Elijah together marks the reception of law, promise, and fulfillment all together (Luke 9:30). The Scriptures, that is, "deliver up" something that is prior to our seeking and our taking. That Christ comes from the Law is part of the Law's divine character (John 4:22), and what we call the canonical shape of the Scriptures as Old and New is at the very core of what we mean by "divine providence." "Divine providence" is an abstracted synonym for "the scriptural canon of Old and New Testaments."

In what follows, then, I want to trace, in an exegetical mode, this peculiar providential character that marks scriptural enunciation. If Scripture is prior to history, as it were, then we should expect that the history of scriptural reception will somehow articulate itself a divine order. To be sure, that is a difficult interpretive task, about which I will say something more as well in the next chapter. But here I want to explore the way that the truth of Scripture that human beings, and the church, articulate in propositional form is not so much "in" the Scripture (either to be extracted from it or logically deduced from its texts) as it is recognized within the life of the world that is scripturally ordered. That is to say, Scripture itself invents dogma within the world, through the power of its figures exerted in time. I am less interested here in redefining "dogma" or "doctrine" in these terms, as in simply watching how in fact Scripture creates such dogma.

We have already seen in the last chapter that, within the well-known example of the so-called Arian controversy, Christological dogma was indeed the product of a contest, a struggle. This is the historical nature of dogmatic articulation. But because historical, it is even more so scriptural. I underlined the combustive character of juxtapositional exegesis as both the intellectual contours and the divine means of such articulation. All of which is to say, however, that it is a *difficult* task, much as life is difficult. Anyone who imagines that the dogmatic propositions the church has "drawn from Scripture" are generally obvious and easily grasped is without historical understanding. By the same token, scoffers who point to such difficulty and contest as a mark of orthodoxy's arbitrary dependence upon human power are without understanding of God's creative priority over all things, including time itself. Providence is the story of a struggle, which is the form of the scriptural ordering of history itself, something we know in fact simply from the figures of Scripture as they are recounted and engaged. That is my theme as we move to an examination of, in this illustrative case of figural exegesis in Isaiah 54, Trinity and Old Testament.

The first thing to point to, then, is the *difficulty* that must attend any attempt or even hope to find the Trinity exposed somehow within the Old Testament alone, as it were, as if it were the object of a search. But the nature of the difficulty, I will suggest, also points to the way that the Triune God we confess as Christians uses the Scriptures to reveal himself, and that way lies precisely in the history of that difficulty and its redemption, an internal act of the Scriptures themselves. Their own strenuous actions, as it were, map the figuratating shape they hold of their own, doing their own work and providing bread from within their own sphere, that is, "from heaven" (Exod. 16:4; Matt. 4:4).

After some general remarks about the character of the language used in Isaiah 54 and its potential nuptial significance for Trinitarian understanding, I will explain how, in fact, Jewish and Christian interpretation of the text moves in an entirely different direction, supplanting nuptial possibilities with the claims of rival loves. This is a figural claim, a claim that arises from the way the text engages, through its form and referents, a range of other related referents, so drawing into itself a wide scriptural and human history. In other words, this is a clear case of Scripture ordering the shape of time. This, I will suggest, ought to indicate to us certain problems with all-too-clean Trinitarian readings of the Old Testament especially; and more particularly, ought to alert us more keenly to what is at stake in affirming the Triune God as the God of two testaments together, that providential reality upon which Christian figural reading is based.

Lest anyone think I have been calling neatly for a reversion to another era's practices, I want here as an aside to issue a warning against simply embracing traditional Patristic discoveries of the Trinity as plain-sense referents within the Old Testament. My aim is not to decouple the Old Testament somehow from the God we confess as Father, Son, and Holy Spirit, as its ultimate author and therefore as its divine referent. Rather, I want to suggest that the disclosure of this referent takes place, but not in a simple correspondence of figure — what often proved the default and wooden figuralism of a worn tradition, already spending itself in a reductionist form of human reference-making. By contrast, the truth of God's being as Trinity is given by God as an actual *act* (or acts over time) in which he brings order to the often knotted and even rival plain-sense referents of both Old and New Testaments in their juxtaposition and conjunction: the Divine Word orders the word that orders our own created time. The God we confess as Father, Son, and Holy Spirit emerges as the *speaker* of Scripture here, as Scripture works upon our lives and churches and history, and only secondarily as first-order referent. Scripture, in God's hands, shapes us, orders us, *uses* us to know him as he speaks; it does not, in the first instance, simply tell us who God is.

I. Stones and the Trinity

Let me return, then, to the question regarding the character of scriptural language, as it speaks of God. Here we revisit issues from the first chapter, on the nature of an otherwise temporally common-sense referent, like "exile"; only now I want to take up a referent not explicitly found in the Bible, that is "the Trinity." What Athanasius struggled to see emerge from the text, after all, soon came to take on an extra-textual substance and meaning, often simply standing over and against the text as an already-defined entity now capable of scrutinizing from its new position of significance the rest of the Bible as a whole. Like "exile" as a thematic-theological trope, "Trinity" could become a hermeneutic key in its own right.

Certainly, this has happened in various ways, as the recent Trinitarian vogue in theological discourse has demonstrated. But it was not always so. If we were to take an early 16th-century catechism used by Portuguese missionaries in West Africa, in what is now Sierra Leone, we would see an example of perhaps a more primary hermeneutic position on the relation of dogma to exegesis. In this case, the catechism is completely ordinary. It was still in use, in an edited version, 300 years later. On the matter of the Trinity, after having repeated the definition of "one God, three persons," the priest would ask, "Can we understand this?," and the answer to be given by the catechumen is "No." It is a "mystery," the catechumen says (in the Susu language) which "we believe because of God's own sharing of it with us, not because we understand it." Why were they taught this, as a basic affirmation, and what did the new converts think about it?

As it turned out, over the next 500 years hardly any of the Soso people ever became Christians, and we can therefore say that the Trinity did not figure much in their imaginations at all. But elsewhere, among those who *do* convert, does, and did, the "mystery" ever get filled out, as it were, over time? And if so, how? Simply by being a part of the church's linguistic life? By hearing or perhaps reading the Scriptures over and over, and letting them seep in, so that the God who is the God of the Scriptures, and whom we call the Triune God, Father, Son, and Holy Spirit, somehow "emerges" and takes over? Perhaps. But if so, what form does this take if any? Most pastors know well that attempts actually to *teach* the Trinity often verge, given the semantic constraints of our conceptualities, into modalistic or Sabellian linguistic frameworks; and devotionally, they can easily slip into a mild and practical tritheism. Were it not for the fact that traditional doctrines of the Christian church and their formulation, like the Trinity, have become increasingly viewed as secondary matters by many new and expanding churches, leaving the doctrine in its somewhat free-floating, if dogmatically imprecise, status would probably remain the default position for many.

But let me try to outline a way in which Scripture itself works to give substance to the mystery's contours as somehow "real." I will take as an example Isaiah 54, a text with traditional Christological (and hence implied Trinitarian) significance, and propose to look at the "work" this text has done in both Jewish and Christian contexts. Out of this work — a divine work of the Word — we shall see how the figurating power of Scripture itself determines the Christian doctrine, although in a way that is less definable than defining of the historical form of the church's apprehension. The Trinity, that is, is not only a "useful" doctrine, but one that expresses the form of God's own use of his creation.

Isaiah 54 (RSV)
[1] "Sing, O barren one, who did not bear;
    break forth into singing and cry aloud,
    you who have not been in travail!

For the children of the desolate one will be more
    than the children of her that is married, says the Lord.
² Enlarge the place of your tent,
    and let the curtains of your habitations be stretched out;
hold not back, lengthen your cords
    and strengthen your stakes.
³ For you will spread abroad to the right and to the left,
    and your descendants will possess the nations
    and will people the desolate cities.
⁴ Fear not, for you will not be ashamed;
    be not confounded, for you will not be put to shame;
for you will forget the shame of your youth,
    and the reproach of your widowhood you will remember no more.
⁵ For your Maker is your husband,
    the Lord of hosts is his name;
and the Holy One of Israel is your Redeemer,
    the God of the whole earth he is called.
⁶ For the Lord has called you
    like a wife forsaken and grieved in spirit,
like a wife of youth when she is cast off,
    says your God.
⁷ For a brief moment I forsook you,
    but with great compassion I will gather you.
⁸ In overflowing wrath for a moment
    I hid my face from you,
but with everlasting love I will have compassion on you,
    says the Lord, your Redeemer.
⁹ For this is like the days of Noah to me:
    as I swore that the waters of Noah
    should no more go over the earth,
so I have sworn that I will not be angry with you
    and will not rebuke you.
¹⁰ For the mountains may depart
    and the hills be removed,
but my steadfast love shall not depart from you,
    and my covenant of peace shall not be removed,
    says the Lord, who has compassion on you.
¹¹ O afflicted one, storm-tossed, and not comforted,
    behold, I will set your stones in antimony,
    and lay your foundations with sapphires.

¹² I will make your pinnacles of agate,
>   your gates of carbuncles,
>   and all your wall of precious stones.
¹³ All your sons shall be taught by the LORD,
>   and great shall be the prosperity of your sons.
¹⁴ In righteousness you shall be established;
>   you shall be far from oppression, for you shall not fear;
>   and from terror, for it shall not come near you.
¹⁵ If any one stirs up strife,
>   it is not from me;
> whoever stirs up strife with you
>   shall fall because of you.
¹⁶ Behold, I have created the smith
>   who blows the fire of coals,
>   and produces a weapon for its purpose.
> I have also created the ravager to destroy;
¹⁷ no weapon that is fashioned against you shall prosper,
>   and you shall confute every tongue that rises against you in
>   judgment.
> This is the heritage of the servants of the LORD
>   and their vindication from me, says the LORD."

If we were simply to read Isaiah 54 through, we would quickly run up against details of seeming irrelevance to dogmatic concerns. For instance, we hear God promise "afflicted" and "storm-tossed" Israel (or so it seems) "stones set in antimony" and "foundations laid with sapphires," "pinnacles of agate, gates of carbuncle," walls of "precious stones" (Isa. 54:11-12). Any reader may wonder about this, but the figural reader will take especial note. In fact, the character of these stones, in their frankly disputed geological reference, has been a matter of interest to most commentators of the past. It is as if these were the first points at which to be snagged by the text. The LXX, for instance, describes the promised gates as being made, not of carbuncles, but of "crystal" — and these, for Christian exegetes, displayed the flashing brilliance of the apostles and prophets, or of the church's miracles. The new Jerusalem or Temple described by Isaiah here, they have said, represents the Christian church. Some Jewish commentators, playing off the root of the Hebrew word translated as a "carbuncle" in the RSV, because associated by some with the verb "to kindle," saw the rock described as being "fiery red," and therefore understood the new gates in terms of their "re-kindled" brilliance, like "coal" or "anthracite," filled with the promise of God's new work yet to be accomplished on Israel's behalf. Yet other Jewish commentators read the root meaning in terms of "boring out," and therefore saw the stone described by Isaiah as, so Rashi, "an expression of a drill, i. e., huge stones of which the entire opening of the doorway is drilled, and the doorposts, the threshold, and the lintel are all hewn from the stone." A single stone, then! And R. Samuel bar Isaac specified it further: "From a single pearl the Holy One will hollow out the east gate of the Temple together with its two wickets!"

We are only talking about a stone, here. Where can this possibly lead? Is it obvious how we should be taking the description of these rocks? Christians might well see in them "shadows" of the church's apostolic ordering and history, but why exactly? For, as we read in one place within the rabbinic tradition, "a certain heretic, a seafaring man, who was present [at a discussion of this matter] said: 'Why, you can't find a pearl even as large as a pigeon's egg, and this person, sitting in a teacher's chair no less, talks like this!'" The man soon after goes on a voyage, his ship is sunk in a storm, and he himself goes down to the bottom of the sea, "where," we are told, "he saw ministering angels hollowing, shaping, and carving designs in an object. He asked them: 'What's that?' They replied: 'It is the east gate of the Temple with its two wickets being made out of one pearl!'" The man miraculously escapes with his life, and makes his way back to the rabbi a year later. "Old man, old man," he cries out, "all that you have to tell us, tell! All the glowing things you say, say. If mine own eyes had not seen what I saw, I would never have believed it." But the rabbi chides him. How then could you ever learn from the Torah? he asks — that is, learning demands faith, not only sight — and "in that instant the man turned into a heap of bones."

But others puzzled over the verse from Isaiah as well. The Pisikta — or homilies for special Sabbaths and feast days — compiled by Rab Kahana goes on: "A pious man, while walking on a beach in Haifa, wondered: Is it possible that the Holy One can hollow the east gate of the Temple with its two wickets out of a single pearl? Whereat a Divine Voice came forth and said: If you were not completely pious, the measure of justice would strike you down. The world — all of it — I made in six days . . . yet you wondered whether the east gate of the Temple can be made out of single pearl?" And then a miracle occurs, and the man is offered a vision of the same act as the "heretic" whose story has just been recounted. "The sea before him was divided, and he saw ministering angels hollowing, shaping, and carving designs in an object. He asked them: What is that? They replied: It is the east gate of the Temple with its two wickets being made out of one pearl."

What a sight: something akin to, bound to the wonder of creation itself! Here, the angels are working beneath the seas, even as we speak, hollowing out a great pearl for a future time, while above them roll the waves and down into their midst fall the remains of the ocean's lost, and the empires of the world draw swords and totter, and the Torah is taught in a corner. What a sight! Yet it is this seeing, this miraculous labor, this vast world, split in two so that its divine truth can be grasped, and where flesh and bone find their way — it is this that the Scriptures open up, at least in the hearing of these men and women.

My point here is this: the reality of the Triune God, the Trinity, can only come to bear within this set of mysterious rocks and their place within God's creative reach, scripturally at least. Yet how does that happen? Amid the storms and stones? Whether the eyewitnesses of Rab Kahana's Pesikta were related in any way to the testimony of the apostles (both Jews and Christians deny they were), and granted the fact that even the gleaming stones described in Isaiah's vision indicate something far greater than their own brilliance, so that we can rightly speak of the "figure" of a text like this — however we answer such things, in a world of many readers, shall we say the Scriptures here speak of the *Trinity* in particular? Or does the Triune God speak these Scriptures? And if these are not exclusive one of the other, how shall this be?

But leaving the rocks aside for now, what of the central image of the chapter, that of a marriage between Israel and God? We might well initially believe that it is the *marriage* imagery of this chapter — God as a husband, covenants of wedlock, procreative abundance or desiccation — that could indeed provide a Trinitarian intersection. On the one hand, what could be more "palpable" in a literal sense than the contours of the nuptial figure, engaged as it is with bodies coming together and giving birth? And on the other, the nuptial figure is one that has traditionally intertwined with Trinitarian impulses. It is true that the Christian tradition has made hardly any direct link between Trinity and marriage, that is, until very recently. Augustine, famously, rejected using as a Trinitarian analogy the male-female *imago Dei*, even in its fruitfulness, for two reasons: first, the image is "corporeal" and hence shared even with the "beasts" — it cannot exhibit the particular *imago* aspect underlined in Genesis; and second, if corporeal analogies or figures are to be used, then their corporeality must be respected, something that in the case of the Trinity would require a child, born of the union of Adam and Eve; but not only does this contradict the dyadic language of the *imago* as described in Genesis, it simply doesn't appear in the historical-corporeal narrative of Scripture itself.

Despite these kinds of concerns, however, the nuptial figure has always given rise to a kind of interplay of relationship, often in a way that works to bridge the kind of corporeal-spiritual logical divide Augustine noted. This is true even in Judaism where the Song of Songs, which evokes Rashi's praise at its most eloquent, quickly found a unique place, from the start, as a legally demanded and exclusive figural text, wherein God and Israel's life were so related, the Creator with creation, as to open up doors for distinctions within the deity itself, later exploited by Kabbalistic writers in the Middle Ages. Israel, in some speculations, incarnates historically the 9th and inclusive *Sefirah*, or emanation, of God known as Beauty, the *Tif-eret*. And the divine marriage of the *Tif-eret* and God's glorying presence, the *Shekhinah* — these being the male and female poles of God's self — became a commonly ritualized Sabbath enactment within Judaism. In this marriage, and in its weekly ritualizations, Israel is gathered into the process itself, the *Shekhina's* own incarnated members, indwelt by a special "spirit" or "soul." This, of course, raises all kinds of questions regarding the monotheistic obduracy frequently associated with Jewish faith. But that is just my point: the Old Testament's nuptial imagery is, at least historically, caught up in elaborations of God's own life, if only indirectly.

Obviously, in Christian interpretations of, e.g., the Song of Songs and its associated and widely scattered New Testament nuptial figures, the relationship of love between Bride and Bridegroom, the church or the Christian soul, or Mary herself as both, and her Lord, bound by the attractive powers of charity — all these provided a fertile soil for at least glimpsing God's Trinitarian life, however fleetingly and unsystematically. The systematizing has come only more recently, and from both the sexually liberalizing to the sexually traditional. It has even given rise to remarkable claims, on a more popular level, like the assertion, made by a host of Catholic and Protestant writers on human relations today, that "'the Trinity, Father, Son, Holy Spirit' is a *family* [emphasis added], and thus man in God's image must be made a family as well." Jewish thinkers, whether tongue-in-cheek or not, can see the ease with which this kind of thinking can be assimilated into pagan notions of human "tripleness" — man, woman, child — that end up being reflected, so they say, in Christian Trinitarianism itself as some "holy family," as the great Elijah Benamozegh pointed out.

So, why *not* the scriptural figure of marriage as a way into the Trinity of God? If it *is* a way in, it is not an obvious one, a way that is without pitfalls and contestation, even among "orthodox" Christians, let alone among those who read the Scriptures as straightforwardly as they can. And in any case, what is striking is that neither Jewish nor Christian exegesis of Isaiah 54 has ever been much interested in this nuptial figure, at least not in terms of what it might say about God. Consistent with Augustine's intuition, the corporeal images in Isaiah 54 seem to hold on to their own meanings apart from their Maker, with their fingers gripping. "Sing, O barren one, who did not bear. . . . For the children of the desolate one will be more than the children of her that is married, says the LORD" (Isa. 54:1). The question posed by traditional exegesis, as it turns out, is therefore instead focused on the question of concretely corporeal love: *whose* wife is she? and which woman is it that God really loves?

II. Wives and the Trinity

So we are in fact invited to deal with these figures, just as we would with the stones, whether pressing into the depths of the sea, or forward into the future, whether spoken of or speaking.

"Sing, O barren one!" (54:1). Of whom *does* the prophet speak? This will be the first and major question, and indeed, it is a question whose answer may seem to drown out the questions we are asking about the Trinity. Who is the barren one? The "congregation of Israel," say Jewish interpreters. This seems clear enough, and we may follow this plain-sense reading through. Yet how does the barren one stand vis-à-vis the "one that is married"? As Israel stands to the nations — "married" to their own gods, to their own idols and idolatries — this is what they answer: the "married" one, with children, is Babylon, or perhaps every nation in which the Jews have been taken. So then, who shall be the children of the barren one? For whom does one "enlarge" one's tent (v. 2)? For the children of Israel herself, for those taken away amid the falsely married, for those who one day, God has promised, will be free of perverted families among the Gentiles.

So we have two figures here, one of Israel and the other of the nations. And what shall become of them? For Jewish interpreters, in general, the nations disappear in this chapter. They are already married, and badly so. They have too many children, poorly raised, destined for destruction, and so they will finally diminish in the shadow of the "desolate" one whose tents are enlarged. They, who have mocked the desolate one, the ruin of the Temple and her seeming rejection by God, will find the coming of the Messiah "harsh," as the people long oppressed take their place, "dispossessing" them in the process (v. 3). And what shall become of the nations? As Rashi explains, in verse 15, if they were not willing to stand with Israel in the time of her barrenness, they will have no place with her in the time of her restoration and blessing: So, "our Rabbis explained it as referring to the proselytes to say that we will not accept proselytes in Messianic times. And even according to the simple meaning of the verse it is possible to explain: whoever became sojourners with you in your poverty, shall dwell with you in your wealth. Comp. (Gen. 25:18) 'In the presence of all his brethren he dwelt.'" Although Ibn Ezra accepts, on the basis of verse 5, that "all nations will accept the divine Law" in this time foretold by the prophet, who, in fact, *will* be left? Only those who "surrender." Those who return to the tents are Jews, not Gentiles. It is *Israel* who shall remain "forever," and the "everlasting covenant" referred to in v. 9, like the covenant made with Noah and all creation, refers to the marriage of God and *Israel*, not to Adam's race as a whole. The Messianic age is an era of particulars restored, not of particulars extended into generalities: God shall teach directly, in v. 13, but not some new or better or broader message, but the Torah itself, in all of its hard specifics. If you wish to live with God, you shall become a Jew.

"Sing, O barren one!" This, finally, is the very *land* of Israel, beset by sin for so long, rendered literally infertile by the failure to keep Sabbath year and Jubilee, contaminated by crime and idolatry, destroyed by divine wrath — yet finally, "married," that is "ruled" by God anew, and bringing forth "children" one after another, Jew by Jew — so says Philo, in one of the most ecologically-oriented exegeses of antiquity. The land of Israel: "mother of a large family."

A Gentile will be uncomfortable here, surely. And so, as we contemplate this traditional Jewish reading of Isaiah 54, going back to the text itself, within its location in the book as a whole, we might note a move towards something new in the actual shift from "Israel" language to "Zion" language used in the latter parts of Isaiah — a "new" people that is defined by something other than the bare lineage of the past. Perhaps here we can see a certain figural opening up of the text to the future, a future somewhat less exclusively Jewish-oriented. And perhaps we will have in mind here, somewhat subliminally, William Carey's famous — but no longer extant — sermon, of May 31st, 1792, on Isaiah 54:2-3: "Enlarge the place of thy tent, and let them stretch forth the curtains of thine habitations: spare not, lengthen thy cords, and strengthen thy stakes; For thou shalt break forth on the right hand and on the left; and thy seed shall inherit the Gentiles, and make the desolate cities to be inhabited" (AV). It was a sermon viewed as launching a missionary movement of Protestant evangelism across the oceans. And, of course, the referents of the figures here are ones we are familiar with as Christians: *ourselves*. Is this not the thrust of the prophecy, then, that Israel opens herself up to, not herself alone, not even herself primarily, but to the *Gentiles*?

Indeed, the Christian reading of the text is well settled from the beginning, and we shall return in a moment to Paul's use of Isaiah 54:1 in Galatians 4:27. And this settled reading more or less took the "barren one" *away* from the Jews and gave her promised blessing to the nations. Who is the "already married"? The Jews, says Theodoret, simply taking the opposite tack to his Jewish co-interpreters. The Jews have had their time, they have had their children, and they have exhausted their families. Now does the barren one of the Gentiles take a husband and bring forth offspring, so as to cover the earth. In Jewish interpretation of the chapter, the nations are simply left out at the end, and disappear as a focus of interest. There are seven "barren" women, says the Pesikta — and Israel takes her life and promise from each of them. But for Theodoret, there are only always two women, for whom God's history is structured so as to reverse their fortunes: there is Peninnah, who seems fertile at first but is barren spiritually and ultimately, and there is Hannah, the church, to be fertile at last for all times.

The figural lines, in all this, are driven by the historical hopes and resentments of the reader's experienced destiny in God's hands. One aspect of this press towards the Gentile wife, as it were, lies in the LXX's peculiar translation of 54:15, used by Greek Christians. The LXX takes the root *gwr* in the sense of "sojourner" rather than as one who "gathers together" for ill. So the verse in the Greek goes like this: "behold! *proselytes* shall come to you through me. . . ." It does *not* read: "if anyone stirs up strife, it is not from me [i.e. God]," as the RSV, based on the Hebrew, has it, along with a number of other Jewish interpretations. The Greek Fathers all took the reading of the LXX, of course, and saw in the streaming of the proselytes to Zion a figure of the Gentile church writ large. The dynamic was well set against which to read verse 3, for instance, when the "inheritance" of the nations represents the nations, in fact, *taking over* the role of bride for God. Jewish exegesis, by contrast and well aware of this possible meaning, becomes clearer as time goes on and as the experience of persecution by the church has become ingrained: no proselytes will come in who were not *already* faithful in the time of Israel's suffering. Those who have heaped misery upon the Jewish people will certainly not be invited to join them when God's blessing returns! (If this sounds rather vindictive in a hoped-for way, it is no different, I should add, from the general Christian approach to the church's persecutors: patience towards them in this world, yes; but there remains to the Christian a great thrill to come in watching persecutors suffer miserably in the arena of God's judgment, just as they themselves once threw believers in with the beasts. Or so say the likes of Tertullian and Lactantius anyway.) To be a "proselyte," in the sense of *joining together as one*, was, for both Jew and for Christian by the time of the 5th century, nothing to be sought: "proselytes" were those who "dispossessed" their hosts, by historical definition. "Proselytes are as bad for Israel as a scab," as one Talmudic sage puts it. And the Christian would probably reply, "even worse!"

The translation of verse 15, however, cannot be seen as singularly crucial in this movement whereby Gentile woos God away from his Jewish bride. Although Jerome, for instance, keeps to the standard Hebrew understanding in his Latin translation, he comments on the LXX, and this is only because its meaning is obviously implied in any case. Whether for Theodoret or Jerome, or even Augustine, there is no continuity among the two wives, the barren and the married, the newly fertile and the newly rejected, the Jew and the Gentile woman, the Jewish and the Christian hearing of the text, except in the language and figure of the promise taken in the abstract. And so for Christian exegetes across the board, the Temple figures the church of the Gentiles; Noah's Covenant, mentioned in 54:9, points to the Gentiles (not the Jews), and so on. Very early, Isidore establishes the Western tradition, despite the Vulgate, upon this basis: "So Israel is slain, and a people from among the Gentiles takes their place. The Old Testament is taken away from them, and the New is handed to us." There you have it: Isaiah 54 is cited precisely to establish the Gentile supersession. Not that, taken as a whole, it is simply triumphant. Rather, the chapter then presents, in the minds of especially Western exegetes, a narrative of the *ecclesia de gentilibus'* history of desolation, past (under the Devil and his angels) and present (under anti-Christ and others vv. 7-9ff.), awaiting final nuptial consummation (an apocalyptic view geared to Revelation).

There is rich material here, to be sure. Material that carries with it, as I have said, elements, words, verbs, phrases, that will fit somewhere into a Trinitarian grammar, later perhaps. For instance, the 9th-century commentator Haymo of Halberstadt opens his discussion of 54:1 with a reflection on the "barren" woman's figuring of Christ's own birth, passion, and death. And in this, he draws out connections, at least subliminally, in his coming discussion of the church under persecution, from Revelation 12. Still, the result is the same, only reversed, from the exclusivist eschatology of Jewish interpretation and its concern with Israel's groaning under the nations' rod, and their waiting for the Messianic age: in each case, the "other woman" stumbles or slinks off the stage, as God turns to the desolate one in order to take her to himself. So, the issue is not just about the historical fulfillment of Isaiah's prophecy — that is, whose interpretation is most historically accurate in its predictions, the Jews' or the Christians'; rather we are dealing with mutually exclusive referents from the start. It is *lex* — the dead law of the Jew — or *Rex*, the living Lord Jesus Christ, as Hervaeus neatly puts it. Which shall it be?

Oddly, our Christian exegetes make no reference to their progenitor in this approach to the text, that is, to St. Paul himself, who quotes Isaiah 54:1 in Galatians 4:27: "Rejoice, O barren one." Here he applies the verse to the "Jerusalem from above" (4:26), who is figured by Sarah and the new "covenant" of freedom in faith, as opposed to Hagar, the wife of Sinai and the enslaving law. It is not clear, as some scholars have more recently queried, whether Paul, in this famous allegory, is contrasting Gentile and Jew as human types, or rather Gentile Christian believer and Jewish-Christian (and circumcision-demanding) believer within the context of the particular Galatian conflict. But whatever the case, the contrast between these two women, wives of a sort, is complete and mutually exclusive in Paul's reading. There are no subtleties about the relation of peoples and covenants in God's providence, as there are, obviously, later in Romans 11.

Exegetically, it keeps coming down to the fact that there appear to be two wives: Jews and Gentiles. And the nuptial imagery, so potently expressed in Isaiah 54:5 — "For your Maker is your husband" — is in fact, in both LXX and Vulgate translations, allowed to drift into indirection at best ("For the Lord is the one who makes you" [LXX], or "For he who made you shall rule over you" [Vulgate]), even though the context, as well as Hebrew usage, makes clear that "rule" here refers precisely to "husband," and to nothing else. A husband, yes; but that is not what is at stake in this argument of interpreters. No, it is the *wife* who is at issue, not God. Which woman does God love more?

Where is the Trinity? Somewhere else, presumably; not directly in a rich text like Isaiah as a whole, let alone Isaiah 54. This is what I want to stress, and what creates the difficulty of the text's Christian depths. Even Isidore, in his *De Fide Catholica*, can gather in references from *elsewhere* in Isaiah that make the specifically *Trinitarian* point (I.4), so it is not the case that no one is looking: "I am the first and the last, my hand laid the foundation of the earth, and the Lord God has sent me and his Spirit" (48:12, 13, 16); "Behold my Servant! I have put my Spirit upon him!" (42:1); "Holy, Holy, Holy, is the Lord God of hosts!" (6:3), and so on, with many more Old Testament texts adduced besides, most of which had already become standard fodder in the Christian Trinitarian apologetic. But all this is at the opening *only* of what turns out to be a very long book; Isidore's treatise on the "Catholic Faith" moves quickly beyond these wooden apologetic tropes, focusing on Jesus' step-by-step rejection at every stage of his life by the Jews, and so marches almost inexorably and with greater and greater momentum away from such mining of divine imagery, and towards the repeated and numbing, and finally triumphant shout of, what?, a woman *chosen* over her rival. Who does God love most? That appears to be of more interest than the love of God itself.

One might answer: all this represents simply the cultural constraints that inevitably inhere in any interpretive tradition. Why not put aside the Isidores and Theodores, the Rashis and Ibn Ezras, as interesting, but ultimately time-bound and therefore blinkered readers of the prophets? Our duty is to read Isaiah afresh, so as to find there the traces of our God in a way that puts aside these kinds of exegetical rivalries that, after all, seem to burden figural reading from the beginning, as if it is the peculiar clothing of the self-concerned. The reduction of Isaiah 54, in the Jewish and Christian traditions, to a battle over who is "chosen" is only a problem if the historicity of the referents — wives, enemies, progenies, and sufferings — is pressed in a wooden fashion, in the midst of contentious debate. After all, metaphors can be variously rearranged depending on the rhetorical place of arguments, and why can we not simply take hold of the nuptial imagery in a renewed way that pulls it back within the orbit of our own Trinitarian revivals?

But historicity is precisely what *is* at issue, both for Isaiah, at least in the plain-sense reading of his words, just as it is for Paul in his stark allegorical contrasts of reversal. We get back to the referential question, and we dare not try to evade it. We are dealing first with a divine promise, tendered to a desolate people, one who *has* a history now redeemed or at least altered, who *will* bear children, who *will* be assaulted by others, yet *will* prevail. One who *will* engage and relate to others in new ways, and who, of course, stands in this history as she stands with God himself. That the referents of Israel and Zion and of the "nations" as they relate to her are to be located in just such a history is obvious from the surrounding chapters of Isaiah, if from nothing else. The issue is not that these referents are misattached, but that their histories demand an interpretation itself that tethers their time to some larger purpose and truth. And *that* is the deeper figural challenge that attempts, imaginative or not, to reframe the character of temporal reference itself, properly addressed. However we approach the prophet, we are asked to "make something" of the referents at play, to make a judgment, if you will, about their fate. Paul can treat his figures of Sarah and Hagar "allegorically," in a technical sense, that is, as *ad hoc* instruments for understanding, and thus as a kind of metaphor for his theological point. But *Isaiah* demands *in addition* a historical, and thus at most a typologically figural judgment.

III. The Bridegroom and the Trinity

We have looked at stones. We have looked at wives. Now let us look at the groom. The *theological* question here, the question of God, the question of the Husband, of the Man, is here in our hearing, as we have seen, a mystery of the wives' coexistence or disappearance, of one or the other and how this happens and what it means. The husband — "your Maker," the "God of the whole earth, [as] he is called" (54:5) — is thus swallowed up, in interest, that is, by the history of the wives. If Hagar and Sarah, why not Leah and Rachel? Ought we to go further, and speak of "brothers" also, as Pope John Paul II spoke of the Jews as "elder brothers" (though we know that the Catholic Church is also "mother," not "sister," according to the Vatican)? But if "brother," of course, Cain and Abel too enter the scene. These are all appropriate figural groupings. And they suggest, rightly, that we should seek the Trinity in such places as these: the ground from which the blood cries out, or Hagar cries aloud, or simply the misery of competing wives like Hannah and Peninnah. A figural reading leads us into such places so as to be discovered by God.

To do that, however, we need to make some major preliminary theological moves. Richard Hays, for instance, speaks to the "logic of reversal" in Paul's reading of Isaiah 54 in Galatians, a "logic" that is central to Christian interpretation of the prophet, and a logic that Hays himself admits goes "well beyond the referential sense envisioned in the original" of Isaiah. How does Paul do this? Hays argues that he does this through a kind of implicit linkage of claims: "you are Christ's," Paul says to the Gentile Christians in Galatians 3:29; but who is Christ himself? Is *he* not the "seed" of Abraham's promise, as he says even earlier in 3:16? *This* is Christ! then, Abraham's heir, and you are his. The logic of reversal — and it is a reversal of the plain sense of Isaiah after a fashion — derives from the Christological logic that makes of the Messiah the bearer of the "mother's" seed, and only thus, through appropriation to this referent, do the Gentiles "dispossess" Israel of her marriage.

It is a logic, however, that even on Paul's terms, continues to go well beyond this point of resolution, and in a way that reverses the reversal, as it were. (Now I move into my own theological reading.) After all, as the "seed" of Abraham, promised prior to the circumcision covenant, the Messiah is also inclusive of that covenant: for "in Him you were also circumcised with a circumcision made without hands, in the removal of the body of the flesh by the circumcision of Christ" (Col. 2:11, NASB). In the Messiah's circumcision are included Jew and Gentile alike, for, as Paul says, he is more than just any man, he is the "second" and the "last" Adam (1 Cor. 15:45), the "Universal Man," in fact, as Pascal put it. And if *this* is so, then all the rivalries of the world are, at least in potency, here taken up; Isaac and Ishmael, Esau and Jacob, Jew and Gentile would, therefore, find their resolution — whatever exactly that means — in Christ Jesus. For he has "created in himself one New Man, in place of two, so making peace" (Eph. 2:15). Shall we not say, then, going back to Galatians (3:28), in a verse that hovers uneasily over the call to "Cast out the slave and her son" (Gal. 4:30, citing Gen. 21:10), that nonetheless "there is neither Jew nor Greek, slave nor free, male nor female, for you are one in Christ Jesus" (Gal. 3:28)? Are not the two wives also, therefore, made one? A figural reading will take each wife seriously in her history of recrimination, and necessarily follow each wife's thread to the Christological source. At this point, history is not so much changed as it is redefined.

And only here is the question of God's being raised properly, we might say; a being that has somehow both given the word and performed that action spoken by the High Priest Caiaphas in John's Gospel, who, "as high priest that year . . . prophesied that Jesus would die for the Jewish nation, and not only for that nation but also for the scattered children of God, to bring them together and make them one" (John 11:51-52, NIV), that is, for *both* wives. It is only within this *historical* press of God's "coming" and bearing the Law that he himself has given to his chosen nation, exposed by its transgression, and somehow bearing-birthing a new people that *he* himself has formed — he, the inseminating Bridegroom as Isaiah would intimate, but also the travailing mother (cf. John 16:21; Deut. 32:18), even the gestating child within (Gal. 4:19) — all images of Christ Jesus himself from the Scriptures that, bound to the prophets' outline of God's history, display him openly: teaching, receiving, obeying. If there is a set of Trinitarian contours that somehow emerges from this press, it is only because of the press itself, the time of its strange enveloping of the human race.

IV. Figural Combustion and the Trinity

It is just this kind of historical press, in the sense of the palpable bearing by God of time's burdens in relation, in part because he is the author of this time, such that the "one new man" could indeed prove to be God's own coming somehow — just this press that motivated the Trinitarian evaluations that began to be made in the early church. One speaks of "economic" Trinitarian reflections among the first Christians, in part because of this; although also, as in the case of Tertullian who first uses the language of "economy," because of the way this ordering of time by God, in which Son and Spirit do their work, discloses something of God's ordering, or "economy" of himself.

My point here is not to enter into outlines of the significance or form of these early Trinitarian reflections, so much as to stress the location of their struggle: not the lurking form of the Trinity, finally uncovered, but the actual imposition of God's Triune act upon the instrinsically irresolvable conflicts of history, of Jew and Greek, of Israel and the nations, of Jacob and Esau, of warring wives, finally, of "old" and "new," the two-testamental character of time: *there* God speaks. Thus, history takes the form of the Scriptures.

Is it going too far to say, even, that the "proper" location of the "Trinitarian" question lies within the interaction of Old and New Testaments together, rather than simply in their proper ordering, or "harmonization" as some have put it? The church, at least in her rival exegesis to the Jews, cannot simply take the place of honor in such disputes, not least because she is always brought up against a plain sense that will not let her relax into an easy figuralism. So Paul warns, "Therefore let anyone who thinks that he stands take heed lest he fall" (1 Cor. 10:12), precisely in the midst of explaining the purpose of figural or "typical" meanings for Scripture's words: not to resolve, but to spur and to warn and drive forward. Only the plain meaning of God's word can prove the figure's power, and often under the sign of contradiction.

Isaiah 54, which is only of course but one limited example, seems to point in this direction, such that we can state several things about such *Old Testament* Scriptures that should probably be extended to all Scriptures, *mutatis mutandis*:

- These are not texts that can stand on their own, and as such "tell us" who God is, in any systematic or fundamental way, let alone a particularly Trinitarian way;
- They remain, in fact, problematic in themselves, so that, if read "in themselves," they not only fail to disclose God clearly, but they perhaps mislead in doing so;
- They challenge in their reading, however, the church's forgetfulness, constantly insisting that their referents are not easily assimilable into the church's self-image (whatever it may be!), and hence they are always subversive in their core, are always sacrificial, being read and heard often poorly, or read and thrown away;
- And so they serve to break the church upon the Scriptures in some real sense, always judging her ability to hear God speak, and *just in this judgment*, revealing God;
- This "breaking" is itself the figural meaning of Scripture as the orderer of history.

Isaiah 54 must take its place within the church's life as a part of a struggle between the Testaments for historical reference and amid a dispute over the claims of such reference. Which woman will you bless? Whose woman are you bound to in covenant? Each effort by the church to answer this is met by some fresh impossibility — which woman? becomes "whose proselyte?" — and the mission of the church begins to totter. The Trinitarian contours of God emerge, or in fact force themselves upon us, as Israel/Gentile (Jew/Christian) are, in all their rivalries, finally and non-polygamously married, and the "many wives" are put away, or rather are made to "come out" (Ezra 10:3), a phrase in Ezra that also means that which is a "going out," a growth, a new life, a fertile birth itself: "I will make you exceedingly fruitful, and I will make nations of you, and kings will *come forth* from you" (Gen. 17:6).

But the marriage takes place, as it were, through Christ in his powerful reach over time, and not through the simple merging of rival loves or making space for rival spouses. Obviously, we speak of the Cross, as does Ephesians here, and of nothing less. And it is this historical demand not to merge the loves that underscores the character of the Christ who is alone able to override such a simple identification. Kendall Soulen, who has done considerable theological work on the Jewish Israel–Christian church relationship, has argued persuasively that we are to affirm "Yahweh" as the "Triune God," for these are the names of the same God, and are thus equivalent signifiers, though in a personal way. It is an affirmation that is moored in the Christian tradition, but it is not one, Soulen says, that has been properly grasped, especially because it has been consistently subjected to the Old/New dichotomy of the Testaments, which has led, in a sense, to a dichotomy of names: once granted his Trinitarian name, of Father, Son, and Holy Spirit, "Yahweh" became "dispensable." Soulen is right, I think. But does he reckon sufficiently with the actual rivalry of loves in this case, a rivalry that is bound to just the dichotomy of Testaments he fears? Does Yahweh love as the Father loves in Christ? What Christian would wish to deny this? Yet how shall we affirm it exactly? To what shall we point, exactly, in the face of the rival claims?

It is easy to slip into inaccurate exegetical habits if we allow the rivalry itself to slip away, flattening scriptural texts and, in effect, simply looking aside from the argument itself. Soulen argues strongly that nowhere "in the entire New Testament" does Jesus "appeal to the authority of this Father to underwrite male privilege."[1] Yet whether we call it "privilege" or not, the Law of Yahweh *is* inscribed with a difference of sexual demand and accountability that many today would describe in terms of just such sexual differentiation and inequality. I am not entering this debate here, except to say that, on the very basis of their plain sense referents, and in the end, the Testaments are *not* equivalent, for they do not always say the same things, even if their divine burden is of a common and singular necessity. Yes, the Yahweh of the Old Testament *is* the same God as the "Father" of Jesus Christ ("our Father, who art in Heaven," says Jesus — though it is a completely non-Trinitarian prayer, in its simple petitions); Yahweh is the same as the Father and Son in their being as "one"; he is the same even as "the Father, Son, and Holy Spirit." All this is most assuredly true. But the historical contours of these names and their personal referents, in each case and in their juxtaposition, and hence the meaning they "deliver" scripturally, are not equal, just as my person as teacher and husband and father are exactly me, are the same, but they are not equivalent. Yahweh is

---

1. R. Kendall Soulen, "Hallowed Be Thy Name! The Tetragrammaton and the Name of the Trinity," in *Jews and Christians: People of God*, ed. Carl E. Braaten and Robert W. Jenson (Grand Rapids: Eerdmans, 2003), 30.

the Triune God, yes; but the Triune God *who speaks in the Old Testament*. And his Triune nature is, as it were, stamped upon the world's consciousness only as this world is forced to confront his looming life, speaking from and in the Old Testament as pressing into the New. The Trinity is given in the combustion of Old and New — not as a dispensational "economy," or as an "unfolding" (with all of its progressivist risks of supersessionism and Marcionism), nor certainly as "rival Testaments" (which is where simply leaving the Jewish-Christian argument alone would land us, and from which it is just the God who is Father, Son, and Holy Spirit who saves us!) but in an almost unstable correlation of the Testaments together, where either, on its own, cannot point.

This is, in fact, the burden of an early Christian like Tertullian's struggle to make sense of the Trinity: Out of the "contradictions" of God's own actions (even in the Old Testament), something is demanded that the New Testament alone cannot quite unravel — the strangeness of a Father hidden, who yet reveals himself, and so on. The New Testament speaks only *into* the difficult demands of the Old to make its own sense. But the New Testament speaks, not so as to resolve these demands, so much as, in the process, to be opened herself as a Testament in her own right. And, as we follow Tertullian's logic, we realize that this is hardly straightforward: he himself stumbles scripturally when it comes to the Spirit — oddly enough, given his own engagement with the New Prophecy. For in *Trinitarian* (as opposed to dyadic) terms, he must turn almost exclusively to the New, although this is something he cannot do apart from having first confronted the dyadic alternatives offered in the Old.

Distinct, non-equivalent, and absolutely necessary: the two Testaments are *necessary* to each other. But they are necessary not as ingredients to something greater, nor as sequential additives to a chemical process of knowledge: "take the Old, then add the New: the Trinity finally comes to view," to coin a false catechetical adage. No indeed: "existences that cause one another exclude one another," as Santayana observed negatively with respect to the modern habit of seeing the past as a "stepping stone" to the present or future. The two Testaments are necessary because this is indeed how and constitutes the fact that God speaks, God does work, and in so doing while doing many things, God "reveals." That is the figural assertion. For if the Trinity is a mystery, as surely it is, far more unsettling historically is the mystery of the two Testaments out of which the very conceptuality arises. Perhaps this is where any catechism, whether to the Susu people or anyone else, should begin (as indeed, in a sense Augustine shapes his own catechetical instructions) not with a statement of the nature of God as Trinity, but with the simple, if intrinsically *difficult* history of a divine creation that opens up to the problem of Israel and the nations.

Let me end this reflection on figural readings as historically combustive by returning to Isaiah 54 in particular. Having initially sought to find at least a vestige, if not more, of the Trinity within the marriage imagery of the chapter, I now join the ranks of those ready to put the brakes on nuptial Trinitarianism altogether. This is an exegetical conclusion that I use simply as an example of what kinds of topical conclusions may come from figural reading. Nuptial Trinitarianism simply isn't true to Scripture, in large measure because it gets the dynamic of the figural reach of the biblical word the wrong way round. We have already gone too far with our relational analogies in any case, and the descent into the maudlin realms of God's home-grown family-life is but one percussive bounce in the long tumbling. "One should renounce the very idea that the point of the doctrine [of the Trinity] is to give insight into God," as Karen Kilby recently put it,[2] and certainly no such insight as would project our struggles for social orderings, fraught amid the rivalries of relationship, onto the divinity.

The nuptial mystery has other theological (and scriptural) moorings, as do most of the forms of our created life with and under God, that do not require them to be squeezed out of his being in a way that in fact ends by distorting the Scriptures themselves (if not truncating them). Where is Wisdom to be found, Job asks, and where is the place of understanding (Job 28:12)? Is it to be found amid the angelic pearls upon the ocean floor? Perhaps not; for the deep and the sea say "it is not in me" (Job 28:14). But even Job must, in a sense, go there also, and discover the "economic" and historical press of God's life within the world, a world that God has made, and which he surveys "to the ends of the earth" (Job 28:23), thereby alone "understanding." This is the world comprehended only by two Testaments. The world of the seas, of angels laboring, of men and women seeking and receiving God's mercy and hard judgment too, on shores and in distant lands, the singularities of God's choices and speech, his coming, and his leaving, Rachel's children crying, and God's own and sole and lonely comforting as he takes this also to himself. And all this is the speaking of the Triune God, to the limits of whose life we are drawn and gathered. As we well know, in Sierra Leone it has been a long gathering even now, whose end is not ours to fathom, only to follow after.

---

2. Karen Kilby, "Perichoresis and Projection: Problems with Social Doctrines of the Trinity," *New Blackfriars* 81 (2000): 442.

CHAPTER 8

The Word's Work:
Figural Preaching and Scriptural Conformance

I. Figural Preaching and Its Constraints

Figural reading is not, as many suspect it to be, in itself a doctrinal prop —
a "reading into" the text of subsequent ecclesial ideas, often self-justifying.
Of course, Christians have and continue to practice the self-justifications of
such eisegesis. But in fact, ongoing figural reading, as I have described it, is
a way of being rattled in and from such postures, over time to be sure. The
time involved in such reading is what I will now explore. Scriptural doctrine
derives from and is embedded within the transformative existence of those
whose lives are themselves willingly enscriptured. The Christian tradition has
long noted this. (One could and should explore the pneumatological aspects
of this, but that involves another and separate study.) As we saw in Chapter 2,
the peculiarly "ascetic" quality of figural reading has always been central to
the discussions of its use. One need not adopt an Origenist anthropology to
accept this, since Protestant emphases on dispositional reading cohere with
the basic reality at issue: humility and receptivity before the creative act of
God within the Scriptures themselves. What is key to realize is the temporal
character of such dispositions. This is a matter not only of their growth "by
degrees," as Hooker would say, or in terms of levels of spiritual maturity, as the
Fathers would note. The temporal character of figural reading, more deeply,
is concerned with the proper engagement of what God is doing through the
Scriptures in the world. We might call this "experience," but this would be too
easily appropriated to contemporary debates over subjectivity. Rather, we are
dealing here with what I have called the artifactual display of the world as it
comes to us and as we apprehend it. The best scriptural figure of such a tempo-

ral disposition is Job, the book about whom is nothing but a long disquisition on providential history as the shape of a human life.[1]

In this concluding chapter, I want to speak to this dispositional question in the context of preaching, and figural preaching in particular. Indeed, I shall argue that the dispositional aspect of humility and receptivity finds its proper expression *just in* the figural reading of the Bible, such that figural preaching is its public face, its witness, commendation, and instruction. It is in such preaching — as speaker and hearer — that we join with all the creatures of heaven, of earth, and under the earth, and proclaim before God, "You have made me!," as Augustine wrote.[2] The Protestant claim regarding the "Word preached" is properly located in this act of created and humbled solidarity in joy before the Creator of all things.[3]

Let us return to simple figural questions of reference. Anyone who reads the Bible will have difficulty in a "plain sense" way of locating the exact meaning of any number of terms. I have suggested already that this must be the case with "exile." And in our last chapter, there was the obvious issue of the "bride" in Isaiah 54. These kinds of questions regarding immediate reference become yet more complicated when they seem to buttress further objects, such as those presented in Revelation 19 and 21 on the bride of the Lamb and the new Jerusalem. The meaning of these objects now in part depends, perhaps, on those earlier referents located elsewhere in the Bible. Not only that, they are given from within what we are told is a vision "in the Spirit" (Rev. 1:1, 9-10) as well as an auditory revelation (Rev. 22:8). Here we come face to face with the ineluctable figural press of the text: who exactly is being talked about here? The Christian church? Israel redeemed? Is this national redemption to be related to Psalm 102, which speaks of "restoring Zion"? If we follow these questions through, we enter into a figural galaxy of vertiginous breadth. For if these links of the book of Revelation's figures with earlier scriptural referents are proper, then the church herself is related to the "rubble" before our eyes, which nonetheless we love (Ps. 102:14). In which case, though, perhaps this church or Jerusalem or Zion "restored" is also related to that of Psalm 80, where the

1. See my chapter "Theology and Listening: Considering Job," in *Developing Ears to Hear: Listening in Pastoral Ministry, the Spiritual Life, and Theology*, ed. Aaron Perry (Lexington: Emeth Press, 2011), pp. 155-68.

2. Augustine, *Confessions* 10.6.9; *Expositions of the Psalms*, on 148, 10 and elsewhere.

3. One might well pursue this point in the context of cultural shifts that have surrounded preaching in our day, and have defined its decline, both in importance and credibility; that is, as preaching has become detached from its continuity with creation's witness to God, and become a specialized and rather narrowly defined theological act — of teaching or event-based experience — it has lost its purchase on the natural receptiveness of human listeners.

"vine" is now trampled and burnt. The church as vine? Yet this vine, is it not Jesus himself, as he himself says in John 15:1? With this in mind, even *he* is torn and trampled, as we know he was, as vine and heir to the vineyard both (cf. Mark 12:7). What then of Revelation 21 and *this* "new Jerusalem" coming out of heaven (v. 2)? What do we see? Is this not the same Vine that "every eye" shall behold in his coming (Rev. 1:7)? When he is "lifted" high (John 8:28)? Thereby "drawing" the world's gaze, and not its gaze only, but its very heart (John 12:32)? Has the bridegroom become the bride, confusing yet further our reading of Isaiah 54, but only because it is now deepened by the words of Ephesians 5:27-32, which presents the self-giving of God to the bride, who has become "one flesh"?

This tumbling out of texts — and I might have added many, many more — is a standard feature of figural reading. Each text is linked to another, not arbitrarily, but by quite distinct equations of forms, which pass from one part of the Bible to another: Jerusalem, vineyards and vines, Jesus and the Cross, husbands and wives, times past and times to come. One text "figures" another, connecting with its referent in a sequence that follows a simple rule of "transitivity," in logical terms: if a = b, and b = c, then a = c. Of course, "a," "b," and "c" each have their own complex properties and relationships. And that is where the richness of the linkages lies, so as to make their exploration always *en route*: tentative in its conclusions, yet driven in its thrust. "This for that," in the Pentecostal phrase, is an extended and processual equation, not a singular one. However one parses the procedure, this kind of concatenation was the common way of reading the Bible until the 16th century, and even beyond for many, as I have argued in Chapter 2.

But by the 18th and 19th centuries, it had begun to disappear as an established approach. By the 20th, it had lost its purchase almost entirely, and the "literal sense," now mostly seen in terms of exact and static historical reference, as something that can be established via critical study, became the only basis for understanding Scripture. The two questions that became the limiting boundaries of scriptural semantics were the following: "What did the writer of the text (whoever that might be, and we must find out) think he was referring to?" and then, "Did it actually happen?" Both questions could be answered, and in theory, through critical historical study. But the implications of the second question — did it happen? — remained contested theological issues, often depending on more and more complex hermeneutical discussions of the first (intention).[4] One can trace the development of modern biblical studies in

4. Cf Benjamin Jowett, "On the Interpretation of Scripture," in *Essays and Reviews* (London: John. W. Parker and Son, 1860), pp. 330-433, for a classic statement of this approach. De-

relation to these two questions, but one can also describe the development of modern preaching in these terms. In fact, most preaching today follows from the straightjacket of these two relentlessly modern questions, whatever the answers one gives to them. And my goal now is to try to show how we might reorient that approach back towards figural reading, so as to reorient, in the end, our preaching as well. It is almost the only means left for our truthful scriptural witness in an era in which time has become, not only the prison of our lives, but one to which we are confined for capital offenses.

Now at least two arguments more recently have been made about the modern "critical" approach to the Scriptures that I just summarized in the form of two ubiquitous questions posed to the text: what was the author's intent, and did it happen that way? We have seen these arguments get elaborated especially in the past couple of decades in increasingly skeptical directions. So, for instance, with respect to the first question, it is now often concluded that we *cannot* accurately tell what the "original authors" really "intended" because of our inability both to figure out who they were (as to discrete human persons who actually "composed" this or that biblical text) and what they thought in their minds (and what unconscious cultural bias influenced them) as they wrote.[5] These are matters both of construing historical method, the philosophy of the past, and socio-political approaches that have generally engaged the "hermeneutics of suspicion."[6] These newer interrogations of historical access

---

spite attempts at undermining this outlook, it remains the default position for popular readings of most documents, including the Bible. A good working example of the method, in literary terms, can be found in M. H. Abrams, "How to Prove an Interpretation" in his volume, *The Fourth Dimension of a Poem and Other Essays* (New York: W. W. Norton, 2012), pp. 106-29. Some of the contemporary attacks on a "hermeneutics of intention" can be accessibly engaged in John Maynard, *Literary Intention, Literary Interpretations, and Readers* (Peterborough, ON: Broadview, 2009). For a creative rebuttal, based on the philosophy of Roman Ingarden (which places works of art in the realm of "intentional" reality, as opposed to other phenomena), see Jeff Mitscherling, Tanya Ditommaso, and Aref Nayed, *The Author's Intention* (Lanham, MD: Lexington Books, 2004).

5. I have mentioned in Chapter 3, Jack W. Meiland, *Scepticism and Historical Knowledge* (New York: Random House, 1965). Meiland, for his part, defends the constructionism of the early Michael Oakeshott (e.g. *Experience and Its Modes* [Cambridge: Cambridge University Press, 1933]). More recent post-structuralist approaches have taken this to the extreme, informed by various political suspicions, e.g. Hayden White, among whose many works, see "The Politics of Interpretation," *Critical Inquiry* 9:1 (Sept., 1982): 113-37.

6. The philosopher Paul Ricoeur seems to have coined the phrase, to describe the approach of Freud, along with Marx and Nietzsche, in interpreting reality as a surface of misleading signs, obscuring deeper realities. In some ways, this could be applied to forms of figural meaning, except that, according to the "school of suspicion," the deeper realities are usually working darker purposes on the whole, and their external clothing usually acts in the

must, by logic, negatively inform the second question regarding historical factuality: it is not only the case that we cannot know what an author of the past "intended," but the construal of an event itself, as coming from the past, is often difficult to define in a universally valid format, because of the deforming forces that obscure intention. That is, accounts of "happening" vary in their form within different contexts, such that the simple dichotomy of "truth" and "fiction" cannot often be applied neatly. A "legend" is not truthful only to the degree that a "core" happening can be extracted from its deformative narrative baggage; but rather, so the theory goes, the very shape of the legendary narrative is designed to engage historical description within certain culturally appropriate (although perhaps morally suspect) parameters.[7] Finally, some scholars have pressed the point that, in any case, such authorial intention does not — historically — constitute the way that the Bible was actually put together or the form that it takes as authoritative "scripture" for a religious community.[8]

It is possible, from a purely historical-descriptive perspective, to locate figural reading within the general concerns raised by these more recent departures from historical-critical orthodoxy. We can say, for instance, that figural reading of the Bible was practiced in the past as a religious commitment that in fact is bound to the character of the Christian (and Jewish) faith itself and its understanding of Scripture. Such a reading of the Bible is part of what it has meant to confess the Christian faith, and it is also intrinsic to the purposes of the Scripture Jews and Christians ordered, preserved, and embraced as a unity: figurative or figural reading is what holds the Bible together as "Scripture" itself. Hans Frei offered a form of this argument, and thus far it has stood the

manner of deceit. See his *Freud and Philosophy* [1965], trans. Denis Savage (New Haven, CT: Yale University Press, 1970), pp. 32-36. Figural realities, by contrast, do not deceive but invite, delight, and transform.

7. Nineteenth-century anthropology consciously sought the kernel of fact within "legends" and folk-stories, and the issue continues to engage debate, especially in students of ancient history. See Emily Baragwanath and Mathieu de Bakker, eds., *Myth, Truth, and Narrative in Herodotus* (Oxford: Oxford University Press, 2012), especially the fine introduction, pp. 1-58, which lays out the ways in which this older approach is now superseded by the more flexible search for cultural "truths" given through the use of story. Narrative theory, more recently, has followed a more formalist path to a similar conclusion. Hans Frei's extreme form of this is given in his narrative-literary version of the ontological argument, in *The Identity of Jesus Christ: The Hermeneutical Bases of Dogmatic Theology* (Philadelphia: Fortress Press, 1975).

8. Brevard Childs, most notably in his *Introduction to the Old Testament as Scripture* (Philadelphia: Fortress Press, 1979), had this theme overshadowing the book as a whole, although he does not ever provide a clear definition of "Scripture" itself in religious terms ; Jon D. Levenson, "The Hebrew Bible, the Old Testament, and Historical Criticism," in a volume of collected essays by the same name, *The Hebrew Bible, the Old Testament, and Historical Criticism* (Louisville: Westminster/John Knox, 1993), pp. 1-32.

test of historical scholarship.[9] I have gone further, however, in founding this historical description of how in fact various Christian readers of the Bible engaged the Scriptures, upon the place of the Scripture itself within God's reality as Creator. That is, I have made a thoroughly theological claim. On the one hand, "intention" with respect to Scripture is properly located with God. But on the other, "history" itself is a subset of that intention, and therefore the question "Did it happen?" with respect to Scripture is irrelevant to the character of created time itself, which, on the subjective level, is nothing but the uses — intended or not — that creatures impose upon God's artifacts as they are presented to them, and, on the objective level, is actually equivalent to the divine intention given in the Scriptures. "To really happen" is in fact to be figured in the Bible; nothing more or less.

Irrespective of my own assertions here, the reappropriation of figural reading of the Scriptures has had its share of recent advocates, among whom are well-known scholars like de Lubac, Childs, Frei, and those after them. But no one quite knows what it means to take this seriously in practice, and none of these writers themselves offered much guidance on this issue. Taking up the topic of the lectionary, from Chapter 6, we can see how confusion over the matter of figural reading has actually driven lectionary reform over the past few decades. Certain Anglican lectionaries, like the Episcopal church's, had, in the 1970s, adopted new Sunday Propers — the appointed set of readings for the day. These had in mind, as part of their intent, a reappropriation of reading habits from the early church, i.e. typological relationships, especially between the Old Testament and gospel readings. Some of the impetus for this unexpected renewal of figural presentation of the Scriptures in lectionary form derived from the "return to the sources" associated with the Liturgical Movement that, since the early part of the 20th century, had been working, especially within Catholic and Anglican circles, to reconnect Christian worship

9. Hans W. Frei, *The Eclipse of Biblical Narrative: A Study in Eighteenth and Nineteenth Century Hermeneutics* (New Haven, CT: Yale University Press, 1974), especially in Chapters 2 and 16. George Lindbeck took this historical argument, and applied it (descriptively) to the way that the Christian faith "in fact" operates: to be a "Christian" is, in a purely definitional ("grammatical") mode, to have a Scripture that operates in a unitary and figural fashion. This is part of his ecclesiological argument for construing the Christian church as "Israel-like." See George Lindbeck, "The Church as Israel: Ecclesiology and Ecumenism," in *Jews and Christians: People of God*, ed. Carl E. Braaten and Robert W. Jenson (Grand Rapids: Eerdmans, 2003), 78-94; "The Church," in Geoffrey Wainwright, ed., *Keeping the Faith: Essays to Mark the Centenary of* Lux Mundi (Philadelphia: Fortress Press, 1988), pp. 178-208; and "'The Story-Shaped Church': Critical Exegesis and Theological Interpretation," in *Scriptural Authority and Narrative Interpretation: Festschrift Hans W. Frei*, ed. Garrett Green (Philadelphia: Fortress, 1987), pp. 161-78.

with its earlier roots.[10] But the new lectionaries of the 1970s, drawn initially from work by Roman Catholic post-conciliar reform, struck many as "unnatural." The Old Testament readings in particular were usually snippets from different books week to week, and were chosen, so it was thought, mainly for their rather forced typological associations. This made it difficult to preach the Old Testament "on its own terms," it was argued, leaving the first lesson mainly as a reinforcing and subordinate appendage to the gospel. This discomfort led the composers of the Revised Common Lectionary, which now represented more Protestant denominations who had returned to the lectionary tradition, to rethink the value of preconceived — either traditional or not — figural associations in the appointed readings.[11] The new lectionary they came up with still has a few of these typological linkages for special days, but far fewer. And even here, there is concern about what to do with this.

In practice, they are concerns that many pastors, and their churches, have not sorted out, except via default. Having Old Testament and New Testament lections and gospel readings that have little thematic unity, because each book is being read more "in course," and thus out of relation to the other books, presents peculiar challenges to hearer and preacher. Usually, that has meant cutting lessons out — no longer three plus the psalm, but perhaps only two, so as to minimize discordance among the readings. But that in turn has meant reading less and less of the Scriptures, and thereby preaching on less and less of the Scriptures. It is an irony of the readoption of the lectionary in contemporary churches that someone like Cranmer's initiating rationale for the lectionary itself — the "whole Scripture" for all the people — should now be seen as an impediment to popular understanding.

But this is perhaps because the very substance of figural reading was never understood from the start of the modern lectionary revival. Instead, we have remained attached to the two modern questions about Scripture, "What did the writer intend?" and "Did it happen?" These linger in the back of our minds, exerting deeply cautionary controls. And thus, when the Scriptures themselves proliferate before us — even if only in the form of three lections and a psalm — our concerns about their origins and meaning in these modern terms silence our imaginations, and tether our textual peregrinations. In general, these worries have led to the flattening out of our sermons: we are fond of single

---

10. For an overview, see John R. K. Fenwick and Bryan D. Spinks, *Worship in Transition: The Liturgical Movement in the Twentieth Century* (New York: Continuum, 1995).

11. See the good overview of the entire process by David R. Holeton, "Reading the Word of God Together: The Revised Common Lectionary and the Unity of Christians," *Communio Viatorum* 48:3 (2006): 223-43.

points on single texts, wrapped up and garnished with our own stories and ramblings, however serious.

This kind of general critique is standard today.[12] One of my simple arguments here, in this light, is that figural reading of the Bible in its homiletic context is a way of putting us back where we belong: into the text itself, away from our own logics (including certain kinds of syllogistic expository frameworks), limitations, and personalities. This puts us back into the text where God's word, in all his creative omnipotence, does *its* work of self-giving and conformation. In order to illustrate how this might be so, let me offer three examples, of different length, with respect to figural homiletics, and aimed at engaging the lectionary juxtapositions themselves. In the course of this, I will try to lift out, and then explain in greater detail, how in fact one of the greatest requirements for the figural preacher is less some kind of method of exegesis (other than the general openness to the figural character of Scripture itself), than the kind of dispositional *ascesis* I mentioned at the beginning of this chapter. To read and to preach figurally, is to read and preach as the creature of the God whose Scripture orders and tends the world. And this is something that modernity has little to say about, and certainly nothing of any value to say against.

II. The Presuppositions of Figural Preaching

Let me begin with an obvious figurally-driven text from the Gospels. It is one that is not actually read in most common lectionaries, a fact that is interesting in itself. But it is a Gospel text that happens to be nicely discussed by St. Augustine in a way that makes it a useful starting point for this discussion:

Matthew 27:3-10
When Judas, his betrayer, saw that he was condemned, he repented and brought back the thirty pieces of silver to the chief priests and the elders, saying, "I have sinned in betraying innocent blood." They said, "What is that to us? See to it yourself." And throwing down the pieces of silver in the temple, he departed; and he went and hanged himself. But the chief priests, taking the pieces of silver, said, "It is not lawful to put them into the treasury, since they are blood money." So they took counsel, and bought with them

12. From conservative Protestants, like John MacArthur, to mainline homileticians and theologians like William Willimon or Stanley Hauerwas, this has been a concern voiced in publications since at least the 1980s.

the potter's field, to bury strangers in. Therefore that field has been called the Field of Blood to this day. Then was fulfilled what had been spoken by the prophet Jeremiah, saying, "And they took the thirty pieces of silver, the price of him on whom a price had been set by some of the sons of Israel, and they gave them for the potter's field, as the Lord directed me." (RSV)

Augustine discusses this text at length in one place.[13] And he does so largely because, as everyone has noted, the part of the Old Testament that Matthew actually quotes as coming from "the prophet Jeremiah" (v. 9) actually comes from Zechariah (11:12-13), at least in the versions of the prophets we now use and that were generally used in the past. Obviously, this has bothered many commentators: did Matthew make a mistake? And if so, what are the implications of such a mistake — ones that clearly touch on issues of scriptural inspiration and veracity.[14] So Augustine takes up the question, and in so doing provides what is ultimately a figural explanation for the discrepancy of prophetic attribution, one that goes to the heart of the figural character of Scripture as a whole.

Augustine first addresses the main question head on: is there a simple scribal mistake at work in quoting the verse as coming from Jeremiah? Here Augustine adopts the method of a good textual critic: since everyone knows that the verse comes from Zechariah, the mistake would have been quickly corrected in most transmissions of the text. But, as he notes, most manuscripts are quite clear that "Jeremiah" is the right word in Matthew 27:9, and thus copyists had consciously insisted on keeping it, knowing full well that it did not cohere with

13. Augustine, *Harmony of the Gospels* III.7:29-31, in *Select Library of the Nicene and Post-Nicene Fathers of the Christian Church*, vol. VI (Grand Rapids: Eerdmans, 1956), pp. 190-93.

14. Contemporary inerrantists have continued to exercise themselves over this text, among many others, and have offered various ways to harmonize it with the Old Testament and with common descriptions of the canon. See, among many, Bodie Hodge and Paul S. Taylor, "Mixed Prophets," in Ken Ham, ed., *Demolishing Supposed Bible Contradictions: Exploring Forty Alleged Contradictions*, vol. 1 (Green Forest, AZ: Master Books), pp. 86-89. Here, various theories regarding the nomenclature of the prophetic books that may have been used by Matthew are explored, all based on, as it were, the two modern questions of "intention" and "facticity": what was Matthew trying to do (e.g. use common ways of naming this or that prophetic book), and did in fact Jews of the time use this nomenclature. There is little theological import to the answers given here, unlike certain earlier attempts to deal with these kinds of documentary inconsistencies, such as Charles Gore's famous argument for a "kenotic" human consciousness applied to Jesus, such that he could, and indeed, *must* make "mistakes" in quoting Scripture just like any other human being, because of the character of the self-emptying incarnation of God in his being. See his essay "The Holy Spirit and Inspiration," in Charles Gore, ed., *Lux Mundi, A Series of Studies in the Religion of the Incarnation* (1889), 10th edition (London: John Murray, 1890), pp. 315-62.

the text of Jeremiah itself. So the real question, for Augustine, is why maintain this incoherence unless, first, it was believed to be Matthew's actual words; and why believe that, unless there was some deeper reason for Matthew to say this?

Augustine then goes on to offer his own interpretation. First, there is a basic truth to be grasped: the Holy Spirit speaks "as one" among all the prophets. Thus, what Zechariah and Jeremiah say *must* be coherent, as a matter of divine truth; their revelatory content, as it were, must be the same. To say "Jeremiah" instead of "Zechariah," is a way of saying "all the prophets," in a kind of figural short-hand, or metonymy, even (in our parlance) a synecdoche. To speak of one prophet in the place of another is actually, Augustine surmises, to say "the Holy Spirit," since the Holy Spirit *is* the author of every prophet's words, *is* their coherence and interchangeability. Hence, if Matthew has said this, it is just because of this pneumatic reality that Matthew was moved by God to say it.

But Augustine goes beyond this kind of general theological explanation, and moves into the question of altered scriptural semantics that results from the framework being applied. There is something then more particular at work in the scriptural revelation that can now be pursued: not only are the words from Zechariah quoted by Matthew, but then there are two more phrases that Matthew adds: the amount of money is fixed as the worth of Christ according to the "sons of Israel"; and then the bit about the "potter's field." Neither of *these* phrases are in Zechariah *or* Jeremiah. But there *are*, Augustine explains, allusions to these phrases: in Jeremiah 32, for instance, we hear about the buying of a field, and putting the property's deed in a pot, an "earthen vessel" (32:15).

Here Augustine makes a complex move. First, he reviews the premise: Matthew deliberately wrote this paragraph as he did, at least pneumatically (that is, his "intention" was subsumed, whatever his consciousness, by the direction of the Spirit). And if this is the case, the association with Jeremiah, whom he mysteriously mentions, was deliberately provoked, as it were, from God's side. Hence, God would have us, the readers, draw what we know of Jeremiah into connection with the account about Jesus in Matthew. We are to do so because this is clearly what God directs us towards doing. In Matthew, then, we hear of the Potter's Field used to bury strangers (27:7). So, the Scripture here provides us with a set of figural artifacts: we have strangers, a field bought at the price of Christ Jesus, and an earthen vessel in which the deed for a future promised land is placed. Augustine draws this all together, by suggesting that in the Matthew text we see the promise of eternal life given to those who die as "strangers" in this world, but are buried in Christ and his death in baptism. That is to say, in this text, we find the "worth" of Jesus explicated theologically, and in nuance and depth. Jesus' coming and death is for you and me, and for our salvation from the despair and confusion of this world. The center of the gospel is announced to us in the immediacy of our experienced lives, in all their concreteness — "strangers" in exile, taken up by the Cross into the life of God.

Is this purely "fanciful," as modern interpreters like Frederic Farrar would say? Only within the limited framework of a certain understanding of what the Bible *is*. Augustine's own understanding, however, demands this kind of movement of reference, and in a way that tracks quite closely with the kinds of arguments I have made throughout this book. In this particular case, there are at least four main elements he brings to bear, each of which grows in complexity of explanation:

1. Scripture is the work of God (Holy Spirit).
2. It is thus utterly coherent and unified, as an expression of the coherence and unity of God. That doesn't mean there is no diversity; only that the diversity is not contingent and contradictory, but deeply demanded and integrated.
3. If Scripture is this kind of divine product, it must be integrated and coherent with the depth of God himself, that is with Christ Jesus. The God who *is* "in Christ" is the one who both orders Scripture and, insofar as Scripture speaks of God, is spoken of by Scripture.
4. The reading of Scripture is about finding this kind of integrated reality within the words, passages, texts, books laid out before one, such that one discovers there the actual shape of one's own self and world, because it is the shape God in Christ has creatively willed.

Augustine is, among the figuralist commentators of Scripture, unusually clear about the *process* side of this reality, and how this process is, in a sense, the important aspect of the interpretive task. That is, it is in *seeking out* the integrated character of the divine scriptural reality, rather than in actually establishing this or that single meaning, that the faithful reader of Scripture does his or her job — is, in fact, "faithful" to the Bible. And while this is an active exercise of the will, it is also one that is dependent upon a prior receptive spirit, one that in seeking "receives," in the dominical sense (Matt. 7:7). That is, in part, why he is often so tentative with his readings: "it seems to me," he will say; or "I offer this as a possibility"; or again, "it may be that this is significant," and "others may think in another way," and so on. But even this kind of *possibility* emerges only from "careful" and "painstaking" study in search of "prophetic unity" brought into relationship with the "evangelical narrative."

So, what does this tell us about preaching, in this case, Matthew figurally? I will list only three general attitudes or formative assumptions, rather than methods here, but they seem fundamentally important to shaping the figural preacher's approach to the biblical text:

1. There is a particular faith that lies behind it, with respect to the nature of Scripture and Scripture's God.
2. There is a work that comes out of this faith, reading, and preaching of a particular kind — pressing one to seek certain kinds of realities that we can trust are indeed given in the text.
3. There is a realm, rather than a single locus, that is the reader's destination; a place to move around, not a place to stand still, insofar as the text's meanings find their contours in relation to the breadth of Scripture and its reach over the entirety of the world.

All three of these elements are pertinent to our preaching, and all three go against very common assumptions about preaching held in our day, such as: To preach a scriptural text, we must approach it neutrally — exegesis, that is, is a matter of criticism. Or again, that preaching is a matter of clarifying a text, resolving its tensions, bringing the work of reading to an end. Or, related to this, that there is a clear place where, in a sermon, we must say, "this is what the text means," and our purpose is to lead our hearers there — from which we get our one point sermons, two or three points perhaps, but always *points*.

III. Figural Preaching and the Lectionary

With this in mind, let us move on, more practically, to another text from Matthew, this time as given within the lectionary proper. In this case we can see how the figural elements of preaching might apply within the juxtapositional framework we have previously examined. And in doing so, we shall also sense the way this must necessarily grate against or even subvert the kinds of common assumptions I have just enumerated. In this case, we can use the Propers from the Revised Common Lectionary for Advent 1A (RSV translation).

Isaiah 2:1-5
The word which Isaiah the son of Amoz saw concerning Judah and
    Jerusalem.
It shall come to pass in the latter days
    that the mountain of the house of the LORD
shall be established as the highest of the mountains,

and shall be raised above the hills;
and all the nations shall flow to it,
    and many peoples shall come, and say:
"Come, let us go up to the mountain of the LORD,
    to the house of the God of Jacob;
that he may teach us his ways
    and that we may walk in his paths."
For out of Zion shall go forth the law,
    and the word of the LORD from Jerusalem.
He shall judge between the nations,
    and shall decide for many peoples;
and they shall beat their swords into plowshares,
    and their spears into pruning hooks;
nation shall not lift up sword against nation,
    neither shall they learn war any more.
O house of Jacob,
    come, let us walk
    in the light of the LORD.

Psalm 122

I was glad when they said to me,
    "Let us go to the house of the LORD!"
Our feet have been standing
    within your gates, O Jerusalem!
Jerusalem, built as a city
    which is bound firmly together,
to which the tribes go up,
    the tribes of the LORD,
as was decreed for Israel,
    to give thanks to the name of the LORD.
There thrones for judgment were set,
    the thrones of the house of David.
Pray for the peace of Jerusalem!
    "May they prosper who love you!
Peace be within your walls,
    and security within your towers!"
For my brethren and companions' sake
    I will say, "Peace be within you!"
For the sake of the house of the LORD our God,
    I will seek your good.

Romans 13:11-14

Besides this you know what hour it is, how it is full time now for you to wake from sleep. For salvation is nearer to us now than when we first believed; the night is far gone, the day is at hand. Let us then cast off the works of darkness and put on the armor of light; let us conduct ourselves becomingly as in the day, not in reveling and drunkenness, not in debauchery and licentiousness, not in quarreling and jealousy. But put on the Lord Jesus Christ, and make no provision for the flesh, to gratify its desires.

Matthew 24:36-44

"But of that day and hour no one knows, not even the angels of heaven, nor the Son, but the Father only. As were the days of Noah, so will be the coming of the Son of man. For as in those days before the flood they were eating and drinking, marrying and giving in marriage, until the day when Noah entered the ark, and they did not know until the flood came and swept them all away, so will be the coming of the Son of man. Then two men will be in the field; one is taken and one is left. Two women will be grinding at the mill; one is taken and one is left. Watch therefore, for you do not know on what day your Lord is coming. But know this, that if the householder had known in what part of the night the thief was coming, he would have watched and would not have let his house be broken into. Therefore you also must be ready; for the Son of man is coming at an hour you do not expect."

In reading these lections through, a range of images emerge. In this case, these can be laid out in terms of contrasts: Terror and light; ignorance and knowledge (out of Jerusalem); destruction and peace, and so on. There is a certain tension, inevitably, that this kind of juxtaposition of texts sets up. But — to go back to our first point — the figural reader will approach this tension with a particular *faith* that it is resolvable, by which is meant not a dissolution of the tensions in themselves, but a reading that can offer *divine sense* of them somehow, as read *together*.

This happens through the figural reader's faith that this sense is given somehow "in Christ." The sense is "given," however, not simply in an instrumental way, as if "in Christ" was a code for saying "Christ helps me make sense of the text." Rather, "in Christ" means that Christ himself is the referent of "terror and light; ignorance and knowledge; destruction and peace" itself. Christ is the referent insofar as the Scriptures refer to the act of God in Christ as creator of all things who conforms the world to his own purpose. Our "task" is to follow this out, and find him in the midst of this array of contrasts (among other things).

As I have insisted, this approach is traditional, and it is even vestigially held, like a fragmentary memory, in much contemporary Christian devotion. But the trace is too often only incompletely grasped, through the tendency to constrict applications to the already-resolved character of our own intuitions. So, Christological readings of Scripture will more often than not take one side of these contrastive forms exclusively: Jesus as light, as knowledge, or as peace, thereby closing down the antinomial force that fuels the figural search and discovery. To exclude one side of the contrastive referents in these particular lections, however, would be to turn our backs on the texts given over to us, even before we begin. To embrace both sides equally as Christologically referring is to be driven beyond the surface of our expectations.

There are in fact numerous possible ways into this deeper reading — a diversity that is part of the nature of the figural task — and here I will pursue only one, and in an effort, homiletically, to engage the appointed gospel, in conjunction with some of the other texts which in this case have acted as agents to stir the figural dynamic into motion. In the context of the contrastive tensions that all the readings present, Jesus claims both ignorance *and* a certain kind of knowledge, or demonstrated truth, one that is clear for all to see: we could call this the "sign of Noah." "Just like the days and acts of Noah." Ignorance and knowledge, as it were, coexist for Christ Jesus in *this* sign. And thus this sign — Noah — is a handle, a "figure," to latch onto, and by which to be drawn through the Scriptures as we seek to understand them "in Christ." Noah becomes the figural vehicle for navigating the antinomial tensions and contrasts whose full significance is given in the form of Jesus.

There are a number of directions in which the sign of Noah might take us. There is, for instance, Hebrews 11:7: Noah is warned of things not seen, and has "faith." Here we find the contrast of ignorance and knowledge given in a particular shape. There is, again, 1 Peter 3:20-22: here, the ark is made a figure of the resurrection of Jesus, such that we are found and saved "in him," through baptism. In the lection from Matthew 24, however, "entering the ark" contains a contrastive warning of destruction. The reading speaks of what lies outside the ark's walls and hull, a "sweeping away" of all things in their ignorance. Likewise, the gospel lection implies the hidden reality behind the warning, the alternative to which Jesus points as well: Noah's "emergence" with all life from the ark as the start of a new world upheld by the unbreakable covenant of God (cf. Gen. 8:1, 18 etc.).

Who then is this Jesus who speaks his words of warning, tied to the sign of Noah? He is *both* the place of safety and the sign of judgment, a convergence (or antinomy) that issues in life itself. The convergence is confirmed in other gospel texts, like John 16:32-33, where tribulation and overcoming are conjoined, where "peace" is given in a newly configured form, and where there is an "hour" that is both "coming" and that "now is." Is this the same "hour" to which Jesus refers in saying that "we do not expect" it (Matt. 24:44)?

One could continue according to various trajectories of texts, touching upon locality, the placement of our bodies, the proximate ties to this or that "city" — in the Lucan parallel to the Matthew Gospel, Jesus says mostly the same things, but now he relates his remarks to Sodom (Luke 17:22-37); and he also adds that "where the body is, there the vultures gather" (v. 37), which is a sign of the Crucifixion itself, such that our exit from the city of this world into the city of God is through the "veil" of Jesus' flesh, the Cross (Heb. 10:20), "a new and living way."

Were we to go this figural route, we would arrive at a kind of resting place: the Cross itself. And in fact, the Cross stands very precisely as the meeting of judgment and mercy, through which life issues. This is the ending point of Matthew 24's discussion of the "hour" and our ignorance of it and difficult preparation for it: the hour and our time is given here, in *this* hour and the new time it offers us. It is not so much that Matthew 24 and the texts of the Propers that accompany it are "about the Cross," although they are in fact. But rather they *lead* us here, and their work together lies in this movement. We can hold on to them, as in the handles in a climbing gym wall, in order to pick our way to such a summit as this, although with different possible routes.

The actual construction of a sermon that is drawn up such a wall will vary with respect to form and rhetoric. In our own culture's habits of cognitive focus, it is unlikely that most listeners could follow the multiplication of figural trails, even if they wished to. Nonetheless, a sermon based on figural reading will necessarily move beyond a single text and, in a way that is suitable both to comprehension and formation, engage some aspect of the network of scriptural forms whose constellation marks the work of God that is his truth. Such a sermon will find some appropriate way by which the biblical texts, in some manner of fertile replication, lead the listener to this resting place of expanded vision.

In my own preaching often, having followed this kind of figural way in my private preparation, I often go back in composition and try to raise questions about the text's treatment of God's life or our own. Doing that allows me to retrace this textual journey in a more ordered fashion. One might take the praying for the peace of Jerusalem in Psalm 122 from the Propers above, or "walking in the light" in Paul's text and start with these scriptural statements and the questions they pose: what *is* the nature of peace, or of the church, or of our moral life itself? These can be raised in ways that are very concrete and perhaps even personal. But having put these forward, I can then lay out in the course of the sermon, as a pathway of understanding, the exploration of those realities that take us from Matthew 24 into the Ark of Christ, and its journey through the world — *these*, as it were, tell us about peace or the church or walking in the light. And we can indeed speak specifically to the reality of such a peace, or church, or walking, in this case as something that must be understood through and as bound to the Cross of Jesus. But in doing this, all (or at least many) of these texts will and *should* find their place in the sermon.

Whatever the rhetorical routes one follows, the founding and engagement of this "figural way" of reading these texts do indeed depend upon the three elements I mentioned above. I must first take the Scriptures themselves — in this case given in a set of lectionary Propers — to be the ordering power of God. I must have faith in this. With the psalmist, I must cry out, "Let your word be my path!" And in this faith, I set myself upon a task: to "search" the Scriptures, to follow this path or paths as they lay them out. The labor of journeying is an essential element of the reading here, and it is something into which we lead others as we preach. And although we want to avoid having people get lost in the texts, as they listen to us, we cannot avoid helping our listeners *work* to find their way within them. Although this is a tricky balance to maintain, the weight should fall on leading people *into* the texts somehow. And we do this because our goal is not to give a definitive or certainly final meaning to the text — a simple "message" or application. Rather, our figural goal is to lead and go with our people into a *realm* of meanings and trace out its parameters and interiors. It should be a realm in which, of course, we do not leave our listeners as disoriented wanderers, but as creatures taken by the scriptural forms themselves, so as to lead them further, or into a clearing, or back out again, in some posture of transformed wonder.

IV. Figural Preaching and the Anvil of the Word

For this is what the Scriptures in fact *do* to us. The agential aspect of Scripture is at the heart of its figural character, as I have been arguing throughout this volume. Time is use, and history is the one use by God of all his creatures. This use is the Scriptures themselves. And these engage the very power of God's life, in mercy and judgment both, whose enunciation from a human side then constitute gospel or blasphemy. To preach, then, is to be taken up by the Scriptures and with those who hear, to be created then and there. Here we find wrapped up and unwound our entire lives. To see, finally, the moral import of this reality, let me end with an extended reflection on one scriptural verse, which will prove to be a point of departure and return both, for the time we call our "life span."

Psalm 118:22-23 (1979 Book of Common Prayer):
The same stone that the builders rejected has become the chief cornerstone.
This is the LORD's doing; it is marvelous in our eyes.

How should we read this verse in this psalm? What does it "refer" to, in
the sense of what the words themselves — the stone, the builders, and so on
— are about? A figural reading, because it submits to the agential power of the
Scriptures, will say simply that these words are about whatever the Bible, as a
whole, says that they are about. Not what you or I say they are about, or what
this or that scholar may say they are about, or what this or that book or historian says that they are about; but rather the Bible itself. It will be the case that
the church in her fullness will rightly say what these words are about through
her "tradition," but only in the sense, as I argued in the last chapter, that this
tradition comprehends the fullness of the times by which readers themselves
have found lives in fact shaped into the forms of the words themselves.

What, then, says the Bible? Matthew's Gospel (21:42) presents it this way:
in the parable of the Wicked Tenants, Jesus caps his story by saying, "Have you
never read in the scriptures: 'The very stone which the builders rejected has
become the head of the corner; this was the Lord's doing, and it is marvelous
in our eyes'?"

What kind of speech is this? Is Jesus himself interpreting Scripture? He
goes on to say, "Therefore I tell you, the kingdom of God will be taken away
from you and given to a nation producing the fruits of it." Here, he (or Matthew, or the early church — for there are some manuscript differences here)
draws from Isaiah 8, "And he who falls on this stone will be broken to pieces;
but when it falls on any one, it will crush him." Are Isaiah, the psalmist, and
Jesus all talking about the same thing? And if so, what is it? The Pharisees,
we are told, recognize that "he was speaking about them." So, according to
Matthew, the psalm and Isaiah together are in fact talking about the Pharisees.
These are perhaps "the builders" mentioned in the psalm. But Matthew at least
implies even more: the psalm and Isaiah together are referring not only to the
Pharisees, but to them in relation to Jesus himself, who is this "very" stone.

The Book of Acts confirms this, when it recounts how Peter says, regarding a healing he has just performed: "be it known to you all, and to all
the people of Israel, that by the name of Jesus Christ of Nazareth, whom you
crucified, whom God raised from the dead, by him this man is standing before you well. This is the stone which was rejected by you builders, but which
has become the head of the corner" (Acts 4:10-11). Again, Peter later writes
something similar (1 Pet. 2:7). And now (in 2:8) he links the psalm with Isaiah
8:14 ("And he" — the Lord of hosts — "will become a sanctuary, and a stone

of offense, and a rock of stumbling to both houses of Israel, a trap and a snare to the inhabitants of Jerusalem"; but also (in 2:6) with Isaiah 28:16 ("therefore thus says the Lord GOD, 'Behold, I am laying in Zion for a foundation a stone, a tested stone, a precious cornerstone, of a sure foundation: 'He who believes will not be in haste'").

All of this — which it seems that Jesus himself, Acts, and 1 Peter (and we could add other related texts) have done — constitutes a "figural" reading of Psalm 118; and of Isaiah; and perhaps of Matthew himself by the writers of Acts and 1 Peter. When one text — Psalm 118 — becomes the means of gathering other texts into a jointly referring ensemble, we are talking about a "figure" — the stone. And this figure reappears elsewhere in its own guise: Zion and its inhabitants, sanctuaries and temples, traps and sins, and judgments and victories, all of which engage each other through the figure, and hence are related "figurally." And all these texts, as they speak, speak also of Jesus, of Pharisees, of people standing around, of churches, of cities and their inhabitants, and of preachers and hearers. And if these Scriptures so speak of the figure, then we too in our preaching must speak to the texts in this way, because in fact we *are* the very things enunciated in the texts.

Let us step aside for a moment and reflect on the significance of this challenge. If we do not preach this way, it is because we think that this is not what biblical texts are, or what they do. We may be willing to apply these texts in variously referring manners as we speak of the Christian message, but that is another matter; that is *us* looking for some kind of useful illustration drawn from Scripture to make a point, however important. Figural reading, by contrast, affirms that these meanings I have just sketched in relation to Psalm 118:22 are what these various texts are not only "really about," but are *actually doing.* And a figural reader will therefore inevitably find herself within the stream of Christians, from the Church Fathers, the medieval commentators, the Puritans and Anglicans who once preached this way, as one who is in fact at one with the same history that God creates through his Scripture. It is a history in which the very question of what Isaiah "intended" in the prophecies that bear his name — did he "intend" Jesus in his discussion of the foundation stone, or did the psalmist? — is of relevance only to the discernment of the vagaries of human desires, ones that the Scriptures themselves put in their proper place — the desires of a narratively reconstructed Israelite prophet from the "8th century B.C." (or B.C.E. which is another time itself), or the desires of those who fabricate such reconstructions, or the desires of those who call this the "true past" of a human being. Instead, the history of the Scriptures is that use by which God "alone canst order the unruly wills and affections of sinful men," the desires of human creatures according to his sin-

274

gle purpose.[15] Indeed, the figural reading of texts, such as Jesus, Acts, Peter, and Paul engage with Psalm 118 — and Psalm 118 and Isaiah conversely — is something we *must* do, if we properly understand *what the Scriptures are*. In a way parallel to Richard Hooker's notion of the public reading of Scripture according to the lectionary as a "witness" to the fact of God speaking, figural reading is an act of declaration of what the Scriptures constitute. It is not just a way of reading, explaining or articulating a "message"; it is a proclamation; and if not a proclamation outright, it is the path towards such a proclamation.

Figural reading is not, in any case, a method of interpretation; it is an un-covering, and "being confronted," and then taken in. And the issue is that the Bible is not the *object* of our varied gazes; rather, it is the *subject*. The Divine Word, the Bible, acts *on us*, not us on the Bible. How do we, as constructing agents of sermons, preach so that we are recipients, rather than givers of the Word? Gregory the Great famously said, long ago, that the Bible is like a "river, both shallow and deep, in which a lamb may walk and an elephant swim"; but his point was that "the divine Word," as he put it, is itself active in different ways for each person: it "causes trouble" for the "learned" with its "mysteries," he says, even while it "brings joy" or "encourages" the "simple" with its "clar-ity"; it "nourishes little ones" and "strikes" the learned with "wonder."[16] The "Word" *does* something to people: grasping this is itself a way of getting at its meaning and the character of God both.

As I have argued, this is in line with most thinking about Scripture through the 17th century. As Scripture came increasingly to be perceived as a textual *object* — the final and least interesting form of the Word's mani-festation in Wycliffe's hierarchy — even the most conservative of Christians began slowly to alter their way of approaching its meaning. Scripture could certainly be considered a literary document of generally supreme authority. But once a documentary object, that authority could be also questioned ac-cording to new modes of historical-documentary analysis, and the question of the Bible's authority — or "power" — drifted out as a separate category of evaluation, distinct from the Scriptures themselves and lodged in any number of proposed extra-biblical realities.[17] So, for instance, one could say that the

---

15. Collect for Fourth Sunday after Easter, in the 1662 Book of Common Prayer.

16. Gregory the Great, "Dedicatory Letter" to the *Moralia*, c. 4. See *Morals of the Book of Job, by S. Gregory the Great, the First Pope of that Name* (Oxford: John Henry Parker, 1844), vol. 1, p. 9.

17. Some of this took place through the scholastic identification of logical categories for understanding, e.g. inspiration as well as the receipt and understanding of Scripture as a pneu-matic event. For an introduction on the Reformed side, see Henk van den Belt, *The Authority of Scripture in Reformed Theology: Truth and Trust* (Leiden: Brill, 2008). But the development

Bible's authority lay in the fact or promise of inspiration, or in the historical relationship between the written text and the Holy Spirit, or between the text and the church and the church and the Spirit, or between created (or uncreated in some cases) human reason and methods of reasoning, or between conscience and social constraint, and so on. This is, in part, the scaffolding of modern interpretive experiments.

Most preachers, even among conservative churches, have been taught within some version of this cognitive structure, and certainly the scholars who teach preachers have been clear about the general "objective" method: to understand the Bible one must *first* figure out rightly the relationship of individual and church, of reason and tradition, conscience and society, science and culture and so on. Only then can one press or squeeze the Bible through this sieve of human knowledge that one has responsibly constructed, and, if lucky, get some potable juice. The Bible as literary object, in this perspective, is to be used; and its character becomes subjectively construed — even if by "subject" we refer to a social subject, like a church commission, an academic guild, or an identity group.

The figural tradition claims that this is an odd and deformed way of looking at the reality of Scripture. And there are some interesting scholarly payoffs to this rediscovery that even scholars of religious traditions that are structured around a "Scripture" more generally, as I indicated, have noted. We know, for instance, that the Desert Fathers spent much of their time in the "meditation" of Scripture (the Greek word from *meletao* — as used in 1 Tim. 4:15). But this meditation was generally far from the word's modern connotation of silent or "mental" reflection. Rather, in the oral, generally illiterate culture of the time (the 4th and 5th centuries) "meditation" for the desert monks meant vocalization of memorized or memorizing verses (cf. the Ethiopian eunuch in Acts 8), as we discussed in the last chapter. And this is why scriptural "meditation" was often urged by the monks as a defense against demonic temptation: *speak* the words of Scripture, and the demons will flee. Sometimes, these words might simply be a quotation from a gospel story, "Jesus, save me!" (cf. Matt. 14:30).

---

of "liberal" theology had a parallel effect, engaging the "Spirit" as a general phenomenon, of which the Scriptures became a subset of encounter. Coleridge is often associated with this view as is Schleiermacher, both with a good deal of unfairness, if also unintended and unfortunate influence. On what was once a standard way of reading that influence, see Alexander Hodge, *Systematic Theology*, vol. 1 (New York: Scribner, Armstrong, & Co., 1873), pp. 151-88. Finally, social and political changes contributed to this evolution of Bible reading, some of which, importantly, were located in the rise of a certain kind of university learning. See Michael C. Legaspi, *The Death of Scripture and the Rise of Biblical Studies* (New York: Oxford University Press, 2011).

Sometimes they could simply be the enunciation of a single word, like "new" from the title "New Testament." But in every case the monks believed there was power in the Scripture's words, an almost "brute power," as someone has put it, capable of exercising its authority purely on its own by being set loose within the world.[18]

And what of "understanding"? This was something to be grasped after, only from a certain perspective:

> To gain . . . protection, it was not even necessary, claimed one elder, for the monk to understand the words upon which he was meditating. A brother who battled with impure thoughts was told: "Watch your thoughts, and every time they begin to say something to you, do not answer them, but rise and pray; kneel down, saying, 'Son of God, have mercy on me.'" But the brother protested, saying, "Look, abba, I meditate but there is no compunction in my heart because I do not understand the meaning of the words." The abba responded: "Be content to meditate. Indeed, I have heard the Abba Poimen and many other fathers uttered the following saying, 'the magician does not understand the meaning of the words which he pronounces, but the wild animal who hears it understands, submits and bows to it.' So it is with us also: even if we do not understand the meaning of the words we are saying, when the demons hear them, they take fright and go away."[19]

The reference to magicians here may well make us think that this apotropaic use of the Scripture — warding off evil by the theurgic incantation of its verses — involves a "magical" way of thinking, negatively associated with both "primitive" and superstitious worldviews.[20] But Jesus himself quotes Scripture to the Devil during his Temptations. And it is not clear that his purpose is to provide a conceptually persuasive or probative response to Satan that thereby convinces him to drop the testing itself — that is, that the power of the Scripture lies in its content being properly applied and understood. At any event, the desert monks' use of Scripture in this case is closer to the Jewish use of the *mezuzah*, the traditional container of the first two verses of the *Shema* attached to a house's doorpost. And rabbinic literature abounds with stories much like those of the Desert Fathers in this regard. The Word has power in itself, like

18. Douglas Burton-Christie, *The Word in the Desert: Scripture and the Quest for Holiness in Early Christian Monasticism* (New York: Oxford, 1993), pp. 123-24.

19. Burton-Christie, *Word in the Desert*, pp. 123-24.

20. On the background to the concept of "magical thinking," as well as engagement with its developments, see Ariel Glucklich, *The End of Magic* (New York: Oxford University Press, 1997), pp. 108-12 and *passim*.

the blood on the Hebrews' lintels in the darkness of Egypt, like blood itself, which has created "life" in it (Lev. 17:11; cf. Gen. 9:4). And what is asked of the monk is not that he understand the Word — written or spoken, it makes no difference — first of all, but that he be open to that power in the Word's work within his life and world. The Bible itself puts it this way: "At the name of Jesus, every knee shall bow, in heaven, on earth, and under the earth" (Phil. 2:10). That is the end point of the Word's purposeful accomplishment.

This broad point raises the question of whether or not "interpretation" is itself really a primary part of a Christian preacher's (and any Christian's) vocation as a creature subject to the Scripture: what is *our part*, and therefore our responsibility, in the Word's work? Does it matter at all — as the monk wondered — if we even understand it? The question of the "efficacy" of the Scriptures entered the Scholastic *loci* by the 17th century within Protestantism especially. And here, the "power" of the Word was defined almost exclusively in terms of the Word being able to accomplish its own saving *cognitive* apprehension on the part of the inquiring subject. Scriptural efficacy was thus tied to categories like "sufficiency" and "perfection" or "perspicuity" and "clarity," and although it is described in the most vital ways as a "power," this power exerts itself in the Spirit as "converting, regenerating, and renewing the *minds* [emphasis added] of men," "convincing them of the truth" in a way that brings salvation.[21] Thus, the "efficacy" of Scripture lies in its interpretability, savingly imposed upon the believer. My point here is to question this primary way of describing Scripture's "power" — that is, as intellectual force — and hence the primary value placed on its interpretation in the first instance. Freedom and authority are exercised or embodied first in terms of what God's Word *does*, and this may or may not involve interpretation as we usually understand the term; and therefore "interpretation" may well fall into an aspect of Christian life where the contemporary notions and values of autonomy and constraint, which so inform debates over scriptural authority today, themselves take on a different sense.

Is it really the preacher's first job to be a master "interpreter"? As a professional theologian who often laments the ignorance and even anti-intellectualism of many clergy, I would want to say "yes"! But honesty about what I take to be the character of the Bible prevents me from going that far. For if the status of the Scriptures is that of subject and not of object, of agent and

---

21. Heinrich Schmid, *Doctrinal Theology of the Evangelical Lutheran Church* (Minneapolis: Augsburg, 1961), Pt. IV.51, p. 501. Schmid is quoting from the 17th-century theologian Johann Andreas Quenstedt, and supplies many other similar citations that stress the positive instrumentality of the Word to save sinners. Larger historical characteristics of the Word, however, are never discussed.

not of passive tool, then we must be open to the reality that the Word of God as Scripture is strong enough to do its work even when men and women are unknowing, perhaps even perversely blind, in their response to it. Like a human civil law, ignorance of which does nothing to provide escape from its sanction, the divine words are inevitable as well; they are inescapable. Though he is wearing chains "like a criminal," the "Word of God," Paul writes, "is not fettered" (2 Tim. 2:9). "For as the rain and snow come down from heaven, and return not thither but water the earth, making it bring forth and sprout, giving seed to the sower and bread to the eater, so shall my word be that goes forth from my mouth; it shall not return to me empty, but it shall accomplish that which I purpose, and prosper in the thing for which I sent it" (Isa. 55:10f.).

In light of all this, I want to make three points about figural reading's dispositional or ascetic posture, and then end with a broad application to the task of preaching that will return us to Psalm 118:22.

First, and to repeat matters I have already stressed, the Bible, precisely in its *words*, as well as its stories and forms, does its own work and wends its own way; it orders its own meaning and presses its own truth. Part of our calling as readers and expositors of the Scriptures is *to let this happen*. Our goal as preachers is, in large part, to *present* the words of the Word — openly and fully, to be seen, heard, and wondered over. If the words of Scripture are God's words, they are powerful for their own purposes and in a way that transcends our own ordering of its textual components. That is simply a matter of taking seriously the intrinsic character of the Bible itself.

All traditional discussions of figural reading, from Origen on — but I would argue, from the formative character of the New Testament on — have stressed a key point: the reading of Scripture is a Holy Spirit-led activity. The Holy Spirit "speaks" as we read — not in some primarily interior space of private cognition, but in ordering texts, and leading us into the path of this ordering. That is the "use" that God makes of us in the Scriptures. Figural meaning is the map or at least the traces, as it were, of this ordering of texts, of their juxtaposition and temporally emergent coherence. It is important to stress this "leading" character, so as to avoid the notion that the Spirit is the shape of our subjective "apprehension," something that emerges more and more in Protestantism in early modernity, as well as in some forms of charismatic reading. The Word is the subject, we are the object.

But obviously, this is not enough to say precisely because an undefined "subject" at work on us tempts us to project our own thoughts upon it. So a second element comes into play. The Scripture wends its way, pneumatically, as the *Word*, that is, the Son, made known as Jesus Christ. Hence, the coherence of the ordering of the Scripture's texts is coherent in and only in this sense that is given in the Word. This marks a key parameter for figural reading: it is essentially Christological. It will always show Christ, express Christ, reflect Christ, or lead to Christ. To be sure, figural reading does this in a myriad of ways: by resemblance, by contradiction, by association, and by questioning. The figures of Scripture are not wooden typologies, easily catalogued into columns and tables, as they came to be presented at various points in the Christian tradition. They emerge, even as they are pursued by the reader: "seek and you will find." But my point here is that this is exactly what we should expect, given the nature of Scripture itself: if prior to our being it is also the end of our seeking, the terminus of any effort or yearning, because it is the very fuel of our temporal movement from beginning to end.

After all, the hard distinction between "the Word" — the Son of God — and the "words" of Scripture that "witness" to this prior and more fundamental reality of God is, as far as I can tell, a relatively recent and modern discrimination. Wycliffe, as we saw, could make the distinction, but only for the purpose of subverting its usefulness. The "word" of the Scripture, in any case, is spoken of by the Scriptures themselves variously with respect to this matter of "words and the Word," and it generally seems to be so bound to the reality of God's own life that prying the two apart is rarely possible. The "words" that Jesus "speaks" are "spirit and life" (John 6:63), and, in the course of his discussions, they become interchangeable with the "bread of life" that is "his own flesh" and that he offers to the world (John 6:33, 35, 51). Similarly, the "word" that God sends in Isaiah is the literal (vocalized) word of his prophets, but it is also God's own personal "counsel," that resides within the interior divine being itself: God "confirms the word" of his servants and "performs" their words, even as these emerge from his own "counsel" that "stands" because it is in fact the very "oath" of God (Isa. 44:26-28; 45:23; 46:10-11). "I have counseled, I have spoken, I will do it" — these are equivalent statements of divine fact.

In a sense, the "word of God" is simply the will of God that takes its form in history — it is the act of creation as it fulfills itself in time. And so, "through him" — the Word — "all things were created" (John 1:3). Yet, as Jewish theology has long insisted, and not only amid the mystic speculations of the Kabbalah, the "him" of the "Word" cannot simply be distinguished from the "words" of Moses and the prophets, for upon the Torah's very syllables, enunciated within the very being of God, dangle the forms of the universe. When God "sends forth his word" to melt the snows and make the winds blow and the waters flow (Ps. 147:18), which "word" is it? Is it not the very "word he declares to Jacob," as the next verse asserts (v. 19)? And must we therefore not say also, the Word "in whom and for whom and by whom" all things are? Who can say exactly how; but they *are* somehow the same. And this "somehow" is the base of figural reading, its permission, its drive, its discovery — we cannot separate the words from the Word; nor must we allow ourselves to do so.

And finally, to speak of what the Word "means" is first of all, perhaps most of all, to speak of what the Word *does*. Hence, we are called to enter into the shape of God's use of time itself, which involves the full range of artifacts by which time is variously construed through our present uses — the confrontations, collisions, and reordering of human apprehension to the one Word. If there is a place for the sharing of "human experience" by the preacher, it is just here, but only here. For what the Word does is what Christians properly call history, or "the past," in which the Word's active creation is grasped, as we examined in our discussion of Isaiah 54, through the traces left among the debris of an encounter that God would confront us with. In a general line with hermeneuticians like Gadamer, Ebeling, and Vanhoozer, this is not "tradition" in some well-defined sense of accumulated and organized authority.[22] Rather,

---

22. One of the philosopher Hans-Georg Gadamer's major points is that, to understand a text well, one must study that text's "history of effects" or *Wirkungsgeschichte* (Hans-Georg Gadamer, *Truth and Method* (1960), 2nd rev. ed., trans. Joel Weinsheimer and Donald Marshall [London: Continuum, 2004], pp. 298-306). This refers to the "influences" a text has had over time upon and against the human traditions regarding its meaning. Only by accepting this history of effects, only by entering into its shape and force, Gadamer argued, can we, situated in our own shaped and influenced contexts, responsibly approach the text itself. So, to understand the Koran, one must properly not just read the Koran, but enter into the worlds that the Koran has helped to shape — in 9th-century Iraq, in 16th-century India, in 21st-century Paris. And, obviously, this kind of study takes a lot of deep and particular engagement. Gadamer's writing did much in the 1960s and '70s to weaken the simple historical-critical approach to texts, including the Bible, which sought meaning solely in terms of an author's or document's "original" intent, often groped after through elaborate experiments of historical reconstruction that quickly took over a text's plain reading. Rather, Gadamer insisted, we must approach the Bible — and this is our only ready avenue anyway — through a willing engagement of its tradition of interpretation. To reverse Gerhard Ebeling's famous phrase, the "history of interpretation is the history of the church." And the "history of interpretation" is now in full swing as a part of the biblical and theological disciplines of the academy. More recently, something called the "history of reception" — how a text has been "heard" and incorporated into a church's or culture's life — has been articulated as a method of interpretation, and Blackwell has inaugurated an entire commentary series on the Bible based on this approach (*Blackwell Bible Commentary*, gen. ed. Christopher Rowland; volumes currently appearing). Here, the history of interpretation is extended beyond just the range of formal exegesis of a given text, to include artistic and popular media, conscious and unconscious social and individual influences, traditional and anti-traditional readings and reactions. "The history of reception" is an almost political method, aimed at "uncovering" the suppressed and hidden effects of a text, so as to expose the dialectical engagement of alternative readers and interpretive communities and, this time upholding Ebeling's claim, demonstrating the "self-contradictions" of the church. (See Gerhard Ebeling, "Discussion Theses for a Course of Introductory Lectures on the Study of Theology,"

it is tradition in the sense that the past reading of the Word's work indicates the emergent contours of time's unfolding. And all this *is* the work of God.

The Word is always a providential Word; it is "providential" in the sense of being a prophecy that inevitably comes to pass, that works its formative power upon events and people. But as Jeremiah tells us (c. 28), prophecies are always read or apprehended as "true" only from behind, from the form of history as we see it already unfolded and unfolding retrospectively. One must wait for the Word to come clean before our senses. To be sure, this poses a problem: if interpretation is the act of submission to the Word, in one form or another, how is this to be done in the present, when the force of the Word's work is still emerging in our time? This dilemma represents the fragile vocation of the Christian reader of the Scriptures. And it indicates how important the "set" of our lives, the pattern of our hearts as being "open" and "humbled" to the Word's work, must be. We are always free to reject this work. We are also always ultimately forced to receive it, that is, to suffer it. This is true on both an individual and a corporate level: we are taken somewhere, willingly or by dragging, but to such a place we go (Jer. 15:2; Rev. 13:10).

Taken together, then, figural reading is based on opening up, being led, and then testing this against the forms of the historical experience that are left in its wake. And this arc itself describes the temporal shape of that ultimate artifact that is the Scripture's own creative work, that is, how creatures "become" who are they are created to be. Reading is becoming, in the sense that it marks the historical form of God's own given creative will in its simple totality. What we have called the "understanding" of Scripture is in fact another way of talking about the dispositional *ascesis* of the Christian recipient of Scripture's divine act.

One can see just this relationship between the Word's doing and the Christian understanding in these terms, in the context of one of the church's greatest

---

in *Word and Faith* [Philadelphia: Fortress Press, 1963], p. 430.) On some of these trajectories, see Mark Knight, "*Wirkungsgeschichte*, Reception History, Reception Theory," *Journal for the Study of the New Testament* 32:2 (December, 2010): 137-46.

These newer approaches to studying the Bible — history of interpretation and history of reception — are absolutely necessary aspects of a responsible reading of Scripture. Similarly helpful have been attempts to understand, in a broader philosophical framework, how "words" actually "accomplish" or "perform" things. This has been an interest taken up by those, like Kevin Vanhoozer, applying "speech act" theory to the scriptural text. (See, among other works of his, Kevin Vanhoozer, *Is There Meaning in This Text?: The Bible, the Reader, and the Morality of Literary Knowledge* [Grand Rapids: Zondervan, 1996], pp. 201ff.) But these, and other new disciplines, are useful only as they contribute to the fulfilling of our Christian responsibility to learn more and more about how God's Word is *in fact* shaping the world, the church, and our own lives.

figural readers himself, Bernard of Clairvaux. His sermons on the *Song of Songs,* not to mention any number of other scriptural and liturgical subjects, constitute a foundational treasure of Christian figural exposition and interpretation of the Scriptures. St. Bernard was also a man of action, who was willing to risk his spiritual capital upon matters that involved both church and state. One of these was what became the Second Crusade, and in the 1140s, Bernard traveled about the countryside of Germany and France preaching sermons to exhort the faithful to go to war against the Saracen. Stories are told that whole villages were emptied by his oratory, and at one point Bernard had to tear off his own clothing to provide fabric enough for the crusading crosses people were rushing to sew upon their cloaks.[23] In some of his recorded exhortations related to the crusading, Bernard urges his listeners on with a citation from Psalm 139:21: "Do not I hate them, O Lord, that hate thee?" This is the deep-seated motivation, welling up from the Old Testament. And it is in line with his notion of the Christian soldier who works for Christ, a new "kind of soldier," in fact, who can now do the work of the sword with an ascetic focus in his killing. "For soldiers of Christ, they can fight the combats of the Lord with all certainty, and without having to fear committing sin if they kill the enemy, or to fear danger if they are killed; for the death one deals or the death one suffers for Christ is not blameworthy, but merits a great glory . . . [I]f he kills, he is serving Christ, for as a minister of God 'he does not carry the sword in vain' [Rom. 13:4] . . . [and] when he extinguishes the life of an evil person, this is not murder: he is the avenger of Christ upon those who have committed evil."[24] In his "encyclical" letter commending the Second Crusade, Bernard writes: "What do you think, brothers? Is the Lord's arm shortened? Has he become too

23. Bernard's sermon to the gathered court and people, as well as his other crusading sermons, have not been preserved. But various fervent, if somewhat literary, pieces he wrote on the matter are extent, and certainly reflect his oratorical scriptural approach to the topic. His *In Praise of the New Knighthood,* on the Knights Templar in Jerusalem, written several years before the Second Crusade, offers a window onto his views at a calmer time, wherein the holy places of Christ's life are now figural settings for the virtues of Christian military life. But they are not without clear practical intent. There is, in addition, his famous Letter 363 to the people of the Rhine, given in Otto of Freisingen, *Gesta Friderici,* I.37-44, see pp. 60-63. See also the *Vita S. Bernardi,* cols. 381-83. I have used the easily accessible *Oeuvres de Saint Bernard,* tome 2 (Bar-Le-Duc: Louis Guérin, 1870), for *In Praise of the New Knighthood* and his later letters, as well as *De Consideratione.* On Bernard and the Crusades, see Jonathan Phillips, *The Second Crusade: Extending the Frontiers of Christendom* (New Haven: Yale University Press, 2007), chapters 4 and 5. It is worth placing Bernard's enthusiasms in a larger context; see Katherine Allen Smith, *War and the Making of Medieval Monastic Culture* (Woodbridge, UK: Boydell, 2011).

24. *In Praise of the New Knighthood,* c. 3, in *Oeuvres,* p. 294.

weak to save his heritage because he is calling you miserable worms to defend him and return what is his? Could he not send more than twelve legions of angels or say only one word to deliver his land? He could, as he chooses. But the Lord your God is testing you, I tell you . . . to see if there is anyone who will understand and cry for him. And for them, he has prepared a salvific remedy. . . ." How so? To "redeem their sins" through "killing the infidel."[25]

Bernard interpreted various verses in a similar vein: "Behold, now is the acceptable time; now is the day of salvation" (2 Cor. 6:2); "O mighty soldier, O man fit for war" (1 Kings 16:18), for you, "to die is gain" (Phil. 1:21). Exodus (16:3) and the psalm (72:19) are quoted to compare the Christian crusaders with the Israelites, warning the former to avoid the cowardice of the latter, and so on. It is all a figural design energizing and ornamenting the divine call specifically to "take up the cross" against the Muslims, by fighting them, killing them, and driving them from Palestine. This was figural reading, literally with a vengeance. Did Bernard rightly interpret these verses from Old and New Testaments? Who was to say at the time? Certainly, it is unlikely that today we would accept Bernard's exegesis even remotely. But why not? As it turned out, the Crusade was a terrible disaster, and led to the death of most of the Crusaders themselves, without accomplishing any of their goals (except, indirectly, in Portugal). Families were decimated, and Bernard's earlier boast that his preaching had left women "widows while their husbands were still alive" was now fulfilled in earnest and in death. God did indeed "breathe one word," but which one was it, and *on whom*? Who was now the pagan, the Moabite, the profaner of the Temple?

In the wake of the Crusade's failure, Bernard himself was crushed, and felt alternately betrayed by men and mortified by his own failure rightly to understand. Whom should he have listened to? And what are we to make of the interpretive outcome? Bernard's own sermons, including texts I have quoted from, were founded on a call to repentance: we live in a time of God's "punishing"; "corruption" covers everything; wickedness lies unchastised; our goal is to "appease" God's anger; our war is a form of "penitence" itself.

And in an odd way — but a very true one — Bernard had indeed been moved to repentance by the failure of the Second Crusade, as had many others left alive. Repentance, ironically, fulfilled through the failure to understand.[26]

---

25. Letter 363, in *Oeuvres*, pp. 33-35.

26. For an illuminating range of Crusader sermons that demonstrate the consistency of this perspective, see the work of Christoph T. Maier, *Crusade Propaganda and Ideology: Model Sermons for the Preaching of the Cross* (Cambridge: Cambridge Univ. Press, 2000); and earlier, his *Preaching the Crusades: Mendicant Friars and the Cross in the Thirteenth Century* (Cambridge: Cambridge University Press, 1994). On the debated question of Bernard's views

Like Lincoln's disturbing intuition regarding the Civil War in his Second Inaugural Address — both sides were praying to the same God, he noted, both sadly but with a certain awe — Bernard finally saw God's will, God's counsel and purpose, God's word, fulfilled even in this calling, where those not taking up the sword are, as Jeremiah says, cursed as much as those who do. Those "taking up the sword will perish by the sword" (Matt. 26:52); and "if anyone slays with the sword, with the sword must he be slain" (Rev. 13:10). We can say, looking at the traces of the Word's work, that Bernard had not gone far enough along the textual paths of figure.

That is one lesson to take from this example. But another is that the Word led him there on its own — "taking him to a place he did not want to go," as Jesus says to Peter (John 21:18). And for us, that is precisely the "tradition" we want our own reading to be tested by. For I use this story as a kind of figural parable itself. In this case, Bernard's reading, its failure, its consequences, all turned him to behold the origin of his quest itself: the Word. It stripped him bare, and led him *back* to another vision that he should have grasped before. Martyrs, saints, the Book of Revelation, and Jesus himself had told him this before: what "repentance" consists of, what "victory" over unbelief amounts to. But now, with this past looming up as the definition of his reading he could enter the figures of the Word's own making. The figural reading of Scripture demands that we too follow this kind of often dangerous course.

All this can be summed up concisely. Figural reading, in this light, emerges *from* the Scripture, in its parts and whole, as God's own active Word, that is the prior agent of all that we are to think and be. It is not a human method of reading brought to bear upon an inert text. And it thus involves an openness, or *being* opened to this priority of divine agency in the ordering of our reading. More specifically, the coherence of our reading is bound to the fact that this Word is *the* word of Jesus Christ, and speaks always of him somehow, in Old and New. And finally, the shape of this speaking is given in the form of our histories, and we can see this from the past, even as we are shaped into it in our presence.

The homiletic implications are straightforward. Since God is the orderer of Scripture's meaning, the preacher, therefore, has a simple and primary task: to *expose* listeners to as much Scripture as possible. The preacher's calling is

about himself in relation to the failed Crusade, I follow in general the judgment of Maria L. Ruby Wagner, "The Impact of the Second Crusade on the Angelology and Eschatology of Saint Bernard of Clairvaux," *Journal of Religions History* 37:3 (September 2013): 322-40. In *De Consideratione*, II.1, Bernard explains to the Pope how God has judged the sins of the church, and this seems to be his view, though one accepted with darkness. See the letter to him from Jean Case-Marie (Letter 386 in *Oeuvres de Saint Bernard*, tome 2, p. 49.

to lead people *into* the Scriptures, and surround them with the Scriptures as fully and profligately as possible, guiding them in and through a kind of luxuriant — if sometimes dangerous, though often beautiful and perplexing — forest or garden.

The preacher will expose them "in faith," a faith that God will act, that he *is* acting there, in this garden of fear and delight. Without insistence, without presupposition. And while there is much to be said about the concrete form in which this can be done, the goal is singular: the preacher at his or her best is leading people through this garden, or at least accompanying them, pointing out this and that, answering questions, a "guide" of some sort. To this degree, furthermore, the preacher must first be someone who has been *led* by the Scriptures into their divine coherence, so as to be a guide in the first place. Here is where the knocking and the seeking come into play. Enter the garden, roam about its range, and be ordered by the very power inherent in the words themselves, which are God's. Then speak: here is where I have been led! How are these plants, in all their confusion, to be *seen*? Can one trace, without argument, the tendrils? How far do they reach? Even unto Christ? And what has become of this growth as we have seen it among our brethren in the church's life? To answer these kinds of questions is to engage the figural process faithfully in a homiletic shape.

Here we can at last return to Psalm 118, as if to the very garden in which we began.

We have seen the stone, and we have learned that this stone is Jesus. It is a stone, we are told, that crushes. How then shall we look at Jesus as such a one? Made the chief cornerstone, it is as if God himself, in all his glory, has come among us and we, alas, stand ready to be struck down. It is as if we ourselves are hearing an announcement of the "day of the Lord": "Blow the trumpet in Zion; sound the alarm on my holy mountain! Let all the inhabitants of the land tremble, for the day of the LORD is coming, it is near" (Joel 2:1).

In the face of Jesus, the "stone that crushes," we are invited to think of such a day in any way we wish, this "day of darkness and gloom, of clouds and thick darkness!" (Joel 2:2). We can think of it politically, looking to Iran and Israel, or North Korea and the strange rustling of nuclear destruction; we can think of it environmentally — of droughts and flooded cities; or epidemiologically — a terrible day indeed. Or simply in the context of our own place in life. . . . The sudden loss of our job and the bills that are there to be abandoned, along with, perhaps, even our home. Or it might be the word that says, "a tumor like this is likely to end things." Or the child who, we have finally to admit, will never get better. Or our marriage, simply and irretrievably ripped apart. These are all horrendous endings, wiping things away — yet here, in Zephaniah, or

Isaiah, or Joel, they are joined to this recognition of something else — of the complete inadequacy of our claims before them, our sense of having been unable to do what needed to be done, even if that somehow escaped us in its form. "O my God," I say in this place, "take me not hence in the midst of my days, thou whose years endure throughout all generations!" (Ps. 102:24). As things are wiped away, we see ourselves more clearly, not necessarily happily; even as we see God as something so far beyond us that, as he meets us, he seems to take away any place we might find stability on our own. "Be silent before the Lord GOD! For the day of the LORD is at hand" (Zeph. 1:7). Simply recognize something: it is God, not another, whom we behold: "I am God; I will testify against you!" (Ps. 50:7).

Who indeed do we stand before? It is in this context, then, that Jesus speaks of the falling stone. The Day that comes, his own day, is the day when the keystone crushes, is it not? So that those who wail, who say aloud, "If you, LORD, were to note what is done amiss, O Lord, who could stand?" (Ps. 130:3), also exclaim "to the mountains, 'Fall on us'; and to the hills, 'Cover us'" (Luke 23:30).

What a place this is, when we cry out, "Fall on me!" It is, after all, as Luke tells us, the place where Jesus himself walks to Golgotha, walks his way to the Cross.

> And as they led him away . . . there followed him a great multitude of the people, and of women who bewailed and lamented him. But Jesus turning to them said, "Daughters of Jerusalem, do not weep for me, but weep for yourselves and for your children. For behold, the days are coming when they will say, 'Blessed are the barren, and the wombs that never bore, and the breasts that never gave suck!' Then they will begin to say to the mountains, 'Fall on us'; and to the hills, 'Cover us.' . . ." Two others also, who were criminals, were led away to be put to death with him. (Luke 23:26-30, 32; RSV)

Behold the Lord! Behold also the Man (John 19:5). They have turned out to be the same. The stone is he who has come among us.

As we follow along with Psalm 118:22, we come face to face with this reality. And dare we say it? "Oh Jesus, fall on me!"? Be thou the stone that finally crushes me! Let it not be any stone, any other mountain, any other rock; let it finally be you! The mountain of the Lord (Isa. 2:3), my Rock and my refuge (Ps. 18:2; 1 Cor. 10:4)!

Find me in the place I have wandered. Fall on me, with every edge and surface and weight that marks your will and your body. For it is your love only that covers a multitude of sins (1 Pet. 4:8).

The promise of figural reading, which is nothing other than following the Scriptures in their own work, is to recognize where we have come within the world: we have found our way.

There is only one reason for figural reading and preaching, just as there is only one reason for this small book: in some small measure, to once again be led, and once again be found.

Four Figural Sermons

The following sermons are given as simple examples of figural preaching. They come from differing periods and contexts of the church's life. I have chosen them because they are typical, short, and accessible within the public domain. But they do not constitute anything like a complete or synthetic set of examples. Indeed, each is deeply tethered to its own place. No matter: within it, the words of Scripture do their work.

I. Aelfric on Palm Sunday

This homily, by Aelfric of Eynsham, probably dates from the late 10th century. Aelfric was one of the most prominent scholars of his time, and his writings in Anglo-Saxon form the core of Christian exegesis from this period. The present sermon, for Palm Sunday, is a modern English translation.[1] *The homily is un-remarkable for its time in its focus. It makes use of traditional figures, drawn from the text of the Entry into Jerusalem by the earlier Fathers, identifying them and explaining them. But while moving towards what became a debased form of figural reading — standard tropes and types applied almost like a catalogue — Aelfric in fact engages the best of this approach: using the figures, he follows their*

---

1. Benjamin Thorpe, F.S.A., editor and translator, *The Homilies of the Anglo-Saxon Church. The First Part, Containing the* Sermones Catholici, *or Homilies of Aelfric. In the Original Anglo-Saxon, With an English Version. Volume 1* (London: Aelfric Society, 1844), pp. 207-220. For modern commentary, see Malcolm Godden, *Aelfric's Catholic Homilies: Introduction, Commentary and Glossary* (New York: Oxford University Press, 2000).

meaning as a way of disclosing the breadth of the gospel message, including Old and New Testament, and the full range of the story of Christ and humankind. Tropology is prominent, but so is its theological shaping by a gospel of grace. As an outline, in any case, the homily provides the scaffolding for any number of rich explorations and elaborations, based on the preacher's command of the scriptural texts.

"And when Jesus drew nigh unto Jerusalem, and were come to Bethphage, unto the mount of Olives, etc."

Christ's passion has just been read before us, but we will first say to you how he came to the city of Jerusalem, and approached his own death and would not by flight avoid his passion.

Jesus went to the city of Jerusalem, and when he approached the mount of Olives, he sent two of his disciples, thus saying, "Go to the town which is before you, and ye shall straight ways find an ass tied and its foal also: untie them, and lead them to me," etc.

It was known to the people that Christ a little before had raised Lazarus from death, who had lain stinking four nights in the grave: then those, who were believing, came to meet Christ with the honours which we have already mentioned. Some also who believed not, came, with no honours, but with great wrath, as John the Evangelist said, That "the chief priests of the people consulted among themselves how they should slay Lazarus, whom Christ had raised from the dead, because many men of the people believed in Jesus, by reason of the dead man's rising."

We will now proceed to the exposition of this text. The two disciples whom Christ sent after the ass betokened the teachers whom God sends to instruct mankind. They were two, because of the character which a teacher should have. He should have learning that he may with wisdom instruct God's people in true belief; and he should, by good works, give good example to the people, and so, with those two things, that is, with learning and good example, ever incline the lay folk to God's will.

The tied ass and its foal betoken two people, that is, the Jewish and the heathen; I say, heathen, because all mankind was yet continuing in heathenism, save only the Jews, who observed the old law at that time. They were tied; for all mankind was bound with sins, as the prophet said, "Every man is bound with the ropes of his sins." Then God sent his apostles and their successors to bound mankind, and bade untie, and lead them to him.

How untied they the ass and the foal? They preached to the people right belief and God's commandments, and also by many miracles confirmed their preaching. The people then inclined from the service of the devil to the worship of Christ and were freed from all sins through holy baptism, and led to Christ. An ass is a foolish beast, and unclean, and stupid, compared with other beasts, and strong for burthens. So were men, before Christ's advent, foolish and unclean, while they ministered to idols, and divers sins, and bowed to the images, which they themselves had wrought, and said to them, "Thou art my God." And whatsoever burthen the devil set on them they bare.

But when Christ came to mankind, then turned he our foolishness to reason, and our uncleanness to pure morals. The tamed ass betokened the Jewish people, who were tamed under the old law. The wild foal betokened all other people, who were heathen and untamed; but they became tamed and believing when Christ sent his disciples over the whole earth, thus saying, "Go over all the earth, and teach all nations, and baptize them in the name of the Father, and of the Son, and of the Holy Ghost, and command that they hold all the precepts which I have taught you."

The master of the asses asked, why they untied his asses? In like manner the chief men of every people would perversely oppose the preaching of God. But when they saw that the preachers, through God's might, healed the halt and the blind, and gave speech to the dumb, and also raised the dead to life, then could they not withstand those miracles, but all at last inclined to God. Christ's disciples said, "The Lord hath need of the asses and sends for them." They did not say Our Lord, nor Thy Lord, but simply, The Lord; for Christ is Lord of all lords, both of men and of all creatures. They said, "He sends for them." We are exhorted and invited to God's kingdom, but we are not forced. When we are invited, then are we untied; and when we are left to our own election, then is it as though we are sent for. It is God's mercy that we are untied; but if we live rightly, that will be both God's grace and our own zeal. We should constantly pray for the Lord's support; seeing that our own election has no success, unless it be promoted by the Almighty.

Christ did not command them to lead to him a proud steed adorned with golden trappings, but the mean ass he chose to bear him; for he ever taught humility, and in himself gave the example, and thus said, "Learn of me, who am meek and very humble, and ye shall find rest for your souls." This was prophesied of Christ, and all the things which he did before he was born as man.

Sion is a hill, and it is interpreted, *A place of contemplation*; and Jerusalem, *Sight of peace*. The daughter of Sion is the congregation of believing men who belong to the heavenly Jerusalem, in which is ever *a sight of peace*, without any strife, to which Jesus will bring us, if we follow him.

Christ's disciples laid their garments upon the ass, because he would not ride on a naked ass. Garments betoken works of righteousness, as the prophet said, "Lord, thy priests are clothed with righteousness." The naked ass is saddled with garments, when the simple man is equipped to the hand of God with the exhortations and examples of wise instructors; and he then bears Christ, as the apostle said, "Ye are bought with great price; glorify therefore, and bear God on your bodies." We bear God on our bodies, because we are a temple and shrine of the Holy Ghost, if we guard ourselves against foul sins: of which the same apostle said very awfully, "He who defiles the temple of God, God will fordo him." He who is not a temple of God is a temple of the devil, and bears a very heavy burthen on his back.

We will say to you a parable. No man may make himself a king, for the people have the option to choose him for king who is agreeable to them: but after that he has been hallowed as king, he has power over the people, and they may not shake his yoke from their necks. In like manner every man has his own choice, before he sins, whether he will follow the devil's will, or withstand it. Then if he bind himself with the works of the devil, he cannot by his own power unbind himself, unless the Almighty God unbind him with the strong hand of his mercy. Of his own will and his own heedlessness he is bound, but through God's mercy he will be unbound, if he afterwards merit his liberation of God.

The people who cast their garments under the feet of the ass are the martyrs, who for Christ's faith gave their own bodies to torments. Some were burnt in fire, some drowned in the sea, and were slain with divers tortures ; and gave us an example, that we should not, for any persecutions or hardships, forsake our faith, and incline from Christ, any more than they did. Many a man is accounted a Christian in peace, who would very quickly deny Christ, if he were sentenced to that to which the martyrs were sentenced: but his Christianity is not praiseworthy. But that man's Christianity is praiseworthy, who will not, for any persecution, incline from Christ, neither for sword, nor for fire, nor for water, nor for hunger, nor for bonds; but ever holds his faith with the praises of God to his life's end.

Those who hewed branches of trees, and with them prepared Christ's way, are the teachers in God's church, who cull the sayings of the apostles and their successors, and with them direct God's people to the faith of Christ, that they may be prepared for his way.

The people who walked before Christ, and those who followed him, all sung "Osanna Filio David!" that is, in our tongue, "Hail, Son of David!" Those who walked before Christ, are the patriarchs and prophets, who were before Christ's incarnation, and those who went after him, are those who inclined to Christ after his birth, and daily incline to him: and all these sing one hymn; because we and they all hold one faith, as Peter the apostle said, when he spake of the patriarchs, "We believe that we shall be saved by Christ's grace as well as they."

They said, "Son of David" because Christ is, according to his human nature, of the great race of David. Of that race was the blessed Mary his mother. They sung, "Blessed is he who is come in the name of God." Jesus came in the name of God, for the Heavenly Father sent him for our redemption; and in all the miracles which he wrought, he praised and glorified his Father's name.

"Hail, Son of David, in the highest!" The Saviour's advent and his passion were salutary both to men and angels; because we increase their host which the fallen devil had diminished; concerning which the apostle Paul said, "That all heavenly and earthly things should be re-established in Christ."

Jesus was staying in the temple from this day till now on Thursday, and both with doctrine and with miracles stimulated the people to truth and to right faith. Then the chief men became envious of his doctrine, and machinated with great deliberation how they might bring him to death. Death could not have approached him, if he himself had not willed it, but he came to men because he would be obedient to his Father till death, and redeem mankind from eternal death by his temporary death. Yet did he not compel the Jewish people to slay him, but the devil instigated them to the work, and God consented to it, for the redemption of all believing mankind. We have often said, and yet say, that the justice of Christ is great, that he would not forcibly have taken mankind from the devil, unless he had forfeited them. He forfeited them when he instigated the people to the slaying of Christ, the Almighty God, and then through his innocent death we were redeemed from eternal death, if we do not destroy ourselves.

Then it befell the cruel devil as it does the greedy fish, which sees the bait, and sees not the hook which sticks in the bait; then is greedy after the bait and swallows up the hook with the bait. So it was with the devil: he saw the humanity in Christ, and not the divinity. He then instigated the Jewish people to slay him, and then felt the hook of Christ's divinity, by which he was choked to death and deprived of all mankind who believe in God.

Christ's passion did not take place on this day, but the four evangelists recorded his sufferings in four narratives: one we read now today, and the others in this week. The Jews took him on Friday evening, and held him that night, and on the morrow fixed him on a cross with four nails, and with a spear wounded him. And then about the ninth hour, when he departed, there came two believing men, Joseph and Nicodemus, and buried his corpse before evening in a new tomb, enwrapt in precious garments. And his corpse lay in the sepulchre the Saturday night and Sunday night; and the Divinity was during that while in hell, and bound the old devil, and took from him Adam, the first-created man, and his wife Eve, and all those of their race who had before given pleasure to God. Then was the devil sensible of the hook which he had before greedily swallowed. And Christ arose from death on the Easter-Sunday, which will now be in seven days, of which it is more fitting then to speak more fully than it is now: but let us now speak of the dignity of this day.

The custom exists in God's church, by its doctors established, that everywhere in God's congregation the priest should bless palm-twigs on this day, and distribute them so blessed to the people; and God's servants should then sing the hymn which the Jewish people sang before Christ, when he was approaching to his passion. We imitate the faithful of that people with this deed, for they bare palm-twigs with hymn before Jesus.

Now we should hold our palm until the singer begins the offering-song, and then offer to God the palm for its betokening. Palm betokens victory. Victorious was Christ when he overcame the great devil and rescued us: and we should also be victorious through God's might, so that we overcome our evil practices, and all sins, and the devil, and adorn ourselves with good works, and at the end of our life deliver the palm to God, that is, our victor, and thank him fervently, that we, through his succour, have overcome the devil, so that he could not deceive us.

The death of sinful men is evil and miserable, because they pass from this short life to everlasting torments: and the death of righteous men is precious, for when they end this life of tribulation they will be brought to the life eternal, and then will their end be as a beginning, for they will not be dead, but will be turned from death to life. The body, which is the garment of the soul, will await the great doom, and though it be rotted to dust, God will raise it, and will bring together soul and body to eternal life. And then will Christ's promise be fulfilled, who thus said, "Then shall the righteous shine as the sun in their Father's kingdom," who liveth and ruleth ever without end to eternity, Amen.

II. John Donne on Christ's Judgment

There are far richer examples of figural exploration in Donne's preaching than the following; and also ones that avoid the extreme anti-Romanism that he exhibits here. Nonetheless, this sermon represents a clear case of the engagement of juxtapositional exegesis in a broad sense, one with, in this case, potential ethical and doctrinal implications that, in the end, focus on a substantive Athanasian-like message. The sermon here constitutes the second of a two-part series on "Christ as Judge." In the first sermon, Donne has treated the text from John 5:22, "The Father judgeth no man, but hath committed all judgement to the Sonne." Here he takes a text that seemingly contradicts this: "I judge no man" (John 8:15). While the ordering has a certain scholastic character, as well as a deep tropological edge, Donne actually moves, with explicit and frequently allusive scriptural breadth, to disclose the full pattern of God's purpose and providence in Christ, using the Son as the great figure of all human life, the "judge" whose "judgment" in its various incarnational and redemptive elements, structures all of human life. It is a marvelous example of the way figural reading opens up vast realms of doctrinal and moral discussion. But these realms, as Donne says, are found within the "field" of Scripture's own variegated "flowers." Donne (1572-1631) became one of the great preachers of England in his later clerical life, arguably therein outshining his earlier poetry. The selection is taken from an early edition of some of his sermons, and preserves the orthography and references almost exactly, with some minor paragraphing changes.[2]

Sermon XIII: Preached at Lincolns Inne.

Epigraph: John 8. 15:
I judge no man.

The Rivers of Paradise did not all run one way, and yet they flow'd from one head; the sentences of the Scripture flow all from one head, from the holy Ghost, and yet they seem to present divers senses, and to admit divers interpretations; in such an appearance doth this Text differ from that which I handled in the forenoon, and as heretofore I found it a usefull and acceptable labour, to employ our Evening exercises, upon the vindicating of some such places of Scripture, as our adversaries of the Roman Church had detorted in some point of controversie between them and us, and restoring those places to their true sense, (which course I held constantly for one whole year) so I think it a usefull and acceptable labour, now to employ for a time those Evening exercises to reconcile some such places of Scripture, as may at first sight seem to differ from one another; In the morning we saw how Christ judged all; now we are to see how he judges none; *I judge no man.*

To come then to these present words, here we have the same person Christ Jesus, and hath not he the same Office? Is not he Judge? certainly though he retain'd all his other Offices, though he be the Redeemer, and have shed his blood

2. John Donne, *Fifty Sermons Preached by that Learned and Reverend Divine, John Donne, Dr. in Divinity, Late Deane of the Cathedrall Church of S. Paul's, London*, Volume 2 (London: Ia. Flesher *for* M. F. I. Marriot, *and* R. Royston, 1649), pp. 101-6.

in value satisfactory for all our sins, though he be our Advocate and plead for us in heaven, and present our evidence to that Kingdome, written in his blood, seal'd in his wounds, yet if hee bee not our Judge, wee cannot stand in judgement; shall hee bee our Judge, and is hee not our Judge yet? Long before wee were hee was our Judge at the separation of the Elect and Reprobate, in Gods eternall Decree. Was he our Judge then, and is hee not so still? still he is present in his Church, and cleares us in all scruples, rectifies us in all errors, erects us in all dejections of spirit, pronounces peace and reconciliation in all apprehensions of his Judgements, by his Word and by his Sacraments, was hee, and is he, and shall he not be our Judge still? *I am sure my Redeemer liveth, and he shall stand the last on earth.* (Job 19:25) So that Christ Jesus is the same to day, and yesterday, and for ever, before the world begun, and world without end, *Sicut erat in principio,* as he was in the beginning, he is, and shall be ever our Judge.

So that then these words are not *De tempore,* but *De modo,* there was never any time when Christ was not Judge, but there were some manner of Judgements which Christ did never exercise, and Christ had no commission which he did not execute; for hee did all his Fathers will. 1. *In secularibus,* in civill, or criminall businesses, which belong meerly to the Judicatures, and cognisance of this world, *Iudicat neminem,* Christ judges no man. 2. *Secundum carnem,* so as they to whom Christ spake this; who judged, as himself says here, according to fleshly affections, *Iudicat neminem,* he judges no man: and 3. *Ad internecionem* [his final destruction in this life], so as that upon that Judgement, a man should despair of any reconciliation, any redintegration with God again, and be without hope of pardon, and remission of sins in this world, *Iudicat neminem,* he judges no man; 1. Christ usurps upon no mans Jurisdiction, that were against justice. 2. Christ imputes no false things to any man, that were against charity. 3. Christ induces no man to desperation, that were against faith; and against Justice, against charity, against faith, *Iudicat neminem.*

First then, Christ judgeth not in secular judgements, and we note his abstinence therein; first, in civill matters, when one of the company said to him, *Master, bid my brother divide the inheritance with me* (Luke 12:14), as *Saint Augustine* says, the Plaintiffe thought his cause to be just, and hee thought Christ to bee a competent Judge in the cause, and yet Christ declines the judgement, disavows the authority, and he answers, *Homo, quis me constituit Iudicem,* Man, who made me a Judge between you? To that Generall, which we had in the morning, *Omne judicium,* the Son hath all judgement; here is an exception of the same Judges own making, for in secular judgements, *Nemo constituit,* he had no commission, and therefore *Iudicat neminem,* he judges no man; he forbore in criminall matters too, for when the woman taken in adultery, was brought before him, he condemned her not; It is true, he absolv'd her not, the evidence was pregnant against her, but he condemned her not, he undertook no office of a Judge, but of a sweet and spirituall Counsellor, *Go, and sinne no more,* for this was his Element, his Tribunall.

When then Christ says of himself, with such a pregnant negative, *Quis me constituit Iudicem,* may not we say so too, to his pretended Vicar, the Bishop of Rome, *Quis te?* Who made you Judge of Kings, that you should depose them, in criminall causes? Or who made you proprietary of Kingdomes, that you should dispose of them, as of civill inheritances? when to countenance such a pretence, they detort places of Scripture, not onely perversly, but senselesly, blasphemously, ridiculously, (as ridiculously as in their pasquils, when in an undiscreet shamlessnes, to make their power greater then it is, they make their fault greater then it is too, & fill their histories with examples of Kings deposed by Popes, which in truth were not depos'd by them, for in that they are more innocent then they will confesse themselves to be) when some of their Authors say, that the Primitive Church abstain'd from deposing Emperors, onely because she was not strong enough to do it, when some of them say, That all Christian Kingdomes of the earth, may fall into the Church of Rome, by faults in those Princes, when some of them say, that *De facto,* the Pope hath already a good title to every Christian Kingdome, when some of them say, that the world will never be well governed, till the Pope put himself into possession of all (all which severall propositions are in severall Authors of good credit amongst them) will he not endure Christs own question, *Quis te constituit?* Who made you Judge of all this? If they say Christ did; did he it in his Doctrine? It is hard to pretend that, for such an institution as that must have very cleer, very pregnant words the carry in; did he doe it by his example and practice? wee see hee abstain'd in criminall causes, when they come to their last shift, that is, that Christ did exercise Judiciary Authority, when he whipped Merchants out of the Temple, when he curs'd the fig-tree, and damnified the owner thereof, and when he destroyed the Heard of Swine, (for there, say they, the Devill was but the Executioner, Christ was the Judge) to all these, and such as these, it is enough to say, All these were miraculous, and not ordinary; and though it might seem half a miracle how that should exercise so much authority as he hath done over the world, yet when we look neerer, and see his means, that he hath done all this by Massacres of millions, by withdrawing Subjects from their Allegiance, by assasinating and murthering of Princes, when we know that miracles are without meanes, and we see the means of his proceedings, the miracle ceases, howsoever that Bishop as Christs Vicar can claim no other power, then was ordinary in Christ, and so exercis'd by Christ, and so *Iudicavit neminem;* In secular judgement, Christ judges no man, and therefore that Bishop as his Vicar should not.

Secondly, Christ judges no man by calumny, by imputing, or laying false aspersions upon him, nor truths extrajudicially, for that's a degree of calumny; We enter into a large field, when we go about to speak against calumny, and slander, and detraction, so large a field, as that we may fight out the last drop of our bloud, preach out the last gaspe of our breath, before we overcome it, those to whom Christ spake here, were such as gave perverse judgments, caluminiating censures upon him, and so he judges no man, we need not insist upon that, for it is *manifestè verum;* but that we may see our danger, and our duty, what calumny is, and so how to avoid it actively, and how to beare it passively, I must by your leave stop a little upon it.

When then we would present unto you that monster Slander, and Calumny, though it be hard to bring it within any compasse of a division, yet to take the largenesse of the schoole, and say, that every calumny is either direct, or indirect, that will comprehend all, and then a direct calumny, will have three branches, either to lay a false and unjust imputation, or else to aggravate a just imputation, with unnecessary, but heavy circumstances, or thirdly to reveale of fault which in it selfe was secret and I by no duty bound to discover it, and then the indirect calumny will have three branches too, either to deny expressly some good that is in another, or to smother it in silence, when my testimony were due to him, and might advantage him, or lastly to diminish his good parts, and say they are well, but not such as you would esteeme them to be; collect then again, for that's all, that we shall be able to doe, that he is a calumniator directly, that imputes a false crime, that aggravates a true crime, that discovers any crime extrajudicially; That he is an indirect calumniator, that denies another mans sufficiencies, that conceales them, that diminishes them; Take in some of Saint *Bernards* examples of these rules, that it is a calumny to say, *Doleo vehementer,* I am sorry at the heart for such a man because I love him, but I could never draw him from such and such a vice, or to say, *per me nunquam innotuisset,* I would never have spoken of it, yet since all the world talkes of it, the truth must not be disguised, and so take occasion to discover a fault which nobody knew before, and thereby (as the same Father says) *cum gravitate et tarditate aggredi maledictionem,* to cut a mans throat gravely, and soberly, and so much the more perswasively; because he seems, and pretends to do it all against his will; This being the rule, and this the example, who amongst us is free from the passive calumny? Who amongst us hath not some other man calumniated? Nay who is free from the active part? Which of us in some of these degrees hath not calumniated some other?

But those to whom Christ makes his exception here, that he judges no man as they judge, were such calumniators, as *David* speaks of, *Sede adversus fratrem tuum loquebaris, Thou sittest and speakest against thy neighbour* (Ps.

50:20), as Saint *Augustin* notes upon that place, *Non transitoriè, non surreptionis passione, sed quasi ad hoc vacans,* not by chance, & unawares, not in passion because he had offended thee, not for company, because thou wouldest be of their minds, but as though thy profession would beare thee out in it, to leave the cause and lay aspersion upon the person, so thou art a calumniator, *They eat up my people as bread* (Ps. 53:4), as *David* says in Gods person: And upon those words of the same Prophet, says the same Father, *De caeteris,* when we eate of any thing else, we taste of this dish, and we taste of that, *non semper hoc olus,* says he we doe not always eate one sallet, one meate, one kinde of fruit, *sed semper panem,* whatsoever we eate else wee always eate bread, howsoever they implored their thoughts, or their wits otherways, it was always one exercise of them to calumniate Christ Jesus, and in that kinde of calumny, which is the bitterest of all, they abounded most, which is in scorne and derision, *David,* and *Iob,* who were slander proofe, in a good measure, yet every where complaine passionately that they were made a scorne, that the wits made libells, that drunkards sung songs, that fooles, and the children of fooles derided them; And when *Saul* was in his last, and worst agony, and had abandoned himselfe to a present death, and prayed his armourbearer to kill him, it was not because the uncircumcised should not kill him (for he desired death, and he had their deadly arrowes already in his bosome) but it was (as it is expressed there) lest the uncircumcised should come and abuse him, he was afraid of scorne when he had but a few minutes of life.

Since then Christ judges no man (as they did) *secundum carnem ejus,* according to the outward appearance, for they thought no better of Christ then he seemed to be, (as Fathers take that phrase, nor *secundum carnem suam,* according to his owne fleshly passions, (as some others take it) judge not you so neither, first *judge not that ye be not judged* (Matt. 7:1) that is, as Saint *Ambrose* interprets it well enough, *Nolite judicare de judiciis Dei,* when you see Gods judgments fall upon a man, when you see the tower of *Silo* fall upon a man, doe not you judge that that man had sinned more then you, when you see another borne blind, doe not you thinke that he or his Father had sinned, and that you onely are derived from a pure generation, especially *non maledicas surdo,* speake not evill of the deafe that heares not (Lev. 19:14); That is, (as *Gregory* interprets it if not literally, yet appliably, and usefully) calumniate not him who is absent, and cannot defend himselfe, it is the devills office to be *Accusator fratrum,* and though God doe not say in the law, *Non erit,* yet he says, *Non erit criminator* (Lev. 19:16), it is not plainely, there shall be no Informer: (for as we dispute, and for the most part affirme in the Schoole, that though we could, we might destroy no intire species of those creatures, which God made at first, though it be a Tyger, or a viper, because this were to take away one link of Gods chaine out of the world, so such vermine as Informers may not, for some good use that there is of them, be taken away) though it be not *non erit,* there shall be none, yet it is at least by way of good counsaile to thee, *non eris,* thou shalt not be the man, thou shalt not be the Informer, and for resisting those that are, we are bound, not onely not to harme our neighbours house, but to help him, if casually his house fall on fire (Prov. 25:23), wee are bound where wee have authority to stoppe the mouthes of other calumniators where wee have no authority, yet since as the North wind driveth away raine, an angry countenance driveth away a back-biting tongue, at least deale so with a libeller, with a calumniator, for he that lookes pleasantly, and hearkens willingly to one libell, makes another, occasions a second; always remember *Davids* case, when he thought that he had been giving judgment against another he was more severe, more heavy, then the law admitted; The law was, that he that had stoln the sheep should returne fourefold, and *Davids* anger was kindled says the text (2 Sam.), and he said, and he swore, As the Lord liveth, that man shall restore fourfold, *Et filius mortis,* and he shall surely dyes *O judicis superfluentem justitiam,* O superabundant and overflowing Justice, when we judge another in passion; But this is *judicium secundum carnem,* according to which Christ judges no man, for Christ is love, and that *non cogitat malum* (1 Cor. 13:5), love thinks no evill any way; The charitable man neither meditates evill against another, nor beleeves not easily any evill to be in another, though it be told him.

Lastly, Christ judges no man *Ad internecionem,* he judges no man so, in this world, as to give a finall condemnation upon him here; There is no error in any of his Judgments, but there is an appeal from all his Judgments in this world; There is a verdict against every man, every man may find his case recorded, and his sinne condemned in the law, and in the Prophets, there is a verdict, but before Judgment, God would have every man sav'd by his book, by the apprehension, and application of the gratious promises of the Gospell, to his case, and his conscience, Christ judges no man so, as that he should see no remedy, but to curse God, and die, not so, as that he should say, his sinne is greater then God could forgive, for God sent not his Sonne into the world to condemne the world, but that the world through him might be saved (John 3:17).

Doe not thou then give malitious evidence against thy selfe, doe not weaken the merit, nor lessen the value of the bloud of thy Saviour, as though thy sinne were greater then it; Doth God desire thy bloud now, when he hath abundantly satisfied his justice with the bloud of his Sonne for thee? what hast thou done? hast thou come hypocritically to this place upon collaterall reasons, and not upon the direct service of God? not for love of Information, of Reformation of thy selfe? If that be thy case, yet if a man hear my words, says Christ, and beleeve not, *I judge him not* (John 12:47), *he hath one that judgeth him*, says Christ, and who is that? *The word that I have spoken*, the same shall judge him; It shall, but when? It shall judge him, says Christ, *at that last day*, for till the last day, the day of his death, no man is past recovery, no man's salvation is impossible: Hast thou gone farther then this? Hast thou admitted scruples of diffidence, and distrust in Gods mercy, and so tasted of the lees of desperation?

It is true, *perpetrare flagitium est mors anima, sed desperare est descensus ad inferos* [Isidore], In every sinne the soule dies, but in desperation it descends into hell, but yet *portae inferi non praevalebunt* (Matt. 16:18), even the gates of this hell shall not prevaile against thee; Assist thy selfe, argue thine own case, desperation it selfe may be without infidelity; desperation as well as hope is rooted in the desire of happinesse; desperation proceeds out of a feare and a horror of sinne, desperation may consist with faith thus farre, that a man may have a true, and faithfull opinion in the generall, that there is a remission of sinne, to be had in the Church, and yet have a corrupt imagination in the particular, that to him in this sinfull state that he is in, this remission of sinnes shall not be applied, so that the resolution of the Schoole is good, *Desperatio potest esse solo excessu boni* [Thomas Aquinas]; desperation may proceed from an excesse of that which is good in it selfe, from an excessive over fearing of Gods justice, from an excessive over hating thine own sinnes, *Et virtute quis malè utitur?* Can any man make so ill use of so great virtues, as the feare of God and the hate of sinne? yes they may, so froward a weed is sinne, as that it can spring out of any roote, and therefore if it have done so in thee, and thou thereby have made thy case the harder, yet know stil, that *Objectum spei est arduum, et possibile*, the true object of hope is hard to come by, but yet possible to come by, and therefore as *David* said, *By my God have I leaped over a wall* (2 Sam. 22:30), so by thy God maist thou breake through a wall, through this wall of obduration, which thou thy selfe hast begunne to build about thy selfe.

Feather thy wings againe, which even the flames of hell have touched in these beginnings of desperation, feather them againe with this text *Neminem judicat, Christ judges no man*, so as a desperate man judges himselfe, doe not make thy selfe beleeve, that thou hast sinned against the holy Ghost; for this is the nearest step thou hast made to it, to think that thou hast done it; walke in that large field of the Scriptures of God, and from the first flower at thy entrance, the flower of Paradise, *Semen mulieris*, the generall promise of the seed of the woman should bruise the Serpents head, to the last word of that Messias upon the Crosse, *Consummatum est*, that all that was promised for us is now performed, and from the first to the last thou shalt find the savour of life unto life in all those flowers; walke over the same alley againe and consider the first man *Adam* in the beginning who involv'd thee in originall sinne; and the thiefe upon the Crosse who had continued in actuall sinnes all his life, and sealed all with the sinne of reviling Christ himselfe a little before his expiration, and yet he recovered Paradise, and Paradise that day, and see if thou canst make any shift to exclude thy selfe, receive the fragrancy of all these Cordialls, *Vivit Dominus,* as the Lord liveth I would not the death of a sinner, *Quandocunque,* At what time soever a sinner repenteth, and of this text *Neminem judicat, Christ judgeth no man* to destruction here, and if thou find after all these Antidotes a suspitious ayre, a suspicious working in that *Impossibile est,* that it is impossible for them, who were once inlightened if they fall away, to renew them againe by repentance, sprinkle upon that worme wood of *Impossibile est,* that Manna of *Quorum remiseritis, whose sinnes yee remit, are remitted,* and then it will have another tast to thee, and then wilt see that that impossibility lies upon them onely, who are utterly fallen away into an absolute Apostasie, and infidelity, that make a mocke of Christ, and crucifie him againe, as it is expressed there, who undervalue, and despise the Church of God, & those means which Christ Jesus hath instituted in his Church for renewing such as are fallen. To such it is impossible, because there are no other ordinary meanes possible, but that's not thy case, thy case is onely a doubt, that those meanes that are shall not be applied to thee, and even that is a slippery state to doubt of the mercy of God to thee in particular, this goes so neare making thy sinne greater then Gods mercy, as that it makes thy sinne greater then daily adulteries, daily murthers, daily blasphemies, daily prophanings of the Sabbath could have done, and though thou canst never make that true in this life that thy sinnes are greater then God can forgive, yet this is a way to make them greater, then God will forgive.

Now to collect both our Exercises, and to connexe both Texts, *Christ judgeth all men* and *Christ judgeth no man,* he claimes all judgment, and he disavows all judgement, and they consist well together, he was at our creation, but that was not his first sense; the Arians who say, *Erat quando non erat,* there was a time when Christ was not, intimating that he had a beginning, and there-fore was a creature, yet they will allow that he was created before the generall creation, and so assisted at ours, but he was infinite generations before that, in the bosome of his Father, at our election, and there in him was executed the first judgment of separating those who were his, the elect from the reprobate, and then he knows who are his by that first Judgment: And so comes to his second Judgment, to seale all those in the visible Church with the outward mark of his baptisme, and the inward marke of his Spirit, and those whom he calls so, he justifies, and sanctifies, and brings them to his third Judgment, to an established and perpetuall glory.

And so all Judgment is his. But then to judge out of humane affections, and passions, by detraction, and calumny, as they did to whom he spoke at this time, so he judges no man, so he denies judgment: To usurpe upon the juris-diction of others, or to exercise any other judgment, then was his commission, as his pretended Vicar doth so he judges no man, so he disavows all judgment: To judge so as that our condemnation should be irremediable in this life, so he judges no man, so he forswears all judgment, As I live, saith the Lord of hosts, and as I have died, saith the Lord Jesus, so I judge none. Acknowledge his first Judgment, thy election in him, Christ his second Judgment, thy justification by him, breath and pant after his third Judgement, thy Crown of glory for him; intrude not upon the right of other men, which is the first, defame not, calumniate not other men, which is the second, lay not the name of reprobate in this life upon any man, which is the third Judgement, that Christ disavows here, and then thou shalt have well understood, and well practised both these texts, *The Father hath committed all Iudgment to the Sonne,* and yet *The Sonne judges no man.*

III. The Sun Do Move[3]

John Jasper (1812-1901) was a former slave turned admired preacher in later 19th-century Virginia. This (deliberately truncated and not exact) transcript of a well-known sermon of his from 1878, recorded by a white colleague and friend of his, William Hatcher, is a good example of several key features of figural preaching, laced with humor: the movement through the Scriptures, on the back of a key figure, the sun; an allowance to let the figure uncover a range of realities about God and human beings that move in diverse directions — mercy, violence, unexpected intimacy; and the overriding ground of divine creative sovereignty.

This part of the sermon, the only part that is really known, is actually de-pendent on the larger theme, based on the verse "The Lord is a man of war" (Exodus 15:3).[4] It is the latter that is really the core of his seemingly anti-scientific posture. And in fact, the rich scriptural allusions that dot the sermon as a whole all move to a crescendo of religious vision that discloses the anti-intellectual jibes

3. William E. Hatcher, LL.D, *John Jasper: The Unmatched Negro Philosopher and Preacher* (New York/Chicago/Toronto: Fleming H. Revell, 1908), pp. 133-149. Another source for the sermon, putting it in, arguably, better context, is E[dwin] A[rcher] Randolph, *The Life of John Jasper, Pastor of Sixth Mt. Zion Baptist Church, Richmond, Va., From His Birth to the Present Time, with His Theory on the Rotation of the Sun* (Richmond: R. T. Hill, 1884).

4. See the discussion by Christopher Z. Hobson, "The Lord Is a Man of War: John Jasper, Covenant, and Apocalypse," *African American Review* 44:4 (Winter, 2011): 619-31.

to be nothing but a rhetorical vehicle for a very different message. The moving sun is a figure in its fullest sense, not at all a scientific claim made to replace Isaac Newton's, as Jasper himself keeps telling us. Jasper's open discussion of the nature of Scripture, while simple, exposes the figuralist conviction regarding the Word rather clearly. The excerpt below begins with Hatcher's brief introduction.

In presenting John Jasper's celebrated sermon on "De Sun Do Move," I beg to introduce it with several explanatory words. As intimated in a former chapter it is of a dual character. It includes an extended discussion, after his peculiar fashion, of the text, "The Lord God is a man of war; the Lord is His name." Much that he said in that part of his sermon is omitted, only so much being retained as indicates his view of the rotation of the sun. It was really when he came into this part of his sermon that he showed to such great advantage, even though so manifestly in error as to the position which he tried so manfully to antagonize. It was of that combative type of public speech which always put him before the people at his best. I never heard this sermon but once, but I have been amply aided in reproducing it by an elaborate and altogether friendly report of the sermon published at the time by The Richmond Dispatch.

Jasper opened his discourse with a tender reminiscence and quite an ingenious exordium. "Low me ter say," he spoke with an outward composure which revealed an inward but mastered swell of emotion, "dat when I wuz a young man and a slave, I knowed nuthin' wuth talkin' 'bout consarnin' books. Dey wuz sealed mysteries ter me, but I tell yer I longed ter break de seal. I thusted fer de bread uv learnin'. When I seen books I ached ter git in ter um, fur I knowed dat dey had de stuff fer me, an I wanted ter taste dere contents, but most of de time dey wuz bar'd aginst me.

"By de mursy of de Lord a thing happened. I got er room-feller — he wuz a slave, too, an' he had learn'd ter read. In de dead uv de night he giv me lessons outen de New York Spellin' book. It wuz hard pulin', I tell yer; harder on him, fur he know'd jes' a leede, an' it made him sweat ter try ter beat sumthin' inter my hard haid. It wuz wuss wid me. Up de hill ev'ry step, but when I got de light uv de less'n into my noodle I farly shouted, but I kno'd I wuz not a scholur.

"De consequens wuz I crep 'long mighty tejus, gittin' a crum hiere an' dar untel I cud read de Bible by skippin' de long words, tolerable well. Dat wuz de start uv my eddicashun — dat is, wat litde I got I mek menshun of dat young man. De years hev fled erway sense den, but I ain't furgot my teachur, an' nevur shall. I thank mer Lord fur him, an' I carries his mem'ry in my heart.

"'Bout seben months after my gittin' ter readin', Gord cunverted my soul,

an' I reckin 'bout de fust an' main thing dat I begged de Lord ter give me wuz
de power ter und'stan' His Word. I ain' bragging an' I hates self-praise, but
I boun' ter speak de thankful word. I b'lieves in mer heart dat mer pra'r ter
und'stand de Scripshur wuz heard. Sence dat time I ain't keer'd 'bout nuthin'
'cept ter study an' preach de Word uv God. Not, my bruthrin, dat I'z de fool
ter think I knows it all. Oh, mer Father, no! Fur frum it. I don' hardly und'stan
myse'f, nor ha'f uv de things roun' me, an' dar is milyuns uv things in de Bible
too deep fur Jasper, an' sum uv 'em too deep fur ev'rybody. I doan't cerry de
keys ter de Lord's closet, an' He ain' tell me ter peep in, an' ef I did I'm so stupid
I wouldn't know it when I see it. No, frens, I knows my place at de feet uv my
Marster, an' dar I stays. But I kin read de Bible and git de things whar lay on
de top uv de soil.

"Out'n de Bible I knows nuthin' extry 'bout de sun. I sees 'is courses as
he rides up dar so gran' an' mighty in de sky, but dar is heaps 'bout dat flamin'
orb dat is too much fer me. I know dat de sun shines powerfly an' po's down
its light in floods, an' yet dat is nuthin' compared wid de light dat flashes in
my min' frum de pages of Gord's book. But you knows all dat. I knows dat de
sun burns — oh, how it did burn in dem July days. I tell yer he cooked de skin
on my back many er day when I wuz hoein' in de corn fell. But you knows all
dat, an' yet dat is nuthin' der to de divine fire dat burns in der souls uv Gord's
chil'n. Can't yer fed it, bruthrin?

"But 'bout de courses uv de sun, I have got dat. I hev dun rang'd thru de
whole blessed book an' scode down de las' thing de Bible has ter say 'bout de
movements uv de sun. I got all dat pat an' safe. An' lemme say dat if I doan't
giv it ter you straight, if I gits one word crooked or wrong, you jes' holler out,
'Hol' on dar, Jasper, yer ain't got dat straight,' an' I'll beg pardon. If I doan't tell
de truf, march up on dese steps here an' tell me U'z a liar, an' I'll take it. I fears
I do lie sometimes — I'm so sinful, I find it hard ter do right; but my Gord
doan't lie an' He ain' put no lie in de Book uv eternal truf, an' if I giv you wat
de Bible say, den I boun' ter tell de truf.

"I got ter take yer all dis artenoon on er skershun ter a great bat'l feil'. Mos'
folks like ter see fights — some is mighty fon' er gittin' inter fights, an' some
is mighty quick ter run down de back alley when dar is a bat'l goin' on, fer de
right. Dis time I'll 'scort yer tet a scene whar you shall witness a curus bat'l.
It tuk place soon arter Isrel got in de Promus Lan'. Yer 'member de people uv
Gibyun mak frens wid Gord's people when dey fust entered Canum an' dey
wuz monsus smart ter do it. But, jes' de same, it got 'em in ter an orful fuss.
De cities roun' 'bout dar flar'd up at dat, an' dey all jined dere forces and say
dey gwine ter mop de Gibyun people orf uv de groun', an' dey bunched all dar
armies tergedder an' went up fer ter do it.

"Wen dey kum up so bol' an' brave de Giby'nites wuz skeer'd out'n dere senses, an' dey saunt word ter Joshwer dat dey wuz in troubl' an' he mus' run up dar an' git 'em out. Joshwer had de heart uv a lion an' he wuz up dar d'reckly. Dey had an orful fight, sharp an' bitter, but yer might know dat Ginr'l Joshwer wuz not up dar ter git whip't . He prayed an' he fought, an' de hours got erway too peart fer him, an' so he ask'd de Lord ter issure a speshul ordur dat de sun hol' up erwhile an' dat de moon furnish plenty uv moonshine down on de lowes' part uv de fightin' groun's. As a fac', Joshwer wuz so drunk wid de bat'l, so thursty fer de blood uv de en'mies uv de Lord, an' so wild wid de vict'ry dat he tell de sun ter stan' still tel he cud finish his job.

"Wat did de sun do? Did he glar down in fi'ry wrath an' say, 'What you talkin' 'bout my stoppin' for, Joshwer; I ain't navur startid yit. Bin here all de time, an' it wud smash up ev'rything if I wuz ter start'? Naw, he ain' say dat. But wat de Bible say? Dat's wat I ax ter know. It say dat it wuz at de voice uv Joshwer dat it stopped. I don' say it stopt; tain't fer Jasper ter say dat, but de Bible, de Book uv Gord, say so. But I say dis; nuthin' kin stop untel it hez fust startid. So I knows wat I'm talkin' 'bout. De sun wuz travlin' long dar thru de sky wen de order come. He hitched his red ponies and made quite a call on de lan' uv Gibyun. He purch up dar in de skies jes' as frenly as a naibur whar comes ter borrer sumthin', an' he stan' up dar an' he look lak he enjoyed de way Joshwer waxes dem wicked armies. An' de moon, she wait down in de low groun's dar, an' pours out her light and look jes as ca'm an' happy as if she wuz waitin' fer her 'scort. Dey nevur budg'd, neither uv 'em, long as de Lord's army needed er light to kerry on de bat'l.

"I doan't read when it wuz dat Joshwer hitch up an' drove on, but I 'spose it wuz when de Lord tol' him ter go. Ennybody knows dat de sun didn' stay dar all de time. It stopt hir bizniz, an' went on when it got thru. Dis is 'bout all dat I has ter do wid dis perticl'r case. I dun show'd yer dat dis part uv de Lord's word teaches yer dat de sun stopt, which show dat he wuz movin' befo' dat, an' dat he went on art'rwuds. I toll yer dat I wud prove dis an' I's dun it, an' I derfies ennybody to say dat my p'int ain't made.

"I tol' yer in de fust part uv dis discose dat de Lord Gord is a man uv war. I 'spec by now yer begin ter see it is so. Doan't yer admit it? When de Lord cum ter see Joshwer in de day uv his feers an' warfar, an' actu'ly mek de sun stop stone still in de heavuns, so de fight kin rage on tel all de foes is slain, yer bleeged ter und'rstan' dat de Gord uv peace is also de man uv war. He kin use bofe peace an' war ter hep de reichus, an' ter scattur de host uv de ailyuns. A man talked ter me las' week 'bout de laws uv nature, an' he say dey carn't poss'bly be upsot, an' I had ter laugh right in his face. As if de laws uv ennythin' wuz greater dan my Gord who is de lawgiver fer ev'rything. My Lord is great;

He rules in de heavuns, in de earth, an' doun und'r de groun'. He is great, an' greatly ter be praised. Let all de people bow doun an' wurship befo' Him!

"But let us git erlong, for dar is quite a big lot mo' comin' on. Let us take nex' de case of Hezekier. He wuz one of dem kings of Juder — er mighty sorry lot I mus' say dem kings wuz, fur de mos' part. I inclines ter think Hezekier wuz 'bout de highes' in de gin'ral avrig, an' he war no mighty man hisse'f. Well, Hezekier he got sick. I dar say dat a king when he gits his crown an' fin'ry off, an' when he is posterated wid mortal sickness, he gits 'bout es commun lookin' an' grunts an' rolls, an' is 'bout es skeery as de res' of us po' mortals. We know dat Hezerkier wuz in er low state uv min'; full uv fears, an' in a tur'ble trub'le. De fac' is, de Lord strip him uv all his glory an' landed him in de dust. He tol' him dat his hour had come, an' dat he had bettur squar up his affaars, fur death wuz at de do'. Den it wuz dat de king fell low befo' Gord; he turn his face ter de wall; he cry, he moan, he beg'd de Lord not ter take him out'n de worl' yit.

"Oh, how good is our Gord! De cry uv de king moved his heart, an' he tell him he gwine ter give him anudder show. Tain't only de kings dat de Lord hears. De cry uv de pris'nur, de wail uv de bondsman, de tears uv de dyin' robber, de prars uv de backslider, de sobs uv de womun dat wuz a sinner, mighty apt to tech de heart uv de Lord. It look lik it's hard fer de sinner ter git so fur orf or so fur down in de pit dat his cry can't reach de yere uv de mussiful Saviour.

"But de Lord do evun better den dis fur Hezekier — He tell him He gwine ter give him a sign by which he'd know dat what He sed wuz cummin' ter pars. I ain't erquainted wid dem sun diuls dat de Lord toll Hezekier 'bout, but ennybody dat hes got a grain uv sense knows dat dey wuz de clocks uv dem ole times an' dey marked de travuls uv de sun by dem diuls. When, darfo' Gord tol' de king dat He wud mek de shadder go backwud, it mus' hev bin jes' lak puttin' de ban's uv de clock back, but, mark yer, Izaer 'spressly say dat de sun return'd ten dergrees. Thar yer are! Ain't dat de movement uv de sun? Bless my soul. Hezekier's case beat Joshwer. Joshwer stop de sun, but heer de Lord mek de sun walk back ten dergrees ; an' yet dey say dat de sun stan' stone still an' nevur move er peg. It look ter me he move roun' mighty brisk an' is ready ter go ennyway dat de Lord ordurs him ter go.

"I wonder if enny uv dem furloserfers is roun' here dis arternoon. I'd like ter take a squar' look at one uv dem an' ax him to 'splain dis mattur. He carn't do it, my bruthr'n. He knows a heap 'bout books, maps, figgers an' long distunces, but I derfy him ter take up Hezekier's case an' 'splain it orf. He carn't do it. De Word uv de Lord is my defense an' bulwurk, an' I fears not what men can say nor do; my Gord gives me de vict'ry.

"'Low me, my frens, ter put mysef squar 'bout dis movement uv de sun. It ain't no bizniss uv mine wedder de sun move or stan' still, or wedder it stop or go back or rise or set. All dat is out er my han's 'tirely, an' I got nuthin' ter say. I got no theory on de subjik. All I ax is dat we will take wat de Lord say 'bout it an' let His will be dun 'bout ev'ry thing. Wat dat will is I carn't know 'cept He whisper inter my soul or write it in a book. Here's de Book. Dis is 'nough fer me, and wid it ter pilut me, I carn't git fur erstray.

"But I ain't dun wid yer yit. As de song says, dere's mo' ter foller, I envite yer ter heer de fust vers in de sev'nth chaptur uv de book uv Reverlashuns. What do John, und'r de pow'r uv de Spirit, say? He say he saw fo' anguls standin' on de fo' corners uv de earth, holdin' de fo' win's uv de earth, an' so fo'th. 'Low me ter ax ef de earth is roun', whar do it keep its comers? Er flat, squar thing has comers, but tell me where is de cornur uv er appul, ur a marbul, ur a cannun ball, ur a silver dollar. Ef dar is enny one uv dem furloserfurs whar's been takin' so many cracks at my ole haid 'bout here, he is korjully envited ter step for'd an' squar up dis vexin' bizniss. I here tell you dat yer carn't squar a circul, but it looks lak dese great scolurs dun learn how ter circul de squar. Ef dey kin do it, let 'em step ter de front an' do de trick. But, mer brutherin, in my po' judgmint, dey karn't do it; tain't in 'em ter do it. Dey is on der wrong side of de Bible; dar's on de outside uv de Bible, an' dar's whar de trubbul comes in wid 'em. Dey dun got out uv de bres'wuks uv de truf, an' ez long ez dey stay dar de light uv de Lord will not shine on der path. I ain't keer'n so much 'bout de sun, tho' it's mighty kunveenyunt ter hav it, but my trus' is in de Word uv de Lord. Long ez my feet is flat on de solid rock, no man kin move me. I'se gittin my orders f'um de Gord of my salvashun.

"Tother day er man wid er hi coler and side whisk'rs cum ter my house. He was one nice Northern gemman wat think a heap of us col'rd people in de Souf. Da ar luvly folks and I honours 'em very much. He seem from de start kinder strictly an' cross wid me, and arter while, he brake out furi'us and frettid, an' he say: 'Erlow me Mister Jasper ter gib you sum plain advise. Dis nonsans 'bout de sun movin' whar you ar gettin' is disgracin' yer race all ober de kuntry, an' as a fren of yer peopul, I cum ter say it's got ter stop.' Ha! Ha! Ha! Mars' Sam Hargrove nuvur hardly smash me dat way. It was equl to one ov dem ole overseurs way bac yondur. I tel him dat ef he'll sho me I'se wrong, I giv it all up.

"My! My! Ha!l Ha! He sail in on me an' such er storm about science, nu 'scuv'ries, an' de Lord only knos wat all, I ner hur befo', an' den he tel me my race is ergin me an' po ole Jasper mus shet up 'is fule mouf.

"Wen he got thru — it look lak he nuvur wud, I tel him John Jasper ain' set up to be no scholur, an' doant kno de ferlosophiz, an' ain' tryin' ter hurt his peopul, but is wurkin' day an' night ter lif 'em up, but his foot is on de rock uv eternal truff. Dar he stan' and dar he is goin' ter stan' til Gabrul soun's de judgment note. So er say to de gemman wat scol'd me up so dat I hur him mek his remarks, but I ain' hur whar he get his Scriptu' from, an' dat 'tween him an' de wurd of de Lord I tek my stan' by de Word of Gord ebery time.

"Jasper ain' mad: he ain' fightin' nobody; he ain' bin 'pinted janitur to run de sun: he nothin' but de servunt of Gord and a luver of de Everlasting Word. What I keer about de sun? De day comes on wen de sun will be called frum his race-trac, and his light squincked out foruvur; de moon shall turn ter blood, and this yearth be konsoomed wid fier. Let um go; dat wont skeer me nor trubble Gord's erlect'd peopul, for de word uv de Lord shell aindu furivur, an' on dat Solid Rock we stan' an' shall not be muved.

"Is I got yer satisfied yit? Has I prooven my p'int? Oh, ye whose hearts is full uv unberlief! Is yer still hol'in' out? I reckun de reason yer say de sun don' move is 'cause yer are so hard ter move yerse'f. You is a reel triul ter me, but, nevur min'; I ain't gi'n yer up yit, an' nevur will. Truf is mighty; it kin break de heart uv stone, an' I mus' fire anudder arrur uv truf out'n de quivur uv de Lord. If yer haz er copy uv God's Word 'bout yer pussun, please tu'n ter dat miner profit, Malerki, wat writ der las' book in der ole Bible, an' look at chaptur de fust, vurs 'leben; what do it say? I bet'r read it, fur I got er noshun yer critics doan't kerry enny Bible in thar pockits ev'ry day in de week. Here is wat it says: 'Fur from de risin' uv de sun evun unter de goin' doun uv de same My name shall be great 'mong de Gentiles. . . . My name shall be great 'mong de heathun, sez de Lord uv hosts.' How do dat suit yer? It look lak dat ort ter fix it.

"Dis time it is de Lord uv hosts Hisse'f dat is doin' de talkin', an' He is talkin' on er wonderful an' glorious subjik. He is tellin' uv de spredin' uv His Gorspel, uv de kummin' uv His larst vict'ry ovur de Gentiles, an' de wurld-wide glories dat at de las' He is ter git. Oh, my bruddrin, wat er time dat will be. My soul teks wing es I erticipate wid joy dat merlenium day! De glories as dey shine befo' my eyes blin's me, an' I furgits de sun an' moon an' stars. I jes' 'members dat 'long 'bout dose las' days dat de sun an' moon will go out uv bizniss, fur dey won' be needed no mo'. Den will King Jesus come back ter see His people, an' He will be de suffishunt light uv de wurl'. Joshwer's bat'ls will be ovur. Hezekier woan't need no sun diul, an' de sun an' moon will fade out befo' de glorius splendurs uv de New Jerruslem.

"But wat der mattur wid Jasper. I mos' furgit my bizniss, an' mos' gon' ter shoutin' ovur de far away glories uv de secun' cummin' uv my Lord. I beg par-dun, an' will try ter git back ter my subjik. I hev ter do as de sun in Hezekier's case — fall back er few dergrees. In dat part uv de Word dat I gin yer frum Malerki — dat de Lord Hisse'f spoke — He klars dat His glory is gwine ter spred. Spred? Whar? Frum de risin' uv de sun ter de goin' down uv de same. Wat? Doan't say dat, duz it? Dat's edzakly wat it sez. Ain't dat cleer 'nuff fer yer? De Lord pity dese doubtin' Tommusses. Here is 'nuff ter settul it all an' kure de wuss cases. Walk up here, wise folks, an' git yer med'sin. Whar is dem high collar'd furloserfurs now? Wat dey skulkin' roun' in de brush fer? Why doan't yer git out in der broad artenoon light an' fight fer yer cullurs? Ah, I un'stans it; yer got no answer. De Bible is agin yer, an' in yer konshunses yer are convictid.

"But I hears yer back dar. Wat yer wisprin' 'bout? I know; yer say yer sont me sum papurs an' I nevur answer dem. Ha, ha, ha! I got 'em. 'De diflerkulty 'bout dem papurs yer sont me is dat dey did not answer me. Dey nevur menshun de Bible one time. Yer think so much uv yoursefs an' so little uv de Lord Gord an' thinks wat yer say is so smart dat yer carn't even speak uv de Word uv de Lord. When yer ax me ter stop believin' in de Lord's Word an' ter pin my faith ter yo words, I ain't er gwine ter do it. I take my stan' by de Bible an' res' my case on wat it says. I take wat de Lord says 'bout my sins, 'bout my Saviour, 'bout life, 'bout death, 'bout de wurl' ter come, an' I take wat de Lord say 'bout de sun an' moon, an' I cares little wat de haters of mer Gord chooses ter say. Think dat I will fursake de Bible? It is my only Book, my hope, de arsnel uv my soul's surplies, an' I wants nuthin' else.

"But I got enudder wurd fur yer yit. I done wuk ovur dem papurs dat yer sont me widout date an' widout yer name. Yer deals in figgurs an' thinks yer are biggur dan de arkanjuls. Lemme see wat yer dun say. Yer set yerse'f up ter tell me how fur it is frum here ter de sun. Yer think yer got it down ter er nice p'int. Yer say it is 3,339,002 miles frum de earth ter de sun. Dat's wat yer say. Nudder one say dat de distuns is 12,000,000; nudder got it ter 27,000,000. I hers dat de great Isuk Nutun wuk't it up ter 28,000,000, an' later on de furloserfurs gin enudder rippin' raze to 50,000,000. De las' one gits it bigger dan all de yuthers, up to 90,000,000. Doan't enny uv 'em ergree edzakly an' so dey runs a guess game, an' de las' guess is always de bigges'.

"Now, wen dese guessers kin hav a kunvenshun in Richmun' an' all ergree 'pun de same thing, I'd be glad ter hear frum yer ag'in, an' I duz hope dat by dat time yer won't be ershamed uv yer name. Heeps uv railroads hes bin built sense I saw de fust one wen I wuz fifteen yeers ole, but I ain't hear tell uv er railroad built yit ter de sun. I doan' see why ef dey kin meshur de distuns ter de sun, dey might not git up er railroad er a telurgraf an' enabul us ter fin' sumthin' else 'bout it den merely how fur orf de sun is. Dey tell me dat a kannun ball cu'd mek de trep ter de sun in twelve years. Why doan' dey send it? It might be rig'd up wid quarturs fur a few furloserfers on de inside an' fixed up fur er kumfurterble ride. Dey wud need twelve years' rashuns an' a heep uv changes uv ramint — mighty thick clo'es wen dey start and mighty thin uns wen dey git dar.

"Oh mer bruthrin, dese things mek yer laugh, an' I doan' blem yer fer laughin', 'cept it's always sad ter laugh at der follies uv fools. If we cu'd laugh 'em out'n kount'nens, we might well laugh day an' night. Wat cuts inter my soul is, dat all dese men seem ter me dat dey is hittin' at de Bible. Dat's wat sturs my soul an' fills me wid reichus wrath. Leetle keers I wat dey says 'bout de sun, purvided dey let de Word uv de Lord erlone. But nevur min'. Let de heethun rage an' de people 'madgin er vain thing. Our King shall break 'em in pieces an' dash 'em down. But blessed be de name uv our Gord, de Word uv de Lord indurith furivur. Stars may fall, moons may turn ter blood, an' de sun set ter rise no mo', but Thy kingdom, oh, Lord, is frum evurlastin' ter evurlastin'.

"But I has er word dis artenoon fer my own brutherin. Dey is de people fer whose souls I got ter watch — fur dem I got ter stan' an' report at de last — dey is my sheep an' I'se der shepherd, an' my soul is knit ter dem forever. 'Tain fer me ter be troublin' yer wid dese questions erbout dem heb'nly bodies. Our eyes goes far beyon' de smaller stars ; our home is clean outer sight uv dem twinklin' orbs ; de chariot dat will cum ter take us to our Father's mansion will sweep out by dem flickerin' lights an' never halt till it brings us in clar view uv de throne uv de Lamb. Doan't hitch yer hopes to no sun nor stars; yer home is got Jesus fer its light, an' yer hopes mus' trabel up dat way. I preach dis sermon jest fer ter settle de min's uv my few brutherin, an' repeats it 'cause kin' frens wish ter hear it, an' I hopes it will do honour ter de Lord's Word. But nuthin' short of de purly gates can satisfy me, an' I charge, my people, fix yer feet on de solid Rock, yer hearts on Calvry, an' yer eyes on de throne uv de Lamb. Dese strifes an' griefs'll soon git ober; we shall see de King in His glory an' be at ease. Go on, go on, ye ransom uv de Lord; shout His praises as yer go, an' I shall meet yer in de city uv de New Jeruserlum, whar we shan't need the light uv de sun, fer de Lam' uv de Lord is de light uv de saints."

IV. The Good Samaritan

The following sermon brings us to the present, and is deliberately used to locate figural preaching in the more mundane confines of normal congregational life. In this case, it is a sermon of my own, drawn from a typical Sunday lectionary and delivered several years ago at a typical urban parish. I place it after the great preachers transcribed above both with tremendous humility, and a sense that it is important for the "ordinary" to be represented in this context. Figural preaching is an ordinary, if divine, task. The sermon speaks for itself: it follows the scriptural figure of the "stranger," and makes use of a variety of modern elements — historical and philological — as well as contemporary tone. It is, I hope, congruent in some measure with the purposes of figural preaching that I have tried to outline.

Luke 10:25ff. — *The Divine Stranger*

One of the hardest things I have had to do as a priest is this: walk into a hospital room, after I have been called in suddenly in an emergency, and not knowing the people there — they are standing around the bed of someone dying, whom they love, they have tears in their eyes, and they look up at you coming through the door, quizzically, sometimes hostilely. As if saying, "Who are you? You don't belong here." And you, in your collar, bearing some invisible and unasked for prayer and mysterious message of grace, which these people may not even believe if told, you are asked to thrust yourself into the midst of their most intimate emotions and pain.

This is what it feels like to be a stranger. And we have all felt it somehow and somewhere. There is this vast gulf, or high wall, that lies between us and "them," that somehow has to be scaled or traversed just to see each other truly eye to eye. And until then? I went to work in Africa for several years right after I was ordained — a young and callow minister. And there, in the middle of the mountains of Burundi, barely following a conversation, watched and stared at . . . this sense of distance often stirred up in me a feeling of panic: no way out.

"Why do you stand so far off, O Lord?" writes the psalmist (Ps. 10:1). It's a question we have all posed, haven't we? We feel alone; everything is crumbling; our own anxiety and sorrow and pain seems inexhaustible and there is no one to quench it. God too is a stranger to our lives, in a way. If only at that moment, so he seems. Perhaps for too long. Perhaps he is a stranger to you even now. And if a stranger, why?

The story of the Good Samaritan, which Jesus tells in our Gospel today, is one of the most astonishing of all his parables. Is it merely about "kindness"? The term "Samaritan," after all, has entered the English language now as almost a synonym for someone who "helps out." (We have "Samaritan" counseling centers, Samaritan suicide hot-lines, Samaritan animal shelters, and the rest.) All appropriate designations, to be sure. But their proliferation and limited focus mask the depth of the reality to which the parable itself would speak.

The discussion into which Jesus injects his story is about being a "neighbor" — loving a neighbor ("love your neighbor as yourself," according to Leviticus 19) and being a neighbor. But then Jesus tells a story about someone who is *not* a neighbor, in any shape or form. This is the first element that should surprise us.

A "neighbor," in English, is literally someone who has settled nearby; it's pretty much the same thing in Greek — a *plesios,* a "nearby person." Or in the Hebrew of Leviticus, which is quoted to Jesus by the lawyer, a "neighbor" is literally a companion and food-sharer, whose life intersects with your own (*rea*) physically and geographically.

Yet this is what is so odd about the example Jesus has chosen for his story: the Samaritan was not any of this at all. He was just "passing through" when he saw the man lying by the road — neither coming close or settling down. He lived north of Jericho, where the man had been going (which itself is north of Jerusalem). And as a member of a people viewed as heretics and syncretists by the Israelites and Jews, the Samaritan was an "outsider" in all respects (John 4:9 — "the Jews have no dealings with the Samaritans"). Even Jesus warns his first disciples whom he sends out, "Enter no town of the Samaritans" (Matt. 10:5). For they have nothing in common with us. The Samaritan, therefore, was *not* a "neighbor" in the strict sense; he did not live nearby; he did not share work or food; he was the quintessential stranger, not in his own land.

Now in Israel, a "stranger" is someone to be distinguished from a "sojourner" (although the terms are sometimes mixed up in English). A sojourner — a *ger* — is someone from abroad who settles among you, a non-Jewish "immigrant," as it were. As an American in Canada, I am a "sojourner," because I am officially a "landed immigrant." And Israel had special responsibilities towards the sojourners, who were to be treated as "guests" (cf. Lev. 17, 19, and 25; Num. 15). (After all, God tells the Israelites, you were once a "sojourner" in Egypt — cf. Deut. 26:5; Ps. 105:23.)

But a "stranger," strictly speaking, was different, and was designated by a different word: called a *zur* or a *neker*, a "stranger" was someone "alien," different, from far away ("scattered"?) or filled with hostility (a "smiter"?) and living with different and perverse customs. In the Old Testament, being a "stranger" is negative and not to be accepted (the prophets speak against "strangers" in the temple, and the "strange" religions that foreigners infect us with). Obviously, in this sense, the Samaritan is not a neighbor, but a stranger. And — let us be clear — to the Samaritan, the Jew is a stranger too. They eye each other from the distance, they judge each other on the basis of their firm and divergent convictions, and they avoid each other. The New Testament Greek translates the word "stranger" by the word *xenos* — which has entered into English itself: and "xenophobia" — fear of strangers and foreigners — is precisely what describes the proper attitude of Jews and Samaritans — indeed of any person who is concerned with the integrity of their own community and of its values. "Don't talk to strangers!" we tell our kids. Fear the stranger, if you would stay healthy.

Yet the Samaritan, passing through, hurrying along to his own distant and separated home, sees the man on the road and responds, not with fear at all, but with "compassion." The stranger looks at the wounded man, and is moved.

How is this possible? You see, it should not be so. I know, you say to me, "oh, it's natural to help . . . what, well to 'help your neighbor.'" But this is my point: they are definitely *not* neighbors, this passer-by from a foreign land and the broken Jew on the roadside. Not neighbors at all; but strangers. Are we to love that which is alien to our values, to our systems, to our structures, to our expectations? Are we to love those who are wrong, those who sin, those who are, perhaps, even *evil*?

We must not jump too soon to the conclusions of a tired humanism. Stop and look at the Samaritan as he pauses and gazes at the unconscious Jew. Who are they, one to another? Jesus is here underlining something fundamental about our life in the world. That is, that we stand, all of us, as *strangers* in the midst of what is most valuable and true. Jesus underlines it, because he *knows* it by heart; he lives it. Because *he*, before all others, is a stranger in the world — driven "outside the gates" (Heb. 13:12f.) and the epitome of those who stand as "strangers and exiles in the world" (Heb. 11:13): "He was in the world, and the world was made through him, yet the world knew him not. He came unto his own" — that is, to his own people, his own countrymen, his own "neighbors" in the strongest sense — "He came to his own place, and his own people received him not" (John 1:10-11). Rightly or wrongly, Jesus is a *zur*, a *xenos* in the world, a stranger in our world, a stranger among us, to you and me. And when he speaks at the Last Judgment to men and women, to you and me, *this* is the persona he adopts: "I was a stranger," he says. And — what? — "you welcomed me or you did not" (Matt. 25:35, 43).

So the Samaritan, when he has compassion on the Jewish traveler, does so as a stranger, not as a neighbor. Which stranger is this? Why, the one who looked upon "the crowds, harassed and helpless, like sheep without a shepherd, and had *compassion* on them" (Matt. 9:36); who looks out on "the crowds," has compassion on them, and heals and feeds them (Matt. 14:14); who, like a "king," forgives his servants' debts out of "compassion" (Matt. 18:27). The Samaritan pauses and looks at the Jew crumpled and bloody on the roadside, and, like the father of the prodigal son, is filled with "compassion" (Luke 15:20); just as is he who, seeing the grieving widow and mother of a dead son, is filled with "compassion" and calls upon the young man to "rise up" and walk again (Luke 7:13).

Is this not all astonishing? That the stranger — the one whom the Samaritan only points to in this story, like a reflection of some great light coming from afar — is it not astonishing that this stranger comes into the midst of the world, the one the world does not know or wish to know, and stands — unknown and derided — and looks upon the multitudes before him, even as they look away or close their doors, or hurl abuse at him, looks at them and *loves* them?

Oh God, why are you so far off from me? You ask that in the midst of some great burden and confusion. Perhaps even today. "Is it I who is far off?" he replies. "Is it I who has wandered far away? Or is it not I who has *come* from far off, come close, and you would not receive me? Is it not I, a stranger to you, who has come and made the stranger my own friend?"

"Remember that at one time you were aliens from the commonwealth of Israel and strangers to the covenants of promise, having no hope and without God in the world. But now, in Christ Jesus you who once were far off have been brought near in his blood . . . no longer strangers, but fellow citizens with the saints and members of God's own household" (Eph. 2:12f., 19).

What is astonishing is how Jesus tells the story of the Samaritan because it is the story about himself. And thus, he tells us that God has become our neighbor, precisely by his willingness to be the stranger who walks through the door uninvited, and we all look up, quizzically and hostilely, and he comes close. You would never know it, would you? We, who look for love from the neighbor we know, from friend and family, from those who are meant to offer it (though often we are disappointed). Yet, the "far off" one, it turns out, has compassion beyond their measure, bringing it to us from the place we thought outside our possibility. He brings us help from the very place we thought incapable of offering grace.

So Martin Luther once wrote concerning God: we too often turn away from his mercy, Luther said, a mercy that comes to us in humility and suffering, strange to our tastes and expectations. We run from suffering, we turn away from difficulty and failure, we hide from our brokenness and that of others. "That the works of God are unattractive," Luther writes, "is clear from what is said in Isaiah 53:2, 'He had no form or beauty,'" this stranger to us because of our hard hearts, who would yet have compassion upon us nonetheless. "And this is what Isaiah (28:21) calls the 'alien' and 'strange' work of God (that is, He humbles us thoroughly, making us despair, so that He may exalt us in His mercy, giving us hope). So the Apostle writes [concerning this strange work] (2 Cor. 6:9-10), "As sorrowful, yet [we are] always rejoicing; as dying, and behold we live (*Heidelberg Disputation*, Note on the 4th Thesis, 1518). "For now I call you friends" (John 15:15).

The "strange work of God," Luther found in Isaiah, is the work, not of the neighbor who treats his neighbor well, but of the stranger, the utterly foreign, the rejected, the repudiated, the ignored alien, who yet comes with compassion and becomes the neighbor of our very souls. All the things — including people! — we are afraid of, that have hurt us, that threaten our securities, so hard-won, that challenge our hearts, that we are certain wear us down — think of health, family, work, spirits — all of them, become neighbors to our very souls.

And so we are caught up in a new life. As St. Paul writes (Col. 3:12-13): "put on, as God's chosen ones, holy and beloved — put on *compassion*, kindness, lowliness, meekness, and patience, forbearing and forgiving one another, *just as the Lord has forgiven you.*"

"Do not neglect to show hospitality to strangers," writes Hebrews and the word is this: *philoxenia*, the "love of strangers." Do not, "for thereby some have entertained angels unawares" (Heb. 13:2). Angels — that is, God himself! "Where is this stupendous stranger?" the poet Christopher Smart wrote in what became a famous hymn: "O most mighty, O most holy/far beyond the seraph's thought; art thou then so mean and lowly?" Thou art the Christ; the one you thought a stranger, yet who is closer than your very breath, the one who has come to you, who is drawing you out of yourself, who is taking you to his own heart. Stranger become friend.

Index of Names and Subjects

Pneumatology, 55, 102n17, 256

Poverty, 153, 154, 156, 159

Prayer Book, 222, 224, 228

Preaching: 214n8, 257n3; Anglican, 149, 222-224; and historicism, 259, 267; and the lectionary, 222-224, 233, 262, 267, 285. *See also* Figural preaching

Presentism, 54, 85, 201n45

Pseudo-Dionysius, 125, 185

Rashi, 241, 242, 244

Reno, R. R., 49, 79n65

Reformed: exegesis, 18-20, 21, 61-62, 75-76, 102; use of lectionary, 226; use of Patristics, 73n55

Ricoeur, Paul, 36-37, 259n6

Scotus, John Duns, 112, 123, 124n30, 136n60

Scripture: as agent, 40, 272-273, 278-279, 285; "allness" of, 209-210, 213-214, 220, 222, 226; as artifact, 100-104, 106-107, 111, 173; and authorial intent, 81, 210, 259-260; authority of, 65, 152-155, 170, 275-277; as Christ, 65, 104; juxtaposition of, 211, 215-220, 269, 274, 279; and naturalism, 75n60, 79-80, 128-129, 134-135, 146; prior to history, 40, 100, 102, 235-236, 251, 261; relation to time, 102, 236, 272. *See also* Figural reading, Language: Scriptural, and Lectionary

Senses (of Scripture). *See* Allegorical sense, Anagogical sense, Analogical sense, Historical sense, Literal sense, Mystical sense, Spiritual sense, *and* Tropological sense

Serapion (monk), 166-168

Simultaneity, 29, 34, 39, 55, 57, 85

Skepticism, 36-37, 84n1, 115n8, 131, 149, 259

Smalley, Beryl, 66, 114, 115, 120n17, 149

Sorrell, Roger, 117n13, 137-139, 140n71, 141-143

Spiritual sense (of Scripture), 7, 55, 149, 196

Steno, Nicolaus, 130, 135n59

Stern, David, 208-209, 212

Substance: in creation, 49, 50, 89; in Ockham, 118, 121, 123-124, 126; and language, 147, 237

Sylla, Edith Dudley, 114, 127-129, 131, 133

Symbol: in exegesis, 123, 149, 157; as moralization, 144-145; in nature, 116-117, 119, 122, 125, 134, 143-144; in Scripture, 141, 157

"Symbolizing mentality": 116, 120, 122, 160; movement away from, 123-124, 129, 139-140, 160

Synecdoche: in Christian speech, 197, 199; definition of, 189-190; incarnational, 189-192, 195; vs. metaphor, 48-49; as natural symbol, 192, 196; in Scripture, 48-51, 265

Tertullian, 21, 22, 254

Theodicy, 32-33, 37, 41-42, 109

Theodoret, 245-246

Thomas Aquinas, 123, 126n34, 185-189

Thomas of Celano, 139n68, 141

Time: as absolute, 85n3, 91n10, 100; beginning of, 47-49; as change, 48-49, 95-96; as conventional, 98; definition of, 98; figural, 33n41, 34; Jewish view of, 39, 67-74; limitations of, 87-88, 96; measure of, 50, 52; medieval view of, 62-63, 65-67; as past/present/future, 37-39, 45, 52, 63, 84, 92, 96-97; Patristic view of, 46-61; and Scripture, 89, 100-104; as unknown, 100; as unreal, 84-85; as usage, 98, 102. *See also* Figural reading: and time, Presentism, Simultaneity

Trinity: as antinomy, 208, 215-216, 254; controversy over, 210-215, 254; figures of, 242, 249-252, 254-255; in Isaiah, 238, 242-244, 248, 252, 254-255; language about, 237-238, 251, 253; in Proverbs, 227-228; relation to time, 50-51, 251

Tropological sense (of Scripture), 7, 44-45, 48, 49-50, 53, 57-58

Tyndale, William, 21-22, 25

Type/Typology: 7, 60; and dispensations, 77-79; and Christ, 62, 104; OT vs. NT, 77-79, 158, 247; in nature, 62-63

Univocity, 112, 122-125, 130, 186

van Helmont, Francis Mercury, 75

CPSIA information can be obtained
at www.ICGtesting.com
Printed in the USA
LVHW110240031022
729815LV00004B/41